Perspectives on Feminist Political Thought in European History

Conventional histories of political thought have sometimes relegated feminist thinking to the footnotes. Yet feminism is central to key notions of modern political discourse such as autonomy, liberty and equality. Also, feminist discussion of morality has been closely linked to major currents in political thought such as republicanism, civic humanism and romanticism.

Spanning six centuries of political thought in European history, this book puts the ideas of thinkers from Christine de Pizan to Simone de Beauvoir in the broader contexts of their time. This intriguing collection of essays shows that feminism is not a variant of modern radical discourse, but is a mode of analysing the issues of authority, power and virtue that have been at the heart of European political thought from the middle ages to the present day.

Perspectives on Feminist Political Thought in European History will be a welcome addition to a growing literature on an area of study that has often been neglected in the past.

Tjitske Akkerman is Assistant Professor in Politics at the University of Amsterdam. She has published on the history of the Dutch welfare state and the history of political thought. **Siep Stuurman** is Jean Monnet Chair of European Studies at Erasmus University, Rotterdam. He has widely published on the history of political thought, European and Dutch history, political philosophy and state formation.

Perspectives on Feminist Political Thought in European History
From the Middle Ages to the Present

Edited by Tjitske Akkerman
and Siep Stuurman

LONDON AND NEW YORK

First published 1998
by Routledge
2 Park Square, Milton Park, Abingdon, Oxfordshire OX14 4RN

Simultaneously published in the USA and Canada
by Routledge
711 Third Avenue, New York, NY 10017

First issued in hardback 2017

Routledge is an imprint of the Taylor and Francis Group, an informa business

© 1998 Selection and editorial matter, Tjitske Akkerman and Siep
Stuurman; individual chapters, the contributors

Typeset in Times by Routledge

All rights reserved. No part of this book may be reprinted or
reproduced or utilized in any form or by any electronic, mechanical,
or other means, now known or hereafter invented, including
photocopying and recording, or in any information storage or
retrieval system, without permission in writing from the publishers.

British Library Cataloguing in Publication Data
A catalogue record for this book is available from the British Library

Library of Congress Cataloguing in Publication Data
Akkerman, Tjitske. Perspectives on feminist thought in European
history: from the Middle Ages to the present/Tjitske Akkerman and
Siep Stuurman.
Includes bibliographical references and index.
1. Feminism–Europe–History. 2. Feminist theory–Europe–History. 3.
Feminist criticism–Europe–History. 4. Women–Europe–Social
conditions. 5. Europe–Politics and government. I. Stuurman, Siep. II.
Title.

HQ1588.A35 1998	97–25914
305.42'094–dc21	CIP

ISBN 13: 978-1-138-16690-5 (hbk)
ISBN 13: 978-0-415-15221-1 (pbk)

Contents

List of illustrations	vii
Notes on contributors	viii
Acknowledgments	x

1 **Introduction: feminism in European history**   1
Tjitske Akkerman and Siep Stuurman

2 **The languages of late-medieval feminism**   34
Miri Rubin

3 **A 'learned wave': women of letters and science from the
Renaissance to the Enlightenment**   50
Brita Rang

4 **L'égalité des sexes qui ne se conteste plus en France: feminism
in the seventeenth century**   67
Siep Stuurman

5 **Reclaiming the European Enlightenment for feminism: or
prologomena to any future history of eighteenth-century Europe**   85
Karen Offen

6 **Culture as a gendered battleground: the patronage of
Madame de Pompadour**   104
Inge E. Boer

7 **A woman's struggle for a language of enlightenment and virtue:
Mary Wollstonecraft and Enlightenment 'feminism'**   122
Virginia Sapiro

8 **French utopians: the word and the act**   136
Claire G. Moses

9 **Equality and difference: utopian feminism in Britain**   150
Ruth Levitas

10 **Liberalism and feminism in late nineteenth-century Britain**   168
Tjitske Akkerman

vi *Contents*

11 Feminists and sex: how to find lesbians at the turn of the century 186
Martha Vicinus

**12 Beauvoir's philosophy as the hidden paradigm of contemporary
feminism** 203
Karen Vintges

13 Contemporary feminism between individualism and community 218
Jet Bussemaker

Guide to further reading 234
Index 237

Illustrations

6.1	Louis Tocqué, *Portrait de Marie Leczinska*	107
6.2	Maurice Quentin de La Tour, *Portrait de la marquise de Pompadour*	108
6.3	Carle Vanloo, *Une sultane prenant du café*	114
6.4	Carle Vanloo, *Deux sultanes travaillant à la tapisserie*	115
11.1	Sarah Bernhardt as Hamlet	192
11.2	Sarah Bernhardt as the Duke of Reichstadt	193
11.3	Natalie Barney as a Hamlet-like page	195
11.4	The Marquis of Angelsey as the Duke of Reichstadt	196
11.5	'The Suffragette: Number 1 in a series of Present Day Types'	198

Contributors

Tjitske Akkerman is Assistant Professor in Political Science at the University of Amsterdam. She has published on the history of the Dutch welfare state and the history of political thought. She is the author of *Women's Vices, Public Benefits. Women and Commerce in the French Enlightenment* (1992).

Inge E. Boer is Associate Professor at the Belle van Zuylen Institute, the Amsterdam Graduate Centre for Multicultural and Comparative Gender Studies. She is interested in literary theory, postcolonialism and art history, and she has edited, with Mieke Bal, *The Point of Theory: Practices of Cultural Analysis* (1994).

Jet Bussemaker is Assistant Professor in Political Science and Public Administration at the Free University in Amsterdam. Her present research is on gender, citizenship and welfare states, and is sponsored by the Foundation for Law and Government of the Netherlands Organization for Scientific Research.

Ruth Levitas is Senior Lecturer in Sociology at the University of Bristol, UK. Her publications include numerous articles on aspects of utopianism and political ideologies. She is the author of *The Concept of Utopia* (1990).

Claire G. Moses is Professor and Chair of the Department of Women's Studies at the University of Maryland, College Park, USA, and editor of the journal *Feminist Studies*. She is the author of *French Feminism in the Nineteenth Century* (1984), winner of the Joan Kelly Memorial Prize for the best book on women's history: *Feminism, Socialism, and French Romanticism* (with Leslie Rabine, 1993); and editor of *U.S. Women in Struggle* (with Heidi Hartmann, 1995).

Karen Offen is a historian and Senior Scholar at the Institute for Research on Women and Gender at Stanford University (California). She has co-edited *Women, the Family and Freedom: the Debate in Documents, 1750–1950* (1983), with Susan Groag Bell, and *Writing Women's History:*

Contributors ix

International Perspectives, with Ruth Roach Pierson and Jane Rendall. She is completing a book on European Feminism, 1700–1950, which will be published in 1997.

Brita Rang was Associate Professor in History of Education at the University of Utrecht, and is now Professor at the University of Frankfurt am Main. She has published widely on the history of higher education and learned women in early modern Europe.

Miri Rubin is Lecturer in Medieval History at Oxford University and Fellow of Pembroke College, Oxford. She is interested in the social and cultural history of late medieval Europe. Her work includes *Charity and Community in Medieval Cambridge* (1987); *Corpus Christi: the Eucharist in Late Medieval Culture* (1991); and with Sarah Kay she has recently edited *Framing Medieval Bodies* (1994).

Virginia Sapiro is Sophonisba P. Breckinridge Professor of Political Science and Women's Studies at the University of Wisconsin, Madison. A political psychologist and feminist theorist, her most recent book is *A Vindication of Political Virtue: The Political Theory of Mary Wollstonecraft* (1992).

Siep Stuurman holds the Jean Monnet Chair of European Studies at the Erasmus University in Rotterdam. He has published widely on the history of political thought, European and Dutch history and state formation. He has recently edited *Les libéralismes: la théorie politique et l'histoire* (1994). His most recent book is on European state formation and political theory.

Martha Vicinus is Eliza M. Mosher Distinguished University Professor of English, Women's Studies and History at the University of Michigan. She has published on Victorian women, the history of sexuality and lesbian history. She is the author of *Independent Women* (1985) and an editor of *Hidden from History: Reclaiming the Gay and Lesbian Past* (1989).

Karen Vintges is Assistant Professor in Philosophy at the University of Amsterdam. She has published widely on theories of ideology, feminist philosophy and on the work of Michel Foucault. She is the author of *Philosophy as Passion: The Thinking of Simone de Beauvoir* (1996).

Acknowledgments

With the exception of the introductory essay, earlier versions of the chapters of this book were originally delivered at the international conference, Six Feminist Waves. Languages of Feminism in Modern History, organized by the Belle van Zuylen Research Institute at the University of Amsterdam in June 1994. We wish to thank the dean of the Belle van Zuylen Institute, Professor Selma Leydesdorff, as well as the manager, Barbara van Balen, for their generous support in preparing, funding and organizing the conference.

The conference has benefited from the financial support of the Royal Dutch Academy of Sciences, the departments of Political Science and Philosophy of the University of Amsterdam, the Department of Political Science of the Free University at Amsterdam, the Amsterdam School for Social Science Research, the City of Amsterdam, the Committee on Female Emancipation of the University of Amsterdam, the Board of the University of Amsterdam, the Geïllustreerde Pers, the Levi Lassen Foundation, the Rosa Manus Foundation, the Ministry of Education and Organon Ltd. KLM Royal Dutch Airlines was the official carrier of the conference.

The editing of this book was supported by grants of the Trust Foundation of the Erasmus University at Rotterdam, as well as the Faculty of the Social and Cultural Sciences of the University of Amsterdam.

We would like to thank Poppy Eveling for the splendid job she did in correcting the book in its final stage. We are grateful to Caroline Wintersgill, then at Routledge, now at University College London Press, who displayed an interest in our 'six waves project' when it was still in its infancy. Our thanks also go to Victoria Smith who, at Routledge, took care of the crucial final stages of the long road from conference to book.

Finally, we wish to express our deep gratitude to our contributors. They agreed to share an intellectual adventure with us, an adventure that turned out to be a highly rewarding one thanks to the quality of their scholarship and the enthusiasm of their response to our project. Without them this book could not even have gotten under way, let alone have been completed.

Tjitske Akkerman
Siep Stuurman
June 1996

1 Introduction
Feminism in European history

Tjitske Akkerman and Siep Stuurman

> What are women? What are they? Are they serpents, wolves, lions, dragons, vipers or devouring beasts and enemies of the human race. . . . But by God! if they are your mothers, your sisters, your daughters, your wives and your companions; they are yourselves and you yourselves are them.
>
> Christine de Pizan

In these flaming words Christine de Pizan decried the prevailing vilification of the female sex. The passage is from an open letter she circulated at the French court in 1401.[1]

Six centuries and the barrier of cultural otherness stand between us and Christine de Pizan. Nevertheless we cannot fail to recognize a feminist voice here. Pizan's text might figure in an anthology, side by side with, let us say, Marie de Gournay, François Poulain de la Barre, Gabrielle Suchon, Mary Astell, Olympe de Gouges, Mary Wollstonecraft, Harriet Taylor, John Stuart Mill, Simone de Beauvoir and Kate Millet. At the same time, however, numerous passages in Christine de Pizan's work are *not* immediately accessible to us. They evoke a mental universe and an intellectual context so different from ours that it cannot be readily located within the orbit of feminist discourse as we at present understand it. Christine de Pizan, then, appears to us as both a familiar and an enigmatic figure, a companion in arms from an alien and distant world, voicing feminist concerns in the forgotten allegorical language of courtly love.

We are facing a dilemma that is unavoidable in any attempt to reconstruct the history of a discourse. In order to trace the intellectual, cultural and political lineages of what we today call feminism, we have to know what we are looking for. The assertion that we recognize a feminist voice in Christine de Pizan necessarily implies that we have embarked on our historical inquiry with some preliminary notion of 'feminism'. On the other hand, we cannot take it for granted that there is one, unambiguous 'history of feminism' that develops along a continuous, evolutionary track from the Middle Ages until the present day. A historical investigation must take into account ruptures as well as continuities in the history of a discourse. In the history of feminist ideas this is especially important since feminism has *not* been one of the major, canonized European intellectual traditions. In the case of feminism,

2 Tjitske Akkerman and Siep Stuurman

the study of silence and forgetting must be an integral part of any historical account that aspires to be more than a collation of great examples and outstanding texts.

The term 'feminism' has been frequently restricted to the women's movements of the late nineteenth century and the contemporary period. When we look at the history of the word, such a restricted use is indeed correct. The word 'feminism' became common towards the end of the nineteenth century, and this conceptual innovation was part of a larger transformation of the European language of politics. From the early nineteenth century onwards, the emergence of the various 'Isms', such as nationalism, liberalism and socialism, coincided with the emergence of modern mass politics, the idea of social change and the expectation of a future better world. The Isms were essentially 'concepts of movement'.[2] In this context, feminism came to be defined as the political articulation of the collective organization of women. In this book, however, the term feminism is used in a much broader sense. That is not to say that we are following the older historiographical tradition stemming from the beginning of the twentieth century, in which feminism was used rather indiscriminately for a variety of ideas, as likely to be found in classical antiquity or ancient Gaul as in the Middle Ages or the nineteenth century. We propose to steer a middle course, limiting feminism to modern European history from late medieval times up to the present day, but not confining it to the nineteenth and twentieth centuries.

In contemporary women's history, terms like 'Renaissance feminism', 'seventeenth-century feminism' or 'Enlightenment feminism' have become almost commonplace. The new historical research of the past decades has convincingly demonstrated that the early-modern history of feminism is not one of isolated examples or lone precursors of a history that 'really' begins only in the nineteenth century. There are, of course, important differences between the nineteenth century and earlier periods, but we feel that a neat dichotomy between a 'history' and a 'prehistory' of feminism is no longer warranted. Hence, our account of European feminism spans the entire modern era, from late medieval times until the present day. Such a long-term historical perspective will enable us to discuss the relation between feminist thought and the making of modernity without *a priori* reducing feminism to a belated effect of Enlightenment egalitarianism.

We propose a provisional periodization containing six major subperiods or 'waves'. The modern history of European feminism, from *c.* 1400 to the year 2000, might be subdivided as follows:

1 Late-medieval and Renaissance feminism (1400–1600)
2 Rationalist feminism (1600–1700)
3 Enlightenment feminism (1700–1800)
4 Utopian feminism (1820–50)
5 Liberal feminism (1860–1920)
6 Contemporary feminism (1960–?)

Introduction 3

This periodization is tentative and hypothetical. It could hardly be otherwise. There is, as yet, no firm empirical grounding for a more precise assessment of the importance of feminist activities in the various periods. Virtually no quantitative research on feminist publishing has been done, and our six periods cannot be more than impressionistic historical constructs. Moreover, there is the complex issue of geographical coverage. All of the chapters discussing the early-modern period have a lot of material on France and French texts. It is important to keep in mind that books published in French were frequently reissued in other European countries, and, more generally, that French culture in early-modern Europe was an international elite phenomenon. By the seventeenth century Paris, that 'magazine of people and things', as John Locke once termed it, had become in many ways the cultural capital of Europe. Brita Rang's contribution refers to Latin texts, which also point to an international audience, but in addition she demonstrates the importance of German-speaking feminist voices from the sixteenth century onwards. The major omission in our treatment of the early-modern period is obviously Italy on which we would have liked to include a chapter. The chapters dealing with the eighteenth century chiefly focus on Britain and France, following most general historical treatments of the Enlightenment. Although the preeminent roles of France and Britain in the Enlightenment cannot be denied, the broader geographical spread of Enlightenment feminism largely remains to be explored. In this volume Karen Offen provides us with a number of fascinating glimpses of Scandinavian, German and Dutch sources.

In the course of the nineteenth century, feminism became a European-wide phenomenon: utopian feminism was, so far as we can see, mainly centred in Britain and France, but after 1850 no clear geographical centres can be discerned except for the greater vigour of feminism in the Protestant nations. Finally, contemporary feminism is an international movement that has left virtually no country untouched.

The contributions in this volume cannot claim any encyclopedic or 'complete' coverage. Other students of feminism will wish to highlight other geographical areas, other periods or episodes. With these *caveats* in mind we feel that it is worth our while to identify and discuss the historical links that are assumed in a growing body of recent and ongoing research. In such an investigation, we need a working definition of feminism that does not prejudice the issue either way. It must be sufficiently broad to be applicable to different historical periods and at the same time sufficiently specific to discriminate between feminist, non-feminist and anti-feminist utterances. Drawing on, but also slightly amending, Nancy Cott's working definition of feminism, we distinguish three core components in feminist discourse:

1 Criticism of misogyny and male supremacy
2 The conviction that women's condition is not an immutable fact of nature and can be changed for the better

4   *Tjitske Akkerman and Siep Stuurman*

3 A sense of gender group identity, the conscious will to speak 'on behalf of women', or 'to defend the female sex', usually aiming to enlarge the sphere of action open to women[3]

As borderline cases, we include texts and forms of behaviour that do not explicitly take a stand against male supremacy but nevertheless transgress the dominant codes of femininity.

We are, of course, aware of the fact that historical reality is always more messy and less clear cut than any definition. Feminist identities are not always to be found ready-made. There are many moments in history in which a sense of gender group identity is fragile, barely visible or on the verge of dissolving. Often a conscious collective identity only emerges when groups have first been identified and labelled by opponents: the term 'feminism', for instance, migrated to England when newspapers began to use it depreciatingly to refer to unwanted continental doctrines.[4] We understand gender group identity as a continuing process of making and unmaking. That implies that our definition cannot be used as a neat, quasi-geometrical standard. Recalling a famous observation in Pascal's *Pensées*, we need not primarily *esprit de géometrie*, but rather an *esprit de finesse* in order to appreciate the often subtle distinctions between feminists and non-feminists. As blurred borders and hybrid identities are fairly common in history, definitions will never dispel all or any doubts about identifying feminists and feminisms.

Our definition covers an enormous variety of theoretical and narrative genres, from allegorical poetry to philosophical treatises and political speeches. Written texts are the main sources used in this book, and our definition is more easily applicable to texts than to visual material. However, as Inge Boer and Martha Vicinus make clear in their contributions, images are often at the centre of cultural struggles about dominant codes of femininity. Even if their meaning is more difficult to pin down, images ought not to be regarded as second-rate sources. The twentieth century has often been called the age of images: representations of womanhood have never before changed so fast or exhibited such dazzling variety.[5] As Martha Vicinus shows in chapter 11, an actress like Sarah Bernhardt was a leading example not only for the growing côterie of fin-de-siècle Paris lesbians, but also for young suffragists. Photographs of suffragists from the period 1903–13 show them dressed in tweed suits, sturdy boots and neat bow ties. A cigarette or cigar, sword or walking stick, or at the very least a tie, were appropriated as symbols for a shorthand masculinity. Likewise, contemporary feminism has exploited the full range of the semiotic arsenal of (post)modern society, from crossdressing and billboards to movies and virtual images. For all that, the importance of iconographic material for the study of earlier historical periods must not be underestimated. We only need to think of the role of engravings and paintings in the representations of femininity. Nicole Pellegrin and Joan DeJean have stressed the importance of the image as a

Introduction 5

source of the discourses of gender in ancien régime Europe.[6] In this volume, Inge Boer reminds us of the important role of paintings and dress codes in the elite culture of eighteenth-century France.

By its very nature, feminist discourse is reflexive and 'theoretical' as well as action-oriented and therefore 'practical'. Women who wrote 'in defence of the female sex' fashioned a public language and constructed a collective identity that might be imagined as well as real and usually was both imagined *and* real although the balance between an imagined female community and a 'real' movement has undergone important changes in the course of modern history. Especially in the nineteenth and twentieth centuries the line between feminist thought and a feminist movement has not always been an easy one to draw. But even in the early-modern period many authors assumed some sort of sympathetic audience, a feminine Republic of Letters that was never taken for granted but always sought after and sometimes passionately desired. The feminist texts discussed in this book were in most cases not self-contained, isolated treatises but rather members of 'families of texts' actively drawing on and presupposing each other. Such series of inter-related texts, like those of the enduring Renaissance controversy on the status of women (usually known as the *Querelle des femmes*), clearly represent more than a number of isolated literary utterances.

FEMINISM AND THE HISTORY OF POLITICAL THOUGHT

Another question that should be addressed is whether it is worth trying to conceive an integral history of European feminism, now that the results of several decades of women's history have brought to the fore a sometimes overwhelming complexity of detail and a welter of subtle differences between groups of women, cultures and nations, and periods. The impressive, multi-volume *Histoire des Femmes/History of Women* project has brought together and synthesized the results of an enormous amount of contemporary research, but it discusses feminist authors and ideas within particular periods and geographical areas, without, however, presenting an overall account of the development of European feminism. One reason for presenting such an overall account is that specialized studies of individual feminists and feminisms tend to draw on more or less implicit presuppositions about what went before or what came after. Arguments about feminism 'now' and feminism 'then' are often used rather routinely, as if there actually is an agreed upon overall history of European, or even 'Western' feminism. It is one of the aims of this book to inquire into the possible contours of such an overall history.

The reconstruction of a long-term history of feminist thought both enables and compels us to consider its relationship to other fields of intellectual history, notably the history of political thought. Feminism has obviously been involved with key notions of modern political discourse, such as autonomy, liberty and equality. Moreover, feminist discussions of

6   Tjitske Akkerman and Siep Stuurman

morality and the tensions between private and civic virtue are closely linked to major currents in political thought, such as republicanism, civic humanism and romanticism. In the recent historiography of political thought, however, the history of feminism is still, with minor exceptions, relegated to the footnotes, if it is discussed at all. In the major twentieth-century handbooks of the history of political theory, feminist thought is virtually absent, or even dismissed out of hand. George H. Sabine's *A History of Political Theory*, a major and frequently reissued textbook, tells readers that John Stuart Mill valued some liberal ideas, 'like the enfranchisement of women, out of all proportion to their importance', and that is *all* the information the book has to offer about Mill's feminism.[7] In many later textbooks, John Stuart Mill's feminism is simply ignored, and feminist authors, such as Marie de Gournay, François Poulain de la Barre, Mary Astell and Mary Wollstonecraft, to name only a few major figures, are not mentioned at all. In the postwar venture of *conceptual history*, the situation is no better. The great multi-volume history of social and political key concepts, the German *Geschichtliche Grundbegriffe* ('Basic Concepts in History'), singles out the emergence of the modern Isms for special attention, but there is no entry for 'feminism'.

Now these examples are drawn from studies published before feminist historiography was rediscovered and the new women's history made its appearance. Yet even in more recently published work the canon of major political theorists has not changed much. The familiar cast of Dead White European Males (DWEMs for short) still reigns supreme. Ian Hampsher-Monk's *A History of Modern Political Thought*, a major new textbook published in 1992, is in many ways an admirable work, but with respect to the exclusion of feminist thought nothing much has changed.[8] In John Dunn's recent *Democracy. The Unfinished Journey. 508 BC to AD 1993*, a short chapter on recent feminist philosophy is added almost as an afterthought.[9] What is perhaps even more astonishing is that these and other authors fail to consider or respond to the critique of the patriarchal assumptions in the 'great thinkers' of the traditional canon formulated by feminist historians over the past twenty years or so, beginning with Susan Okin's *Women in Western Political Thought* (1979).[10] A reconstruction of the history of European feminism in the modern age will enable us to identify the parallels as well as the differences between the trajectories of feminism and male political theory. The historiography of political thought must come to terms with the fact that feminism is *not* simply a variety of recent 'radical discourse' but a specific mode of discussing the issues of virtue, power and authority that are at the heart of political thought. The realization that feminist thought has been a part of the self-reflection of European society right from the beginning, may in due course lead to a reconsideration of the key concepts underpinning the history of political philosophy itself.

Introduction 7

INVENTING A TRADITION OR RECOVERING SUPPRESSED EVIDENCE?

At the end of the nineteenth century feminists began to reconstruct their past systematically and sometimes professionally. For the first time in history they sought to create a female and feminist historical memory in order to prevent their history from being forgotten again.[11] These feminists established journals and libraries in order to support professional research and to inform a wider public. We could even say that they 'invented' a feminist tradition by searching for ancient documents which would reveal moments of former female glory and power, by publicly celebrating the memory of their predecessors, and by putting up statues or naming streets and marking places with memorial plaques.[12] Our project follows in the professional footsteps of this late nineteenth-century feminist fascination with history, but today we do not wish to found a tradition of charismatic historical worthies such as Amazons, Matriarchs, Gauls or Britons. That historical genre tended to flow over into myth, frequently set in a nationalist framework. Charlotte Stopes, for instance, began her general history *British Freewomen: Their Historical Privilege* (1894) with the exemplary 'feminism' of ancient Britain and Anglo-Saxon England.[13] This fascination with 'ancient history' and ultimate origins was not, of course, confined to feminism. It was found in much nineteenth-century historical narrative, especially in the historiography of nations and peoples. In recent critical studies of nationalism, these evocations of a mythical past have been deconstructed as 'invention'. The 'invention of tradition' has by now become a commonplace in cultural history and it has frequently been associated with uncritical use of sources, with bold sweeps of the imagination, or even with fraud or ideological manipulation. While acknowledging the force of this criticism, we feel that it must not lead us to a premature dismissal of the very idea of a long-term feminist tradition: after all, Christine de Pizan, Marie de Gournay and Mary Astell were no mythical Amazon queens (neither was the somewhat Amazon figure of the Princess de Montpensier at all mythical, as Louis XIV was to find out to his cost). It is not invention, but rather recovery and reconstruction that are called for in the case of feminism.

A brief comparison of the cases of feminism and nationalism can serve to clarify the point. Nationalism is, of course, one of the major traditions of modern Europe. Nationalist ideologies have penetrated European societies more successfully than any other type of discourse, for the elementary reason that societies and states were organized as nations. Written history was before all else national history, and even today historiography is dominated by the canon of the nation-state. It is therefore understandable that the myth of the ancient origin and smooth permanence of the homogenous nation has been subjected to harsh criticism in an age that has witnessed the murderous consequences of this particular ideology. The recent upsurge of the invention of tradition approach was actually occasioned by the critique

8   *Tjitske Akkerman and Siep Stuurman*

of traditional nationalist historiography.[14] The case of feminism is, however, far different. Prior to the first wave of women's history around the turn of the last century there existed precious little knowledge of feminist attitudes and writings before the mid-nineteenth century. In the most literal sense, there *was* no European feminist tradition, there were only the scattered remains and traces of earlier feminisms, mostly buried in the less frequented recesses of the great libraries and archives of European cities and states. The French historian Henri Piéron, who, at the turn of the last century, rediscovered the treatise on the equality of the sexes by the seventeenth-century feminist Poulain de la Barre, had to cut open the copy of the *Egalité des deux sexes* in the Bibliothèque Nationale where it had lain unread for over a century.[15] Many similar examples could be adduced. The process of historical retrieval, the recovery of supressed evidence, as Karen Offen calls it in her contribution to this book, is still going on today. New research continually uncovers feminist writings which were previously unknown, and sometimes unsuspected. Time and again, the conclusion imposes itself that the amount of feminist activity over the past six centuries has been consistently underestimated, even by historians sympathetic to the feminist cause. The issue of a feminist tradition is, then, almost the opposite of the case of nationalism. The point is not to demystify a dominant ideology but rather to reconstruct the elements of a forgotten and fragmented tradition of European discourse. The question is not, in our opinion at least, whether we ought to reconstruct a history of European feminism(s), but *how* we may do so.

Instead of the traditional emphasis on the difference between the nineteenth century and the prior history of feminist discourse, we propose to discuss each period in its own right, putting an equal emphasis on the historical specificity of particular forms of feminism and on the issue of their linkages with earlier and later parts of the trajectory of European feminism. In this way, we want to avoid the twin pitfalls of a facile evolutionism and a narrow historicism (in the Rankean sense of the latter term). Our approach is inspired by the critique of anachronistic and teleological genres of intellectual history that has been developed in fields such as political thought, the historical study of literature and the arts, and the history of natural science. The advocates of a contextual treatment of authors and texts, such as, for example, the 'Cambridge School' in the history of political thought, have convincingly argued that the historical meaning of a text can only be recovered by situating it in its contemporary lexical, intellectual and political contexts. Others have called for a 'social history of ideas' in which forms of sociability and channels of communication are studied as part of the process of the cultural and political 'making' of ideas. In the historical study of ideas, texts and discourses there exists at present a great variety of theoretical approaches which is also reflected in this book. Nonetheless, the views presented here share a broadly conceived historical and contextual approach: on the one hand, they privilege political languages over the tradi-

Introduction 9

tional, more philosophical focus on individual 'great' or 'canonical' texts; on the other hand, they eschew a purely semiotical, immanent textual analysis and opt instead for an historical study of texts and their multiple contexts. The latter point perhaps deserves some emphasis: usually there is not one unequivocal context, but a plurality of contexts. To cite a well-known example, John Locke, who was traditionally seen as a classical, natural-rights liberal, has been in turn portrayed as a late-medieval natural-law philosopher, a Calvinist moralist, a Baconian theorist of agrarian improvement, and a near-democratic revolutionary. Likewise, Christine de Pizan can be situated in the context of allegorical poetry and aristocratic courtly life, and in the intellectual tradition of the constitution of fame by means of historical exempla.

The same words do not convey the same meanings to authors and readers living in different ages. Notions like liberty, authority and equality are gendered in all historical epochs, but they are gendered in different ways in different periods. In our opinion, the different feminisms must be contextualized and, so to speak, restored to their own historical milieu, before we can attempt to reconstruct the long-term trajectory of European feminism. Such a reconstruction implies an analysis of the various ways in which feminists have drawn on earlier texts, as well as the cycles of forgetting and recovery of both ancient and recent events and texts. The links between earlier and subsequent feminist texts are seldom straightforward and clear; authors frequently appropriate and deploy elements of earlier texts, forging something new in the process by means of subtle shifts and new combinations, deleting some parts of previous discourses and adding new ones where they feel compelled to do so. Ideas and languages from a remote past can be routinely used or consciously redeployed. Reconstructing the trajectory of feminist ideas therefore means that we have to trace the ways in which authors have read and understood earlier feminist as well as non-feminist writings, albeit in their own highly idiosyncratic ways.

FROM THE LATE MIDDLE AGES TO THE ONSET OF THE ENLIGHTENMENT

More than fifteen years ago, Joan Kelly put forward the bold thesis that there was a European feminist tradition that antedated the era of the French Revolution and could be traced all the way back to the beginning of the fifteenth century. She saw the Renaissance *Querelle des femmes* as the principal genre of early-modern feminism. According to Kelly, early feminist theory was 'rooted in the humanistic form of literacy some women acquired while it was being denied to women as a sex'.[16] Right at the beginning of this line of thinking Kelly situated the imposing figure of Christine de Pizan who was the first to draw attention to the sexist partiality implicit in the whole extant body of misogynist literature, from classical antiquity to Latin Christendom. Pizan's work marked a turning point because she refocussed

10 *Tjitske Akkerman and Siep Stuurman*

the old medieval debate on marriage and female vices onto the issue of misogyny itself and because she did so as a woman speaking on behalf of the entire female sex. A new debate was opened, and it was opened to women as active participants.[17]

Our approach is obviously indebted to Kelly's pioneering insights. It is therefore useful to ask at this point which parts of her argument still stand today and what revisions have to be made as a result of the new research of the past decades. One major departure from Kelly's argument concerns periodization. Instead of lumping the whole 1400 to 1789 period together, we should at least distinguish two major subperiods: a first one that spans late-medieval and Renaissance times and ends somewhere in the seventeenth century; and a second one that more or less coincides with the Enlightenment. The feminism of the first period is fairly well represented by the genre of the *Querelle*, which was above all a discourse on morality and manners with philosophical concerns occasionally intruding. Enlightenment feminism, however, was exemplified by an altogether different mode of discourse, underpinned by a few key philosophical notions, such as reason, progress and, above all, equality, which is of course not to say that the older emphasis on manners and morals was absent from it. In this perspective, the seventeenth century appears as a time of transition in which different feminist genres existed side by side, even in the writings of individual authors. Marie de Gournay is a case in point: it is impossible to assign her work in an unequivocal way to either the *Querelle* literature or the genre of egalitarian-rationalist feminism.

Let us start with the first period. In her contribution to the present volume, Miri Rubin calls our attention to a variety of settings in medieval society, ranging from craft guilds to courtly high society, in which women contested the limitations put upon their activities by the prevailing masculinist practices and ideologies. The female critique of the dominant notions of gender came in many forms. What emerges from the sources, Rubin tells us, 'is a set of reflections and arguments, ranging in subject matter from homiletics, vernacular literature, to theories of just price and notions of public action, in which some writers valued women *despite* gender difference and others *because* of it'. The literary defence-of-women genre, sometimes amounting to scathing attacks on misogynist prejudices, was not absent from the late-medieval intellectual scene, and as such predated Christine de Pizan. Rubin's argument makes clear that we must not engage in a vain quest for ultimate origins. We should rather acknowledge the separate presence of elements of the three modes of discourse that, according to our working definition, went into the making of a distinct feminist voice. It may be impossible ever to identify the first 'really feminist' utterance in European history, but it seems highly plausible that it was well before Christine de Pizan. Pizan is one of those emblematic figures who mark a provisional ending as well as the beginning of something new. Rubin rightly points to the numerous elements in medieval culture that made

Introduction   11

Pizan's work possible. It remains true, however, that Pizan, by fusing these disparate elements into a synthesis, and by deploying all the means of courtly high culture and refined literacy at her disposal, produced a feminist discourse unprecedented in its aesthetic power and theoretical consistency. The precise valuation of Christine de Pizan's work, at the juncture of medieval and renaissance culture, is likely to remain a matter of dispute for some time to come.[18]

The literature of the *Querelle* proper expanded considerably during the fifteenth century. The introduction of printing gave birth to a new kind of literary world, wider in scope than anything that went before. In her seminal study of Renaissance feminism, Constance Jordan confines her sources to the printed texts in the vernacular languages, arguing that a fairly large, partly female audience as well as the multiplication and repetition of similar arguments were the defining characteristics of the *Querelle* and that this made it into more than a series of isolated intellectual events.[19] The sheer number of feminist printed texts over the entire period 1450–1650 is impressive. It seems to grow in volume over time, although no reliable quantitative data are at present available. Likewise, it would probably be premature to delineate the precise contours of the geographical spread of Renaissance feminism. Jordan demonstrates the major importance of Italian authors and texts in the fifteenth century. Thereafter, the centre of gravity appears to shift to the north-west and especially to France and the French-speaking Republic of Letters. In chapter 3, Brita Rang shows, however, that the contribution of the German-speaking lands was not negligible either. A comprehensive study of the European geographical pattern and its evolution over time would be extremely welcome.

The sense of standing in a tradition is clearly present in many of the *Querelle* authors, who frequently voiced the conviction that they were not alone, but many. One way of doing this was the compilation of enormous lists of famous, valiant or learned women from the remote past up to the times of the authors themselves. Brita Rang's chapter discusses the important genre of catalogues and lexica of 'learned women', a literary genre that went on well into the eighteenth century. According to Rang, these authors were addressing a central issue of the *Querelle*: the claim that women were intellectually capable and therefore entitled to enter the Republic of Letters. At the same time, their discourse was in line with some major features of Renaissance culture, such as the high cognitive status of the historical example and the validity of fame, the *Pantheon des Weltruhmes* ('Pantheon of World Fame') as Brita Rang calls it, following Jacob Burckhardt.

Of course, the *femme savante* ('learned woman') was not the only feminist role-model available to Renaissance authors. The Amazon heroine was also very much present as an historical example, an iconographic symbol and a protagonist of the female novel, as Joan DeJean has recently shown in the case of seventeenth-century France.[20] We may well ask, however, if the Amazon ideal was of more than symbolic significance, except for a tiny

12   Tjitske Akkerman and Siep Stuurman

minority of aristocratic ladies like the *Grande Mademoiselle* and her friends during the turbulent *Fronde* years in mid-seventeenth-century France. For the overwhelming majority of feminist authors, the ideal of the learned woman was by far the most attractive, as it directly concerned themselves in their quality as female writers who wanted to be heard and recognized in the male community of letters. Christine de Pizan is, once more, exemplary: in her *Livre de la cité des dames* ('Book of the City of Ladies') she dwells at length on famous queens and Amazon warriors, but when it comes to actually building the City of Ladies, its bastions and ramparts are raised on 'the field of letters'.

Moreover, the feminist struggle for recognition in the sphere of culture and letters was to some extent successful. By the middle of the seventeenth century, the female author had become a part of the European intellectual landscape, even though the status of women as writers and intellectuals remained a highly contested one. In the thriving salon culture, especially but not exclusively in France, the value of female conversation and, more generally, the contribution of women to politeness and literary refinement were greatly appreciated. Old-style rude misogyny did not completely disappear but it was more and more confined to the retarded culture of a backwoods aristocracy.[21] The power of this new female intellectual culture is, so to speak, proved in reverse by Molière's famous diatribes against the *précieuses* and the *savantes*; ridiculing female intellectual aspirations on the stage guaranteed a packed house in late seventeenth-century Paris, the then cultural capital of Europe. This fact alone goes far to prove that feminism had become much more than a marginal phenomenon. Furthermore, Molière illustrates the significance of manners and style for feminists and their enemies. His plays do not engage in any serious discussion of the ideas of the women he puts on the stage, the focus is rather on their behaviour, their language and gestures. For the première of the *Femmes savantes* Molière hired a male actor for the part of Philaminte, the chief *savante*, whereas the other female characters were played by actresses, and Chrysale, the timorous and harassed husband of Philaminte, by Molière himself.[22] The woman who ventures into the masculine realm of science was impersonated by a man who postured as a woman.

The association of feminism with crossdressing, trespassing and the violation of accepted codes of behaviour was, of course, no special prerogative of the critics of feminism. Nor was it a peculiarity of the seventeenth century: feminists, and more generally, women who felt estranged from the prevailing conventions of gendered correctness, have time and again experimented with subtle, challenging or ironic variations in manners, speech and dress (see especially the chapters by Inge Boer and Martha Vicinus in this volume).

Having succeeded in gaining access to the world of letters, many women ardently wished to win membership in the new institutions of scientific learning that were emerging all over Europe in the course of the seventeenth

Introduction 13

century. By and large, they failed. Nor did the spread of the modern theory of natural law benefit the feminist cause in an immediate way: just as women were refused access to the new scientific academies, they were conveniently forgotten in the greater part of the most influential statements of the 'natural equality of mankind'. Admittedly, the new discourse of 'natural equality' was potentially critical of masculine authority and it demolished old-style biblical patriarchism, but very few male theorists were ready to face the full implications of an egalitarian critique of gender hierarchy. In most cases, they were more concerned to establish in some, usually rather illogical way the 'naturalness' of the authority of the family father, so that the political contract could then be ratified by the male heads of families instead of the isolated, as yet ungendered individuals found in the famous 'natural condition of mankind'. It is well known that Locke in the final analysis opted for a 'foundation in nature' of male superiority, therewith violating one of his own basic axioms, while Hobbes first admits that male supremacy is not natural, then gets himself into a logical tangle and finally walks out as if nothing ever happened. Poulain de la Barre was one of the very few, perhaps the only, seventeenth-century author to point out in explicit terms the contradiction involved in the use of the term 'natural' by the theorists of natural jurisprudence.

A fundamental egalitarian critique of mainstream natural-rights thought was thus at least thinkable in the seventeenth century. And Poulain, as Siep Stuurman shows in chapter 4, did not stand alone – he was in many ways drawing on the large and multifarious corpus of extant feminist writing. Many seventeenth-century feminist authors, from Marie de Gournay and Anna Maria van Schurman, by way of Elisabeth Clement and Marguerite Buffet, to Poulain and Gabrielle Suchon fashioned and reworked the egalitarian critique of traditional arguments for male supremacy, usually pitting 'reason' against 'custom' and 'prejudice'. More generally still, sixteenth- and seventeenth-century feminism surely must be counted among the European cultural and intellectual currents that have contributed to the making of the modern idea of equality. On the other hand, the rise of 'natural equality' as a generally agreed standard during the 'crisis of the European mind'[23] at the close of the seventeenth century enabled eighteenth-century feminists to enlist this prestigious element of Enlightenment discourse in their cause. It is thus apparent that we must look at the relation between feminism and Enlightenment philosophy from two angles: apart from the standardly asked question, 'what was the significance of the Enlightenment for feminism', we should also inquire into the significance of feminism for the emergence of Enlightenment egalitarianism.

ENLIGHTENMENT FEMINISM

The Enlightenment is still passionately debated today. Its legacy has come to represent some of the most cherished but also most challenged elements of

14 *Tjitske Akkerman and Siep Stuurman*

modern Western culture. The liberation of men and women from the bonds of traditional authority has been traced back to the core values of the Enlightenment, but at the same time the modern cult of abstract and instrumental rationality is frequently blamed for the darker sides of twentieth-century politics. In the historiography of feminism as well as in contemporary feminist philosophy the heritage of the Enlightenment is highly contested. Against the traditional view of science and reason as liberating forces, the postmodern critique of the Enlightenment maintains that abstract rationality led to an eradication of difference and finally to a marginalization of female experiences and values.

The question then arises whether feminist authors like Olympe de Gouges and Mary Wollstonecraft were mistaken to stress natural equality and women's rationality, and more generally, to ground their feminist argument in an appeal to reason? We do not think so: the postmodern critique of 'abstract scientific rationality' fails to consider the intellectual and political contexts in which Enlightenment feminists voiced their appeals to reason. Feminists were used to counterpoise reason against various arguments of their opponents. Ever since the seventeenth century they had called upon reason in order to dismiss custom and tradition, and this particular opposition of reason versus prejudice was still important to Mary Wollstonecraft when she countered Edmund Burke's reverence for 'the rust of antiquity' in his *Reflections on the Revolution in France*. Burke had predicted in 1790 that the French Revolution would lead to tyranny, because of the revolutionaries' lack of respect for tradition. Like many of her intellectual friends, Wollstonecraft was no unqualified defender of the French Revolution, but she nevertheless felt that Burke's argument was indiscriminately used by conservatives to fend off all attempts to reform society, and to disqualify all those who supported the cause of liberty and equality.[24]

In this volume, Karen Offen and Virginia Sapiro both address the question of how the belief in reason shaped Enlightenment views of gender. They contend that we must attempt to extricate and understand the eighteenth-century connotations and shades of meaning of 'reason' instead of looking through the lenses of late twentieth-century philosophical quarrels. In chapter 7, Virginia Sapiro shows that for Wollstonecraft, reason was not an abstract, mathematical concept, but that it referred to the process of reaching understanding from experience. Her belief in the development of a rational disposition in the minds of women and men induced her to stress the importance of education, which meant to her a rich development of the individual personality through all her experiences, including not only formal education, but also learning by experience in other institutions, ceremonies and rituals, from dress codes to table manners. According to Sapiro, Wollstonecraft was well aware that one should not expect too much of reason until society was differently constituted. The judgment that she overrated the power of reason and underestimated the importance of social and political institutions, a standard Tocquevillean argument against Enlightenment

Introduction 15

philosophers ever since the nineteenth century, is based on a superficial and unsympathetic reading of Wollstonecraft's writings.

In chapter 5, Karen Offen points out that the characterization of the Enlightenment in terms of abstract reason and equality easily leads to a caricature of eighteenth-century feminism. Even though feminist authors emphatically claimed reason for themselves, they also emphatically invoked female values, seeking to find a balance between the sentiments of the heart and the demands of rationality. To highlight only the element of rationality is to miss the complexity as well as the emotional temper of Enlightenment feminism. Offen's argument raises the issue of the complex intellectual texture of the Enlightenment which cannot be reduced to a single philosophical formula. Reason was certainly central to it but its meaning was not always the same, and Enlightenment intellectual culture was by no means confined to rational*ism* in a restricted sense. A similar observation can be made about the concept of equality. 'Natural equality' was dear to many Enlightenment authors, and not least to feminist writers, but that is not to say that they did not consider or theorize difference. Moreover, and this is perhaps the decisive objection to any reduction of the Enlightenment to a 'rationalist project', social and political matters were discussed in a variety of settings and in disparate intellectual idioms, some of which had only a tenuous relation to the discourse of reason and equality. Besides rationalism, the modern historiography of the Enlightenment has identified at least three other major modes of discourse: the Protestant language of spiritual equality before God; the republican or 'civic humanist' language of virtue and citizenship; and finally the discourse of commercial society and self-interest. All three have implications for the theorizing of gender, and all three were on various occasions taken up by feminist authors.

In Northern Europe, particularly in the English-speaking world, feminist discourse was frequently couched in the Protestant language of spiritual equality. For English feminists like Mary Astell and Mary Wollstonecraft, the moral idiom of Protestant dissent, with its vehement rejection of idolatry and hypocrisy, was a major source of inspiration. Wollstonecraft's call for 'a revolution of manners' was strikingly akin to Mary Astell's late seventeenth-century criticism of women's idle conversation and their passive way of life 'as Tulips in a Garden'.[25] The Protestant criticism of the reigning cult of upper-class femininity in terms of idolatry inspired Astell's and Wollstonecraft's call for a reform of manners as much as their enlightened notion that reason should prevail over the 'tyranny of custom' and blind prejudice. For all that, the importance of the Protestant tradition for European feminism as a whole should not be overrated. The thesis, defended by Richard Evans, Olive Banks, Jane Rendall and others, that the Protestant ethos has been a necessary condition for the emergence of strong feminist movements may be plausible when applied to the second part of the nineteenth century when the movement for the emancipation of women was indeed most impressive in England, the Netherlands and the Scandinavian

16   Tjitske Akkerman and Siep Stuurman

countries (and the United States), but it does not work so well for feminism in the early-modern period. Renaissance feminism was particularly strong in Catholic countries like Italy and France, and seventeenth- and eighteenth-century feminism was probably stronger in France than anywhere else in Europe. Surveying the long run of the history of European feminisms, there seems to be no convincing case for a selective affinity between feminism and one particular religious culture.

The importance of the republican language of the civic virtues in late eighteenth-century feminism has by now been widely acknowledged.[26] While Protestantism focussed on the private character of morality, republicanism stressed the *public* nature of virtue. In some feminist writings, religious themes were mixed with ideas about civic morality. It has been observed, for instance, that the rise of a new ideal of motherhood in the late eighteenth century frequently exhibited such a mixture of republican and Protestant values. In the American and French revolutions, feminist authors extolled the virtues of the mothers of the republic, whose duty it was to bear sons and raise them to become virtuous citizens who loved their fatherland above all.[27] Karen Offen indicates that the ideal of militant citizenship informed republican proposals in France to turn the education of women into an affair of state. She quotes Mably who warned that in a republic women should not be forgotten: 'You must choose, either to make men of them as at Sparta or condemn them to seclusion.' The Enlightenment brought about an ever-widening debate about the education of women, and numerous authors, both female and male, both feminist and non-feminist, discussed female education in terms of the cultivation of patriotic attitudes and values.[28] The dominant 'Spartan' strand in republicanism tended to identify civic virtue with militant and 'manly' qualities such as heroic self-sacrifice. It was the Spartan mother, who cared more about the fate of the state than that of her sons, on which Rousseau, Baudeau, Mably and others modelled their ideal of motherhood. But the traditional republican discourse of the patriotic, armed citizenry might also be enlisted in a more direct way by militant feminists, such as one encounters in the demands of the *citoyennes republicaines revolutionnaires* ('republican revolutionary female citizens') who in 1793 claimed the right to participate in the armed defence of the republic.[29]

Finally, a more positive view of the 'feminine' virtues emerged with the rise of a commercial ethos and the notions of enlightened self-interest and polite manners. The eighteenth-century preoccupation with manners was linked to the theory of 'commercial society' as a new and higher stage of human civilization that called for a reappraisal of traditional standards of civility and politeness. With the emergence of the new political and economic language of manners, feminine values traditionally condemned as 'luxurious' and 'effeminate' came to be praised for their utility.[30] The love of luxury, fashion and a refined taste were applauded and upgraded by writers who promoted a commercial mentality and who despised the uncouth warrior ethos of the traditional sword nobility. The 'destruction of the hero'

Introduction 17

and the new ideal of politeness went together, and the origin and early development of this transformation of elite culture can be traced back to the seventeenth-century French salons. In the light of these developments, it is not surprising that critics of a commercial morality, of which Rousseau was the paramount representative, frequently turned against certain feminine values as well, and particularly detested the French elite culture [31]

On the other hand, most female authors and feminists, two categories that overlap but do not coincide, found a natural habitat in salon culture. The same can be said of female patronesses of the arts. In the world of the salon, women 'naturally' played a leading role as teachers of the subtleties of rank, etiquette, taste, dress, manners and conversation. Very often, the power and visibility of these women made them into objects of admiration by some and of hatred and abuse by others. The world of the salons was extremely fluid and the boundaries between 'respectable' and 'unlicensed' behaviour were not always easy to perceive, especially for women. Madame de Pompadour was such a *salonnière* who transgressed existing boundaries of rank and gender, even though her stance was not explicitly feminist in any commonly accepted sense of the word. In her contribution to this book, Inge Boer carefully analyses her position as a court salonnière, comparing it to that of women in the typical Enlightenment salon.

Madame de Pompadour is a borderline case when it comes to identifying who was a feminist and who was not. Inge Boer's chapter 6 helps us to appreciate the importance of the social milieu and the different modes of sociability for Enlightenment feminism. What women, feminist or not, were able to say or write, depended as much on the immediate social setting and on political culture as on the intellectual context. Feminism changed its colours and its language as it moved from the relatively secluded world of the early salons to the more open and dangerous world of 'public opinion' that emerged all over Europe in the course of the eighteenth century. The Enlightenment salon developed out of the older salon culture in the middle decades of the century, when court control over elite culture was relaxed after the death of Louis XIV. It was invented and presided over by women of letters like Marie-Therèse Geoffrin, Jeanne-Julie de Lespinasse and Suzanne Necker.[32] Until the 1780s, these salons provided the channel for a successful entry of elite women in the Republic of Letters. But, just as in the seventeenth century, women were not admitted to the great national institutions of learning like the academies. We would need more comparative research to explain why women were not successful in this respect, in contrast to the situation in Italy where many female intellectuals gained admission to academies from the early seventeenth century onwards. Emilie du Châtelet, for instance, was elected to the Bologna Institute, but she did not manage to get a seat in the Académie Française or in any other French academy.[33] Women like Emilie du Châtelet and Madame de Lambert played an important part as mediators in getting some of the *philosophes* elected in the

18 *Tjitske Akkerman and Siep Stuurman*

academies, but they themselves remained excluded. Thus, the most prestigious institutions of learning remained closed to women.

The feminism of the typical Enlightenment salon must be sharply marked off from that of the feminist *journals*, especially the *Journal des dames*.[34] These journals were everything other than established; more or less tolerated but not formally licensed by the authorities they had a very uncertain existence. Compared to the situation in countries such as England and Germany, in France feminist journals were far more harassed; fifteen *libraires*, ten royal censors, and five police and book-trade directors were involved in working against the *Journal des dames*.[35] According to Gelbart, the radical oppositional mentality of the feminist journalists linked them to the revolutionary feminism of Olympe de Gouges and other women militants in the *Grande Révolution*. However, other students of eighteenth-century political culture have argued that the Enlightenment salon was no less important as a precursor of revolutionary feminism, even though by the 1780s the salons were losing their exclusive position in the making of public opinion because new institutions of intellectual sociability, such as museums and political clubs, had emerged.[36] At present, there is no scholarly consensus about the relation between Enlightenment and revolutionary feminism.

The French Revolution itself is sometimes regarded as predominantly masculinist and anti-feminist. Various scholars have stressed the repressive features of the Revolution, notably the masculine 'Spartan' political culture of the Jacobin dictatorship culminating in the outlawing of the clubs of female citizens in October 1793. Nobody will deny that Jacobin rule with its gendered public roles for male citizens and exclusively domestic roles for women, inspired by a Rousseauist ideal of motherhood, represented a ferocious backlash against feminist aspirations to a public voice for women. Yet, the eventual defeat of feminism should not be read back into the 1789–93 period, in which feminist political presence was actually quite impressive. The work of Darline Levy, Harriet Applewhite and others has demonstrated that women's political participation in the early phase of the French Revolution was not the preserve of a small elite group.[37] Moreover, the French Revolution created a new public space and a novel political culture that called forth new and multiple repertoires of political action on the part of women. In contrast to the salons, the new women's clubs excluded men and were thus able to formulate the idea of a collective political interest of women. They frequently followed the organizational model of the Masonic movement with its gendered separation of lodges.

In the open political atmosphere of the first years of the French Revolution, when political women's clubs flourished and censorship had broken down, feminists voiced an impressive array of political claims, including demands for political participation, equal treatment in civil law, the legalization of divorce, and a wholesale reform of family law. In the early years of the Revolution the winning of civil and political rights for women sometimes appeared to be nearly within reach. Lynn Hunt has underlined

Introduction   19

the importance and *the novelty* of the appearance of a feminist political discourse which, in her view, 'distinguished the French Revolution from all previous such upheavals, including the American Revolution of the 1770s and 1780s and the Dutch Revolution of 1787'.[38] The debates of the National Assembly in 1789 and 1790 were dominated by a democratic discourse that employed a radicalized, frankly egalitarian language of natural rights. A feminist like Olympe de Gouges sought to legitimate her demands for women's rights in terms of the political language of the *Declaration of the Rights of Man and the Citizen*, a document invested with the august authority of the National Assembly. In particular Article Six of the 1789 Declaration, proclaiming the right of *all* citizens to partake in the formation of the general will, opened up a unique historical opportunity to place the demand for female suffrage on the political agenda. Olympe de Gouges' *Declaration of the Rights of Woman and the Citizen* boldly declared that all the rights mentioned in the Declaration, including Article Six, ought to apply to all men *and* women.[39] In July 1790 Condorcet had submitted a proposal for equal political rights for both sexes to the National Assembly, but his views were shared by only three other deputies.[40] For the overwhelming majority of the male revolutionaries female suffrage was altogether unacceptable, but it is striking that the principle of equality as such was acknowledged by several of them. In his *Observations on the new Organization of France*, submitted to the National Assembly in October 1789, the Abbé Sieyès ironically observed:[41]

> In the present state of customs, opinions and human institutions, one sees women called upon to wear the crown, and, by a bizarre contradiction, they are nowhere included among the active citizens, as if it were not an axiom of sound politics to enlarge more and more the proportional number of real citizens, and as if it were impossible for a woman ever to be useful to the commonwealth. Following a prejudice that does not even allow for doubt in these matters, we are thus compelled to exclude at least half of the entire population. At a single stroke, twenty-six million souls are reduced to twelve and a half million.

In this early phase of the Revolution, the idea of sexual equality was not yet entirely supplanted by the Rousseauist republican discourse of motherhood and domestic virtues. Admittedly, the upsurge of feminist aspirations was a shortlived phenomenon that lasted only for a few years. It is undeniable that much of the new feminist politics did not survive the Jacobin dictatorship. Finally, the principles of female subordination and an exclusively domestic role for women were enshrined in the *Code Napoléon* which heavily influenced early nineteenth-century legislation in the greater part of continental Europe. On the other hand, the memories of eighteenth-century and revolutionary feminism, and the revolutionary language of female citizenship were not completely erased by the early decades of the nineteenth century. The egalitarian and democratic legacy of the French Revolution remained a

20 *Tjitske Akkerman and Siep Stuurman*

powerful source of inspiration for the succeeding generations. An active public political role for women had been claimed at a climacteric moment in European history and this and other powerful vindications of the rights of women could be recovered and reasserted by nineteenth-century feminists, even though, at the present time, we cannot identify precisely the channels through which the message was transmitted to the generation of the 1820s and 1830s.

THE NINETEENTH CENTURY: UTOPIAN FEMINISM

The political history of the nineteenth century is made up of two great periods of a markedly different nature. Before the revolutions of 1848, certain parts of Europe were already passing through the first phase of the industrial revolution, but politically the continent was still living in the aftermath of the French Revolution and the Napoleonic Wars. After 1848, another era began, characterized by intermittent struggles for the democratization of state and society, successful in some parts of Europe, doomed to failure in others. By and large, nineteenth-century feminism fits into the same pattern: the utopian-socialist feminism of the earlier part of the century and the liberal-feminist movements that emerged in various countries after the mid-century decades show striking differences of theoretical discourse and political culture and style.

Utopian-socialist feminism flourished in the 1820–48 period, especially in France. From France it spread to other European countries, for example Italy and Spain. In Britain it developed in a more autonomous fashion, even though the influence of French ideas and figures is undeniable. The French utopian-feminist movement was preeminently inspired, but also haunted, by the past. As late as 1848, in response to the February Revolution of that year, feminists who had participated in Saint-Simonian and Fourierist circles looked back to the Revolution of 1789. In the *Voix des femmes* ('The Women's Voice'), a feminist journal founded in the crucible of the 1848 upheaval, one of them exclaimed:

> Arise! Look to the past and march to the future. . . . In the first Revolution women acted politically by using posters, pamphlets, clubs, stormy debates, heated discussions – they took part in all and often were the impetus for them. Their spirit was not deterred by obstacles.[42]

The biographies of 'femmes célèbres' ('famous women') and the memoirs of earlier generations of feminists did, however, not only evoke positive images and examples. The spectre of '1789' could also be used to conjure up a disquieting association of women's collective action with unruliness and mob violence. The utopian feminists were frequently compelled to defend themselves against the accusation of being the spiritual granddaughters of the 'furies' of 1789.

Not only feminist movements, but French politics as a whole was haunted

Introduction 21

by the legacy of 1789. As Ernest Renan once stated, comparing the history of France to the old Hebrew legend of Rebecca: revolutionary France remained 'an unborn child, struggling in the womb of the country'.[43] According to de Tocqueville, the Revolution had been a political movement that took the form of a religious upheaval, and this aspect of the Revolution explained the dramatic and passionate antagonism between a 'black' Catholic France and a 'red' revolutionary France. In this context it is not surprising that French feminism had to relate in some way or other to the question of the place of religion in the society of the future, and to the Catholic view of women as well.

While late nineteenth-century French feminism was preeminently secular and anti-clerical, the feminism of the pre-1848 period was not. The Saint-Simonian feminists were deeply committed to a religious view of the human predicament, as Claire Moses points out in chapter 8. They called themselves 'apostles', their 'Church' was to be headed by a couple-Pope, they awaited a female Messiah, and their writings resonated with New Testament rhetoric. Their religion must indeed be called 'red': the Saint-Simonian feminists were mostly working-class women, trying to extend the class analysis of the Saint-Simonian doctrine to the relations between women and men. They set up cooperative associations, but extended them beyond the workplace. They practised what they preached, establishing co-directorships of women and men in their health-clinics, cooperative workshops for tailors and seamstresses, and communal dining halls.

Owenite feminism in Britain was in some ways related to the French utopian tradition, but it developed an altogether different political style. The British feminists' radical critique of bourgeois marriage, analysed by Ruth Levitas in chapter 9 in this volume, was framed in terms of women's slavery. Especially in England, such language reflected the influence of the anti-slavery movement on utopian feminism, for instance through Anne Knight and Frances Wright. The links between abolitionist and feminist movements have a long tradition that originates in the Enlightenment and continues into the late nineteenth century. Even before Mary Wollstonecraft, who expressed her abolitionist sympathies in several of her books, feminists had compared the lot of women to that of slaves.[44] In Britain in particular, the anti-slavery campaigns were an important vehicle for the entry of women into public life. The anti-slavery petitions in the early 1830s occasioned the first large-scale intervention of women in British parliamentary politics.[45] Since the second half of the eighteenth century the mobilization of British public opinion and its use in influencing parliamentary politics had become increasingly important. This male prerogative of putting pressure on the national government was now claimed by women's organizations as well.

It was only with the benefit of hindsight that the pre-1848 movements in Britain and France came to be labelled 'utopian'. The denigrating term 'utopian' was applied by Marx and Engels to discredit the cooperative organization of the workplace as an immature form of socialism. However, these

22 Tjitske Akkerman and Siep Stuurman

early feminists and socialists were only 'proved wrong' by a history they could not possibly have foreseen. The political theories of the Saint-Simonians, Fourierists and Owenites were conceived in a society confronted with the beginnings of the industrial revolution. Perhaps it was not 'unscientific' but quite realistic to believe that the cooperative artisan workshop and the medium-sized farm formed the model for a socialist society (John Stuart Mill was still thinking along such lines when he drafted his 'Chapters on Socialism' in the early 1870s!). Confronted with a still chiefly artisan capitalism, utopian feminists naturally arrived at the conclusion that small-scale, locally organized socialism would offer the opportunity to change the sexual division of labour, and perhaps even to reorganize domestic work.

THE NINETEENTH CENTURY: LIBERAL FEMINISM

In the second half of the nineteenth century a new wave of feminist activity began. In the 1860s, following the lead of the United States, organizations for the emancipation of women were founded in France, Germany and Britain, soon to be followed by most other European countries. The type of feminism they articulated was markedly different from that of their predecessors. While the utopian feminists had appealed to working-class women, the new feminism was a predominantly middle-class movement. And whereas the pre-1848 feminists had adapted the language of utopian socialism to their own purposes, their post-1848 sisters voiced their demands in the language of liberal reform. When applied to these feminist movements, the term 'liberal' is used rather vaguely to refer to various middle-class groups who shared beliefs in reform and progress. As such, the demands of these women's organizations were not altogether new. The reform of matrimonial legislation, equal access to the labour market, the opening of secondary and higher education to women, and finally the right to vote – all these had, at one time or another, been discussed by Enlightenment feminists. What was new, however, was that such demands now became part of a political platform supported by formal, eventually nation-wide organizations. Moreover, these women's organizations soon acquired a fairly large following. At the end of the century, when women began to organize on an ever larger scale in moral reform societies, trade unions, political parties, suffrage organizations and so on, feminism had developed into an authentic mass movement. At the same time it was spreading across the social spectrum, once again including working-class women.

In the historiography, the feminists of the period from 1860 to 1920 are frequently depicted as middle-class, liberal and Protestant. It is probably correct to call the movement middle-class in the ecumenical and rather vague sense in which the term was used by many nineteenth-century observers, but not in any precise sociological sense. However, we have to take note of the fact, already indicated above, that the social composition of

Introduction 23

feminism broadened around the turn of the century. Turning to the political character of the movement, it has most often been designated as 'liberal'. It is certainly true that liberal ideas set the initial agenda for late nineteenth-century feminism, but towards the end of the century the movement became ideologically more diversified. Nonetheless, there are good arguments for the thesis that in most European countries liberal ideology remained central to the politics of feminism. In Britain this was certainly the case, as Tjitske Akkerman shows in chapter 10.

Especially in Britain, progressive liberal ideas easily mixed with other political languages. One of the foremost liberal feminists in Britain, John Stuart Mill, was well acquainted with Saint-Simonian leaders. This should remind us of the fact that the feminist movement of the second half of the century was not a complete world apart from the earlier utopian movements. Although the utopian-socialist experiments with cooperatively organized households and workplaces were rather marginal to the later feminist movement, a radical and 'socialist' inspiration remained part of liberal feminism in Britain. This should also be taken into account when we try to explain the development of British feminism at the turn of the century. When feminism grew into a mass movement the potential for internal class tensions increased, but in Britain these tensions were more successfully bridged than on the continent. In 'lib-lab feminism', like lib-lab politics in general, we encounter the ideals of democracy and radical equality, which were part of a tradition that ran from Chartism by way of Gladstonian Liberalism to the New Liberalism after the turn of the century. The political nature of British feminism is to be contrasted with the sometimes acrimonious relations between socialist and liberal feminists in other European countries, especially Germany where the division between liberal and socialist women became manifest in 1894 with the foundation of the *Bund Deutscher Frauenvereine* ('League of German Women's Associations').

Apart from middle-class culture and liberalism, evangelical Protestantism has been identified as a major influence in nineteenth-century feminism. In the case of Britain and the United States, the moral language of Protestantism and the evangelical networks provided the linkages between early nineteenth-century abolitionism and the emergence of liberal feminism. According to Jane Rendall the lack of such a Protestant culture in France explains the slow growth of French liberal feminism, compared with Britain and America. In the latter two countries, anti-slavery was a broad social movement, using mass propaganda, while in France it was small and elitist.[46] However, the importance of abolitionism should not be overrated. Even in the absence of a large-scale anti-slavery movement, Protestant culture goes a long way towards explaining the success of feminism in the Netherlands and the Scandinavian countries. Generally speaking, late nineteenth-century feminism encountered greater resistance in Catholic countries than in Protestant ones.[47]

The major idiom of late nineteenth-century feminism is made up of

24 Tjitske Akkerman and Siep Stuurman

various mixtures of Protestant and liberal discourse. Feminists freely drew on the liberal discourse of 'equal rights', but they were by no means committed to a radical claim of gender equality in all fields of life, and they also took up the theme of a special civilizing mission of the female sex. Within feminism, there developed a discourse of a particular elevated and morally worthy 'feminine nature', of separate spheres, of the designation of women as key agents in the moral order, and the need for a female effort towards the domestication or civilization of 'masculine politics'. This way of thinking frequently inspired 'the call to women to . . . identify with their fellow [sic] sisters as women'.[48] Until quite recently, historians were inclined to identify such ideas as conservative tendencies within nineteenth-century feminism, on the assumption that an appeal to sexual difference was almost by definition contrary to the feminist ideals of Reason and Equality. Thanks to the theoretical and historical debate about 'difference' and 'equality', which is still on the agenda of feminist historians today, we have come to understand that there were various ways in which commitments to equality and difference coexisted without necessarily leading to a conservative stance. Taking the suffrage struggle, for instance, it is now well known that feminists often combined a commitment to equal rights with the belief that women as mothers had a special mission to civilize the sphere of 'male politics' and to purge it from its destructive and warlike qualities. Such beliefs in a moral duty to civilize the world were found in several types of reform movements in the nineteenth century, notably in evangelical Protestantism, but in many varieties of liberalism and socialism as well.

That an appeal to sexual difference in itself cannot be taken as a sign of conservatism becomes particularly clear when we look at feminist ideas about social reform. At the turn of the century, women's movements in several European countries, often sustained by personal contacts across national borders, formulated demands for the amelioration of the condition of mothers, especially working-class mothers. While stressing the elevated dignity of maternity and its important function for society, they not only asserted the duties but also the rights of mothers. Though this meant that feminists relinquished earlier ideals of individual rights and now formulated claims on behalf of their contribution to the community as wives and mothers, this does not imply that such an appeal to motherhood can be termed conservative. Feminist historians have by now well established that such distinctions are far too crude to draw a line between feminist ideas on one side and non- or anti-feminist ideas on the other.

In our discussion of nineteenth-century feminism we have dealt with three main intellectual traditions: utopian socialism, evangelical Protestantism and liberalism.[49] Some caution is needed, however. Our view is predominantly derived from the history of feminism in Britain, the United States, France and a few other countries, such as the Netherlands and Belgium. In other European countries feminism followed different trajectories. In the German lands and in Eastern Europe, many women were

Introduction 25

inspired by nationalist ideals, especially in the 1840s. In the 1848 German revolutions, women dressed in the national colours black-red-gold, while the most courageous among them summoned women to form a regiment 'um für's Vaterland zu kämpfen und zu streiten' ('to fight and struggle for the Fatherland').[50] Women such as Narcya Zmichowska in Poland, Clara Maffei, Cristina Trivulzio Belgiojoso and Ester Martini Currica in Italy, and Karolina Svetlà in Bohemia all voiced nationalist aspirations.[51] These regional differences within European feminism do not only concern nationalism, but also religion. In some Southern European countries, Catholic movements played an important role in the development of feminism.[52] The history of nineteenth-century feminism cannot be separated from these diverse contexts, and historians of Southern and Eastern or Central European feminism have warned against compressing the history of European feminism into one single model.

Nevertheless, it is hard to deny that feminism was more successful in Northwestern Europe than in the rest of the continent. When we trace the most favourable conditions for the emergence of feminist mass movements at the end of the nineteenth century, it is very plausible that Protestantism on the one hand and a liberal-democratic culture on the other were the crucial factors. Generally, feminist organizers and authors in Northwestern Europe forged their own ideas in a continuous critical dialogue with liberalism, Protestant thought and, later on, with socialism. In these parts of Europe, late nineteenth-century feminism was part of a broad movement of ideas that accompanied the democratization of society and the state.

CONTEMPORARY FEMINISM(S)

As Jet Bussemaker observes in chapter 13, contemporary feminism is multifarious and hard to define. The movement we have provisionally christened 'the sixth wave' is still continuing today, and there is, as yet, no consensus about its historical significance and eventual results. Contemporary feminism encompasses an extremely broad range of substantial issues, organizational forms and political styles. Its kaleidoscope of programmes seems to condemn all definitional exercises and neat taxonomies as so much vanity. Its manifold languages have appropriated and transcended almost all previous feminist discourses. It sometimes appears in an outright abstract-philosophical and even anti-historical guise, but at the same time it has probably produced a greater awareness of women's past and the history of feminism than has ever existed before. The cultural and intellectual variety of contemporary feminism is matched by its organizational diversity, ranging from informal consciousness-raising groups to single-issue campaigns and huge, nation-wide formal organizations. Moreover, contemporary feminism has from its very beginning been an *international* movement, far more so than any of its predecessors in European history.

For all its kaleidoscopic variety, the major historical coordinates of contemporary feminism can be determined with some precision. It originated in advanced industrial society, mainly but not exclusively in the North-Atlantic world. It emerged as part of broader cultural and political transformation in the 1960s and 1970s which one might characterize as a deepening of the democratic sentiment in all spheres of social life. Tocqueville famously observed that equality by its very nature engenders a passionate desire for more and more equality. Living in the aftermath of the French Revolution, Tocqueville was thinking of the nineteenth century, but his observations about the propensity of the egalitarian ethos to feed upon itself are even more true of the contemporary age. After the defeat of Nazi Germany, Western society was reconstructed on the foundations of a democratic consensus that left no legitimate place for traditional, non-functional forms of authority. Bussemaker's observation about the Netherlands can be generalized: the ideal of the responsible autonomous citizen gained ground everywhere, albeit in different ways, sometimes enthusiastically welcomed and in other places and at other times only reluctantly accepted. A less authoritarian model of the nuclear family gained ground as well, as the imposing figure of Doctor Spock hovered over the mid-Atlantic. Finally, a new culture of consumption, full employment and the welfare state encouraged women and men in all walks of life, but especially in the middle strata of society, to look for enjoyments and opportunities that had in previous historical periods been reserved for the upper classes. Ancient ideals like self-development, autonomy and authenticity now entered the imagination of ever broader layers of society. They were fuelled, and partly channelled by the new welfare-state agencies attuned to psycho-cultural and social regulation. New psychological needs were articulated, or manufactured as some critics contended, but new forms of political opposition emerged as well. In the final analysis, the psychotherapist and the rebellious youngster were two sides of the same coin. The grave, reassuring rhetoric of the Cold War and the mixed economy went together with the frenzied rhythm of the new styles in music, clothing and behaviour. In the long run, the mixture proved quite unstable.

The traditional division of labour, social roles and psychological traits between the sexes sat ill with the prevailing ethos and style of the postwar democratic, advanced industrial society. Women were full political citizens, at least in theory, but they were clearly not full participants in social, political and economic life. They were told by Doctor Spock and other well-meaning experts to raise their children in a non-authoritarian, modernized way, but they themselves were apparently not to take part in the welter of new opportunities laid before their sons and, to a lesser extent, their daughters. In postwar Europe and America, girls enrolled in secondary and higher education en masse, but it was less clear what they were going to do with the certificates and grades they obtained in such impressive numbers. Huge changes were transforming society; women were part of that process, and yet they were not. The same ambivalence was, of course, to be found in the lives

Introduction 27

of many men, but for women the contradictions and tensions were perhaps more difficult to deal with and harder to diagnose. The myriad manifestations of these tensions and contradictions constituted, in the famous words of Betty Friedan in *The Feminine Mystique* (1963), 'the problem that has no name'. It was the new feminist movement that gave the problem a name, or rather, as it turned out, a bewildering variety of names.

In the 1970s, terms such as sexism, the patriarchal system, sexual politics, coercive heterosexuality, the sex-gender system, and so on and so forth became commonplaces of feminist discourse, and some of them gained the status of household words in the mass media. By the 1980s, sexism was, in the liberal and progressive parts of Western society, generally felt to be a grave moral and political offence, whereas twenty years before most people would not even have understood the meaning of the term. The prohibition of gender discrimination began to be written into constitutional law and judicial decisions. Feminism became a more or less accepted part of the political vocabulary of Western society, and it was also taken up by many Third World movements and, finally, by the United Nations and other international organizations. Gender equality remained, however, a highly contested issue, and in most spheres of society discrimination against women continued, although frequently in muted and self-ashamed ways.

As noted above, any attempt to identify a single feminist language as the representative discourse of contemporary feminism is doomed to failure. In their respective contributions to this volume, Jet Bussemaker and Karen Vintges underline the multiplicity of discourses that together make up recent feminist thought. They handle that multiplicity, however, in different ways. Bussemaker stresses the polarity of egalitarian individualism and differential communitarianism, arguing that a generic egalitarian critique of all kinds of male dominance provides a consensual background to the otherwise widely divergent feminisms of the last decades. Communitarian, socialist and postmodern feminists may despise hard-core liberal individualism, but they usually subscribe to at least some basic egalitarian notions. Likewise, those feminists who claim a particular feminine identity in terms of 'difference' and the affirmation of 'otherness' usually take for granted the notion of an equal value or dignity of different life projects, be they female, male or androgynous. Vintges, on the other hand, puts more emphasis on the other side of the equality/difference polarity. In her view, contemporary feminism is above all an 'identity politics', an ongoing series of life-experiments in which women probe the limits of the possible in a male-dominated world. She singles out the trend towards a postmodern fluidity as the most conspicuous feature of contemporary feminist thought, arguing that the enduring fascination of feminists with Simone de Beauvoir can best be explained by the necessity and the freedom for women to choose their own identity, and the romantic longings for personal authenticity that are at the core of *The Second Sex*, as well as of the personality of Beauvoir herself. We feel that the approaches of Bussemaker and Vintges do not necessarily exclude each

28 Tjitske Akkerman and Siep Stuurman

other, and that both furnish useful starting-points for a fuller historical analysis of contemporary, 'sixth-wave' feminism.

FEMINISM, MODERNITY AND EUROPEAN HISTORY

It is generally agreed that the roots of European modernity reach back into medieval times, and that the 'origins of modern freedom' must be sought in the protracted transition from late antiquity to the Renaissance.[53] The plural is important; there was not one single origin of liberty, neither in social and political practice nor in the field of culture and ideas. Multiple tensions and influences gave rise to the drive towards equality and liberty that eventually became the hallmark of the liberal view of European history.

Modern liberty thus has a long history. It is the contention of this book that feminism has been a part of that history right from its beginning. At the present time, it is impossible to give reliable quantitative indications of the 'historical weight' of feminism over the centuries, but it seems warranted to predict that future research will uncover a greater rather than a lesser feminist presence in modern European history. Lest we be misunderstood, we do not for a moment want to deny that the feminist voice has been a 'marginal' one during the greater part of the past six centuries. However, it must be realized that, in the eyes of an overwhelming majority of Europeans, 'democracy' was a term of abuse until the late nineteenth century, and that liberal and egalitarian ideas were also 'marginal' during the greater part of modern history. Yet nobody will deny that the rise of liberal thought and democratic rule are central to our understanding of the long run of European history. We propose to treat feminism in the same way as democracy: for the greater part of modern history, it has been a highly contested, marginal discourse, articulated and disseminated by a small minority of dedicated women and men who often despaired of their own endeavour. Just like the German peasant leaders who drafted their anti-feudal programme in 1524 or the Leveller pamphleteers who dreamed of a more egalitarian England in 1647, for several centuries the feminists were not on the winning side of history. And just like other democratic and iconoclastic movements, they sometimes appealed to ancient rights and liberties, or to famous examples from the annals of antiquity or the sacred history of Christendom. In the course of the seventeenth and eighteenth centuries, however, such traditional languages were more and more accompanied by the universalist discourse of reason, equality and liberty. Once more, the comparison with the Levellers, and beyond them with the entire tradition of radical politics in ancien régime Europe, comes to mind. In many feminist texts we encounter a mixture of political languages: they routinely juxtapose Amazon queens or female senators in ancient Gaul with the equalizing force of reason, in the same way as the Levellers would combine the language of abstract natural right with an appeal to ancient Saxon liberties trampled down under the 'Norman Yoke'.

Introduction 29

The languages of feminism have at all times been part of, and interacted with other political and cultural discourses. As an intellectual and social phenomenon, feminism has never been isolated from its cultural surroundings. During the protracted transition from Renaissance humanism to the Enlightenment and beyond, the epicentre of European intellectual culture has slowly shifted from the south to the northwest. The changing geographical contours of feminist discourse are clearly linked to the larger movement of the centre of gravity of European culture. Throughout modern history, feminist movements and informal groups have interacted with other cultural and political formations, sometimes borrowing ideas and organizational practices or even forging alliances, but also engaging in acrimonious polemics and bitter contestation. In the process, feminists influenced others as well as being influenced by them. The history of European feminism is also the history of these *mutual* influences. The dialectic of feminism and 'non-feminism' is perhaps not sufficiently acknowledged, especially when it comes to the question of the influence of feminism on other cultural and political formations. As is observed elsewhere in this book, we should not only look at the impact of the Enlightenment on feminism but also at the role of feminist thought in the making of the Enlightenment. Likewise, the inquiry into the causes of the nineteenth-century emancipation movements, be it in terms of industrialization, liberalism or evangelical Protestantism, should be complemented by a study of the significance of nineteenth-century feminism for the formation of a democratic culture in Western societies. In the contemporary age, the importance of the two-way relationship between feminism and advanced industrial society can be demonstrated in many fields, from the welfare state to the world of the visual arts. When we come to understand why and how feminisms arose in the succeeding periods of European history, we shall arrive at better comprehension of both the history of feminism and European modernity.

We would like to argue, then, for a historical interpretation of feminism as an integral element of the making of modern Europe. Insofar as there is a 'European exception', feminism has always been part of it. For all their 'marginality', feminist ideas and movements have made a difference in European history. At the present time, it is of course difficult to say to what extent European feminism has been 'essentially' different from the contestation of gendered culture and power in other parts of the world. The process of historical retrieval of which this book is a part has hardly begun in the historiography of Asia, Africa and pre-Columbian America. We think it probable that there are important differences, but without comparative studies of European and extra-European feminisms it would be unwise to go beyond such a provisional judgment.

The presence of feminism in the long history of European modernity is of more than antiquarian interest. Today we look back from an enormous historical distance on medieval and Renaissance misogyny: the utter vilification of women found in many texts of those periods strikes us as weird and

30 Tjitske Akkerman and Siep Stuurman

ridiculous, to the extent that we tend to forget how commonplace such arguments once were. In the view of many, if not the majority of male authors before the seventeenth century, women had a nearly subhuman status. Feminist authors, from late medieval times onwards, challenged those views, and to a large extent they succeeded in discrediting old-style misogyny. That is not to say, of course, that women were now considered as the *equals* of men, but inequality could no longer be simply assumed or founded upon a supposedly divine injunction. Modern sexism had to voice its claims for male superiority in the language of reason and science: 'ancient difference', grounded in religion and the authority of tradition, gave way to 'modern difference', purportedly based on the findings of empirical sciences such as biology, anthropology, medicine and psychology. But such 'scientific' claims necessarily remained contested ones. The vast and heterogeneous movement of ideas we call the Enlightenment, produced the claims of egalitarian feminism as well as those of a new, 'scientific' sexism, *and* it bequeathed the legacy of the essential contestability of *all* claims to truth and power.

Between the Enlightenment and the present age, feminists have argued both in terms of equality and in terms of difference, but they have always challenged the advocates of masculine superiority and male privilege. Once again, they have been remarkably successful: women have gained access to secondary and higher education, and they have acquired at least formal equality in the civil law as well as the status of full citizens. In some states the equality of the sexes has been written into constitutional law. That is not to say, of course, that we are living in an egalitarian utopia. But the terrain of contestation has been displaced in favour of issues of political economy and administrative power on the one hand, and the realm of culture, personal identity and symbolic communication on the other. The displacement is undoubtedly linked to the profound and unsettling transition Western societies are passing through. At the present time, as in previous historical periods, feminist thought is both an active force in that transition and a continuing critical reflection upon it.

NOTES

1 Quoted in Pierre-Yves Badel, *Le Roman de la Rose au XIVe siècle*, Genève, Droz, 1980, p. 446.
2 Reinhardt Koselleck, 'The temporal structure of conceptual change', in Willem Melching and Wycher Velema (eds), *Main Trends in Cultural History*, Amsterdam, Rodopi, 1994, p. 11.
3 Cf. Nancy Cott, *The Grounding of Modern Feminism*, New Haven and London, Yale University Press, 1987, pp. 4–5.
4 Cott, *Grounding*, p. 14.
5 F. Thébaud, 'Introduction', in G. Duby and M. Perrot (eds), *A History of Women in the West*, 5 vols, Cambridge MA, Belknap Press, 1992–1995, vol. 5.
6 Nicole Pellegrin, 'L'androgyne au XVIe siècle: pour une relecture des savoirs', in Danielle Haas-Dubosc and Eliane Viennot (eds), *Femmes et pouvoirs sous l'ancien régime*, Paris, Rivages, 1991, pp. 24–5; Joan DeJean, *Tender*

Introduction 31

Geographies: Women and the Origins of the Novel in France, New York, Columbia University Press, 1991, pp. 24–42.

7 G. H. Sabine, *A History of Political Theory* (1937), London, Harrap and Co., 1968, p. 711; the quoted sentence was retained in Thomas L. Thorson's 'updated' edition of Sabine's book, *A History of Political Theory*, Hinsdale Illinois, Dryden Press, 1973, p. 643.

8 Iain Hampsher-Monk, *A History of Modern Political Thought. Major Political Thinkers from Hobbes to Marx*, Oxford, Blackwell, 1992.

9 John Dunn (ed.), *Democracy. The Unfinished Journey: 508 BC to AD 1993*, Oxford, Oxford University Press, 1993.

10 Susan M. Okin, *Women in Western Political Thought*, Princeton, Princeton University Press, 1979; see also e.g. Ellen Kennedy and Susan Mendus (eds), *Women in Western Political Philosophy*, Brighton, Wheatsheaf, 1987; Carole Pateman, *The Sexual Contract*, Cambridge, Polity Press, 1988.

11 See Billie Melman, 'Gender, history and memory: the invention of women's past in the nineteenth and early twentieth centuries', *History and Memory*, 1993, 5, pp. 5–41.

12 L. Klejman and F. Rochefort, *L'égalité en marche. Le féminisme sous la Troisième République*, Paris, Presses de la Fondation Nationale des Sciences Politiques, 1989, pp. 319–26.

13 Charlotte Carmichael Stopes, *British Freewomen: their Historical Privilege*, London, Swan Sonnenschein and Co., 1894, quoted in Joyce Senders Pedersen, 'The historiography of the women's movement in Victorian and Edwardian England: varieties of contemporary liberal feminist interpretation', paper presented at the ISSEI Conference, Graz, August 1994.

14 Cf. the classic work by Eric Hobsbawm and Terence Ranger (eds), *The Invention of Tradition*, Cambridge, Cambridge University Press, 1983, 1985, which is almost exclusively about national and state-sponsored traditions.

15 Henri Piéron, 'De l'influence sociale des principes cartésiens: un précurseur inconnu du féminisme et de la révolution', *Revue de Synthèse Historique*, 1902, 5, p. 155n.

16 Joan Kelly, 'Early feminist theory and the *Querelle des femmes*, 1400–1789', *Signs*, 1982, 8, pp. 4–28, p. 7; reprinted in *Women, History and Theory: The Essays of Joan Kelly*, Chicago, University of Chicago Press, 1984.

17 *Ibid.*, p. 15.

18 Cf. the contributions in Margaret Brabant (ed.), *Politics, Gender, and Genre. The Political Thought of Christine de Pizan*, Boulder CO, Westview Press, 1992.

19 Constance Jordan, *Renaissance Feminism. Literary Texts and Political Models*, Ithaca and London, Cornell University Press, 1990, pp. 2, 9–10; see also Beatrice Gottlieb, 'The problem of feminism in the fifteenth century', in Julius Kirshner and Suzanne Wemple (eds), *Women of the Medieval World*, Oxford, Basil Blackwell, 1985, pp. 337–64, esp. pp. 357–61.

20 DeJean, *Tender Geographies*.

21 Cf. Ian MacLean, *Woman Triumphant. Feminism in French Literature, 1610–1652*, Oxford, Clarendon Press, 1977, pp. 151–2.

22 Gustave Reynier, *Les Femmes savantes de Molière*, Paris, Mellottée, 1948, pp. 243–4.

23 Cf. Paul Hazard, *La Crise de la Conscience Européenne*, Paris, Fayard, 1961.

24 See M. Wollstonecraft, 'A vindication of the rights of men, in a letter to the Right Honourable Edmund Burke' (1790), in J. Todd and M. Butler (eds), *The Works of Mary Wollstonecraft*, New York, New York University Press, 1989, vol. 5, pp. 1–266.

25 M. Astell, *A Serious Proposal to the Ladies for the Advancement of Their True and Greatest Interest*, 1694, cited in J. K. Kinnaird, 'Mary Astell: inspired by

32   Tjitske Akkerman and Siep Stuurman

ideas', in D. Spender (ed.) *Feminist Theorists*, London, The Women's Press, 1982, p.33.

26 J. B. Landes, *Women and the Public Sphere in the Age of the French Revolution*, Ithaca, Cornell University Press, 1988; V. Sapiro, *A Vindication of Political Virtue. The Political Theory of Mary Wollstonecraft*, Chicago, Chicago University Press, 1992; L. K. Kerber, *Women of the Republic. Intellect and Ideology in Revolutionary America*, Chapel Hill, University of North Carolina Press, 1980.

27 R. Bloch, 'The gendered meanings of virtue in revolutionary America', *Signs*, 1987, 1, pp. 37–59; R. Bloch, 'American feminine ideals in transition. The rise of the moral mother, 1785–1815', in *Feminist Studies*, 1978, 2, pp. 101–27.

28 J. H. Bloch, 'Women and the reform of the nation', in E. Jacobs (ed.), *Woman and Society in Eighteenth-Century France*, London, Athlone Press, 1979, pp. 3–27.

29 D. Godineau, 'Masculine and feminine political practice during the French Revolution, 1793–Year III', in H. B. Applewhite and D. G. Levy (eds), *Women and Politics in the Age of the Democratic Revolution*, Ann Arbor, University of Michigan Press, 1990, pp. 61–81.

30 J. G. A. Pocock, 'Virtues, rights and manners. A model for historians of political thought', in Pocock, *Virtue, Commerce and History*, Cambridge, Cambridge University Press, 1985, pp. 37–51.

31 T. Akkerman, *Women's Vices, Public Benefits. Women and Commerce in the French Enlightenment*, Amsterdam, Spinhuis, 1992.

32 D. Goodman, *The Republic of Letters. A Cultural History of the French Enlightenment*, Ithaca, Cornell University Press, 1994.

33 Erica Harth, *Cartesian Women. Versions and Subversions of Rational Discourse in the Old Regime*, Ithaca, Cornell University Press, 1992, p. 205.

34 N. Rattner Gelbart, *Feminine and Opposition Journalism in Old Regime France. Le Journal des Dames*, Berkeley, University of California Press, 1987.

35 Gelbart, *Feminine and Opposition Journalism*, pp. 1–2; Suzanne Van Dijk, *Traces de femmes. Présence féminine dans le journalisme français du XVIIIe siècle*, Amsterdam, APA-Holland University Press, 1988; S. Schumann, 'Das "lesende Frauenzimmer": Frauenzeitschriften in 18. Jahrhundert', in B. Becker-Cantarino, *Die Frau von der Reformation zur Romantik*, Bonn, Bouvier Verlag Herbert Grundmann, 1980, pp. 138–70; A. Adburgham, *Women in Print*, London, George Allin, 1972.

36 Harth, *Cartesian Women*; Goodman, *The Republic of Letters*.

37 See Applewhite and Levy (eds), *Women and Politics in the Age of the Democratic Revolution*.

38 Lynn Hunt, 'Forgetting and remembering: the French Revolution then and now', *American Historical Review*, 1995, 100, pp. 1119–35, esp. p. 1131.

39 Olympe de Gouges, 'The declaration of the rights of woman and the citizen', in D. G. Levy, H. B. Applewhite and M. D. Johnson (eds), *Women in Revolutionary Paris 1789–1795. Selected Documents*, Urbana, University of Illinois Press, 1979, pp. 87–97.

40 See Olivier le Cour Grandmaison, *Les Citoyennetés en Révolution (1789–1794)*, Paris, Presses Universitaires de France, 1992, p. 273.

41 Emmanuel-Joseph Sieyès, *Ecrits politiques*, ed. Roberto Zapperi, Editions des Archives Contemporaires, Paris and Montreux, 1985, p. 255.

42 *Voix des femmes*, June 10–13 1848, p. 276, cited in L. S. Strumingher, 'Looking back: women of 1848 and the revolutionary heritage of 1789', in H. B. Applewhite and D. G. Levy, *Women and Politics*, pp. 259–87.

43 R. H. Soltau, *French Political Thought in the Nineteenth Century*, New York, s.l., 1931, p. 486.

Introduction 33

44 See K. M. Rogers, *Feminism in Eighteenth-century England*, Brighton, Harvester Press, 1982; M. Ferguson (ed.), *First Feminists: British Women Writers, 1578–1799*, Bloomington, Indiana University Press, 1985.

45 C. Midgley, *Women against Slavery: the British Campaigns, 1780–1870*, London, Routledge, 1992, p. 69.

46 Jane Rendall, *The origins of Modern Feminism: Women in Britain, France and the United States, 1780–1860*, London, Macmillan, 1985, p. 247.

47 R. Evans, *The Feminists*, London, Croom Helm, 1977.

48 L. Davidoff, *Worlds Between: Historical Perspectives on Gender and Class*, Cambridge, Polity Press, 1995, p. 262.

49 See also Olive Banks, *Faces of Feminism: A Study of Feminism as a Social Movement*, Oxford, Robertson, 1981.

50 *Stuttgarter Neues Tageblatt*, 27 April 1849, cited in C. Lipp *et al.*, 'Frauen und Revolution. Zu weiblichen Formen politischen Verhaltens in der Revolution von 1848 und den Schwierigkeiten im Umgang mit einem complexen Thema', in *Die ungeschriebene Geschichte*. Dok. 5, Historikerinnentreffen Wien, Himberg bei Wien, 1984, p. 387; U. Gerhard, *Unerhört. Die Geschichte der Deutschen Frauenbewegung*, Reinbek bei Hamburg, 1992, p. 56.

51 A. Käppeli, 'Episoden uit het feminisme', in G. Duby, M. Perrot, *Geschiedenis van de vrouw. De Negentiende Eeuw*, Amsterdam, Agon, 1993; U. Gerhard, 'Uber die Anfänge der Deutschen Frauenbewegung um 1848. Frauenpresse, Frauenpolitik, Frauenvereine' in K. Hausen, *Frauen suchen ihre Geschichte: historischen Studien zum 19. und 20. Jahrhundert*, München, Beck, 1983, pp. 196–220.

52 On Spanish feminism: Mary Nash, *Defying Male Civilization: Women in the Spanish Civil War*, Denver, Arden Press, 1995.

53 See e.g. R. W. Davis (ed.), *The Origins of Modern Freedom in the West*, Stanford, Stanford University Press, 1995.

2 The languages of late-medieval feminism

Miri Rubin

The quest for origins is a quest for a place in the world, it is an exercise in self-definition, self-understanding and self-fashioning. It is both generous and exploitative, as privileges and rights are claimed in the name of others long dead. Yet origins must be posited as an initial stage of participation in discourse: they are the counters which we bring to the terribly serious game of politics and exchange. Moreover, origins are almost always linked to a metaphor of procreation, of generation, of birth with all the implicit pain and severing that these life-giving processes imply.

Feminists, in their struggle for recognition, for a space in the political and cultural debates of their days, have always been preoccupied by the question of origins, as their putative mothers could not only lend a sense of viability and credibility to their struggles, but also provide examples of lives lived under the demands and pressures which radical intellectual or political commitments necessarily bring to bear. Within intellectual traditions – philosophy, literature, history – that privilege powerful canons, the thoughts and writings of 'mothers' could offer a counter-canon, women who had been as important, thoughtful and articulate as those men which the canon hallowed. There is a particular *frisson* when encountering a mother-figure who also earned the recognition and respect of her contemporary male counterparts: a Christine de Pizan, a Harriet Martineau, a Mary Wollstonecraft – women who gained the paternal approval of what are seen as the more acceptable sections of unreconstructed male establishments. Many of the great and inspiring writings of feminism have opened with the tracing of such a tradition emanating from originary figures: not so long ago Joan Kelly traced a grand historical trajectory of feminism starting with the *Querelle des femmes*, from Christine de Pizan to Rachel Speght, and finally to Mary Astell and the Enlightenment; Judith Bennett began a reflection on feminist historiography with de Pizan's *City of Ladies* as the originator of the genre of defence of women.[1] In our lecture halls, conferences and casual debates we are empowered by the knowledge that women far away in time and place, women whose lives in many ways remain a mystery to us, could still speak words that we would be happy to pronounce ourselves. It is heart-warming and empowering to hear those complaints

The languages of late-medieval feminism 35

which we have voiced sounded in Middle English, written in Old High German or penned in the secretary hand of cultivated Elizabethans. And it is not only heart-warming, but effective, since so many of our interlocutors respect the notion of a canon and the charisma and power of historical worthies, particularly when their writing is witty and solidly located within an intellectual world of high culture.

Yet the moment of vindication and reclamation, though never over, recedes in its primacy as confidence grows, institutional implantation is achieved and as the arguments, once fragile and unfamiliar, increasingly resonate within our political culture. The moment has produced the space and the resources for reflection not only on aims but also upon strategies, not only on bold pronouncements and inspiring gestures but also on the intricate work of change within institutions, families, communities. History can be a source and a resource for reflection and realization of change just as it offers the material from which our origins were moulded. History moreover, at this stage of the century, is a discourse about relations of power embedded within social practices, practices which must be contextualized to be interpreted, and which are amenable to change – historical change. Important rewards will follow from the unlocking of structures and their possibilities, of discursive frames. Tracing the cracks and fissures seems as important an intellectual task as the bolstering of the walls around the City of Women.

The capacity to imagine the different arrangements of gender relations which this chapter will trace concerns a period as 'different' as can be: the Middle Ages. These 'arrangements' will be identified not in so many pronouncements emanating from lofty institutions of learning and reflection, but rather as ideas embedded in possibilities, in life-choices within social structures. Here one would part company not only with a totalizing feminist view of patriarchy but also with the very Worthy Feminist Mothers of the past.

DOMINANT DISCOURSES ON WOMEN AND FEMININITY

Before tracing some of the feminist moments and the dialects within which they were set, let us quickly trace some of the pervasive understandings about women and femininity. Here a series of discourses overlap, if not totally then in interesting and reinforcing ways. By the thirteenth century a forceful Aristotelian paradigm offered a robust frame for the understanding of society, personhood and nature. The human person resided and emerged from and within a body, a body conceived in Galenic terms as a cocktail of humours and complexions, a never-fixed combination of tendencies within a psychosomatic whole.[2] Women's bodies were seen as cooler and wetter, thus lacking in the dry warmth which was vital for action and health. Women were understood to be more physically morbid, even if some writers, such as Albert the

36   *Miri Rubin*

Great in the mid-thirteenth century, demurred against such accepted truths.

Conception was a process of impregnation, where a single male seed was received into a passive female uterus, although a counter-view about a two-seed theory was powerfully present in Galenic writings. Woman's body and constitution were ruled by a mobile and active uterus which could induce disease from head to toe.[3] Woman's sexuality was seen as a warm, gentle fire compared to the male blaze, and her rational capacities were similarly limited, producing an imperfect, if necessary, human complement to man, one which was in need of guidance and open to influence. As we shall see, this greater tractability, her openness to influence, could also be turned into a benefit, as women were deemed more open to religious and moral teaching. Their suggestibility called for vigilance, guidance and discipline from better informed and more morally robust persons: fathers, brothers, husbands, sons or priests. Such understandings also explain the limited role which women were allowed to play in politics, administration, legislation and leadership. This was the theory.

These views constituted mainstream knowledge which was developed and discussed in texts ranging from university-level natural philosophy to theology, medicine and the more popularized and widespread pastoral guides and manuals on manners and moral formation. Other genres of explicit misogyny also existed, particularly those produced by clerical pens, and well traced in the work of Howard Bloch.[4] In these writings, which were based on the two colossal pillars of the early Christian writers and the classical Ovidian tradition, a more pointed misogyny was rationalized: here women appear as sources of riotous behaviour, confusion, hypocrisy and disorder, as a danger to man, to his physical, economic and moral well-being. In the clerical anti-matrimonial satire and the vernacular of some *fabliaux* a male strategy is formulated, a strategy for survival: in order to outwit the dangerous temptress and shrew, man must be wily and cautious, lest he be ensnared, destroyed, cuckolded, emasculated.

Within this variety of attitudes, all based on the possibilities of an inherent female malleability, in a perceived absence of a moral and rational core to her behaviour, were embedded two possible evaluations of femininity, which coexist in intersecting and opposing contemporary discourses. Female malleability, openness to persuasion, disqualified women from holding positions of leadership, guidance and responsibility. But that was not all: women's openness to persuasion also made them better recipients of codes of morality and honour which patriarchs and priests purveyed and supervised. Femininity was thus a state of innocence as well as a state of disorder, both produced by the absence of a rational core, a strong motivating will to power and domination, and the related libidinal energies. Within this world of possibilities, literature on women, legislation, and moral and social attitudes of a very wide variety were constructed, and thus conditioned and moulded the possibilities of women's lives.

WOMEN, WORK AND AUTHORITY

Throughout the medieval economy, in the towns and in the countryside, women were visible at work. Insofar as much production was organized within the framework of the household-workshop or the household-rural tenancy, family and work were tightly interwoven. The lines of public and private were drawn quite differently from their spheres in other periods.[5] The urban workshop where production took place under the aegis of a male craft-master, member of guild, enfranchised and empowered through this institution, was also the centre of training, exchange and the employment of many labourers. As wife to the master, the woman of the household participated in production and training; she also often sold the wares produced at a retail outlet facing the street.

In exploring the experiences of work we should bear in mind some salient pairs of categories which interact vigorously in constructing women's experiences: that of gender and class, that of the public and the private, and that of the normative and the real. Women's work experiences differed dramatically according to their social and economic position (which I shall call by the shorthand of class) and yet even that 'socio-economic' position was gendered. Their work was spoken of as primarily private, to do with the hearth and domestic chores and yet women worked hard and long in other positions outside the house. Their work was always counted on and yet barely acknowledged and badly remunerated. Even though there were some clear prescriptive schemes about how work ought to be organized in the household, women's lived experience was produced at the intersection of such ideas and the raw demands of resources and circumstance. Work within the medieval household was on the whole divided by sex, as well as by age and status, and women's work was generally less specialized, less skilled and lower paid.[6] The husband's work was the defining work of the family economy, to which the work of women and children was supplementary. That this was so is clear from the returns of late fourteenth-century English poll-taxes, where the husband's occupation is mentioned, except for the households headed by women, which is to say widows or spinsters. The nature of women's work was supplementary and accommodated that of the husband: for example, the making of candles from the tallow produced by the husband's butchering. Accordingly, women usually shifted occupation with marriage and remarriage. This is recognized in some late-medieval labour legislation such as that in England in 1363 which restricted artisans to one trade but allowed women to pursue many. On the other hand, the defining characteristics of work organization and political participation which followed from craft membership in guilds were mediated through the husband's craft and thus through his craft-guild.[7]

It is exactly the measure of women's integration into dense routines of work and management which explains the elaborate and widespread arrangements for childcare and nurturing which developed in medieval

38   *Miri Rubin*

society. For a variety of legal and conceptual reasons already outlined above it is difficult to come to know women at work in a very comprehensive way, so many of their activities being masked by the *persona* of their husbands or guardians, but occasionally a glimpse is permitted. We possess a fascinating picture of work in Paris in the collection of Parisian guild statutes compiled *c.* 1270 by Etienne Boileau, the provost of the merchants of the city, in the *Livre des métiers* ('Book of Trades').[8] The variety of crafts and trades of working men and working women was unparalleled by any other city. With around 200,000 inhabitants at the turn of the thirteenth century, Paris was the richest, most varied, most magnificent city in France, and perhaps in Europe. Of the one hundred crafts mentioned by Etienne Boileau, six were crafts in which women only were engaged in Paris, while in another eighty they worked side by side with men. The exclusive female crafts were spinning silk on a broad loom (which was done at home with materials supplied by a merchant), the making of elegant head-coverings decorated with gold thread (*chapeaux d'orfroi*) and expert working of embroidered purses (*aumonières sarazinoises*). The purse-makers and the headdress-makers worked in *ateliers* and their labour was organized into women's guilds headed by a male provost called the *praepositus*.[9] The statutes of women who worked in the eighty mixed professions (and in some of these, such as ribbon-making, scarf-making, wig-making and work in feathers, they made up the majority) made them members of the guild of the said craft, and allowed them to train apprentices in the same way as male craft-members, but they could not become guild officers.

Production was centred in household-workshops, a world explored so effectively by Merry Wiesner and Lyndal Roper for a slightly later period.[10] Guild privileges of price and quality control, and training monopolized and set the number of workshops operating in the area. Production was carefully monitored in order to maintain the level of prices and profits. It is this primary guild preoccupation which produced a vast area for female activity: at the death of a master-craftsman, his wife would continue to maintain the workshop, train apprentices, sell wholesale and retail, in fact fulfil all the functions of the craft-master, that core figure of the productive and enfranchised citizenry. There was one exception: she did not have the right to gain access to guild offices and be elected through them to urban political and administrative office.[11] We thus find that the formal, explicit rule excluding single women workers from running a workshop, with all that entailed in terms of authority, judgment and financial independence, was frequently bypassed for practical reasons. In the name of corporate health and guild viability, in the name of streamlined production and stability of profit, women were in fact allowed to function as effective workshop heads, as long as they remained widows and complied, like all guild members, with the guild's rules. Once such a woman remarried, however, she disappeared into a new household-workshop in the trade of her new husband.

The prerogatives of patriarchy could produce further contradictory forms

The languages of late-medieval feminism 39

of organization and privilege. For example, in the city of Cologne, the foremost imperial trading city on the Rhine with strong links with Venice and other Italian towns, women were allowed into the citizenship of the city, to enjoy both rights and duties, primarily that of taxation. But we find few women in the citizenship registers, as entry required a hefty payment, and for married women such an expenditure would have been seen as an unnecessary and unsuitable luxury. In Cologne, famed for its production of the silver and gold thread which supplied the brocade workshops in Venice, we find a number of guilds which accepted female members and even allowed them to be elected to office. The gold-spinning guild had two men and two women as guild-masters every year.[12] Here family structure was very important, and the craft family assumed the blood family, with the apprenticeship of daughters, and the dual membership of husbands and wives. The guild incorporated women in this very lucrative trade, in which a partnership between the spinning wife and the husband who sold the yarn was evidently at work. But Cologne was precocious and exceptional.

WOMEN AS MORAL GUIDES AND PREACHERS

The guidebooks to married life would recommend that all major decisions be reached in consultation, and under the aegis of the husband. But preachers and priests, from their daily contact in pastoral care and in confession, were only too aware that whatever the formal image, women were in fact sensible and hard-working, and could be far wiser than their husbands. It is striking that among moral theologians of the twelfth and thirteenth centuries, and later among preachers, there developed a new emphasis in the approach to moral influence within marriage.[13] These favourites of so many female patronesses, these hearers of thousands of confessors, were only too aware of the beneficial and subtle influence which women could have on the moral tone of the household. This produced some interesting ideas among pastors and teachers who attempted to penetrate the household and inculcate Christian values.

An important example is Thomas Chobham's *Manual for Confessors* of c. 1215–16, an encyclopedic guidebook to priests on the intricacies of the confessional encounter. In the section on the types of penances, Thomas recommended that wives be approached as preachers ('praedicatrices') to their husbands:

> In imposing penance, it should always be enjoined upon women to be preachers to their husbands, because no priest is able to soften the heart of a man the way his wife can. . . . Even in the bedroom, in the midst of their embraces, a wife should speak alluringly to her husband, and if he is hard and unmerciful, and an oppressor of the poor, she should invite him to be merciful; if he is a plunderer, she should denounce plundering. . . .
> For it is permissible for a woman to expend much of her husband's

40 *Miri Rubin*

property, without his knowing, in ways beneficial to him and for pious causes.[14]

Numerous *exempla*, illustrative religious tales, recounted cases of male souls delivered from purgatory by a wife who had given clandestine alms for her spouse. This is, of course, an area of some ambiguity: the age-old issue of female moral force, of women's overt or covert access to informal power and influence. In the sexual order were rooted the most fundamental notions of hierarchy and authority; its subversion was always disturbing and a source of collective and communal action.

And yet, subvert the norms of obedience they did, and never more so than in the arena of marital guidance, and powerfully in discussions of the marriage or conjugal debt. Here, from the twelfth century onwards, a strong pastoral position on the mutual obligation of husband and wife to participate in sexual intercourse, for the furtherance of the aims of procreation and for the satisfaction of human needs, was elaborated. Although much of the pastoral literature emphasizes particularly the woman's duty to fulfil this debt, even sometimes in situations which are life-endangering, the later Middle Ages see the development of a contrary formulation, which encourages women in their desire to withdraw from sex, and joins in a vitriolic attack on unbridled male sexuality while praising feminine decorum and greater sensibility. It is hard to gauge the degree to which such views empowered women in their marital strategies, but their presence in the writings of some very influential preachers, such as Bernardino of Siena and Antoninus of Florence (who were hounded for their views by leading patricians), is a striking one.[15] Rather than female concupiscence we have here a critique of an unbridled male sexuality which does not pay attention to the moods and needs of women.

WOMEN AS RELIGIOUS INSPIRATION

Many experiments in religious life took place in the burgeoning towns of the high and later Middle Ages, as the laity sought forms of religious perfection and initiative which were not totally dominated by parochial practice, nor as rigorous and limiting as monastic routines. The participants in these new forms could range from members of the urban patriciate to the poor female weavers and spinners. When the mendicant orders developed in the towns of early thirteenth century, they soon recognized their counterpart in the order of Poor Clares, who were not itinerant like the male Franciscans, but enclosed and disciplined, and who attracted in their urban houses the daughters of merchants and craftsmen. Furthermore, less disciplinary forms of religious communal living developed in very loose organizations such as the Beguinage, the houses of Beguines. Beguines is a generic term for religious women who lived in urban communities which were neither enclosed nor based on a rule, but rather informally regulated and in coexistence with

The languages of late-medieval feminism   41

other social frameworks, much like the women who inhabited the Beguinages which can still be seen today in Dutch and Belgian towns. Such houses would welcome maidens, widows or married women who had taken a vow of chastity and were ready to engage in communal living based on simple manual labour and works of charity.

These organizations posed serious dilemmas to church authorities. When they were more formally organized and maintained routines of prayer under the watchful eye of a confessor, they were tolerated; in some areas they gained the admiration and support of local bishops, for example in thirteenth-century Liège, an important Beguine centre.[16] But in cases where they were not officially protected, and especially in periods of moral panic about unorthodox forms of religion, such as the early fourteenth century, strong legislation against them might result in persecution and, in some cases, even in the execution of Beguines who were seen to be simply out of control – women on spiritual quests who evaded normal parochial and institutional tutelage. By the fourteenth century some of them came to be known as 'Free Spirits': persons who claimed a certain freedom in their mystical quests, and who vaunted the ability to reach union with God through means of their own perfection and contemplation, and without the aid of sacramental religion and parochial governance.[17]

However, it was the very susceptibility of women to sensation and sensibility, their very lack of mediating reason in an age when intellectual speculation was seen by many as most threatening to the edifice of faith, that suggested women as vehicles of religious sentiment and even revelation. In its great attempt to christianize and evangelize, the great internal mission of the Church of the twelfth and thirteenth centuries as it turned its attention from the elites in monasteries or castles to ordinary folk in urban and rural parishes, the Church was investigating and reconsidering the standing of such women and such enthusiasms. Some observers were sceptical, but others were open and impressed, identifying some useful material and didactic inspiration in these enthusiasms. One such important observer of female religiosity was James of Vitry, theologian, preacher, historian and ecclesiastical grandee. In the early thirteenth century he gave a description of the Beguines of the diocese of Liège and their piety, which centred particularly around the Eucharist:

> Many had the taste of honey sensibly in their mouth because of the gift of spiritual sweetness in their hearts. . . . Another's flow of tears had made visible furrows down her face. . . . Some in receiving the bread of him who came down from heaven obtained not only refreshment in their hearts but palpable consolation in their mouths sweeter than honey and the honey-comb. . . . They languished with such desire for the sacrament that they could not be sustained . . . unless their souls were frequently refreshed by the sweetness of this food. Let the infidel heretic blush, who do not partake of this food whether by faith or by love.[18]

42   *Miri Rubin*

In an atmosphere of religious diversity there was sufficient receptivity to such female religiosity, which centred on the bodily reception of Christ through the sacrament, that the visions of one such woman, Juliana of Cornillon, could be mediated through the enthusiasm of a local bishop and the interest of recently arrived Dominicans into a celebration which was to become a universal calendar feast of the Christian church. But in other circumstances such enthusiasms were disciplined, controlled and quashed.

Particular interests could find their place in those special frameworks for religious and social activity, the fraternities. But even here the conventional and hierarchical structure of adherence was strongly circumscribed. Women's religion is probably much more powerfully understood in the practices which can sometimes be considered as magical: in amulets, incantations, practices which have to do with household devotional and private prayers. At the higher end of the social scale, from the thirteenth century onwards, we encounter the development of a religious literature of guidance which was meant for those who could read the vernacular: English, Italian, French and German Books of Hours for the recitation of prayers and for private and home-bound devotion. Such books were frequently made for women, with a profusion of female saints and the use of feminine pronouns. But here too a household chaplain or a parish priest would have punctuated and contributed to the definition of boundaries and the control of permissible initiatives. The female impulses were frequently channelled towards charitable donations and the support and patronage of religious orders.

A FEMINIST LANGUAGE

Thus some churchmen subverted the ideal of female obedience in suggesting collusion between priest or confessor and wife. This image flew in the face of a powerful and far more traditional *topos* of the woman as the unmaking of man. Finally, let us look at a number of literary traditions which contained differing constructions of gender relations. In one of Geoffrey Chaucer's *Canterbury Tales*, that told by the Nun's Priest, the hero, the cock Chaunticleer speaks to his favourite wife-hen Pertelote:

> For al so siker as *In principio*,
> *Mulier est hominis confusio* –
> Madame, the sentence of this Latyn is,
> 'Womman is mannes joye and al his blis'.[19]

Here the clever cock moves neatly between the misogynistic Latin discourse ('In the beginning, woman is the confusion of man') to a popular and more friendly companionable discourse which cherishes the wife.

The power of literary representations to spread and sustain misogyny was at the heart of the discussion which came to be known as the *Querelle des femmes* ('the dispute about women'), an early part of which was the *Querelle de la rose* ('controversy about the *Romance of the Rose*'). This debate, which

The languages of late-medieval feminism   43

involved leading courtly and ecclesiastical figures in the years following 1400 in France and in French, passionately considered the relation between literature and truth, and between literature and experience, through the case of the representation of love and women in the great French allegorical poem, the *Roman de la Rose*, written by Guillaume de Lorris around 1237, continued by Jean de Meun around 1275–80, and translated into other European languages in the fourteenth century.[20] Women were maligned in this immensely popular epic poem, and this was a real offence, one which Christine de Pizan (1363–1429x34), the animator of the debate, aimed to highlight and decry. She claimed that these were not 'only words' but vicious acts, which attacked women and which also reflected a pathology in the writer himself, a sinner who inverted his own sexual excesses into so many universal claims about feminine wile and duplicity.

Christine de Pizan, a woman of letters who followed her father into the service of Charles V of France from 1368, married to a courtier, and widowed at the age of twenty-five, lived the rest of her life as a single mother, working at her writing for her family's support. On the Feast of Lovers, 1 May 1399, she produced a poem which contains the ideas which would unfold in the future polemic. This is the *Epître au dieu d'amours* ('Letter to the God of Amorous Sentiments'), a letter by Cupid to all true lovers about the many complaints which he had received from women of all estates about the abuse which they suffered from their male love-objects.[21] These were to be sharpened further in the debate which was to follow the publication of a treatise about the Roman de la Rose in May 1401, and to which Christine de Pizan responded in July. Epistolary exchanges followed over the next two years. The Roman de la Rose was encyclopedic in its recycling of the tales of poets of antiquity such as Ovid, Virgil and Catullus, as well as patristic writers, and more recent sages like Alan of Lille and John of Salisbury. The Roman contained countless stories of love and seduction, lost honour and suicides; in particular, the second part of the poem abounds with malicious and poisonous misogynist vitriol.[22] Women are made into either ugly and cunning or beautiful and wounding creatures, and the only way to treat them is with deceit, so as never to fall into their hands, be seduced and discarded. This venomous position in the Rose section of Jean de Meun made him the target for Christine de Pizan's attacks.

Christine took up her eloquent pen to write against Jean de Meun, she quarrelled with the *Rose* and with those who enjoyed the literature, and failed to see the pain and insult which it inflicted on women. She marshalled great examples of constancy and virtue: the Virgin Mary, female martyrs, heroines of antiquity which she developed into the *Le livre de la cité des dames* ('Book of the City of Ladies'), which was completed in 1405.[23] The debate continued in an exchange of letters with leading humanists and courtiers, but on her side were moralists as well as cultivated men of court, such as Jean de Boucicaut, the Marshal of France. In response to her literal complaint came some sophisticated rebuttals, focussing on the autonomous

44   *Miri Rubin*

role of aesthetics and the dramatic voice. Christine's critics contended that no sensible person reads a poem either as autobiography or as an endorsement of the actions discussed in it; that a dramatic voice, even a wildly misogynistic one, could be ironic, subversive and playful. Her opponents defended artistic freedom and appealed to the discerning reader, while Christine and her moralizing supporters marshalled the language of morality in defence of victimized and vilified women.

Male writers entered the debate, or at least had to take a position within its parameters, as they recycled the French romance tradition as the basis for the formation of other vernacular traditions, such as the English one, forged in these very years by Geoffrey Chaucer. In Chaucer, who died in 1400, a year after the beginning of the *Querelle*, Christine de Pizan may have had an ally, of whom she would have never known. In the next century, Chaucer came to carry the epithet 'ever women's friend'. He had probably harboured such sympathetic sentiments when he embarked upon the translation of the great French poem, to produce the earliest of the three fragments now known as the *The Romaunt of the Rose*, written in the 1360s.[24] Chaucer was at once a fine judge of literary taste and fashionable opinion, and he was a most original subverter of pieties as well as prejudice through his irony, keener than any knife. In his *Legend of Good Women* he attempted to extol the virtues of female martyrs of love rather than to revel in the seduction and betrayal of their trust. Neither he nor the translators of other parts of the *Roman* into English (still held by some to have been Chaucer himself!) approached this most famous of European poems, written in the language of polite secular society, as a subordinate provincial author. They had recourse to the creative work of trans-cultural exchange and free interpretation, as we have already seen other users of European symbols and texts had.[25] The *Romaunt* includes the first half of Guillaume de Lorris' poem and two extracts of Jean de Meun's work. It steers away from the most misogynistic passages of Jean de Meun's continuation. We know that Chaucer considered the French style of denigration of women and extolling of duplicitous amorous conquest to be something in the way of a 'French disease'.[26] Neither his own temperamental inclination nor his sense of his audience allowed him to include those hateful lines, which would be so painful to Christine, in the English version of the *Rose*. So the English knew a *Rose* by the same name, but which was indeed *not* the same *Rose*. Within the European-Christian culture of misogyny there were some strikingly familiar themes, and yet the experience of it must have been different in England and in France.

Thomas Hoccleve (*c.* 1370–1450), that long-standing clerk of the Privy-Seal and poet extraordinaire, contributed to the debate in his own way. He chose to translate Christine de Pizan's *Epître* in his 476-line long poem *Letter of Cupid* (1402).[27] Hoccleve was very loyal to Christine's poem, although he shortened it here and there, and dropped references to famous Gallic seducers whom the English audience simply would not have known.

The wit of Christine's defence of women comes through loud and clear in Cupid's opening:

In general we wole þat yee knowe
Þat ladyes of honur and reverence,
And othir gentil wommen, han I-sowe,
Swich seed of conpleynte in our audience,
Of men þat doon hem outrage & offense,
Þat it oure eres greeueth for to heere,
So pitous is theffect of hir mateere.[28]

(In general we wish you to know
That ladies of honour and reverence,
And other gentle-women have sown
Such seeds of complaint in our hearing,
About men who have outraged and offended them,
That it hurts our ears to hear it,
So piteous is the effect of their complaint)

Hoccleve's translation is realistic and bawdy, and yet serious and balanced. He even puts forth the theory of the Fortunate Fall, not only exculpating Eve for responsibility for Adam's temptation, but even explaining that it was a happy choice, a *felix culpa*. So misogyny, one of the most powerful ideas of medieval European culture also had divergent forms and formulations: it was a discourse familiar to all and yet specific in its disparate articulations and contextual constructions, as well as in the lived experiences which it drew on and helped to shape.

CLASHING AND INTERSECTING DISCOURSES

Thus an awareness and an anger, as well as a sort of resistance, did exist in some areas of medieval culture. Admittedly, many of the sources of that resistance are as yet uncovered, and they will always be embedded in materials which offer great difficulties of interpretation. The examples of Alison, the wife of Bath, and of Christine de Pizan, fiction and fact, demonstrate a more general point: the great differences between women's lives according to their respective social positions. Here is another cautionary signpost: we will not be able to distil a standardized image of *the* medieval woman's life. There were multiple lives and varieties of position. Women differed from each other according to region, age, occupation, status, health and talent, just as men did. Moreover they were caught up in a variety of contexts of living, sometimes consecutively in the course of an individual's life cycle, sometimes parallel as they participated in disparate social contexts: as mothers, daughters, wives, lovers, employers and employees. Furthermore, their lives were shaped by a whole series of roles and expectations which raised of necessity the need to make choices and to compromise, sometimes

46   *Miri Rubin*

in confusion, sometimes in harmony. I shall call these different bodies of knowledge about life 'discourses': we may discern the clerical and the theological discourse, the discourse of medical science, the popular and the professional discourses, as well as the discourses of work and play. In all these discourses we encounter images, visions and expectations of women which corresponded and intersected but always differed slightly from each other. Most of them advocated a general view of women as subordinate, needy of tutelage and protection, demarcating and limiting in different ways the proper and accepted areas of female activity. The task of historical interpretation is a sort of archaeology of all these forms of knowledge about sexual difference.

Gendered discourses could clash, sometimes dramatically. Obligation to kin was keenly felt and enshrined in customs of inheritance and marriage. Sometimes familial duties would conflict with the entire string of axioms that stressed female inferiority, the unsuitability of woman to exercise power or public office, and above all functions of rulership and military command. The nobility was particularly aware of the overriding importance of dynastic continuity, and from around the eleventh century it steered towards the custom of primogeniture, the protection of the familial patrimony through the rule of impartible inheritance by the eldest male. In most cases this worked, but as is well known, it failed when a male heir could not be found. To whom should the patrimony go in such an eventuality? Among the nobility of Western Europe a strong customary practice developed of preferring a daughter over more distant male kinsfolk. This can be seen as a powerful triumph of the discourse of kinship over that of misogyny, and one which created blatant exceptions to the general rule that was restated at the beginning of every tract about feudal law from the thirteenth century onwards: that a woman should not hold office or command men since she lacked *auctoritas* ('authority').[29] Numerous women actually exercised political authority, among them some very powerful countesses of Flanders, Western Lorraine and several Northern French counties. Female rule was, however, never formalized, except in the inheritance customs of the Kingdom of Jerusalem. Thus some women could exercise considerable power. They would, of course, almost always marry, and their husbands would fulfil the military side of their commitments but the women nonetheless acted as the formal holders of power and authority: they issued charters, they pronounced sentences in their feudal courts, they received oaths of fealty negotiated with foe and friend, with kings, towns and vassals, they even had their own seals. The call of the blood thus frequently resulted in a modification of the powerful axiom which insisted on women's unsuitability to govern.[30] Such examples illustrate the important truth that no ideological system can be totally closed, and that human lives are lived at the intersection of multiple discourses, producing a reality that is far more complex than the textbook image would suggest.

Particular languages of feminism, containing critiques of the patriarchal

The languages of late-medieval feminism 47

order which favoured man in so many spheres, were thus available in certain niches of medieval experience and action. To acknowledge and trace them is to uncover and distinguish the meaning of gender relations in the past. It is to identify locations from which more effective onslaughts on prejudice and limitation could be launched. What is also to be appreciated is the force of certain intellectual procedures within our own historical research in further identifying such possible areas of contentious ambiguity: a recent example would be Roberta Krueger's study of French courtly literature, which is not an attempt at deconstructing it, but rather an attempt to identify it as a place from which gender relations could be problematized, questioned, lampooned and reconsidered.[31] Her interpretation moves away from the endorsement of courtly literature as female-friendly, but she is also reluctant to reject it as wholly misogynist and disabling. She focusses instead on the ambiguity and agency that can be found in the unfolding and collective making of a literary genre, highlighting the historicity of the writing and reading of texts.

Other possibilities arise from the intellectual onslaught on the inherited binary formulation which still informs so much of our thinking about the past. Recent work on medieval perceptions of the body has uncovered a far greater variety in the combinations of gender and bodily attributes than could be accounted for by the traditional sexual dichotomies. The new research displays a mingling of imageries of femininity and bodily vulnerability with some of the most powerful ideas of spiritual progress.[32] These trends in medieval history are moving in interesting harmony with other new developments in historical research and interpretation. The languages of feminism and the past experiences which they reflected continue to provide the subject matter as well as the motivating force for much new and exciting work. This book's comparative thrust will help to bring all of these into sharper focus.

NOTES

1 Joan Kelly, 'Early feminist theory and the *Querelle des femmes*, 1400–1789', *Women, History and Theory: The Essays of Joan Kelly*, Chicago, University of Chicago Press, 1984.
2 For an introduction to this medical paradigm see N. Siraisi, *Medieval and Early Renaissance Medicine: An Introduction to Knowledge and Practice*, Chicago and London, Chicago University Press, 1990, chaps 4, 5 and 8. Joan Cadden, *Meanings of Sexual Difference in the Middle Ages: Medicine, Science and Culture*, Cambridge, Cambridge University Press, 1993.
3 For an introduction to medieval gynaecology and an illustrative text see R. Barkaï, *Le Infortunes de Dinah ou la gynécologie juive au moyen-âge*, Paris, Cerf, 1991.
4 R. Howard Bloch, *Medieval Misogyny and the Invention of Western Romantic Love*, Chicago, University of Chicago Press, 1991.
5 For an attempt to discuss women's space see B.A. Hanawalt, 'At the margin of women's space in medieval Europe', in R. R. Edwards and V. Ziegler (eds),

48　*Miri Rubin*

Matrons and Marginal Women in Medieval Society, Woodbridge, The Boydell Press, 1995, pp. 1–17.

6　J. M. Bennett, 'History that stands still: women's work in the European past', *Feminist Studies*, 1988, 14, pp. 269–83; J. M. Bennett, 'Medieval women, modern women: across the great divide', in D. Aers (ed.) *Culture and History, 1350–1600: Essays on English Communities, Identities and Writing*, New York, Harvester Wheatsheaf, 1992, pp. 147–75.

7　For a study of women's work which pays much attention to conjugal companionship see P. J. P. Goldberg, *Women, Work and Life Cycle in a Medieval Economy: Women in York and Yorkshire c. 1300–1520*, Oxford, Clarendon Press, 1992.

8　*Règlements sur les arts et métiers de Paris rédigés au XIIIe siècle, et connus sous le nom du Livre des Métiers d'Etienne Boileau*, G. B. Depping (ed.), 3 vols, Paris, Firmin Didot, 1837, pp. 80–5.

9　*Ibid.*, pp. 80–5, 99–101.

10　Merry Wiesner, *Women and Gender in Early Modern Europe*, Cambridge, Cambridge University Press, 1993; Lyndal Roper, *The Holy Household: Women and Morals in Reformation Augsburg*, Oxford, Oxford University Press, 1989, esp. chapter 1.

11　Steven A. Epstein, *Wage Labor and Guilds in Medieval Europe*, Chapel Hill NC, University of North Carolina Press, 1991.

12　Edith Ennen, *Women in the Middle Ages*, Oxford, Basil Blackwell, 1989, pp. 181–2.

13　Sharon Farmer, 'Persuasive voices: clerical images of medieval women', *Speculum*, 1986, 61, pp. 517–43.

14　Thomas of Chobham, *Summa Confessorum*, F. Broomfield (ed.), Louvain, Nauwetaerts, 1968, p. 375, translation from Farmer, 'Persuasive voices', p. 517. For an interesting comparison see David Wallace, *Chaucerian Polity*, Palo Alto CA, Stanford University Press, 1996.

15　Dyan Elliott, 'Bernardino of Siena versus the marriage debt', in J. Murray and K. Eisenbickler (eds), *Desire and Discipline: Essays on Sex and Sexuality in Premodern Europe*, Toronto, Toronto University Press, 1996.

16　M. Rubin, *Corpus Christi: The Eucharist in Late Medieval Culture*, Cambridge, Cambridge University Press, 1991, pp. 166–74.

17　Robert E. Lerner, *The Heresy of the Free Spirit in the Later Middle Ages*, Berkeley CA, University of California Press, 1972.

18　James of Vitry's Life of Mary of Oignies, as translated in Caroline W. Bynum, *Holy Feast and Holy Fast: The Religious Significance of Food to Medieval Women*, Berkeley CA, University of California Press, 1987, p. 13.

19　*Riverside Chaucer*, gen. ed. L. Benson, third edn., Boston MA, Houghton Mifflin, 1987, 'Nun's Priest's Tale', pp. 253–61; lines 3163–6, p. 257.

20　For the materials of the debate see *Le Débat sur le Roman de la Rose*, E. Hicks (ed.), Paris, Librairie Honoré Champoin, 1977. See also *La Querelle de la Rose: Letters and Documents*, J. L. Baird and J. R. Kane (eds), North Carolina Studies in the Romance Languages and Literatures 199, Chapel Hill NC, University of North Carolina Press, 1978; P.-Y. Badel, *Le Roman de la Rose au XIVe siècle. Etude de la réception de l'oeuvre*, Genève, Droz, 1980.

21　*Oeuvres poétiques*, M. Roy (ed.), Paris, 1891, II, pp. 1–27.

22　John V. Fleming, *Reason and the Lover*, Princeton NJ, Princeton University Press, 1984.

23　In English translation see *The Book of the City of Ladies*, E. J. Richards (trans.), New York, Persea Books, 1982.

24　See *The Romaunt of the Rose and Roman de la Rose: A Parallel Text Edition*, R. Sutherland (ed.), Oxford, Basil Blackwell, 1967.

The languages of late-medieval feminism   49

25 On this see D. Wallace, 'Chaucer and the European *Rose*', *Studies in the Age of Chaucer*, 1984, 1, pp. 61–7.

26 R.F. Green, 'Chaucer's victimised women', *Studies in the Age of Chaucer*, 1988, 10, pp. 3–21, esp. pp. 7ff; R. Howard Bloch, 'Medieval Misogyny', *Representations*, 1987, 20, pp. 1–24. Note below that the 'Epistle of Cupid', Hoccleve's translation of Christine's poem *Epître au dieu d'amours*, claims that 'Albioun draws most complaint for misogyny', (lines 15–16), see below n.27.

27 *Hoccleve's works. II: the minor poems*, I. Gollancz (ed.), EETS Extra Series 73, London, 1925; 'Lepistre de Cupide' is on pp. 20–34.

28 *Ibid.*, lines 8–14, p. 20.

29 Shulamith Shahar, 'Family prerogatives and the limitation of patriarchy: a medieval case', *Tel Aviver Jahrbuch für deutsche Geschichte*, 1993, 22, pp. 105–15.

30 For the activities of some women, single or widowed, and in possession of movable goods see M. C. Howell, 'Fixing movables: gifts by testament in late medieval Douai', *Past and Present*, 1996, 150, pp. 3–45.

31 Roberta L. Krueger, *Women Readers and the Ideology of Gender in Old French Verse Romances*, Cambridge; Cambridge University Press, 1993.

32 *Framing Medieval Bodies*, Sarah Kay and Miri Rubin (eds), Manchester, Manchester University Press, 1994.

3 A 'learned wave'
Women of letters and science from the Renaissance to the Enlightenment

Brita Rang

The Renaissance *Querelle des femmes* evolved from a 'moral point of view'. The participants in the debate were especially concerned with the notion of women's *intrinsic* inferiority to men. Moral equality or even excellence was claimed by those who spoke in favour of women, but their discourse moved within the particularistic and hierarchical assumptions of premodern thought. Generally, they took for granted the existence of a natural and historical gender difference. What they objected to was the denigration and negative evaluation of female difference by men and in the written record. Women's moral rights *as women* were the crucial issue in the early *Querelle* literature: Christine de Pizan envisaged a 'city of virtuous ladies', not an egalitarian meeting-place for both sexes.

The discourse of gender began to change during the seventeenth century when a new philosophical universalism emerged, offering an image of women's equality and potential interchangeability with men. The theoretical conjecture of a natural equality of mankind allowed, at least theoretically, the critique of hierarchical conceptions of birth, rank and gender. At the same time, the forum of public debate broadened, and sometimes even university faculties became participants in the *Querelles*. The wide-ranging discussion about the *savantes* in the seventeenth and eighteenth centuries offers an intriguing perspective on what might be called 'an intellectual or learned feminist wave' in early-modern Europe. In presenting this 'learned wave', I shall refer to seldom-used sources, chiefly encyclopedia, lexica or catalogues containing short biographies (*vitae*) of learned women, mostly published in the seventeenth and eighteenth centuries. Scholar's catalogues are not unknown as a genre, but research in this field has been largely confined to the male *vitae*.[1]

THE RENAISSANCE DISCOURSE ON 'FAMOUS WOMEN'

The encyclopedias of learned women constitute a subspecies of an older and broader genre that predates the coming of the printed book. As early as the fourteenth century, we find catalogues of 'famous women', in which women renowned for their *scientia* ('knowledge') and *sapientia* ('wisdom') were

A 'learned wave' 51

included.[2] It was not before the seventeenth century that encyclopedias dealing mainly with learned women became a separate genre. The oldest and most influential of the early catalogues is Giovanni Boccaccio's *De claris mulieribus* ('On Famous Women', *c.* 1360).[3] Boccaccio stands at the beginning of a literary genre that took issue with the traditional Christian emphasis on female weakness, and promoted a more assertive image of women. Boccaccio's famous heathen women were strong, courageous, intelligent, creative, sometimes dangerous, defying fate and the gods. They hardly fitted into the theological view of women playing a 'negative' and very 'sporadic' role in creation, canonized by Thomas Aquinas in the late thirteenth century.[4] Although Boccaccio's descriptions were by no means unambiguous, his book bears witness to an early discussion of female status in society and culture. His influence is, for instance, apparent in Christine de Pizan's writings, roughly one generation later.[5]

Christine de Pizan was, however, by no means the only one to be influenced by Boccaccio. In the fifteenth and sixteenth centuries, several voluminous catalogues appeared, containing the biographies of powerful women. Just like Pizan's, these collections were frequently more comprehensive, encompassing *vitae* of the strong Renaissance queens, as well as women from biblical and the later Christian sacred history. Frequently, these books were dedicated to learned aristocratic women, such as Beatrice of Aragon or Bianca Maria Sforza. In most cases, even the title is a panegyric to exceptional women: *De laudibus mulierum* ('In Praise of Women'); *De mulieribus admirandis* ('On Women Worthy of Admiration'); *De memorabilibus et claris mulieribus* ('On Memorable and Famous Women'); etc. Authors such as Giovanni Sabadino degli Arienti (1483), Jacobus Philippus Bergomensis (1497), Johannes Ravisius Textor (1521), Baptista Fulgosus (1521), Giuseppe Betussi (1545), Juan Perez de Moya (1583) and others extolled these 'mulieribus admirandis' to their Italian, French or Spanish audiences.[6] One also finds references to fifteenth-century manuscript catalogues, one of them by the famous biographer Vespasiano da Bisticci.[7] These older encyclopedias were extremely important sources for the seventeenth- and eighteenth-century authors of collections of learned women's biographies.[8] They were adduced to buttress the claims that Renaissance humanism had already valued female learning. In the collection of ancient catalogues edited by Textor in 1521 there is even one exclusively dedicated to learned women, written by the above-mentioned Baptista Fulgosus, doge of Genoa in the early fifteenth century.

In my opinion, these early authors intended the inclusion of eminent women in what Jacob Burckhardt has called an *allgemeines Pantheon des Weltruhmes* ('General Pantheon of World Fame').[9] Presented to an aristocratic or patrician public, these divine, mythological, queenly, aristocratic-learned and biblical women were portrayed as exalted figures inhabiting a late-medieval hierarchical cosmos. They were not really intended as models to be imitated, but rather as 'objects of demonstration',

52   *Brita Rang*

exemplifying potential rather than actual capabilities. This is precisely why it is almost irrelevant whether they were portrayed as mythical or divine figures, or as women who had historically existed. They showed what might be possible for a few, but theirs was not an attainable ideal, not even for the great majority of upper-class women. It is precisely this aspect of the catalogues that was to change considerably in the seventeenth and eighteenth centuries.

FROM FAMOUS TO LEARNED WOMEN

I would like to interpret the rise of the catalogues of learned women in the seventeenth and eighteenth centuries as a 'realistic turn'. The older genre, presenting a miscellaneous assortment of women, famous in one way or another, slowly faded into the background.[10] In the new catalogues learned women were no longer imputed a divine lineage, nor were they primarily appreciated for their noble birth or high rank. The women to whom the authors now wanted to pay tribute derived their elevated status from their own intellectual efforts. Although they were frequently of noble or even royal blood, more than that was required to be included in the select company of learned women. The underlying conception of human abilities was clearly influenced by modern ideas of individual desert and natural rights.[11] To many authors this meant that in the final analysis, men and women had the same rational faculties.

This shift of perspective coincided with the transition from *famous* women to *learned* women. At the same time, the nature of the catalogues changed: from the 'pantheon' we move to the lexicon and the dictionary. Furthermore, the *savantes* ('learned women') became a model to be followed. Breathless exaltation gave way to a more prosaic desire for emulation. The authors presented 'their' female scholars as 'precedents', literally to be equalled; *Imitatio et emulatio* was their motto. In this context they drew attention to the importance of education in general, and to the crucial role of parents in particular. Most of the authors of the catalogues considered it no more than 'fair to accept women into the republic of scholars'.[12] Eventually, this became one of the central issues of seventeenth-century feminism (see also Siep Stuurman's chapter 4 in this book).[13]

Finally, there is a shift in the geography of the genre. During the fourteenth, fifteenth and sixteenth centuries catalogues had been published in France, Spain and, above all, in Italy, the ancient centre of humanism. But these books, frequently written in Latin, also attracted a humanist reading public in northern countries, as can be seen when we consider the places where, for example, Boccaccio was published. This is confirmed by the European-wide interest in the texts edited by Textor in Paris. The early catalogues were mainly published in Renaissance Italy, while most of the newer catalogues appeared in the northern countries. I even found one Swedish and three Danish catalogues.[14] The shift in the place of publication coin-

A *'learned wave'* 53

cided with the onset of the scientific revolution, in which the main centres of scientific activity moved to the north and the west.

It may sound surprising that in an age in which learned women were generally seen as an anomaly, voluminous books were published portraying hundreds of *savantes*. It is no less astonishing that nowadays these encyclopedias are largely forgotten and hard to come by.[15] This may be due to the fact that they were published for particular purposes. The overriding aim of the authors was to demonstrate that women were capable of engaging in scholarly work. The biographies are usually embedded in detailed argumentation in favour of the scientific pursuits of women, while the individual *exempla* 'proved' that women could actually do scientific work. There had therefore to be as many of these as possible. Johan van Beverwijck, for example, stated that he had mentioned 'all the learned ladies, of whom we could gain any knowledge'.[16] In the eighteenth century, the Cartesian Riballier, who listed more than a thousand learned women, asserted that he had presented every woman he could identify in the 'Histoires générales & grands dictionnaires', adding that there were probably still more to be found.[17] For Riballier, the sheer number of learned women was the strongest of proofs for the thesis that women and science were not mutually exclusive.

It is hard to say how popular these catalogues were. They were published in great numbers, frequently reissued, and internationally renowned. There must have existed a rather large public interest in these publications.[18] But who were the readers? Judging from the list of subscriptions to George Ballard's catalogue *Memoirs of Several Ladies* (1752), many of the readers were women.[19] This squares well with the fact that these works were usually dedicated to outstanding learned ladies of noble rank, for many subscribers came from the same Estate. It is also interesting to note who the authors were. They were mostly men, although there were female authors as well, such as Marguerite Buffet, Leonara von Ulfeld and Charlotte Cosson.[20] The writers usually were Third Estate professionals: they were lecturers, such as Menage and Thomasius, doctors, such as Van Beverwijck and Paullini, theologians, such as Eberti and De la Porte, lawyers, such as Della Chiesa and Corvinus, and, let us not forget, librarians such as Lehms.

There are several questions I would like to examine. In the first place, how did these women acquire their knowledge, given their exclusion from the institutions of formal education? Second, who were the learned women, who trespassed onto the 'male' territory of science? Can we say anything about their social origin and their way of life? Finally, we would like to know in which fields of knowledge they were chiefly engaged, and whether there were changes or shifts in their interests in the course of time? To sum up, can anything like a specific feminine culture of learning be distilled from our sources?

The authors of the catalogues were, of course, inspired by a contemporary perspective. The questions thus remain how *they* regarded the women they portrayed, which concepts of female erudition they presented to their

54 *Brita Rang*

public? Their objective was the demonstration of female abilities, in an age when concepts of universal rights and equality were discussed, and the social importance of science was rising sharply. But even the most brilliant learned women were hardly admitted to the male republic of letters where the new science was surging ahead.[21] It is therefore important to inquire whether the catalogues themselves suggest an explanation for this persistent exclusion.

THE SEVENTEENTH-CENTURY CATALOGUES

Dictionnaire or *Catalogus* did not refer solely to a collection of short biographies, sometimes it was just a list of names. One of the first extensive lists with biographical notes was the *Catalogus doctarum virginum et foeminarum* ('Catalogue of learned Virgins and Women'), published in 1606 in Prague.[22] The author, Martinus a Balthoven, lists around seventy names of learned women from antiquity, the Middle Ages and the Renaissance. Indirectly, he pleads for female education. The catalogue is dedicated to a learned noblewoman, Elisabeth Johanna Westonius, whose poems are printed in an introductory chapter. In the following decades the *vitae* were increasingly embedded in treatises on women's intellectual abilities.[23]

Two early examples of the genre can be found in the writings of Johann Frawenlob and Johan van Beverwijck.[24] Both placed the biographies (Frawenlob *c.* 120, Van Beverwijck *c.* 185) within a coherent string of arguments. Frawenlob demanded that parents give their daughters a better education, while van Beverwijck stated among other things that 'the true happiness of mankind consists in learnedness and virtue'.[25] This conception of learnedness as a common aim of mankind, implies that striving for it should not be the monopoly of privileged men. Van Beverwijck rejoices at someone like Vossius, who educated his young daughters in the humanities. He himself taught his own daughters, aged four and seven, classical and modern languages. In his view, female learning was to be acquired within the context of family life. The women 'of all peoples and centuries' he cited are thus not necessarily the lonely, unmarried inhabitants of a 'book-lined cell'.[26] Science and virtue in women do not imply social isolation; the women he lists are usually married and play their part in the intellectual education of their children. Moreover he regards them as members of the intellectual community. Van Beverwijck especially admires intellectual families such as that of Thomas More, citing Erasmus who admonished others to follow their *exemplum.*[27] In this context, biblical women are no longer relevant to van Beverwijck and Frawenlob. As in Boccaccio, science and virtue in their work are by no means necessarily linked to Christian virtues.

The same is true of Aegidius Menagius, author of the best-known catalogue of the late seventeenth century, dedicated to one of the foremost French *savantes*, Anne Dacier.[28] It is one of the first catalogues concerned with just one discipline – classical philosophy.[29] It is striking that Menagius concentrated solely on classical philosophy. He does not deal with women interested in the philosophy of his own day, for example that of Descartes, even though he refers to contemporary learned women like van Schurman, de Gournay, Christine of Sweden and Madame de Sevigné. As for Van Beverwijck, the women he presents did not lead an isolated existence. This applies especially to the philosophers of antiquity. Speaking of women belonging to the schools of Pythagoras, Peripathes and Epicurus, he reports that they were mostly married and that they moved in the circles of learned men.[30]

THE EIGHTEENTH-CENTURY CATALOGUES

The catalogues published in the first half of the eighteenth century form a diverse group.[31] What they have in common, compared to those of the seventeenth century, is greater bibliographical precision. Sometimes Eberti, for example, mentions more than forty references for one biography.[32] In his *Istoria* Alberti seeks to provide precise chronological data.[33] Ballard (1752) was one of the first to present his entries in *chronological* order, from the fifteenth century to his own time. Latin, still the predominant language of the seventeenth-century catalogues, loses ground to the vernacular. Another novelty was the sometimes exceptional number of short biographies, more than a thousand in one case.[34] Some catalogues now had a regional focus, probably enhancing reliability as well as guaranteeing denser coverage.[35]

The content of the biographies also changed over time. In the seventeenth century they dealt mostly with the relatively abstract question of whether or not women had the same intellectual abilities as men. The authors in the first half of the eighteenth century tended more and more to attack contemporary prejudice against female learnedness. In this context the parents were criticized as well. According to Lehms, they were often so foolish as to tear books from their daughters' hands.[36] The new catalogues were thus deliberately designed as instruments of enlightenment. Finally, it is noteworthy that around 1700, a number of dissertations were published in Germany, mainly in the fields of theology, philosophy and medicine, in which short *vitae* of learned women were included, demonstrating that the issue of female learning had become an academic subject.

In the second half of the eighteenth century interest in the catalogues and *savantes* waned.[37] By this time, two distinct views had emerged. Cartesian authors such as Riballier championed an egalitarian scientific education for women and girls, encompassing all sciences and all arts.[38] We may conclude that Riballier did not attribute special aptitudes for literary and aesthetic disciplines to women. On the other hand there were authors, such as de la Porte or Triller, for whom the learned woman as poetess was the central figure. In a certain sense we may consider this to be a narrower and more conservative view, tied to the older, humanistic literary culture of the Renaissance.

56 *Brita Rang*

'SHE WAS THE DAUGHTER AND PUPIL OF THEON OF ALEXANDRIA'[39] – HOW WOMEN ACQUIRED THEIR SCIENTIFIC KNOWLEDGE

In most of the catalogues, little attention is devoted to the question of *how* women acquired their scientific knowledge.[40] At first sight this seems surprising: weren't these catalogues inspired by the struggle for higher education for girls and women? It is striking that one of the simplest and oldest forms of tuition, namely by private tutors, is hardly mentioned in the catalogues, with the exception of Ballard's. An unusual form of academic training is exemplified in the biographies of the Greek female philosophers. These women often attended public lectures by well-known philosophers, together with men. By far the most common solution cited in the catalogues was, however, tuition by fathers. They were, at least according to the catalogues, the key figures in the informal academic education of women. Thus Theon of Alexandria, Melanchthon, Thomas More, the Florentine humanist and aristocrat Bartholomeo Scala, the painter Tiepolo and the less well-known lecturer Reichenbach of Helmstedt passed their knowledge on to their daughters. According to the catalogues, this applied to a fifth of all women: a high percentage, when one keeps in mind that in 60 per cent of all cases no explanation whatsoever is offered. There are several stories of father-daughter relationships of mutual intellectual support, and of daughters who delivered their father's lectures when he was ill: 'Francisca Nebrissensis, daughter of the highly learned Antonius Nebrissensis, royal historiographer and professor, was so learned that she often held public lectures instead of her father.'[41] The authors attached great importance to this fatherly upbringing. The parental or marital home not only formed a closed and sheltered institution, but domestic education also guaranteed a relative monopolization of knowledge. In this way, knowledge, though in principle attainable for many women, could hold on to its exclusiveness. The improvement of higher education for women was considered desirable, but preferably within a 'private' setting, the family of the intellectual elite. Only a few authors wanted to admit women to the learned societies, the universities and the academies. One such was Riballier who asserted in 1779: 'If we admit women to the schools for rhetoric, politics, philosophy and mathematics, like the Athenians, we shall find eloquent women, able politicians, inspired philosophers and astute mathematicians among them.'[42]

'SHE CLAIMED THAT SHE COULD PULL THE MOON DOWN FROM HEAVEN'[43] – THE TYPE OF KNOWLEDGE POSSESSED BY LEARNED WOMEN

On the whole, the catalogues do not privilege one particular form of knowledge and skill. The arts and the subjects taught in universities (theology, law, medicine, the *artes liberales* and languages) are often mentioned, but on the

A 'learned wave' 57

other hand we encounter references to practical abilities such as needlework, or to astrology and prophecy. Paullini mentions a woman who 'could discover hidden things and foretell the future – in the year 1620'.[44] The talents of Aganice, who 'was very experienced in stargazing' and who could make others believe 'that she . . . could pull down the moon from heaven' are not doubted by Van Beverwijck.[45] The knowledge of learned women is therefore by no means restricted to the kind of rational knowledge we associate with the Enlightenment. So how much ground did their knowledge actually cover? Roughly 15 per cent of the learned women were presented as universal scholars, learned in a broad, humanistic sense. More than 20 per cent were accomplished in languages and literature, or music and aesthetics. The learning of a large group, nearly 20 per cent, took a religious and theological direction. The majority of these women wrote religious tracts, prayers or hymns, but some were trained in theology.[46] Less than 10 per cent occupied themselves with medicine, including obstetrics. The percentage of women in mathematics, astronomy and history was still lower.

Judging from their description of female learning, the authors do not seem to have been aware of living in the age of the scientific revolution. Illustrative are the biographies of women who took part in the development of modern science, for example Maria Cunitz, who attempted to ameliorate Kepler's tables of planetary motion.[47] Eberti says: 'Maria Cunitz could speak seven languages and could draw well. Moreover she took great pleasure in astronomic speculations. . . .'[48] Note that the author mentions her linguistic and aesthetic abilities first, while her astronomical abilities are mentioned last. But we must bear in mind that by doing this, he is merely following a general trend. The women themselves and nearly all the authors put great value on the acquisition of literary and humanistic culture. This is true even of Riballier: even though he explicitly rejects the traditional canon in his introduction, it nevertheless crops up again and again in his biographies. This standard of a broad humanistic learning should, however, not be confounded with the humanism of the early modern universities, for the traditional university was an institution characterized by a strong degree of specialization. The true 'universitas litterarum', on the other hand, flourished *outside* the universities in the informal circles of the humanists and the salons. It had no fixed institutional form. The emphasis the catalogues placed on the humanistic-literary and religious-theological genre leads one to suppose that the authors preferred to associate women with open, informal modes of acquiring and transferring knowledge, rather than with more institutionalized forms of education such as universities. The father who tutored his daughter in the sciences and the husband who encouraged his wife to 'help' him with his studies were important alternative models.[49] Both gave access to the 'universitas litterarum', but not to universities.

Vitae presented in the catalogues from the second half of the eighteenth century confirm this view. In Ballard's catalogue a close link between female learnedness and the literary-humanistic tradition is evident. The

58   *Brita Rang*

fifteenth-century women he names seem to lag behind the intellectual accomplishments of their time, in the sixteenth century they move to the forefront of intellectual life, but as soon as the importance of the humanistic concept of education diminishes we find women falling behind again: most of the seventeenth and eighteenth-century women listed by Ballard took no part in the new empirical scientific developments in England, for the large majority received a predominately literary-humanistic education.[50] These tendencies are not only to be found in the work of the chroniclers, they are also manifest in the published work of many of the learned women themselves.[51] More than 80 per cent were 'authors' in one way or another, or there were letters or other writings mentioned or published by other authors. The lists not only comprised many titles of religious works, but also titles of books on other subjects concerning women: education, obstetrics, 'harmony of women', women who had been queens, theological investigations about women and their position. For example: 'Marie de Romieu, a young lady from Vivarets in the Languedoc, has published in a poem, printed in Paris in 1581, that women are superior to men, and in prose an instruction for the young ladies, printed in Diepe in 1573'.[52]

'SHE WAS LEARNED, RICH, BEAUTIFUL AND OF A NOBLE FAMILY'[53] – THE SOCIAL BACKGROUND AND THE LIFE OF LEARNED WOMEN

The relationship between beauty and knowledge, the harmony of body and mind, is an ancient leitmotif. It crops up frequently in writings about women in the Renaissance, apparently under the influence of Neoplatonism. 'She was a very beautiful Lady of great spirit . . . ', Ballard writes about a woman from the fifteenth century.[54] Even the Cartesian Riballier informs us of learned women, whose beauty surpassed that of the most beautiful women of their time.[55] Still more important than the combination of beauty and wisdom, is the combination of learnedness and noble origin. A large portion of the women mentioned in the catalogues (about 40 per cent) were nobles. Considering that in a third of the women's *vitae* no information is disclosed about their origin, it is quite probable that the percentage of noble women was actually higher. In Ballard's catalogue, for example, the percentage of noble women is over 80, although his data for the seventeenth century display a slightly higher share of bourgeois women. In the catalogues I studied systematically, 23 per cent of the women came from the intellectual bourgeoisie. Only a very small group is reported to have come from humble circumstances. This was obviously so rare that the authors thought it necessary to give heart-rending accounts of how these poor girls had acquired their knowledge with the help of rich benefactors.[56]

Female learnedness went hand in hand with a certain degree of prosperity, which allowed women some leisure. The privileged life of female scholars was not criticized by the authors of the catalogues. Only the less wealthy citizens of the second half of the eighteenth century referred to female learnedness – because it was so closely connected to some degree of affluence – as a silly waste of time for wealthy women.

In *Beyond Their Sex* Margaret King describes the life of learned women in the Renaissance as a lonely, secluded existence.[57] According to her account, these women lived in a state of monastic recluse, the famous 'book-lined cell'. Moreover, they were regarded as asexual beings. King maintains that the male authors who presented the learned women to the public were also prejudiced in this way: 'When learned men praised learned women they undermined them as women. They regarded them as sexless beings or women with a disturbed sexuality.'[58] Apart from the question of whether this gives us a complete picture of the complex situation of learned women in the Italian Renaissance,[59] we should also examine the validity of such a statement for women from later periods and other countries. Furthermore, the question of how the women themselves saw their own lives remains to be answered. According to King, they internalized the opinions of their contemporaries and voluntarily led a kind of celibate, monastic life: 'The learned women, conquered from within, capitulated and withdrew from battle. They withdrew from study altogether, into marriage, or into grief. They withdrew to convents, and to good work and to silence.'[60] The catalogues of the seventeenth and eighteenth centuries, however, do not confirm this dreary picture. Learned women now seem, on the contrary, to have lived in fairly good harmony with their surroundings. According to the *vitae*, they were mostly married and often active in science even after their marriage. For example: 'Elisabeth Margaretha von Keil, wife of the famous physician Andreas von Keil ... was very well-versed in pharmacy and chemistry and wrote a good book about obstetrics, which her husband wished to publish.'[61] Unfortunately, the biographies give very little information about a learned woman's way of life. When they contain detailed information, such as in Ballard's case, we get the impression that the percentage of married women was high: about 90 per cent in Ballard's catalogue, compared to some 60 per cent among the overall population. This is due to the comparatively secure economic situation of these learned Englishwomen. Therefore it is doubtful whether the image of the lonely woman defying marriage, or the married woman giving up science, is a correct one. At any rate it is not confirmed by the catalogues.

The authors of the catalogues did not formulate learnedness, marriage and motherhood as alternative paths of life. Their examples do not convey the impression that they regarded the life of a learned woman as socially and emotionally repressed or limited. The question remains whether the 'normality' of these women's lives, which they so strongly emphasize, was always in agreement with the concrete existence of early-modern learned women. An imaginary dialogue, taken from an English book about astronomy for young ladies from 1768, leads one to suspect otherwise. A student just home from Oxford tells his sister:

60   *Brita Rang*

> Philosophy is the darling science of every man of sense and is a peculiar
> grace in the fair sex; and depend on it, sister, it is now growing into
> fashion for the ladies to study philosophy; and I am very glad to see a
> sister of mine so well inclined to promote a thing so laudable and
> honourable to her sex.

His sister's answer shows something of the problems so generously ignored
by her brother:

> I often wish that it did not look quite so masculine for a woman to talk of
> philosophy in company. . . . how happy will be the age when the ladies
> may modestly pretend to knowledge, and appear learned without singu-
> larity and affection.[62]

Nevertheless, the many women who, according to the catalogues, combined
their female existence with learnedness without becoming socially isolated,
give us something to think about. A surprisingly great number of women
obviously did not choose the combination 'children, husband and kitchen'
but 'children, husband and science' instead. It is remarkable that this has
been forgotten in our century. All things considered, I do not think it justified to speak of learned women, especially in the seventeenth and eighteenth
centuries, in terms of 'absence' and 'isolation'.

EPILOGUE

In this chapter, only a small selection out of the hundreds of brief biographies could be dealt with. Nevertheless, my hypothesis seems to be
confirmed: there were probably many more of such learned women than is
sometimes assumed. The large number of *vitae* in itself, especially from the
fifteenth to the eighteenth centuries, endorses this hypothesis. Furthermore
I, like Riballier, suspect that there were far more learned women than the
catalogues list. For example, only a few of the sixty-four poets of the
Pléiade, a French literary group from the sixteenth century, still known by
name today, are mentioned in the catalogues.[63] And of the seventeenth
century Dutch female painters the biographers seem ignorant.[64] Thus we
may speak of a 'learned wave', at least as far as the quantitative side of the
problem is concerned. I also disagree with Sylvia Bovenschen's thesis that
the idea of women of intellect (*schönen Verstand*: 'beautiful intellect') can be
regarded as a 'modern' achievement of the eighteenth century.[65] On the
contrary, it seems to me to be the continuation of an older tradition in a
different form. A learned wave moved through European history in times
when learnedness was not yet bound to universities and when new concepts
of equality stimulated the questioning of traditional views.

Questions about the specific female modes of practising science are not
so easy to answer. I have tried to formulate some tentative conclusions. One
important aspect was the informal way in which science was almost always

passed on to girls and women, in an intellectual culture that developed outside the universities. It should perhaps be recalled that the early-modern scientific revolution also largely bypassed the traditional universities. The specific position of women in the history of modern science can therefore not be ascribed just to their exclusion from formal or institutionalized education. By arguing in this way, we would be blotting out aspects of education which were extremely important for the women concerned (and for many men) throughout several centuries.

Another facet concerns the scientific subjects studied by women. A number of the women described as learned gave their own emphases, and managed, for example, to express productively their poetic and literary abilities in religion. The range of female learnedness we find in the catalogues is very broad, and not as well-defined as that of male learnedness. A third aspect of the problem is whether women were isolated by their academic interests. Was the life of learned women in the seventeenth and eighteenth centuries a 'no man's land' or a book-lined cell? I have treated this question in detail, and I think it goes to the heart of the matter. The catalogues of learned women do not support such a thesis for the early-modern period. Rather they contain instructions for *enlarging* the scope of action, possibilities for expression and study for (predominantly married) women. But perhaps I have allowed myself to be influenced too much by the authors' wish to show that a learned woman, who is indeed 'extraordinary', can also be quite 'ordinary'. Whatever the case may be, the sheer number of women described in the catalogues lead us to conclude that being learned was by no means unusual, but rather an almost 'everyday' phenomenon.

It is sometimes asserted that the concept of the 'female scholar' in the seventeenth and eighteenth centuries was in accordance with, or even disciplined by, the Enlightenment 'gospel of reason'.[66] For this to be the case, surely the catalogues pleading most ardently for female education in those times must bear witness to it? But I find no evidence supporting such claims. Neither is there any mention of a distinct, rationalistic idea of science on which female learnedness is modelled. On the contrary, from the eighteenth century onwards, the growing importance of the modern empirical and rationalistic model of the sciences led to a marginalization of the learned 'beautiful souls'.

Moreover, interest in women's learnedness was undermined by the rise of the middle classes. For this new social group it was unacceptable to grant women the freedom and leisure to practise science. For the average burgher of modest means, it was economically impossible to exempt women from housework, allowing them time for developing the kind of intellectual lifestyle that the wealthy humanist patrician classes had pursued for their women. But instead of admitting this, they rationalized the problem, stating, like the premodern misogynists, that learning conflicted with women's 'nature'.[67] Towards the end of the eighteenth century the resplendent image of the *savante* was slowly supplanted by the image of the neurotic, frustrated

62 *Brita Rang*

learned woman.[68] It is therefore hardly surprising, in the light of the growing social and cultural importance of the middle classes, that the interest in catalogues with examples of learned women decreased and finally almost disappeared in the course of the nineteenth century.

NOTES

1 See, for example, Guillaume de Roville, *Promptuarium iconum insigniorum a seculo hominum, subjectis eorum vitis, per compendium ex probatissimis autoribus desumptis*, Lyon, Rovillius, 1553; Paulus Jovius, *Elogia doctorum virorum ab avorum memoria publicatis ingenii monumentis illustrium . . .* , Antwerp, Bellerus, 1557 (first edn., 1536); Theodorus Beza, *Les vrais portraits des hommes illustres en* piété *et doctrine*, Genève, Laon, 1581.

2 Cf. G. A. Guarino, 'Introduction', in Giovanni Boccaccio, *De claris mulieribus (1355–1359) ('Concerning Famous Women')*, New Brunswick, 1963.

3 See also A. Hortis, *Studj sulle opere latine del Boccaccio*, Trieste, Base, 1879; Latin versions of Boccaccio's book were published in 1473, 1475, 1487, 1531, 1539; French editions 1476, 1483, 1493, 1515, 1538, 1551, 1578; German 1473, 1479, 1488, 1541, 1543, 1545, 1566: A. Bacchi della Lega, *Bibliografia Boccacesca. Serie delle Edizioni delle opere di Giovanni Boccaccio*, Bologna, Romagnoli, 1875.

4 J. MacLean, *The Renaissance Notion of Woman*, Cambridge, Cambridge University Press, 1980, pp. 6ff.

5 Christine de Pizan, 'Epistre au dieu d'amours', (1399), in M. Roy (ed.), *Christine de Pisan. Oéuvres poetiques de Christine de Pisan. In three volumes*, Paris, Firmin Didot, 1891, vol. 2, p. 23; A. Jeanroy, 'Boccace et Christine de Pisan. Le De claris mulieribus, principale source du Livre de la Cité des Dames', *Romania*, 1992, XLVIII, 51, pp. 93–105.

6 Giovanni Sabadino degli Arienti, *Gynevera de le clare donne di Joanne Sabadino de li Arienti (1483)*, a cura di Corra de Ricci e. A. Bacchi della Lega, Bologna, Romagnoli, 1888. Joannes Ravisius Textor (Jean Tixier, seigneur de Ravisy), *De memorabilibus et claris mulieribus: aliquod diversorum scriptorum opera*, Paris, Colinaeus, 1521; Jacobus Philippus Bergomensis (Jacopo Philippo Foresti), *Opus de claris selectisque plurimus mulieribus*, Ferrara, De Rubeis, 1497. Other catalogues were published by Bathelemy de Chasseneux (Lyon, 1529, 1549), Guiseppe Betussi (Venice, 1545); Johannes Ireneus (Frankfurt, 1569), Alexandre Vandenbussche (Rouen, 1574, 1603), Andreas Hondorff (Frankfurt, 1575), Juan Peres de Moya (Madrid, 1583), Petruccio Ubaldini (London, 1591), Francesco Sardonati (Florence, 1596).

7 Vespasiano da Bisticci, Delle lodi delle donne (MS Ricc. 2293); Antonio Cornazzano, *De mulieribus admirandis, in terza rima* (MS Est. ital. 177, Alpha J.6.21).

8 The catalogues cited most often are those of Bergomensis, Textor, Peres de Moya, Fulgosus, Betussi, Sardonati and Boccaccio.

9 J. Burckhardt, *Die Kultur der Renaissance in Italien*, Leipzig, Seemann, 1891, vol. I, p. 177.

10 In France, publications in the Renaissance tradition continued into the seventeenth century: Pierre Le Moyne, *La Gallerie des Femmes Fortes*, Paris, Antoine de Sommaville, 1647; Madeleine (and George) de Scudéry, *Les femmes illustres, ou les harangues heroïques, avec les veritables portraits des ces heroïnes*, 2 vols, Paris, 1644 and 1646.

11 E. Bloch, *Naturrecht and menschliche Würde*, Frankfurt a. Main, Suhrkamp, 1961.

A 'learned wave' 63

12 'Jus fasque esse in Rempublicam litterariam foeminis adscribi', Johann Thomasius, *Diatribe academica de foeminarum eruditione, revisa et emendatior prodit*, Diss., Leipzig, Hahn, 1676 (first edn. 1671), Prooemium.

13 J. Kelly, 'Early feminist theory and the *Querelle des femmes*', *Signs*, 1982, 8, pp. 4–28, reprinted in *Women, History and Theory: The Essays of Joan Kelly*, Chicago, University of Chicago Press, 1984; L. M. Richardson, *The Forerunners of Feminism in French Literature of the Renaissance from Christine de Pisa to Marie de Gournay*, Baltimore and Paris, John Hopkins, 1929.

14 Johannes Eßbergius, *Mulieres philosophantes*, Upsala, 1699; Albert Thura, *Gynaecaeum Danmiae litterarum, foeminis Danorum, eruditione vel scriptis claris conspicuum*, Altona, Korte, 1732; Frederik Christian Schønau, *Samling af danske learde fruentimer, som ved deres leerdom, og udgivne eller efterladte skrifter have giort dercs navne i den laerde verden bekiendte*, Kopenhagen, 1753; Von Ulfeld, *Den fangne Grevinde*. See note 20 below.

15 Recent reprints or translations of those catalogues have been published (Ballard 1752, 1985; Eberti 1700, 1986; Lehms 1715, n.d.; Menage 1690–1692, 1984). See further J. Woods and M. Fürstenwald, *Schriftstellerinnen, Künstlerinnen und gelehrte Frauen des deutschen Barock*, Stuttgart, Metzler, 1984; L. Traeger, *Das Frauenschrifttum in Deutschland von 1500 bis 1650*, Diss., Prague, 1943; Giana Pomata 'Storia particolare e storia universale in margine ad alcuni manuale di storia delle donne', *Quaderni Storici*, 74, 1990.

16 Van Beverwijck, *Van de Wtnementheyt des Vrouwelicken geslachts*, Dordrecht, Boy, 1643; *De excellentia foemini sexus*, 1636, p. 88.

17 Riballier, *De l'éducation physique et morale des femmes, avec une notice alphabe-tique de celles qui se sont distinguées dans les differentes carriéres des Sciences & des Beaux-Arts, ou par des talens & des actions mémorables*, Bruxelles and Paris, Estienne, 1779, pp. 87, 93.

18 Georg Christian Lehms, *Teutschlands galante Poetinnen. Mit ihren sinnreichen und netten Proben*, Frankfurt, Hocker, 1715.

19 George Ballard, *Memoirs of Several Ladies of Great Britain who have been cele-brated for their writings or skill in the learned languages, arts and sciences*, Oxford, W. Jackson, 1752, pp. ix–xvii.

20 Marguerite Buffet, *Nouvelles observations sur la langue françoise, ou il est traitté des termes anciens et inusitez, et du bel usage des mots nouveaux. Avec les éloges des illustres sçavantes, tant anciennes que modernes*, Paris, J. Cusson, 1668; Leonora Christina von Ulfeld, *Den fangne Grevinde Leonora Christinas Jammers Minde*, Kopenhagen, facsimile Udgave, bekostet af Apoteker A. E. Sibbersen, 1931.

21 See Brita Rang, ' "Een maeght kan eerbaer zijn en niet te min geleerd" (Cats). Discussies over vrouwen, wetenschap en studie in de 17de en 18de eeuw', *Comenius*, 1986, 6, pp. 272–91.

22 Martinus a Balthoven, *Catalogus doctarum virginum et foeminarum. Appendix of: Parthenicon Elisabethae Westoniae*, Prague, Paul Sesse, 1606.

23 See Francesco Agostino Della Chiesa, *Theatro delle donne letterate con un breve discorso della preminenza, e perfettione del sesso donnesco*, Monte Reguli, Rossi, 1620; Giulio Cesare Capaccio, *Illustrium mulierum et illustrium litteris virorum elogio*, Napoli, Carlinus/Vitalis, 1608; *Mulieres virtutibus et scientia praedita cum praefixis authoribus qui earum laudes scripserunt. Item traité de la perfection des femmes comparée a celles des hommes*, 1617/18 (MS, Maz 4398); Thomas Heywood, *Tuneikeion: Or, Nine bookes of various history, concerning women; inscribed by the names of the nine muses. Written by Thom Heywoode*, London, Adam Islip, 1624; Hilarion de Coste, *Les eloges et vies de reynes, princesses, dames et damoiselles illustres en pieté, courage et doctrine, qui ont fleury de nostre temps, et du temps de nos péres*, Paris, Cramoisy, 1620 (second edn. 1647); Louis

64 *Brita Rang*

Jacob, *Dictionnaire biografique des femmes écrivains, depuis l'antiquité jusqua'au XVIIe siècle*, 1646 (BN, FF 22865).

24 Johann Frawenlob (pseud. Israel Clauderus?), *Die lobwürdige Gesellschaft der Gelahrten Weiber/ oder Kurtze historische Beschreibung der fürnehmsten/ gelahrten/ verstandigen/ und kunst-erfahrenen Weibes Personen/ so in der Welt biß auf diese Zeit gelebet haben*, n.p., 1631; Van Beverwijck, *Van de Wtnementheyt.*

25 Van Beverwijck, *Van de Witnementheyt*, chapter 2, p. 17.

26 *Ibid.*, pp. 18 ff; see also G. D. J. Schotel, *Letter – en oudheidkundige avondstonden*, Dordrecht, Blus & Van Braam, 1841, pp. 160–1.

27 Van Beverwijck, *Van de Wtnementheyt*, p. 64.

28 On Madame Dacier: F. Farnham, *Madame Dacier, Scholar and Humanist*, Monterey, Angel Press, 1976; P. Mazon, *Madame Dacier et les Traduction d'Homère en France*, Oxford, Clarendon Press, 1936.

29 *Historia Mulierum Philosopharum*, Lyon, 1690; reprinted Amsterdam, 1692; I use the 1692 edition.

30 Besides the catalogue of Menagius, a whole lot were published in the second half of the seventeenth century, of which Juncker's became very famous internationally. See Jean Fronteau, *Dissertatio philologica . . . de virginate honorata, erudita, adorata, foecanda*, Paris, Cramoisy, 1651; Johann Herbinius, *Duabus dissertationibus de Foeminarum Illustrium eruditione*, Diss., Wittenberg, 1657; T. H. Gent (Thomas Heywood), *The Generall History of Women, containing the Lives of the most Holy and Prophane*, London, W. H., 1657; Antoine Baudeau de Somaize, Grand dictonnaire des priétieuses, Paris, 7. Ribou, 1661. Buffet, *Nouvelles Observations*; Thomasius, *Diatribe academica. Johann Friedrich Heckel, Dissertatiuncula de foeminis litteratis*, Rudolphstadt, Schulz, 1686; Andreas Planerus and Johann Pasch, *Gynaecaeum doctum, sive dissertatio historico literaria. Vom gelehrten Frauenzimmer*, Wittenberg, Fincel, 1686; Christoph Christian Haendel and Magnus Daniel Omeis, *De eruditis Germaniae mulieribus*, Diss., Altdorf, Meyer, 1688; Christian Juncker and Abraham Gottleber, *Centuria foeminarum eruditione et scriptis illustrium*, Diss., Leipzig, Fleischer, 1692; Christian Frantz Paullini, *Zeitkürzende Erbauliche Lust* (Cap. 193: 'Das gelahrte Frauen-Zimmer in Teutschland'), Frankfurt, Fr. Knoch, 1695, pp. 1097–1122; Eßbergius, *Mulieres philosophantes*; Van Ulfeld, *Den fangne Grevinde*; Cornelis von Beughem, *T'Lof deer Doorlugtige Vrouwen siiende een historisch verhaal aller gelarden Vrouwen*, Amsterdam, s.a. (mentioned in *Philotheens Frauenzimmer*, see n.37).

31 Johann Dietrich Stark and David Schulte, *De feminis prima aetate eruditione ac scriptis illustribus ac nobilibus*, 2 vols, Diss., Wittenberg, Gerdes, 1703; Christian Frantz Paullini, *Hoch- and Wohlgelahrtes Teutsches Frauenzimmer*, Frankfurt and Leipzig, Stössel, 1705; Johann Kaspar Eberti, *Eröffnetes Cabinet dess gelehrten Frauenzimmer, Frankfurt, Rohrlach, 1701*; Johann Gerhard Meuschen, *Curieuse Schaubühne durchlauchtigst gelehrter Damen*, Frankfurt and Leipzig, Bielcke, 1706; other catalogues were published by Christian Heinrich Engelcken and Johan Bernhard Weppling (Rostock, 1707), Johann Christian Blum and Gottfried Olarius (Leipzig, 1708), Gustav Georg Zeltner (Nürnberg, 1708), Johann Konrad Zeltner (Altdorf, 1708), Gottlieb Siegmund Corvinus (Leipzig, 1715), Georg Christian Lehms (Frankfurt, 1715), Anonymous (Leipzig, 1716), Ambrosius Scheumader (Altdorf, 1717), Johann Stengel (Altdorf, 1724), Johann Kaspar Eberti (Breslau, 1727).

32 Eberti, *Eröffnetes Cabinet*, p. 99 (Hildegard of Bingen), 184 (Jeanne d'Arc).

33 Marcello Alberti, *Istoria delle donne Scientiate. Naples 1740.*

34 Alberti lists about 900 names; Eberti, *Eröffnetes Cabinet*, 600, Riballier more than 1000.

35 See Lehms, *Teutschlands galante Poetinnen*; Eberti, *Schlesiens Frauen-Zimmer,*

A 'learned wave' 65

Thura, *Gynaeceum*; Ballard, *Memoirs*; Schønau, *Samling*. National pride is shown by collecting as many names of learned women of one's own country as possible.

36 Lehms, *Teutschlands Galante Poetinnen*, 'Vorrede'.
37 See, among others, Ballard, *Memoirs*, 1752; Schønau, *Samling*; Thomas Armory, *Memoirs of Several Ladies of Great-Britain*, 2 vols, London, 1755; Finauer, *Allgemeines historische Verzeichnis*, 1761; Johann C. K. Oelrichs, *Historische Nachricht vom Pommerschen gelehrten Frauenzimmer. Historisch-Diplomatische Beyträge zur Geschichte der Gelahrtheit, besonders im Herzogthum Pommern*, Berlin, Reimer, 1767; *Les vies des Hommes & des Femmes illustres d'Italie depuis le Retablissement des sciences & des beaux Arts*, 2 vols, Yverdon, 1768; Pierre-Joseph Boudier de Villemert, *Le nouvel ami des femmes, ou la Philosophie du sexe . . . avec une notice alphabétique des femmes célèbres en France*, Amsterdam and Paris, Monory, 1779; De la Porte and De la Croix, *Histoire litteraire*; Riballier, *De l'éducation*, 1779; *Philotheens Frauenzimmer*, 1783; *The Promenade*, Dublin, Byrne, 1788 (with lives of Irish poetesses); Jean Francois de la Croix, *Dictionnaire portatif des femmes célèbres: contenant l'histoire des femmes savantes, des actrices & generalement des dames qui se sont rendues fameuses dans tous les siècles*, Paris, Belin, 1788; Samuel Baur, *Deutschlands Schriftstellerinnen*, Ulm, Stettin, 1790.
38 Riballier, *De l'éducation*, p. 5; see Brita Rang, 'Männlicher Bewußtseinsdiskurs and existentielles Weiblichkeitskonzept', *Das Argument. Zeitschrift für Philosophie and Sozialwissenschaften*, 1986, 28, 155, pp. 86–92.
39 Quotation from the life of Hypathia, Menagius, *Historia*, p. 52.
40 Figures calculated from: Van Beverwijck (1643); Menagius (1690); Paullini (1705); Eberti (1706), Alberti (1740) and Riballier (1779).
41 Van Beverwijck, *Van de Wtnementheyt*, chapter 2, p. 50.
42 Riballier, *De l'education*, p. 90.
43 This is part of a sentence from the life of Aganice ('persuavit se lunam caelo posse deducere'), Menagius, *Historia*, p. 25.
44 Paullini, *Hoch- and Wohl-gelahrtes Frauen-Zimmer*, p. 60.
45 Van Beverwijck, *Van de Wtnementheyt*, chap. 2, p. 28.
46 Life of Anna Lavaggi: Riballier, *De l'éducation*, p. 331.
47 Maria Cunitz, *Urania propitia, sive Tabulae Astronomicae mire faciles, vim hypothesium physicarum a Keplero propitiarum complexae . . . Das ist: Newe and langgewünschte / leichte Astronomische Tabelln . . . dem Kunstliebenden Deutscher Nation zu gut herfürgegeben*, Oels, Seyffert, 1650.
48 Eberti, *Eröffnetes Cabinet*, p. 127.
49 Van Beverwijck, *Van de Wtnementheyt*, p. 61.
50 An exception is Catherine Chidley who was politically modern and took part in the English Revolution: Ballard, *Memoirs*, p. 281.
51 See P. O. Kristeller, 'Learned women of early modern Italy: humanists and university scholars' in P. Labalme (ed.), *Beyond their Sex: Learned Women of the European Past*, London and New York, New York University Press, 1980, p. 95.
52 Van Beverwijck, *Van de Wtnementheyt*, chap. 2, p. 59.
53 Menagius, *Historia*, p. 25: 'Mulier docta, dives, formosa, generosa'.
54 Ballard, *Memoirs*, p. 5.
55 Life of Madeleine Acciaivoli: Riballier, *De l'éducation*, p. 97.
56 E.g. Emerentia Fulbicke and Eva Juliana Gräserin: Paullini, *Hoch- and Wohl-gelahrtes Frauen-Zimmer*, pp. 63, 71.
57 King, 'Book-Lined Cells'; King, 'Thwarted ambitions: six learned women of the early Italian Renaissance', *Soundings*, 1976, 76, pp. 280–300; King, 'The religious retreat of Isotta Nogarola (1418–1466)', *Signs*, 1978, 3, pp. 807–22.

66 Brita Rang

58 King, 'Book-Lined Cells', p. 79.
59 A. R. Jones, 'City women and their audiences: Louise Labé and Veronica Franco', in M. W. Ferguson, M. Quilligan and N. J. Vickers (eds), *Rewriting the Renaissance. The Discourses of Sexual Difference in Early Modern Europe*, Chicago and London, University of Chicago Press, 1986, pp. 299–316.
60 King, 'Book-Lined Cells', p. 74.
61 Paullini, *Hoch- and Wohl-gelahrtes Frauen-Zimmer*, p. 86.
62 Benjamin Martin, 'The Young Gentleman and Lady's Philosophy' (second edn., 2 vols, London, 1772), cited in M. Alic, *Hypathia's Heritage. A History of Women in Science from Antiquity to the Late Nineteenth Century*, London, W. Owen, 1986, p. 81.
63 L. Feugère, *Les femmes poètes au XVIe siècle*, Paris, 1860 (Genève, Slatkine, 1969).
64 A. Sutherland & L. Nochlin, *Women Artists 1550–1950* (Exhibition Catalogue), Los Angeles, Austin, Pittsburg, New York, Alfred A. Knopf, 1977.
65 S. Bovenschen, *Die imaginierte Weiblichkeit. Exemplarische Untersuchungen zu kulturgeschichtlichen and literarischen Präsentationsformen des Weiblichen*, Frankfurt, Suhrkamp, 1979, p. 220.
66 Bovenschen, *Imaginierte Weiblichkeit*, p. 81.
67 J. H. Campe, *Vaderlyke Raad aan myne Dochter . . . aan de huuwbare jufferschap gewyd*, Amsterdam, J. Doll, 1790, p. 49.
68 Campe, *Vaderlycke Raad*, p. 68, states that all learned women suffered 'in some degree from a nervous illness'.

4 *L'égalité des sexes qui ne se conteste plus en France*
Feminism in the seventeenth century

Siep Stuurman

In 1720 Mehmed Efendi, ambassador of the Ottoman Empire, visited France on a fact-finding mission for the Sublime Porte. One of the many things that baffled him was the position of women in French society. The women in France, he observed, 'can do what they want and go where they desire . . . so much that France is the paradise of women'.[1] Some twenty-five years before, the Abbé DuBos even saw reason for alarm: 'it seems to me that women have forgotten that they belong to another sex than men, so eagerly are they seeking to adopt masculine manners'.[2] The visitor from the Islamic world and the habitué of the Parisian salons were in many ways worlds apart, but both men apparently felt that the evolution of French manners in the seventeenth century had called into question old patriarchical certainties. According to many seventeenth-century feminist authors, that was indeed what was happening, and in their eyes this was, of course, an eminently desirable change in the ways of the world.

Seventeenth-century French feminism was a broad and vigorous, though not organized, intellectual movement. Thanks to the new women's history of the last decades we can now see that it was more than a handful of daring and exceptional individuals.[3] Jeannette Rosso has compiled a list of publications on the 'woman question', from 1600 to 1789. For the whole seventeenth century she lists 142 publications (her list is, as she herself admits, far from complete). The distribution over the decades shows a steady increase in the number of publications, peaking in the 1640s, and subsequently continuing at a somewhat lower but fairly regular rate.[4] The pro-woman texts are in clear majority, especially in the latter half of the century. The picture tallies quite well with Ian McLean's conclusion that the 1640s mark an important transition. An autonomous feminist discourse emerged which was more vigorous and self-assured than the old *Querelle* literature.[5] Feminists, as well as their enemies, were found chiefly in the upper classes: only 10 per cent of the authors in Rosso's list are bourgeois, against 30 per cent clericals, 20 per cent male nobles, and 20 per cent, mostly aristocratic, women.[6] Carolyn Lougee has shown that the rise of salon culture was linked with a progressive intermingling of the older sword nobility with the newer *noblesse de robe* (ennobled state

68 *Siep Stuurman*

servants and magistrates) and the upper strata of the Third Estate, with the various types of nobility remaining in a clear majority.[7]

Seventeenth-century feminism, like its counterparts in other ages, was highly contested. Reactions to it varied from enthousiastic endorsement to ferocious hostility. The spectacular role played by some aristocratic women in the military actions of the *Fronde*, the violent social and political upheaval that shook the French state from 1648 to 1653, had elicited both celebrations of 'heroic women' and mysogynist vituperation against 'sexual disorder', linking the misfortunes of the French nation to female transgression. Of the two feminine ideals – the heroic, strong woman and the *savante* ('learned woman') – the former waned together with the political culture of the old sword nobility to which it was related.[8] The ideal of the cultivated and learned lady, on the other hand, flourished as never before: the 1650s and 1660s were the heyday of the *précieuses*[9] who extolled literary refinement and female independence. The same period, however, saw a vicious anti-feminist reaction, epitomized in the popular playwright Molière's famous diatribes against the *précieuses* and the *femmes savantes*.

It has been suggested by Ian McLean and Joan DeJean that the beginning of the personal reign of Louis XIV (1661) was accompanied by a decline in feminist activity and writing.[10] We shall see, however, that feminist writing, as well as the intellectual aspirations of numerous elite women, flourished in the 1660s and 1670s, and that the radical, egalitarian work of the Cartesian philosopher Poulain de la Barre, published in the early 1670s, was not so exceptional and isolated as is sometimes assumed. For all that, we must be careful not to overstate our case: in these decades, feminism took part in the general upsurge of French culture but at the same time reached its limits as the world of male science and letters was institutionalized in the new academies that, by and large, closed their ranks to women.

EQUALITY AND KNOWLEDGE: FROM MARIE DE GOURNAY TO MARGUERITE BUFFET

As the century progressed, egalitarian arguments drawing on reason, 'nature' and divine justice became more and more common. As early as 1621, Louys LeBermen asserted that sexual difference was an 'accidental quality' only pertaining to certain bodily features.[11] In 1622, the same argument was used by Marie de Gournay in her *Egalité des hommes et des femmes* ('Equality of Men and Women'), probably the first resolutely egalitarian feminist treatise in European history. According to Gournay, the soul formed the real essence of the human being whereas the sexes were made solely for the function of bodily propagation and therefore '*secundum quid* [for a particular purpose], as the Scholastics have it'.[12] In Gournay's time, such an unflinching assertion of gender equality was still rather exceptional, and the majority of her contemporaries rejected these claims out of hand. For all her intellectual assurance, Marie de Gournay did not write in a victo-

Feminism in the seventeenth century 69

rious mood. In the *Grief des dames* ('The Ladies' Complaint', 1626), an embittered tone predominates, and she lashes out at 'the moustached Doctors' who so arrogantly dismissed the woman of letters.[13] Throughout her life, Gournay had to defend herself against misogynist slander.[14]

Furthermore, it is important to point out that Gournay did not rely entirely on the egalitarian argument. She also invoked the authority of the great philosophers of antiquity, even of Aristotle (sic!), as well as the Fathers of the Church, and finally the example of the Amazons and other outstanding women. There was no clear hierarchy among these arguments, and this remained so in most seventeenth-century feminist writing: next to general arguments for equality and female participation in intellectual life, the vindication of a special, feminine contribution to gentle manners and civilized culture, as well as the display of long lists of 'famous and learned women' remained highly popular genres. Almost all feminist tracts drew on the historical and mythical record. The seventeenth-century galleries of famous women, however, contained far more contemporary examples than the older *Querelle* literature (see also chapter 3 of this book).[15]

In the following decades, the egalitarian argument was taken up by some other authors, among them the anonymous author of *La femme généreuse* ('The Generous Woman', 1643) who declared that the soul was neither male nor female.[16] The case for gender equality was usually linked to the older demand for participation in intellectual life. This is especially clear in the famous exchange between the Dutch *savante* Anna Maria van Schurman and the Huguenot minister André Rivet, published in Latin in the Dutch Republic in 1641, in a French translation in Paris in 1646, and in English in London in 1659.[17] The point of contention was whether it was fitting for women to devote themselves to the pursuit of learning. Schurman asserted that it was, and, more generally, that one ought to follow 'the voice of reason and not that of a bad custom'. To buttress her claim, she referred to Marie de Gournay's *Egalité*.[18] In her reply to Rivet's objections she invoked the Italian feminist Lucrezia Marinelli and, again, Gournay.[19] Although Schurman herself did not dwell at great length on the egalitarian argument, it is obvious that she knew that it had been used by others and assumed her opponent to be familiar with it. Moreover, the way she put reason in opposition to 'bad custom' would recur in many later feminist tracts. References to both Gournay and Schurman are rather common in subsequent feminist writing (Schurman was one of the two seventeenth-century *savantes* to be mentioned in the article 'femme' ('woman') in Diderot's *Encyclopedia*).

After the *Fronde* there emerged a new feminine intellectual culture that was highly critical of traditional marriage and, more generally, of the prevalent masculine style. The salons and the novel were its main vehicles. Madeleine de Scudéry and her circle forged a new ideal of womanhood, independent of marriage. It must be recalled that marriage was tantamount to legal slavery: several of the great heroines of the *Fronde* were, on the orders of their husbands, literally imprisoned in provincial castles for long

70 *Siep Stuurman*

periods, in some cases for the rest of their lives.[20] As so often in later centuries, the vindication of the single woman and of female friendship were crucial matters for these feminists. They also advocated women's psychological independence within marriage, and some of them envisaged reforms ranging from 'trial marriage' and 'free liaisons' to modes of terminating unworkable unions.[21] One of the *précieuses* is quoted by the Abbé de Pure as saying: 'The greatest delight of our France is the liberty of women'.[22] These extremely visible feminists attracted a lot of attention, often hostile. The first documented use of the anti-feminist catchword *prétieuse* was in 1654,[23] the Abbé Michel de Pure's *La Prétieuse* appeared in the years 1656–58, and Molière's infamous satirical play, *Les Prétieuses ridicules*, was first staged in the autumn of 1659.

Meanwhile, feminist discourse became bolder and more egalitarian than before. The high output of feminist publishing in the 1640s and 1650s is well documented in the historiography, but in the 1660s this trend continued apace. Major publications include: an anonymous *Apologie pour la science des dames* ('Defense of the Learning of Ladies', 1662);[24] a fourth, enlarged edition of Jacques Dubosq's *L'honneste femme* ('The Honest Woman', 1662);[25] *Le cercle des femmes savantes* ('The society of learned women', 1663, re-issued 1667),[26] by Jean de la Forge, probably a brother of the well-known Cartesian Louis de la Forge; a *Dialogue de la princesse sçavante et de la dame de famille* ('Dialogue of a Learned Princess and a Housewife', 1664), by Elisabeth Marie Clement;[27] *Les dames illustres ou par bonnes et fortes raisons il se prouve que le sexe féminin surpasse en toutes sortes de genre le sexe masculin* ('The illustrious ladies wherein it is demonstrated by good and solid proofs that the female sex is in all respects superior to the male sex', 1665), by Jacquette Guillaume;[28] a fifth edition of Dubosq's *Honneste femme* (1665);[29]; Louis Leslache's *Les avantages que les femmes peuvent recevoir de la philosophie* ('The utility of philosophy for women', 1667);[30] and finally the *Nouvelles observations sur la langue française avec les éloges des illustres sçavantes tant anciennes que modernes* ('New observations on the French language followed by the praise of illustrious learned women in ancient and modern times', 1668), by Marguerite Buffet.[31] Some of these books, especially Lesclache, were fairly moderate, but others, notably Clement, Buffet, and the anonymous author of the 1662 *Apologie*, were frankly egalitarian.[32]

The 1662 *Apologie* and Clement's book are particularly interesting because they are written in the form of a polemical exchange of views between different personages. In both publications, the feminist side eventually emerges victorious. The first part of the *Apologie* is written in the form of a polemic of 'Cléante' against 'Aristide' who stands for vulgar sexist opinion, but in the second, more radical part, the debate is joined by a collective female voice, identified as 'the ladies who are indebted to Cléante for the key to the sciences'. The ladies' main point is that Cléante, for all his magnanimity, stops short of full equality.[33] He had advocated the cause of

Feminism in the seventeenth century 71

the learned women on the condition that they would not display their knowledge openly, nor forget their femininity. Generally, women would be permitted to acquire all sorts of knowledge but they were not to exercise any kind of public authority.[34] The ladies in the second part of the book will have nothing of this:

> But by grace, why do you affirm that Themis does not entrust us with her balance, whereas you yourself have asserted that *among our ancient Gauls we commanded the government of the towns.* . . . Why is it that you swim between two waters, as the saying goes, & that you deprive us of the sovereign authority you admit us to have exercised in an earlier age?[35]

The ladies go on to dispute the inequalities Cléante has left untouched. The balance of Justice is now turned into a metaphor for gender *tout court*: 'Ha! Cléante; had the Ladies governed the balance, they would definitely have maintained a better equilibrium.'[36] With Aristide, the champion of male supremacy, they will have no trade at all. He lays claim to sovereign rights over the realm of the sciences but such a claim manifestly goes against the liberality of God who has bestowed the gift of reason on all human beings alike. The light of knowledge must shine equally on both sexes:

> With men we partake in life's journey, and thus we need the same *lumières* as men to illuminate our path . . . If you will have knowledge, so will we, & to withhold it from us, is to thrust us back into the darkness.
>
> All of nature lies open before our & your mind alike. . . . On her treasures we have the same rights as you, & since nature does nothing in vain, we cannot see why she has inspired us with such an avid curiosity, were it not as a faculty to acquire knowledge about her.[37]

Knowledge is not like material wealth: women can become rich in knowledge without impoverishing the men. There is thus no cause for alarm: 'Finally, what harm would be done if women would become as learned as men? Would the heavens cease their revolutions?'[38] The war between the sexes has endured long enough, peace is now at hand. If the men will agree to put an end to their usurpation, the two sexes shall live in peace, in the state of equality God's grace has bestowed upon them.[39]

In Elisabeth Clement's *Dialogue of a Learned Princess and a Housewife* we encounter the learned Pauline and the solid, down-to-earth Penelope. Pauline is dressed in green, silver and gold; in her right hand she holds a globe and some mathematical instruments, and in her left hand a great book, entitled *general science*. Penelope's attire is modest, and her physiognomy more robust: she too holds a book, entitled *economy of the household*, and in her other hand a full purse adorned with the device *I am the bulwark of the house*.[40] In the presence of a male Judge the two ladies engage in a lively debate about the utility of learning in women. After a heated exchange of views the Judge is called upon to pronounce his verdict. Pauline, who expects a sentence in favour of the *savantes*, is crudely rebuffed: women,

72 *Siep Stuurman*

according to the Judge, need prudence and 'economy'. What use is to them the knowledge of the Arctic pole or Stoic philosophy? If they continue along that road, their next demand will be to become members of the senate (*senatrices*).[41]

Pauline resolutely refuses to accept the verdict. Angrily she turns against the Judge. She charges him with vanity, and goes on to say that he would not treat her in such an unjust way if he were really so wise as he thinks he is. The discussion now takes a new turn: the robust Penelope quietly fades into the background, and the rest of the *Dialogue* is really a series of exchanges between Pauline and the Judge. Time and again the Judge concedes some ground to Pauline, but every time she presses him still further. In the course of the discussion, Pauline marshals all the main feminist arguments we have encountered so far: women are 'capable to found and govern cities', woman was created from Adam's flesh, 'in order to be neither the master nor the slave of the male, but his companion, his equal & his helpmate', Molière merits the criticism of the female sex, and his *Ecole des femmes* ('The School of Women') is a 'very ignorant sort of school'.[42] Her chief accusation is that many men are malignant: 'The only language they hold about us, is aimed at banishing us from the learned academies, the scientific cabinets, & finally from all those places where one gets instruction in the sciences.'[43]

The Judge reluctantly gives way, and in the end he comes around to Pauline's position, calling her 'a princess of learning'. The full, contemporary meaning of the *Dialogue* is only disclosed in the final section when the reader is told that the Judge is none other than *Monsieur de Conrat*, one of the founders and the long-time secretary of the Académie Française. The historical background seems evident: in the 1650s Gilles Ménage and Gervais Charpentier had nominated a number of *savantes*, notably Madeleine de Scudéry, Antoinette DesHoulières and Anne Dacier, for membership of the French Academy, pointing to the example of the *Academia dei Ricovrati* in Padua. Their proposal was, however, rejected.[44] Elisabeth Clement's book can thus be read as an imaginary alternative scenario in which the feminist cause wins out.

The patriarchal interpretation of the Bible, and especially the book of Genesis, was a major obstacle in the way of any feminist author. The authority of scripture had, of course, to be respected, but interpretation was free, at least within certain limits. Jacquette Guillaume cleverly turned the argument about Eve and the snake upside down: Eve, she contended, was the stronger of the two since it took a devil to lure her into sin whereas Adam was easily seduced by a mere mortal woman.[45] Many variations can be found: Eve was created last and was thus the 'summit of Creation', Eve was created from Adam's rib, while Adam was made out of mud and slime, definitely less noble material, and so on and so forth. On the other hand, there was the equality of souls before God, a venerable Christian topos that could easily be given a feminist turn. Thus Marguerite Buffet, having maintained that women stand in the same relation to God as men, drew the

Feminism in the seventeenth century 73

following conclusion: 'The souls having no sex whatsoever, it follows that the quality of the mind [*beauté de l'esprit*] does not share in the difference between man and woman.'[46]

According to Buffet, the two sexes were 'equal in everything': there were no greater differences between men and women than those found between individuals of the same sex. Just like Gournay, she maintains that the biological differences between the sexes are confined to procreation, and have no importance for human agency dependent on the will.[47] Buffet explains the misogynist biology of Aristotle as a product of hurt masculine pride: Aristotle was somewhat dwarfish, with short arms and crooked legs; women found him repellent and it was therefore understandable that he wrote against them.[48] Regrettably there were still some men around who, moved by an unjust envy, were conducting a continuous war against women: they sought to keep them 'imprisoned in ignorance', even though they were perfectly aware of the real capabilities of women.[49]

Clement, Buffet and the author of the *Apologie* are crossing an important line when they openly proclaim that the prevailing standard of polite manners is only a hypocritical cloak for the male monopoly of knowledge, and that women are kept ignorant in order to keep them in perpetual subjection. Instead of subtly adapting to so-called good manners, they uncover it as 'merely' custom, based only on masculine prejudice.

THE QUEST FOR KNOWLEDGE AND EQUALITY: PUBLIC DEBATES AND LECTURES

The question of the *femmes savantes* was not only treated in books. On occasion, it entered public debate as well. As early as 1636, the weekly conference at Théophaste Renaudot's *Bureau d'Adresse* addressed the issue 'whether it is expedient for women to be learned'. One of the participants in the debate answered in the affirmative: the 'veritable servitude' of women was bad enough, and it would be utterly unjust also to deprive women of the precious commodity of knowledge. His opponent retorted that women already exercised enough power over men, even without the help of science.[50]

It is possible that women participated in Renaudot's conferences but this cannot be proved.[51] On this score, we are better informed about the public conferences set up in 1654 by Jean de Soudier de Richesource, a one-time visitor of Renaudot's *Bureau d'Adresse*. By 1660, Richesource's *Académie des Orateurs* ('Academy of Rhetoric') had become quite a successful undertaking, attracting numerous young men embarking on a career in the Parisian magistracy (the 'robe').[52] Active participation was restricted to men but women were admitted to the gallery.[53] The politics of gender were frequently discussed in Richesource's conferences. Apart from the question of learning, discussed below, topics included: whether the passions of women were more violent than those of men; whether an orator would

74   *Siep Stuurman*

encounter more obstacles in persuading a man or a woman; and whether it was preferable to grant women liberty, as in France, or to keep them in confinement (*enfermées*) as in some other countries. The conclusions of the Academy, drawn up by Richesource himself, usually took the pro-woman side of the question at issue.[54] During one session, probably in the early spring of 1661, the Academy took up one of the central demands of early-modern feminism: whether the study of the sciences was fitting for ladies. The anti-feminist party took the lead in the debate. According to Monsieur de Godonville, the heart of the matter was simply a question of power: if women seek to uncover (*éplucher*) the secrets 'that we keep hidden from them', he contended, 'they will become more arrogant and presumptuous, and we, the men, shall be reduced to utter subjection'. Knowledge was power, Godonville contended, and he warned his audience of the dire consequences of granting knowledge to women:

> As their constitution is much less constricted than ours, their organs far purer, and the spirits that nourish their brain more subtle, they perceive light where we stumble in darkness ... they sink their nails into the tightest knots & the most abstract ideas will not escape their penetrating gaze.[55]

The next speaker, a monsieur Prieur, did not agree. In the first place, there was the example of great men who willingly dispensed knowledge to women, like Pythagoras and Cicero, and, more recently, the great Montaigne who assisted Marie de Gournay in becoming learned. There had been many learned women in the past. History could thus be summoned in support of the cause of the *femmes savantes*. Finally, it was fitting for women to be learned because nature herself had willed it so, having given imagination, mind and memory to women as well as men. By way of conclusion, Prieur forcefully addressed his fellow men (at this point, I imagine him raising his voice): 'Yes, Gentlemen, women have the ability to become learned, just like ourselves.'[56] Prieur's speech was followed by an even more pro-feminist broadside delivered by a lawyer, Philippe Cattier. Like Prieur, Cattier referred to illustrious historical examples: Istria, queen of the Scythians, taught her son Greek; and in his own time there was the great example of 'that illustrious maiden, the Dutchwoman Marie Anne de Schurman'. Cattier speaks scornfully of the *barbarie* of those men who want to exclude women from knowledge. He would welcome action on the part of women and he offers to speak on their behalf: 'I would like them to establish a syndicate, so that their agent might charge me with the defence of their cause.'[57]

The final verdict of the academy, signed by Richesource himself, was in favour of intellectual equality since the practice of the sciences was perfectly respectable and useful for women who, after all, were rational beings only differing from men in some physical organs, and in some degrees of hotness and humidity.[58] The last addition shows that Richesource's egalitarian argu-

Feminism in the seventeenth century 75

ment is still mixed up with the traditional explanation of sexual difference in terms of the bodily humours.

What to make of these feminist and anti-feminist voices in a Parisian academy in the 1660s? In the debates, feminist and anti-feminist positions are distributed rather evenly, but this only reflects the organizational pattern of the conferences. In the debate on women and knowledge, Cattier intimated that the majority of the academy supported his feminist line, but it seems hazardous to generalize from such a remark.[59] Richesource himself usually takes a middle course, in favour of intellectual equality of the sexes and liberty for women within the confines of the established institutions of marriage and civil society. Such a middle-of-the-road position may well be representative of an important current of moderate, enlightened opinion in the Parisian magistracy and the intellectual circles associated with it. The point to emphasize is that here were men, who were not known as feminist authors, but who, as a matter of course, defended feminist positions in a public debate. This tells us something about the intellectual climate in the early days of the reign of Louis XIV.

In the 1650s and 1660s, many women frequented salons and lectures. The university was, of course, closed to them, but they could, and did, visit public lectures. Louis de Lesclache's lessons of philosophy seem to have attracted such a large number of women that he became known as a professor for the ladies. He sometimes let his pupil, Mademoiselle Girault, stand in for him.[60] Lesclache was an anti-Cartesian,[61] but Gassendists and Cartesians, such as De Launay, De Fontenay and Rohault attracted a lot of female interest as well. The weekly lectures of Jacques Rohault, probably the best course in experimental physics then to be had in Paris, were especially popular: the seats in the front rows were reserved for the ladies.[62] There was also a great vogue for astronomy, and many women paid a visit to the new Parisian observatory.[63] The savantes benefited greatly from the rather open, as yet not firmly institutionalized, setting in which the new science was then taught. In this light, it is all the more significant that women were from the outset excluded from the new Royal Academy of Sciences, founded in 1666.

As is well known, the question of gender and science was also a popular topic in the theatre. Apart from Molière, the topic of women and learning was put on the stage by Samuel Chappuzeau. His second comedy, *L'Academie des femmes* ('The Academy of Women'), was published in Paris in 1661 and re-issued in 1662. The final act of the play ends with the complaint of the learned Emilie when her supposedly dead husband returns and at once orders her to throw all *her* books out of *his* house: 'Quel est nostre malheur! maudite obeissance!/Et que l'homme a sur nous une injuste puissance!'[64]

Both Molière and Chappuzeau exemplify a new, modernized response to feminist discourse. They have abandoned the old misogynist language: they admit that woman should be treated with dignity and fairness, but they marginalize (Chappuzeau) or ridicule (Molière) feminist aspirations to real

76 *Siep Stuurman*

social and intellectual autonomy. At the same time, the obsessive recurrence of these themes in their plays betrays a deep ambivalence about the status of women in seventeenth-century French society.

FEMINISM AS SOCIAL CRITIQUE: POULAIN DE LA BARRE

We can now see that François Poulain de la Barre's three feminist treatises, published in 1673, 1674 and 1675,[65] did not come out of the blue. The thesis that 'the mind has no sex', for which Poulain is chiefly known, was hardly new in his time. His assertions about the ability of women to participate in intellectual life, or even in military affairs and government were all prefigured in the literature and the debates of the 1650s and 1660s. In this regard, it is certainly relevant that Poulain had frequented Richesource's Academy for some time.[66] His egalitarian argument, in terms of an ungendered faculty for reason grounded in a common human 'nature', was by the 1670s almost a commonplace of feminist thought. Like his predecessors, Poulain submits that sexual difference resides solely in the body, and then qualifies that statement, limiting it to 'that part of the body that serves procreation'.[67] But he adds a 'materialist' argument for equality: drawing on contemporary biology, he states that 'the most meticulous anatomical research' has failed to establish any difference between the male and the female brain.[68]

Poulain, however, went beyond his predecessors by formulating his feminist argument as an integral part of a systematic, egalitarian social philosophy. The full title of his first book was already a little philosophical manifesto: *On the equality of the two sexes. A physical and moral treatise, wherein one sees the importance of overcoming prejudices.* Prejudice stands for virtually all received opinion, while the 'physical and moral' philosophy Poulain draws upon, is chiefly taken from Descartes. His feminist philosophy is therefore best characterized as *social Cartesianism.* Beyond the issue of gender, Poulain extended his critique of 'prejudice' to other fields, such as rank and race. In the preface to the *Egalité* he observed that male superiority was the oldest, most widespread and deeply ingrained prejudice of all; if that could be brought down, all other prejudices would become questionable too.[69]

The chief methodical rule Poulain took from Descartes was the critique of ordinary experience. Right at the beginning of the *Egalité* he refers to the example of heliocentric astronomy which is contradicted by the commonsense view of the immovability of the earth. Just as the apparent revolution of the heavens is no reliable guide in astronomy, so our daily experience of the behaviour of women and men does not reflect the true nature of the sexes. To arrive at a correct explanation, we must therefore investigate the mechanism 'behind the phenomena'. Poulain thereupon introduces 'conjectural history': he urges his readers to imagine how men in an early stage of human history subjected women by brute force, have kept them in servitude ever since, and have finally succeeded in shaping women's behaviour and

Feminism in the seventeenth century 77

consciousness in the image of their degraded state. From this vantage point, the vulgar historical view that seeks to justify male supremacy in terms of the universal consensus of past generations can easily be dismissed as spurious sophistry.[70] Moreover, the ancient adversaries of women were *men* just like those of today. Therefore everything they say must be suspect, 'because they are both judges and interested parties'. This last argument was, of course, not new – it was often used in the feminist polemics of the 1660s – but Poulain links it to a general critique of prejudice and customary authority.

Poulain then turns to the philosophers of natural law ('jurisconsultes') who assert that male supremacy is *natural*. Their mistake is to attribute to nature a distinction that originates in custom: 'They would be quite embarrassed when called upon to explain in plain language what they mean by nature in this context.'[71] What is more, they can be slain with their own weapons:

> For they themselves recognize that subjection and servitude are contrary to the state of nature in which all human beings are equal.
>
> Dependency being a purely material and civil relation, it must be considered merely as a consequence of chance, power [*violence*] and custom.[72]

Poulain is perhaps the only seventeenth-century thinker to expose the contradictory use of the concept of 'nature' in the modern theory of natural law. Likewise, he conceives of marriage as the result of reciprocal promises and conventions, and observes that not nature but the civil law endows the male sex with marital power.[73] He envisages a reform of matrimonial law, establishing a *conseil souverain my-party d'hommes et de femmes* ('a mixed sovereign council of men and women') to judge marital conflicts.[74]

The real crux of Poulain's discourse of the accessibility of the new philosophy is, however, the question of method. Real knowledge begins with self-knowledge. Poulain stresses the importance of the knowledge of body and mind (in that order!).[75] He employs the dualism of Descartes but, like the master himself, continually emphasizes the inseparability of mind and body. This is of crucial importance for our understanding of his main conclusion on the equality of the sexes. His striking and often quoted aphorism, *l'Esprit n'a point de Sexe* ('the mind has no sex'), comes at the end of his exposition of method. He employs the postulate of the equality of reason to demonstrate that women are equally capable as men, not only in intellectual pursuits, but in all other fields of social activity as well. He does this by showing time and again that the only condition of efficient participation in a given art is the mastery of the rules governing it; that is, the mastery of a specific kind of knowledge. Discussing the art of military command, Poulain stresses that this is not a question of physical prowess but of applied intelligence; well, he asks rhetorically, can't women read maps, and can't they conceive of strategy and tactics?[76] For the same reason

78 *Siep Stuurman*

women can participate in political life: the science of politics is founded upon 'the notion we ought to have of the equality of men according to nature, and of their obligation to preserve each other through mutual support'. There is nothing mysterious about the theory of the political contract that women could not understand as easily as men.[77] All this is a far cry from the references to Amazon heroines and Scythian queens found in much previous feminist writing. Poulain is thus not postulating an equality of 'abstract reason', but rather the equality of practical reasoning. His educational programme, outlined in the *Education des Dames* ('The Education of Ladies'), is entirely consistent with this approach. It is definitely not of a literary sort, but rather reads like a systematic introduction to the new philosophy, comprising, *inter alia*, Descartes' *Meditations*, the Port Royal *Logic* and Jacques Rohault's *Traité de physique*.

Coming to the crucial topic of the division of labour between the sexes, Poulain definitely passes beyond most feminist writing of his time. At first, he declares that the fact of equal capability does not necessarily imply an equal sharing of all positions, provided only that there is no 'abuse' of power contrary to the meritocratic rule of equality.[78] As for pregnancies and childbirth as obstacles to the employment of women, Poulain points to anthropological evidence: it is well known, he writes, 'that all over America and in the greater part of Africa women labour just like men, without being hindered by their pregnancies'.[79] Discussing the objection that the participation of women in the 'emplois' will surely cause many inconveniences, Poulain retorts:

> [Our opponents] rely entirely on custom, and they only look at the present state of civil society, as it is governed and ordered by the male sex. People do not pay enough attention to the fact that civil society has not always and everywhere been organized in the same way, without being any the worse for it. If the women had governed, they would have ordered the callings and professions in their fashion.[80]

These hints at social change are related to Poulain's dismissal of tradition and custom: one must not become a slave of the past, the Ancients are not infallible for they were young in their time. People judge the present and the future by the standards of the past, that is 'the capital error that prevails in the entire world'.[81] Poulain thus envisions social change, at least as a possible future. Here, his feminism is tied up with cultural relativism, drawing on Jansenist moralism and travel literature, and with an incipient sense of historical change, derived from the *Querelle des anciens et des modernes* ('quarrel of the ancients and the moderns').[82]

CONCLUDING OBSERVATIONS

During the final decades of the seventeenth century, learned women continued to attract the attention of the public, and the 'equality of the sexes' became something of a standard expression. The September 1678 issue of the *Mercure Galant* treated its readers to a vivid relation of an academic ceremony at Padua where Helena-Lucrezia Piscopia Cornara had obtained the doctorate in philosophy (Cornara was the other woman who was mentioned in the article 'femme' in the *Encyclopedia*). 'The equality of the two sexes', the *Mercure* concluded, is now demonstrated in practice, 'as it has been demonstrated for some time by solid arguments'.[83] In 1682, Antoinette de Salvan de Saliez, an aristocratic *savante* living in southern France, confidently proclaimed that 'the equality of the sexes is not any more contested among honest people'. But she went on to complain about 'the injustice and the envy of men' who deprived women of the opportunity to display their true capacities.[84] Five years later, a certain Decrues treated the 'famous question' of the two sexes in *Les Entretiens de Theandre et d'Ismenie* ('Conversations of Theandre and Ismenie'). Those who always wanted to hear something new would not like his book, he warned his readers, so often had the issue already been discussed before.[85] In 1698, Charles Guyonnet de Vertron published *La nouvelle Pandore ou les femmes illustres du siècle de Louis le Grand* ('The new Pandora, or the illustrious women of the century of Louis the Great'), which, among other things, contained an epistolary exchange with Antoinette de Salvan. Vertron concluded the second volume with a list of 'illustrious ladies'; he listed in total the names of 183 learned women, of which 112 were still living when his book went to the press.[86]

The passages just quoted could be replaced by many others. The very least that can be inferred from them is that the issue of the equality of the sexes did not disappear from public debate. What is also clear, is that egalitarian arguments and historical examples were habitually juxtaposed: in most seventeenth-century feminist discourse, Scythian queens happily coexisted with natural equality. Likewise, many authors appealed to rationalist philosophy without renouncing the venerable notion of a special feminine contribution to civilization. It must be noted, however, that the warrior queens, but for the significant exception of the great aristocratic *Frondeuses* (aristocratic ladies who took part in the military actions of the mid-century civil disturbances known as the *Fronde*), were mostly situated in a distant past, whereas the more recent examples of 'famous women' were increasingly confined to the cultivated and peace-loving *savantes*. After the Fronde, the robust culture of the sword nobility had once and for all lost its attraction. If the female sex were ever to be victorious, it would be on the field of letters. It is surely no coincidence that in the *Querelle des anciens et des modernes*, the feminists by and large sided with the moderns who preferred French over Latin and the world of the arts and sciences over the virtues of the battlefield.[87]

80 *Siep Stuurman*

Feminism, especially aristocratic feminism, had developed its own type of sociability in which polite conversation among equals, women and men, was the main vehicle for the communication of both elite gossip and philosophical truths. In this respect, feminism was part of a broader trend in French culture, the formation of an independent civil society that was to become the breeding ground of the Enlightenment.[88] Women did not however, gain access to the formal institutions of letters and science, these remained the domain of an exclusive male sociability. Neither were women allowed to enter the institutions of higher education. On the other hand, they were able to attend all sorts of informal lectures and experimental demonstrations where the latest scientific discoveries and inventions were discussed.[89] As we have seen, many literate women reacted with considerable bitterness to these arbitrary limitations on their sphere of activity. The violent diatribes against male prejudice and the radical egalitarianism of seventeenth-century feminism are largely explained by the ambivalent situation of women who were conscious participants in elite culture and whose abilities frequently surpassed the opportunities open to them.

Poulain de la Barre's social egalitarianism remained exceptional. Although he was probably read by quite a lot of women and men, even outside France, only one seventeenth-century feminist that I know of, Gabrielle Suchon, quoted him extensively and made real use of his philosophical argument.[90] Others, like Antoinette de Salvan, optimistically noted that 'several of our best authors have thoroughly discussed the equality of the sexes which is no longer contested in France'.[91] Poulain's treatises were re-issued several times.[92] All this does not, of course, prove that Poulain was 'influential' but it demonstrates that there were women and men who thought alike or who, at any rate, were willing and able to understand his argument. The significance of Poulain's thought is not that it was 'representative' of the main current of feminist writing but rather that it exemplified the limits of the thinkable in late seventeenth-century France, or even Europe. At the same time, it is important to see that Poulain's work would have been impossible without the feminist tradition on which he drew so abundantly. Thanks to his Cartesian training, Poulain went beyond other feminist authors, but it was not simply a matter of applying Cartesian method to the issue of gender: it was feminism that enabled him to formulate a critique of the shortcomings of the philosophy of natural law, and it was feminism that occasioned him to give a *social* turn to Cartesianism in the first place. Insofar as Poulain can be said to have formulated a first and tentative version of themes usually associated with the Enlightenment, feminism must count as one of the ingredients that went into the making of the Enlightenment.

What goes for Poulain, is also true in a more general sense – by their criticism of ancient patriarchal certitudes, the feminist writers of the seventeenth century helped to clear the way for an overall attack on traditional morality and customary authority. That the Enlightenment had important implica-

Feminism in the seventeenth century   81

tions for feminist thought is by now well established and commonly accepted (see chapter 5 in this book). That feminism was also instrumental in bringing about the Enlightenment has perhaps not been sufficiently appreciated.

NOTES

1 Quoted in Fatma Müge Göçek, *East Encounters West. France and the Ottoman Empire in the Eighteenth Century*, Oxford, Oxford University Press, 1987, p. 45.
2 Letter to Pierre Bayle, 19 November 1696, quoted in Boileau, *Oeuvres complètes*, Bibliographie de la Pléiade, Paris, Gallimard, 1966, p. 933n.22.
3 See Carolyn C. Lougee, *Le Paradis des Femmes. Women, Salons, and Social Stratification in Seventeenth-Century France*, Princeton, Princeton University Press, 1976; Maité Albistur and Daniel Armogathe, *Histoire du féminisme français*, Paris, Des Femmes, 1978; Ian MacLean, *Woman Triumphant. Feminism in French Literature, 1610–1652*, Oxford, Clarendon Press, 1977; Joan Kelly, 'Early feminist theory and the *Querelle des femmes*', *Signs*, 1982, 8, pp. 4–28, reprinted in *Women, History and Theory: The Essays of Joan Kelly*, Chicago, University of Chicago Press, 1984; Evelyne Berriot-Salvadore, *Les Femmes dans la Société Française de la Rénaissance*, Genève, Droz, 1990; Constance Jordan, *Renaissance Feminism*, Ithaca and London, Cornell University Press, 1990; Joan DeJean, *Tender Geographies. Women and the Origin of the Novel in France*, New York, Columbia University Press, 1991; Erica Harth, *Cartesian Women*, Ithaca and London, Cornell University Press, 1992; Danielle Haase-Dubosq and Eliane Viennot (eds), *Femmes et pouvoirs sous l'ancien régime*, Paris, Rivages, 1991; of the older literature, Gustave Reynier, *La Femme au XVIIe siècle. Ses ennemis et ses défenseurs*, Paris, n.p., 1929, is still quite useful.
4 Jeannette Geffriaud Rosso, *Etudes sur la féminité aux XVIIe et XVIIIe siècles*, Pisa, Libreria Goliardica, 1984, pp. 189–211; she states that her list is limited to works she considered relevant, and available in the Bibliothèque Nationale, but she did not privilege a particular decade.
5 McLean, *Woman Triumphant*, pp. 79, 151–2.
6 Rosso, *Etudes sur la féminité*, pp. 178–82.
7 Lougee, *Paradis des femmes*, chaps 8–10.
8 DeJean, *Tender Geographies*, pp. 33–66.
9 *Précieuses*: term used to designate women of refined (literary) taste and delicate manners, frequently unmarried. Often employed as a term of abuse, implying that these women were definitely overdoing it, thus becoming 'artificial' or 'unnatural' in their manners and, especially, their convoluted, hyper-refined ('precious') language.
10 McLean, *Woman Triumphant*, pp. 118, 265; DeJean, *Tender Geographies*, p. 63.
11 Louys LeBermen, *Le Bouclier des dames*, Rouen, 1621, quoted in Lougee, *Paradis des Femmes*, p. 14.
12 Gournay, *Egalité*, Mario Schiff (ed.), *La Fille d'alliance de Montaigne: Marie de Gournay*, Paris, Champion, 1910, p. 70.
13 'Grief des Dames', originally published in *L'ombre de la Damoiselle de Gournay*, Paris, Jean Libert, 1626; quoted from *Egalité des hommes et des femmes*, Paris, Côté Femmes, 1989, p. 120.
14 See Marjorie H. Ilsley, *A Daughter of the Renaissance. Marie le Jars de Gournay: her Life and Works*, The Hague, Mouton, 1963.
15 Berriot-Salvadore, *Femmes françaises*, p. 355.
16 Quoted in McLean, *Woman Triumphant*, p. 49.

82 Siep Stuurman

17 The English translation is mentioned by Ruth Perry, *The Celebrated Mary Astell, an early English Feminist*, Chicago and London, University of Chicago Press, p. 15.

18 *Question celèbre s'il est necessaire, ou non, que les filles soient sçavantes, agité de part and d'autre*, par Mlle Anne Marie de Schurman, Holandoise, and le Sr. André Rivet, Poitevin, le tout mis en François par le Sr. Colletet, Paris, Rolet le Duc, 1646, pp. 14–15.

19 *Question celèbre*, pp. 73–4.

20 See Nicole Aronson, *Mademoiselle de Scudéry, ou le voyage au pays de tendre*, Paris, Fayard, 1986, p.19.

21 Lougee, *Paradis des femmes*, pp. 22–5, and DeJean, *Tender Geographies*, pp. 148–56, see these feminist ideas partly as a response to the harsher enforcement of marriage law as the state increasingly supplanted ecclesiastical jurisdiction in the field.

22 Quoted in Francis Baumal, *Le Féminisme au temps de Molière*, Paris, s.d., p. 27.

23 See Donna C. Stanton, 'The fiction of *préciosité* and the fear of women', *Yale French Studies*, 1981, 62, pp. 107–34.

24 Lyon, B. Coral.

25 The work went through numerous editions. MacLean, *Woman Triumphant*, pp. 278–9, gives the first edn. in 1632, followed by a second in 1633, and supplements in 1634 and 1636; a third edn., not mentioned by MacLean, was published in 1640 [Ars. 4 Sc. A 582]; I have used the fourth edn. of 1662 [Ars. 8 S 2083].

26 Paris, Jean-Baptiste Loyson. This was a reply to Chappuzeau's first play, the *Cercle des femmes* (Lyon, 1656) which was reissued in Paris in 1663. De la Forge's *Cercle* was reprinted in 1667, see Samuel Chappuzeau, *Le cercle des femmes et l'académie des femmes*, ed. critique par Joan Crow (University of Exeter, 1983), pp. xv–xvi, xxvi; see also Pierre Clair, *De la Forge*, Paris, Presses Universitaires de France, 1974, p. 63.

27 Paris, Loyson.

28 Paris, Thomas Iolly.

29 Paris; the text is identical with the 1662 edition.

30 Paris, Laurent Rondet.

31 Paris, Jean Cusson.

32 Rosso's bibliography (*Etudes*, pp. 197–9), mentions some more publications but these are of a moralistic genre and not openly feminist. She does not mention Clement and the *Apologie de la science des dames* of 1662. Nor are these two referred to in the studies by McLean, DeJean, Harth, and others cited above (notes).

33 *Apologie*, p. 49; Cléant(h)e may stand for Barbier d'Aucour.

34 *Apologie*, pp. 19, 41, 47.

35 *Apologie*, p. 59, italics in original; the story of the female senate in ancient Gaul is also found in other authors, cf. DuBosq, *Honneste femme* (1662 edn.), pp. 118–119; see also Le Président Rolland, *Recherches sur les prérogatives des dames chez les Gaulois*, Paris, Nyon l'aîné, 1787.

36 *Apologie*, p. 65.

37 *Apologie*, pp. 81–2.

38 *Apologie*, p. 85.

39 *Apologie*, p. 102.

40 Clement, *Dialogue*, pp. 8–9.

41 Clement, *Dialogue*, pp. 77–9.

42 Clement, *Dialogue*, pp. 120, 160–1, 165.

43 Clement, *Dialogue*, p. 134.

44 Londa Schiebinger, *The Mind has no Sex? Women in the Origins of Modern*

Feminism in the seventeenth century 83

Science, Cambridge MA, Harvard University Press, 1991, p. 22; DeJean, *Tender Geographies*, p. 234–5, n52.

45 Guillaume, *Dames illustres*, pp. 202–203; a related argument is found in *Apologie*, p. 100.

46 Buffet, *Nouvelles observations*, p. 200.

47 Buffet, *Nouvelles observations*, pp. 223–4.

48 Buffet, *Nouvelles observations*, pp. 234–5.

49 Buffet, *Nouvelles observations*, p. 271.

50 *Recueil général des questions traitées ès Bureau d'Adress, sur toutes sortes de matières, par les plus beaux esprits de ce temps*, 4 vols, Paris, 1666, vol. 3, pp. 59–62; for other gender-related topics, see vol. 1, p. 140; vol. 4, p. 96. The debate on the *savantes* was conference no. 106, on the dating see Howard M. Solomon, *Public Welfare, Science, and Propaganda in Seventeenth-century France: The Innovations of Théophraste Renaudot*, Princeton, Princeton University Press, 1972, p. 66.

51 Solomon, *Public welfare*, p. 69.

52 Ch. J. Revillout, *Un maître de conférences au milieu du XVIIe siècle: Jean de Soudier de Richesource*, Montpellier, 1881, pp. 49–52.

53 See 'advis de l'Académie' in *La première partie des conférences académiques et oratoires sur toutes sortes de sujets problématiques, utiles et agréables, accompagnées de leur décision où l'on voit l'usage des plus belles maximes de la philosophie et les plus beaux preceptes de l'éloquence*, 'par I. D. S. Escuyer, Sieur de Richesource, moderateur de l'académie, & *La seconde partie etc*', in one vol., Paris, 'chez l'Autheur, à l'Académie des Orateurs', Place Dauphiné, 1661 (Henceforth quoted as: Richesource I–II); followed by *La troisième partie etc.*, Paris, etc., 1665 (quoted as Richesource III).

54 Richesource I–II, pp. 383–92, 409–18; Richesource III, pp. 75–86.

55 Richesource III, p. 26.

56 Richesource III, p. 31.

57 Richesource III, p. 32.

58 Richesource III, pp. 35–6.

59 Richesource III, p. 32.

60 Reynier, *La Femme au XVIIe siècle*, pp. 160–5.

61 He thought the kind of philosophy that aimed 'at doubt rather than positive knowledge' pernicious; *Les avantages*, p. 18.

62 See Pierre Clair, *Jacques Rohault (1618–1672). Bio-bibliographie*, Paris, CNRS, 1978, p. 46; Reynier, *La Femme au XVIIe siècle*, pp. 149–64.

63 Gustave Reynier, *Les Femmes Savantes de Molière*, Paris, Mellottée, 1948, p. 32.

64 'How great is our misfortune! Accursed obedience!/And what unjust power men exercise over us!': Chappuzeau, *Cercle des femmes*, p. 112.

65 *De l'égalité des deux sexes. Discours physique et moral où l'on voit l'importance de se défaire des préjugez*, Paris, Jean Dupuis, 1673; *De l'éducation des dames pour la conduite de l'esprit dans les sciences et dans les moeurs. Entretiens*, Paris, Dupuis, 1674; *De l'excellence des hommes, contre l'égalité des sexes*, Paris, Dupuis, 1675.

66 See Poulain, *Essai des remarques particulières sur la Langue Françoise, pour la Ville de Genève*, Genève, n.p., 1691, preface.

67 Poulain, *Egalité*, pp. 109–10.

68 Poulain, *Egalité*, p. 112.

69 Elsewhere I have discussed these aspects of Poulain more fully: Siep Stuurman, 'Social Cartesianism. François Poulain de la Barre and the origins of the Enlightenment', *Journal of the History of Ideas*, forthcoming.

70 Poulain, *Egalité*, p. 90, 235.

71 Poulain, *Egalité*, pp. 94–5.

84 *Siep Stuurman*

72 Poulain, *Egalité*, p. 96.
73 Poulain, *Egalité*, p. 97.
74 Poulain, *Education*, p. 6.
75 Poulain, *Education*, pp. 234–5.
76 Poulain, *Egalité*, p. 169.
77 Poulain, *Education*, p. 321.
78 Poulain, *Excellence*, pp. 76–7.
79 Poulain, *Excellence*, p. 270.
80 Poulain, *Excellence*, pp. 268–9.
81 Poulain, *Education*, p. 293.
82 The 'quarrel between the ancients and the moderns' was a prolonged polemic debate in several European countries over the relative merits of the literature and science of classical antiquity and 'modern' Europe. The moderns contended that Europe was in the process of surpassing the highest achievements of ancient Greek and Roman civilization. The debate could thus spill over into an emergent sense of history as progress and change.
83 *Mercure Galant*, September 1678.
84 'Reponse de Mme de Saliez', *Mercure Galant*, January 1682.
85 D. I. B. Descrues, *Les entretiens de Theandre et d'Ismenie sur un ancien et fameux differend*, Paris, Robert Pepie, 1687, Préface.
86 Ch. Guyonnet de Vertron, *La nouvelle Pandore*, Paris, 1698, vol. II, pp. 470ff.
87 See Béatrice Didier, 'Perrault féministe?', *Europe. Revue mensuelle*, 1990, 86, 739–40, pp. 101–13.
88 This section draws on Daniel Gordon, *Citizens Without Sovereignty. Equality and Sociability in French Thought, 1670–1789*, Princeton, Princeton University Press, 1994; Gordon mentions 'aristocratic feminism', but he contrasts it too forcefully with 'modern feminism' (p. 109), thereby underestimating its critical and polemical egalitarian impulse.
89 See Geoffrey V. Sutton, *Science for a Polite Society. Gender, Culture, and the Demonstration of Enlightenment*, Colorado and Oxford, Westview Press, 1995.
90 G. S. Aristophile [Gabrielle Suchon], *Traité de la morale et de la politique*, Lyon, B. Vignieu, 1693, troisième partie, pp. 67–8, 103, 137.
91 Letter to the *Academia dei Ricovrati* at Padua, 1689, *Lettres de Mesdames de Scudéry, de Salvan de Saliez, et de Mlle Descartes*, Paris, 1806, p. 223; this letter was also published by Vertron, *Nouvelle Pandore*, vol. 1.
92 See Madeleine Alcover, *Poullain de la Barre: une aventure philosophique*, Papers on French Seventeenth-Century Literature, Paris/Seattle/Tübingen, 1981, p. 29.

5 Reclaiming the European Enlightenment for feminism

Or prologomena to any future history of eighteenth-century Europe[1]

Karen Offen

The European Enlightenment was a privileged time for debate on the 'woman question', as the controversy over relations between the sexes only later became known. Enlightenment inquiry was 'feminocentric' in the sense that male writers focussed intensively on 'woman', and subsequent interpretation has typically focussed on views of women expressed by its leading figures – Montesquieu, Voltaire, Diderot, Rousseau, Condorcet, and Kant. If one examines the broader spectrum of Enlightenment debate by decentring these leading male *philosophes*, however, it becomes evident that it offered women and their male allies an arena to develop in print an impressive arsenal of concepts, vocabulary and arguments capable of challenging what some women in 1789 would call the 'aristocracy of sex'.[2]

Enlightenment debate can thus be seen as a spawning ground not simply for positioning 'woman' as some have complained, but for asserting women's equality to men, for criticizing male privilege and domination, for analysing historically the causes and constructions of women's subordination, and for devising eloquent arguments for the emancipation of women from male control. These were all defining features of that critical tradition we now call feminism, but which at the time remained a critique that had no name.

The issues of choice in this debate were not restricted to topics in formal philosophy; they addressed fundamental aspects of societal organization, beginning with marriage and the socialization of children. In the efforts of learned men (*savants*) and philosophers (*philosophes*) to understand what we know and how we know it, they posed many important questions about the world in which they lived. Their attempts to distinguish, through comparisons, what was 'human' from what was 'animal', what was 'social' or 'cultural' from what was 'natural', to probe the difference between 'laws' and 'morals', quickly confronted them with the distinctions their own societies prescribed between men and women, and the rationales offered to support these distinctions. Critiques of women's status provoked an awareness that the relations between the sexes were neither God-given nor determined exclusively by 'Nature', but socially constructed; in other words, they understood the concept that we today call 'gender'. Madame d'Epinay in fact spoke in the 1770s of 'genre masculin' and 'genre féminin' and insisted that

86   *Karen Offen*

she was not speaking only about grammar but about socialization. Such criticism led quickly to disagreements about what relationships between the sexes should look like and stimulated visions of alternative arrangements. Assertive claims for sexual hierarchies and male dominance, invoked in the name of tradition, were countered by equally vehement claims for sexual equality and the emancipation of women from male control.

Eighteenth-century feminists claimed a 'natural' equality of the sexes prior to all social and political organization, and demanded, accordingly, full equality of the sexes in organized society. They highlighted women's disadvantaged legal and economic situation in institutionalized marriage and called for an acknowledgment of women's rights *as women*. They criticized women's inadequate education and lack of economic alternative to marriage, and – despite these disadvantages – the importance of their influence and societal role. Such arguments led in several directions. First, they pointed to the necessity of women's full spiritual/moral and intellectual development as individuals, a goal embedded in a discourse of *rights*. Second, they led directly to a reassertion of so-called women's values, the claims of the heart and of the emotions – of *sentiment*, in short, as the complement to 'masculine' rationality – even as women claimed reason for themselves. Third, they precipitated a rethinking, in the name of *public utility*, of women's strategic societal importance as mothers, and they asserted their centrality as child nurturers and partners with men in the project of 'civilization.'

This debate did not begin with the Enlightenment, as is clear from the earlier chapters in this book. Yet by the mid-eighteenth century the number of participants had expanded and the audience had grown dramatically. By this time educated Europeans were experiencing, along with great prosperity, a veritable explosion of printed criticism of the existing gender order. Books, periodicals, tracts, broadsides poured forth from the presses. Growing literacy among women as well as men of the privileged classes in urban settings guaranteed a sizeable audience for these works. In France alone, according to Roger Chartier, the literacy rate for both women and men had nearly doubled (for women, from 14 to 27 per cent) in the course of the eighteenth century, and many more people owned books.[3] The rise of the novel itself was closely intertwined with this debate over sexual politics.

THE CRITIQUE OF INSTITUTIONALIZED MARRIAGE

Let us enter the Enlightenment debate by examining the critique of institutionalized marriage. In most European states at this time, in the aftermath of the Protestant Reformation in the sixteenth century, the formalization and dissolution of marriage remained the prerogative of Christian religious institutions. Each denomination endorsed some structural form of male control over women. The Roman Catholic Church had declared marriage to be an indissoluble sacrament, a position that some Protestant denominations

Reclaiming the Enlightenment for feminism 87

never adopted (and which in consequence allowed them to tolerate divorce, rather than concocting elaborate religious annulment procedures in ecclesiastical courts). Moreover, churches – acting as agencies of the state – kept track of births, deaths and marriages, and exercised moral authority over family relationships. Throughout the seventeenth century French legal authorities had exhibited interest in claiming direct control of these functions as well as in secularizing the institution of marriage, in order to exert an even more direct control over male-headed families. Thus, in eighteenth-century France, and in those countries which modelled themselves on France, church and state appeared to be on a collision course over the control of marriage. Civil divorce was one item over which agreement seemed impossible.

Male domination was also inscribed in most Protestant approaches to marriage. With the exception of the Quakers in England, who acknowledged an important degree of equality for women, most Protestant sects had reverted to Old Testament precedents on which to base new assertions of male authority over women in marriage. The leaders of Protestant churches appreciated neither Mary Astell's criticism of the submission required of English women in marriage (and her celebration of spinsterhood) in her *Reflections Upon Marriage* (third edn., 1706) nor Daniel Defoe's even more scathing characterization of marriage without love in 1727 as 'conjugal lewdness', a condition Mary Wollstonecraft would later label outright as 'legally prostituted'.[4] This critique of arranged and loveless marriages, often accompanied by a celebration of love itself, would reverberate through the arguments of many subsequent feminist writers in various countries. In France, women writers took up this issue early, challenging the abuse of women by families and husbands.[5]

By the time Montesquieu published his *Spirit of the Laws* (1748), one of the salient issues in his political theory was the subordination of women in male-headed families, and its relationship to three types of governments: republican, monarchical and despotic. In monarchies, he postulated, women were 'subject to very little restraint', while under despotic governments women were an 'object of luxury', 'in servitude'. Under republics, 'women are free by the laws and restrained by manners'.[6] As critics identified themselves increasingly with republican ideas, this set of observations provoked a new round of reflection on the woman question in terms of the 'politics' of marriage. Enlightenment thinkers and writers of fiction appeared on both sides of the issue. Prominent legal theorists, notably Samuel von Cocceji, Prussian compiler of a legal code for Frederick the Great, Robert Pothier, author of several influential French legal texts on marriage and William Blackstone, commentator on the British common law, opted for circumscribing women's place in order to realize nature's plan.[7] On the dissenting side could be found writers such as Louis de Jaucourt, who in volume 6 of the enormously influential French *Encyclopédie* (1756) raised the point that 'the reasons that can be alleged for marital power could be contested,

88 *Karen Offen*

humanly speaking'. Jaucourt then went on to argue that the authority of husbands was arbitrary: it ran 'contrary to natural human equality'. Men were by no means superior to women, and the extant rules were the contributions of 'positive' or man-made, as distinct from 'natural', law. Marriage, Jaucourt proposed, was nothing more than a contract, and as a contract it could conceivably be organized in a variety of ways by the individual parties concerned.[8] A new wave of published fiction by women novelists in France extended and deepened this critique, as Joan Hinde Stewart has ably demonstrated for the period from 1750 onwards. The actress-turned-novelist Marie-Jeanne Riccoboni, in particular, astutely explored the politics of love, marriage, and remarriage, and did not hesitate to address issues of adultery, independent widowhood and even illegitimacy.[9] Another French novelist, Jeanne-Marie Le Prince de Beaumont craftily argued the case for opting out of the 'uterine economy' of love and marriage, privileging mother-daughter relationships over male-female relationships, and seeking 'final liberation . . . in and through the single life'.[10]

THE CRITIQUE OF WOMEN'S EDUCATION

The critique of women's education became a commonplace of Enlightenment thought. Earlier Protestant leaders and Catholic reformers of the Counter-Reformation had concerned themselves with the education of girls of all social classes, primarily in the interest of encouraging their piety. Advanced instruction for women of the upper classes was a different matter, and the critique levelled at the 'learned ladies' of Elizabethan England and especially at the *femmes savantes* of mid-seventeenth century Parisian high society, was vicious and unprecedented, as is reflected in Molière's widely known comedies, *Les Précieuses ridicules* (1659) and *Les Femmes savantes* (1672). 'You've been writing!. . . . You've ink stains on your fingers! Ah! Cunning Signora', Beaumarchais had Dr Bartholo exclaim, in his comedy *The Barber of Seville* (1775), when he suspects his ward Rosina of writing to a suitor. 'Women think they can safely do anything if they are alone'.[11]

The seventeenth century saw the culmination of the scientific revolution, but the accession of women to the new scientific learning was hotly contested in some quarters. Defenders of women's innate intellectual capacities, following Poulain de la Barre's claim (1673) that 'the mind has no sex', reiterated and elaborated this claim in various forms throughout the next century. Nicolas Malebranche, in his treatise on the search for truth (first published in 1674), acknowledged that women's brains were characterized by 'delicate' fibres, which accounted both for their great intelligence and taste, but also made them less good at abstractions; he nevertheless acknowledged that there was no such thing as absolute masculinity and femininity. Bernard le Bovier de Fontenelle framed his best-selling *Conversations on the Plurality of Worlds* (1686), a work explaining the new physics in simple language, as a dialogue between a philosopher and an aristocratic lady, the Marquise.[12]

Reclaiming the Enlightenment for feminism 89

Comparable defences of women's reasoning capacity had already been sharply expressed in England by Mary Astell, who in her *Serious Proposal to the Ladies* (1694) proposed founding a women's university and community for women who did not wish to marry, but preferred to pursue life-long learning in the company of other similarly disposed women.[13] Another who insisted on the equal capacities of women and men was the 'father' of the Spanish Enlightenment, the Roman Catholic cleric Benito Feijoo, author of a *Defence or Vindication of the Women* (1739).[14] It is in the context of this debate that the 1732 conferral of a doctoral degree in philosophy on the brilliant Laura Bassi by the University of Bologna took on added significance for studious women throughout Europe.

The discussion of women's education had already taken a distinctly anti-feminist and utilitarian turn in France with the publication of Archbishop Fénelon's very influential *Treatise on the Education of Daughters* (1687).[15] As part of a comprehensive plan for reforming the French aristocracy, Fénelon designed a programme intended for daughters of the impoverished nobility, to direct them away from the frivolity of court and salon society and towards the serious business of training to become wives, mothers and estate managers who would be useful to their husbands, their families and thereby to the French state. This tract by Fénelon – and the subsequent establishment by Madame de Maintenon, morganatic wife of Louis XIV, of the girls' school at St Cyr – influenced the development of secular girls' education for the family among the elites throughout eighteenth-century Europe.[16]

Following a celebrated exchange with the encyclopedist Jean Le Rond d'Alembert on the subject of women's education and place in 1758–9, Jean-Jacques Rousseau published his didactic works, *Julie* (1761) and *Emile* (1762), to drive home in a more popular form the bald point that women's education must prepare them to serve men – even as he underscored the enormous influence women could and did wield within the family.

> The search for abstract and speculative truths, principles, axioms in the sciences, and everything that tends to generalize ideas is not within the compass of women: all their studies must deal with the practical. Their job is to apply the principles that men discover and to make the observations that lead men to establish principles.[17]

Many women writers published critiques of the superficiality of girls' education during the eighteenth century and, in the course of their arguments, defended women's right to reason and to acquire knowledge in the best Enlightenment tradition, often arguing (as did the pseudonymous 'Sophia', in 1739) that in the state of nature women and men were equally reasonable creatures: 'In a word, were the *Men Philosophers* in the strict sense of the term, they would be able to see that nature invincibly proves a perfect *equality* in our sex with their own.'[18] Such claims were reiterated in radical tracts such as *Female Rights Vindicated* by 'A Lady', published in

90   *Karen Offen*

London in 1758, who framed her insistence on the natural equality of the sexes and her defence of women's abilities with an attempt at a historical account of how men had subordinated women.[19] In the Paris-based *Journal des dames* ('Ladies' Magazine'), the feisty *éditrice* Madame de Beaumer insisted in 1761 that 'We women think under our coiffures as well as you do under your wigs. We are as capable of reasoning as you are. In fact,' she added, with what must have been a broad grin, 'you lose your reason over us every day.'[20] Under Beaumer's successor, Madame de Maisonneuve, the *Journal* went on to cultivate and celebrate women's intellectual prowess.

Male-dominated culture, these women knew, contrasted with what they saw as the natural (or pre-social) state of things. Some eighteenth-century feminist critics sensed then, as others have repeatedly rediscovered since, that the relationship of the sexes is a socio-political or 'cultural' construction; they understood intuitively the distinction French philosophers, in particular, were making between natural law (God's law) and positive law (man-made law). Indeed, some feminists went directly to the heart of the matter, as did Madame de Beaumer, who – addressing unnamed male critics of the *Journal des dames* in 1762 – issued this indictment:

> I love this sex, I am jealous to uphold its honor and its rights. If we have not been raised up in the sciences as you have, it is you who are the guilty ones; for have you not always abused, if I may say so, the bodily strength that nature has given you? Have you not used it to annihilate our capacities, and to enshroud the special prerogatives that this same nature has bounteously granted to women, to compensate them for the material strength that you have – advantages that we would surely not dispute you – to truly appreciate vivacity of imagination, delicate feelings, and that amiable politeness, well worth the strength that you parade about so.[21]

Madame de Beaumer and her readers were well aware of the significance of socially imposed educational norms for the cultural construction of gender, even as they acknowledged certain differences between the sexes as inherent and complementary.

Depending on the country and the cultural context, various criticisms of women's education could be and were made. British feminists criticized the frivolity of an ornamental and 'useless' education for aristocratic and wealthy girls. The 1780s works of Catharine Macaulay and Mary Wollstonecraft, among others, eloquently express this set of complaints.[22] The Spanish reformer and educational writer Josefa Amar y Borbon argued in 1790 that a better, more substantive education for women, a cultivation of the mind and of talents, rather than of personal appearance and coquetry, would greatly enhance the quality of a couple's relationship in marriage as well as a woman's personal satisfaction in life.[23]

Well before these women critics, however, the Swedish poet and essayist, Charlotta Nordenflycht, had confronted the arguments for male supremacy

Reclaiming the Enlightenment for feminism 91

put forth by Jean-Jacques Rousseau in a set of clever verses published in Stockholm in the early 1760s:

Woman is prevented from grasping any truth,
people amuse themselves by laughing at her stupidity.
But when the seeds of stupidity finally grow into sins
then much poison is spread and much blame assigned.
Then there is no appealing to the suppression of her intellect,
then she is the embodiment of weakness and a woman.
Nature, then, is blamed, and blood and heart decried
for what has its roots in the manner of upbringing only.
The source of a gushing well is obstructed
and then the question asked: why does not the water flow?
They set a trap for the Eagle's foot and break his wings,
and then they blame him for not reaching the sun.
Thus is the energy of women suppressed by upbringing and custom,
They are left to fight each other in stupidity's narrow arena,
And as an ornament drag the heavy yoke of ignorance,
Because it is seen as an affront to women to be wise and learned.
Oh, cruel tyranny, will this our world improve,
that half of mankind is by narrow folly chained
When lack of brains is evident in every task?[24]

The Abbé de Mably would subsequently stress the *political* importance of the education of women. 'The Republic,' he warned in 1776, 'is not composed of men alone, and I warn you that you will have done nothing if you neglect the education of women. You must choose, either to make men of them as at Sparta or condemn them to seclusion.'[25] In France, the education of women had been reframed – by Mably and others – as an affair of state; it was no longer sufficient to argue that it was necessary merely for a woman's personal happiness or that of her husband. This notion of educating women to form citizens was a momentous development for the history of European feminism.

WOMEN'S POTENTIAL: WHAT SHOULD WOMEN BE? WHAT COULD WOMEN DO?

Critiques of marriage and of women's education quickly led to discussion of the central issue of what women should be, of what they should be trained to do in a well-organized society. In the developing market economy of early modern Europe, questions began to be posed concerning possibilities for new roles for elite women within the family, and also concerning possibilities for economic independence and freedom of movement for women beyond the control of fathers, husbands and brothers. Issues about women's options were increasingly framed in terms of 'liberty' and 'emancipation', in this case from familial control. The English businessman and political

92 Karen Offen

pamphleteer Daniel Defoe, seemingly in ignorance of Fénelon's proposals in his treatise on the education of daughters, argued in his *Essay on Projects* (1697) that women should be educated to become good companions to their husbands, not 'only Stewards of our Houses, Cooks and Slaves'.[26] A few women, mostly of the emerging middle classes, watching the freedoms and opportunities enjoyed by their brothers, eloquently expressed a sense of constraint, envy and injustice. In 1779, for instance, the young German poet and housewife from Göttingen, Philippine Gatterer Engelhard, published her 'Girl's Lament':

> How oft with damnation
> And tears of frustration
> My gender I curse!
> Its ban ever dooms
> Us girls to our rooms;
> How freely men move!
> Even youngster and serf.[27]

Women of the lower classes had always worked, and in early modern European cities many worked for pay. But the sexual division of labour that stipulated not only different, more sedentary jobs, but also lower pay for women than for men had deep roots in European societies.[28] Nevertheless, women could be found engaged in a wide range of commercial craft activities including rug-making, clock-making, taxidermy and lens-grinding – even journalism, as the *Journal des dames* reported in the 1760s.

The French monarchy had already attempted to address the 'problem' of women's work in the seventeenth century by stipulating that certain trades would be reserved for women's guilds (or corporations), even as restrictions on women's entering the male trades were tightened. When these regulations were overturned during the monarchy's brief experiment in liberalizing commerce in the early 1770s, men began to infiltrate a number of lucrative women's trades. Louis-Sébastian Mercier, a writer and social commentator who thought poorly paid married women should be eliminated from the labour force and sent back to their households, nevertheless argued that single women who needed employment should have it. It was absurd, he argued, for men to become women's hairdressers, to engage in needlework, to sell lingerie and items of fashion, when young women who could not find work in these suitable trades were forced to do heavy labour or resort to prostitution. He insisted, as did women pamphleteers into the mid-nineteenth century, that the monopoly of such trades should be restored to women as their rightful due.[29] The reformist playwright Beaumarchais inserted a comparable protest, this time couched in a protest against men's victimization of women, through the voice of Marceline in his subversive comedy, *The Marriage of Figaro* (1784).

Women's aspirations to participate in the learned professions were highly problematic for men and rarely successful. In France Poulain de la Barre

Reclaiming the Enlightenment for feminism   93

had squarely proposed the possibility of access for women to university education, including theology, medicine and law. But even in Italy, where a few exceptional women had occupied chairs in universities since late medieval times, their role was questioned. In Padua, the Academy of Ricovrati (which had elected a number of French women writers to membership *in absentia*) sponsored a debate in 1723 between two professors on the question of 'whether women should be admitted to the study of science and the noble arts'.[30] In Germany, Dorothea Leporin Erxleben learned of Laura Bassi's doctorate at Bologna, and determined to attempt to do the same at Halle. In 1742 she published a tract arguing that women should be permitted to undertake university studies. She convinced allies at the Halle University and in 1754 she presented her doctoral thesis in medicine, written (as was the custom) in Latin.[31] Dorothea Erxleben was an extraordinary exception, like Laura Bassi, but news of the accomplishments of both continued to inspire other talented and ambitious women.

The universities, with their classical learning available only to men, by no means monopolized learning or the development of the arts and sciences at this time. In other settings, a few highly intelligent women made celebrated contributions to the advancement of knowledge. Madame du Châtelet was applauded for her experimentation in physics but especially for her masterful translation into French of Newton's *Principia*. In England Elizabeth Carter received respect and praise for her translations from the ancient languages. In the so-called Bluestocking circle, a cluster of well-known intellectual English women gathered regularly to discuss ideas.[32] In the Low Countries, Betje Wolff and Aagje Deken pioneered the Dutch novel by publishing *Sarah Burgerhart* in 1782. This novel, which told the story of a spunky young Dutch girl's life in epistolary form, espoused Enlightenment values of reason, knowledge and tolerance, and advocated women's access to life as free and independent persons.[33] A few talented women became famous painters: the names of the German-born Angelika Kauffmann in England and Elisabeth Vigée-Lebrun in France remain celebrated. Nevertheless, these women who derived such public renown – and affluence, in the case of Vigée-Lebrun – from their talents, were few and far between.

There was no question, however, that a series of women played extraordinary roles in developing what was known at the time as the 'Republic of Letters'. The Parisian *salonnières*, Madame du Deffand, Madame Geoffrin, Julie de Lespinasse, Madame Necker (and later, their counterparts in Berlin), stood strategically at the very heart of the Enlightenment project; indeed, Dena Goodman has argued that the ambitions of the *philosophes* converged with those of a small and select group of 'intelligent, self-educated, and educating women who . . . reshaped the social forms of their day to their own social, intellectual, and educational needs'. Goodman claims that in these new social spaces, 'the primary relationship . . . was between female mentors and students, rather than between a single woman and a group of men'.[34] She makes a strong case for the centrality of

94　*Karen Offen*

women's governance, through the organization of salon sociability, in the emerging French Republic of Letters.[35]

GENDERING AUTHORITY: CONTROVERSY OVER WOMEN IN PUBLIC AFFAIRS

The area where most eighteenth-century men drew the line was with respect to the 'threat' of women's participation in governance and military affairs. Poulain de la Barre's treatise, *The Woman As Good As the Man* (1673), had put into circulation a strong and daring argument for women's capacity to fill positions of political and military authority as well as all other public offices.[36] This was a contentious claim, and one which Enlightenment writers would address frequently, especially during the highly visible reigns of Maria Theresa in Austria (1740–80) and Catherine II in Russia (1762–96). Pro-woman historians dredged up legends of the Amazons and, of course, the example of Joan of Arc to support arguments for women's inclusion even in military matters, based on past example, while the French dramatist Marivaux would insist, in his comedy, *The Colony* (1750), on their fundamental pacifism.[37] In the 1780s a cluster of utopian novels by French women addressing the issue of women's rule were published; only recently have these been identified and analysed by literary scholars.[38]

Some French critics, who strongly supported the principle of male rule, were particularly incensed by such claims on women's behalf; had France – alone among the great powers of Europe – not excluded women from succession to the throne! 'I defy you to name me a State where women have held power without destroying morals, laws, and the Government', asserted the same Abbé de Mably who had nevertheless underscored the need for women's education, in 1776. But British sages were little better: 'Nature has given women so much power that the law has wisely given them little', insisted the redoubtable Samuel Johnson.[39] Even Montesquieu noted that 'except in special cases, women have almost never aspired to equality: for they already have so many natural advantages that equal power always means empire for them'.[40] This is a different perspective on power than we are accustomed to today. Some eighteenth-century male writers deemed women so powerful, so influential, so effective by virtue of their sexual allure, that only outright suppression or sequestration could keep them under control. All the more reason why men should be determined to retain a deliberate hold on *authority*. This may not have been a mere symbolic move, but rather an eruption of outright fear. The most retrograde expression of this point of view was perhaps Restif de La Bretonne's tract, *Les Gynographes* (1777), in which he argued that 'women should be forbidden to learn to read and write in order to limit them to useful domestic labour'.[41] Not all prescriptions for repression were this severe, but nevertheless it can be said that the sheer volume of eighteenth-century prescriptive literature addressed to girls, exhorting them to be meek, respectful, virtuous, obedient,

Reclaiming the Enlightenment for feminism 95

etc., may be understood as a gauge of the extent to which some highly visible and articulate women were already perceived by some anxiety-ridden men as powerful forces about to escape from male control.[42]

Not all men felt that way, however. Madame du Châtelet's friend Voltaire, in particular, had long celebrated the mixing of the sexes that contributed so much to the vivacity of French society: 'Society depends on women. All the peoples that have the misfortune to keep them locked up are unsociable.'[43] Voltaire ridiculed the exclusion of women from the French throne. It was left to the Marquis de Condorcet, however, to restate Poulain's claims with reference to representative government in a republic by claiming that property-owning women should be both entitled to vote and to hold office. 'The facts prove,' he argued in 1787, 'that men have or believe they have interests that are very different than those of women, because everywhere they have made oppressive laws against them, or at the least have established a great inequality between the two sexes.' Women, especially single adult women and widows, he believed, should be fully able to exercise the rights of citizenship; with respect to married women, the civil laws subordinating them in marriage should be changed. 'Consider that we are speaking of the rights of half the human race', Condorcet insisted.[44] Thus did Condorcet put the issue of women's citizenship squarely on the table, just two years before the calling of the Estates-General and the beginning of the French Revolution.

WOMEN'S CIVILIZING MISSION: THE PROJECT OF FORMING FUTURE MOTHERS

Citizenship for women was still a radical idea that even the most enlightened Europeans were generally unwilling to countenance. But it was clear to some that women did have a significant public role to play in the advancement of civilization as it was then understood. Indeed, more than one eighteenth-century historian attributed a central role to women in the formation of culture and civilized progress, as Sylvia Tomaselli, Jane Rendall and others have reminded us.[45] The formula, too often attributed to Charles Fourier, which identified advances in the condition of women as the index of societal progress had many spokesmen in the 1770s and 1780s, especially among historians of the Scottish Enlightenment. Side by side with such arguments, another body of prescriptive literature addressed to women emerged in the course of the European Enlightenment. This literature was also an outgrowth of the concern about women's power and influence, but it was designed to harness that power and influence on behalf of societal progress. This was the mother-as-educator literature. This current of thought – like the prescriptive literature aimed at curbing girls – developed increasing magnitude and impact, and attached itself like a leech to the secular reformulation of citizenship.

'It is so important for a household to have a virtuous and intelligent

96 *Karen Offen*

mother [*mère de famille*] that I have willingly adopted the proverb, "women make or break households" [*ce sont les femmes qui font & qui défont les maisons*].' Thus wrote the Abbé de Saint-Pierre in 1730, arguing further that the education of women should be given just as much attention as the education of men, and that well-ordered states should assure its effective organization. Several years later he proposed a plan for a network of girls' *collèges*, or secondary schools, based on the model of St Cyr.[46] Pierre-Joseph Boudier de Villemert, author of *Women's Friend*, insisted on women's role as a civilizing force, portraying them as the complements to – and the tamers of – men, and arguing for the cultivation of their intelligence to this end.[47] Writing in 1762, Nicholas Baudeau strengthened the argument, when he argued for national education that fully included female citizens (*citoyennes*): 'We must pose as a fundamental maxim that the Daughters of the Nation are destined each to become within their class, *Citoyennes*, Wives, and Mothers.'[48] And Rousseau consecrated a more subordinate, deliberately channelled, privatized vision of such motherliness in the public interest with his portraits of Julie – his vision of the new Héloïse – and, of course, Sophie.[49]

The mother-educator perspective made a deep impression in a wide variety of circles, and well outside France, though certainly within the circle of French influence, including the 'enlightened' despots of Prussia and Russia. 'I must admit being surprised,' wrote Frederick the Great in 1770, 'that persons of the highest class would raise their children like chorus girls.'

> What! Was their destiny not to become mothers? Should one not direct all their instruction toward this goal, should one not inspire them early on against anything that could dishonor them, or make them understand the advantages of wisdom, which are useful and long-lasting, instead of those of beauty, which will pass and fade? Should one not render them capable of instilling good morals in their children?[50]

The king's observations were echoed in 1782 by the reforming Polish prince Adam Czartoryski, who likewise insisted on the importance of mothers, and the necessity that they be well-educated, conversant with public affairs, promoters of 'citizenship, courage, capacity for public service', and in particular that they teach their children Polish and promote Polish (not French) culture. Mothers were, for Czartoryski, the very keystone to the future success of any Polish state.[51]

Motherhood, then, was no purely domestic matter; it was clearly seen as a desirable and important socio-political or public function by these progressive, socially minded men. Civic motherhood could be women's form of citizenship; indeed forming mothers could be construed as a national obligation! What may surprise modern audiences is that many elite women thought this new role quite wonderful. What men and women of the Enlightenment were criticizing was a set of customary practices that had allegedly denied women of rank and wealth the opportunity to mother.

Reclaiming the Enlightenment for feminism 97

Consider, for instance, the critique by Madeleine d'Arsant de Puisieux, who in 1749 criticized mothers who palmed off their daughters' education on uneducated governesses or on convents.[52] Moreover, the arguments directed at women in the 1760s to encourage them to nurse their own babies, rather than employing wet-nurses, struck a responsive chord among many elite women. Rousseau was not alone in touting the virtues of breastfeeding for his *Julie*. Madame d'Epinay expressed in her fictionalized memoirs her great regret at being prevented from nursing or rearing her own two children.[53] In the mid-1770s Madame de Montanclos raised the theme of enlightened motherhood to new heights in the *Journal des dames*, even as she insisted that women could be both mothers and pursue careers of their choosing.[54]

In the 1780s, in a tract entitled *How Women Should be Viewed, or Perspectives on What Women Have Been, What They Are, and What They Might Become*, Madame de Coicy rearticulated Madame d'Epinay's complaint, pointing out that French women of the highest ranks were not even allowed to mother; their children were taken from them, turned over first to nurses, then to governesses, then tutors. In this critique of court life, she speaks of motherhood as 'the most beautiful and important occupation,' but one denied to women of rank in France.[55] In the context of the eighteenth century, breastfeeding one's own infant had become, for these women, an aspect of what Joan Hinde Stewart has since called 'the struggle of these heroines for self-ownership'.[56] Nor was the subversive quality of nursing as a threat to male control lost on Prussian lawmakers; under the consolidated Civil Code of 1794, healthy wives would be 'required' to nurse their babies, but their husbands would be given the legal right to tell them when to stop![57]

MOVEMENTS, MOMENTS, AND OTHER POSSIBILITIES

In her novel *Voyage de Milord Céton dans les sept planètes* (1765–6) Marie-Anne de Roumier (dame Robert) wrote:

> I am always astonished that women have not yet banded together, formed a separate league, with an eye to avenging themselves against male injustice. May I live long enough to see them make such profitable use of their minds. But up until now, they have been too coquettish and dissipated to concern themselves seriously with the interests of their sex.[58]

In 1784 the anonymous author of a one-act comedy *Le Club des dames* ('The Women's Club', attributed to Madame de Genlis) called Descartes back from the grave to preside over a women's club engaged in reforming the status of women.[59]

It would certainly be misleading to make exaggerated claims either for the size of the feminist following during the European Enlightenment or for its level of organization; indeed, as Roumier Robert's utopian novel makes clear, despite many and repeated flashes of insight, there was no formally

98 *Karen Offen*

organized feminist movement as such during these years. Indeed, there were few organized reform movements of any kind in eighteenth-century Europe. Such organizations existed, at this time, only in the realm of fiction, though for men (and a few women) freemasonry did offer one possible channel.[60] But there was clearly a full-blown feminist consciousness in existence among some privileged women and men, in dialogue with a mounting backlash. A number of tracts were published by women and by men that spoke specifically to the emancipation and equality of women; what is perhaps surprising and even more significant, however, is the extent to which the woman question – and thus the issue of gender – was regularly addressed in works whose main subjects ostensibly concerned other topics. Imaginative fiction, plays and poetry complemented full-length books, philosophical treatises, essays on political economy, aesthetics, polemical pamphlets, and even treatises on law, physiology and animal taxonomy.[61] The woman question permeated a full range of other subjects. Leading Enlightenment critics participated enthusiastically in this debate, along with many other, lesser known analysts of both sexes.

Reclaiming the Enlightenment for feminism – and claiming a feminist Enlightenment – is not a difficult task. Abundant textual and contextual evidence clearly demonstrates not only the centrality of the so-called woman question to Enlightenment debate, but also the extent of support by eighteenth-century reformers, female and male alike, for ending women's subordination to men. Equality between the sexes was a key theme for feminist advocates in eighteenth-century Western Europe, especially in France, but also in a variety of countries influenced by French thought. While they claimed equality, however, European feminists acknowledged women's difference from men – in physical strength, in reproductive physiology, even in ways of thinking – and they celebrated womanhood, women's contributions, even 'women's ways of knowing,' etc., as significant. They rejected sexual hierarchy even as they embraced sexual difference. The thrust of Enlightenment feminism was not sameness, but equality, understood as equity and equality of opportunity, based on Reason. This was neither paradoxical nor contradictory within the context of the times.

Even as Enlightenment feminists argued for equal opportunity for full human development for women, they framed their arguments with reference to women's relationship to men, to children, to others, and to the community and the state. This tendency became more pronounced in the 1760s and 1770s, as reformers increasingly argued a case for women's important civic role as mother-educators and socializers, and insisted on the centrality of women's status as a measure of civilization itself. What I am suggesting here, in other words, is that the arguments became increasingly 'relational' in character as the debate moved from a level of philosophical argument to an engagement with contemporary socio-political possibilities.

Embedded in the foregoing treatment are two implicit arguments that should perhaps be made explicit. First, it is my contention that our under-

Reclaiming the Enlightenment for feminism 99

standing of eighteenth-century European feminism is not well served when we view it through the clouded lenses of late twentieth-century theoretical concerns, whether postmodernist, post-colonialist or post-feminist. Neither is it helpful to frame analyses of Enlightenment feminism in contemporary terms such as 'liberal individualism' versus 'socialism' or 'public' versus 'private'. Nor is it helpful, as is the current fashion in critical theory – including some contemporary feminist critical theory – to follow the lead of the Frankfurt School and its acolytes in blaming the Enlightenment for launching all sorts of diabolical mischief, capped by universalizing the subject category 'Man' and reifying or instrumentalizing Reason. We cannot begin with 'modernity' or with Kant's 1784 essay on *What is Enlightenment?* Historical analysis reveals that Reason provided the essential underpinning for feminist arguments for sexual equality, while pre-Kantian claims for the universality of the category 'Man' were repeatedly contested by Enlightenment feminist theorists, who reclaimed and celebrated the category 'Woman', as well as insisting that 'Man' included both women and men. In speaking so, I intend to reconnect my analysis with an earlier historiography that has made deliberate claims for Enlightenment feminism, and, in so doing, endorses Gerda Lerner's insistence on the necessity and utility of a historical understanding of feminism. The evidence I have consulted suggests that we can and must speak in terms of a feminist historical tradition, irrespective of whether it meets someone else's definition of a proper academic subject. It is less a question of 'inventing a tradition' than of retrieving and reclaiming a well-buried but surprisingly well-documented aspect of the European past.

A second point follows from the first. I believe it to be incumbent upon feminist historians to write the history (or histories) of feminism by reading and analysing *in extenso* – and with careful attention to context – the multiple sources of the period in question, not just those of the canonical *philosophes* or counter-*philosophes*. Chronology, geography and context must all be taken into account; this kind of research and analysis is painstaking but fascinating work. It is the sort of detailed reconstructive work that previous generations of historians did, but they were too few and thus unable to unearth more than partial evidence. In the 1990s we now have more personnel, more access to sources, and we can now work in greater depth, more comparatively and cross-culturally, within the European context. Only by working in this manner can we approach a comprehensive understanding of what advocates and opponents of women's emancipation were saying, the way they said it; and only then can we grasp the key points in their debates. A return to the sources demonstrates unequivocally that the European Enlightenment is far richer in content and scope on gender issues, indeed far more explicitly 'feminist' in its claims and aspirations than has been generally acknowledged.

100 *Karen Offen*

NOTES

1 This essay has been adapted from chapter 2 of my forthcoming book, *European Feminism, 1700–1950*. I am grateful to many colleagues who have read and criticized the chapter as well as suggesting additional sources. Space does not permit adequate citation of the voluminous secondary literature on which I have relied in revisiting the Enlightenment debates; these materials will be provided in the bibliographical essay appended to my book.

2 Quotation from *Requête des dames à l'Assemblée Nationale* (1789), reprinted in *Les Femmes dans la Révolution française, 1789–1794*, présenté par Albert Soboul, vol.1, Paris, EDHIS, 1982.

3 Roger Chartier, *The Cultural Origins of the French Revolution*. Translated from the French by Lydia G. Cochrane, Durham NC, Duke University Press, 1991, p. 69.

4 Mary Astell, *Reflections on Marriage* (1700). The third edition (1706) is reprinted in Bridget Hill (ed.), *The First English Feminist: Reflections on Marriage and other Writings by Mary Astell*, New York, St. Martin's Press, 1986; Daniel Defoe, *Conjugal Lewdness; or Matrimonial Whoredom: A Treatise concerning the Use and Abuse of the Marriage Bed* (1727), reprint edn., introduction by M. E. Novak, Gainesville, Florida, Scholar's Facsimiles and Reprints, 1967; Mary Wollstonecraft, *A Vindication of the Rights of Woman*, New York, Norton, 1967, p. 104.

5 See Joan DeJean, 'Notorious women: marriage and the novel in crisis in France, 1690–1715', *The Yale Journal of Criticism*, 1991, 4, 2, pp. 67–85. Important additions to the literature are Joan DeJean, *Tender Geographies: Women and the Origins of the Novel in France*, New York, Columbia University Press, 1991; and Joan Hinde Stewart, *Gynographs: French Novels by Women of the Late Eighteenth Century*, Lincoln, University of Nebraska Press, 1993.

6 *The Spirit of the Laws, by Baron de Montesquieu*, translated by Thomas Nugent, New York, Hafner Publishing Inc., originally published 1749. See especially Book VII, Section 9, pp. 102–3.

7 *The Frederician Code* (Edinburgh, 1761) Part I, Book I, Title VIII, pp. 37–9. Originally published in German, Berlin, 1750.; Sir William Blackstone, *Commentaries on the Laws of England*, 11th edn., London, 1791, Book I, chap. 15, p. 433, 442–5. Lectures presented at Oxford, 1756. Originally published in Oxford, 1765–9. Pertinent parts reproduced as docts 4 and 5 in Susan Groag Bell and Karen Offen (eds), *Women, the Family, and Freedom: The Debate in Documents, 1750–1950*, Stanford, Stanford University Press, 1983, vol. 1.

8 Louis, Chevalier de Jaucourt, 'Femme (Droit Nat.)', in *L'Encyclopédie*, VI, Paris, 1756, pp. 471–2. Translated in Bell and Offen, *Women, the Family, and Freedom*, vol. I., doct 6.

9 See Joan Hinde Stewart, *The Novels of Mme Riccoboni*, Chapel Hill, University of North Carolina Press, 1974.

10 On Le Prince de Beaumont, see Stewart, *Gynographs*, p. 47.

11 Pierre-Augustin Caron de Beaumarchais, *The Barber of Seville* (1775), in Beaumarchais, *The Barber of Seville/The Marriage of Figaro*, translated with an introduction by J. Wood, London, Penguin, 1964, p. 64.

12 Bernard le Bovier de Fontenelle, *Conversations on the Plurality of Worlds*, translated by H. A. Hargreaves, introduction by Nina Rattner Gelbart, Berkeley and Los Angeles, University of California Press, 1990.

13 Astell, *Reflections on Marriage*.

14 Benito Jeronimo Feijoo y Monetnegro, *Three Essays or Discourses on the Following Subjects: A Defense or Vindication of the Women, Church Music, A*

Reclaiming the Enlightenment for feminism   101

Comparison between Antient [sic] and Modern Music, transl. from the Spanish of Feyjoo by a Gentleman [John Brett], London, 1778.

15 Fénelon, *Treatise on the Education of Daughters*, in H. C. Barnard (ed.), *Fénelon on Education*, Cambridge, Cambridge University Press, 1966.

16 See Carolyn C. Lougee, *Le Paradis des femmes*, Princeton, Princeton University Press, 1976, chaps 11–13.

17 From Jean-Jacques Rousseau, *Emile*: as quoted in Michèle Crampe-Casnabet, 'A sampling of eighteenth-century philosophy', in Natalie Zemon Davis and Arlette Farge (eds), *A History of Women: Renaissance and Enlightenment Paradoxes*, Cambridge MA, Harvard University Press, 1993, p. 329.

18 Sophia, A Person of Quality (pseud.), *Woman Not Inferior to Man or, A Short and Modest Vindication of the Natural Right of the Fair Sex to a Perfect Equality of Power, Dignity, and Esteem, with the Men*, in Bell and Offen, *Women, the Family and Freedom*, vol. I, doct 1, p. 27.

19 *Female Rights Vindicated* by 'A Lady', London, G. Burnet, 1758. My thanks to Gary Kates for bringing this text to my attention.

20 Madame de Beaumer, in the *Journal des Dames* (November 1761), as translated by Nina Rattner Gelbart in *Feminine and Opposition Journalism in Old Regime France*, Berkeley and Los Angeles, University of California Press, 1987, p. 107.

21 Madame de Beaumer, 'Avant-propos', *Journal des dames*, March 1762; in Bell and Offen, *Women, the Family and Freedom*, vol. I, doct 2, p. 28. This text is discussed fully in Gelbart, *Feminine and Opposition Journalism*.

22 See the texts by Catharine Macaulay-Graham, *Letters on Education* (1787); and Mary Wollstonecraft, *A Vindication of the Rights of Woman* (1792), in Bell and Offen, *Women the Family and Freedom*, vol. I.

23 Josefa Amar y Borbon, 'Prologo' to *Discurson sobre la educacion fisica y moral de las mugeres* (1790). Thanks to Constance A. Sullivan for sharing her translation of this text.

24 Hedvig Charlotta Nordenflycht, *Fruentimrets Försvar, emot J. J. Rousseau medborgare i Geneve* (1761), as translated by Stina Katchadourian, 1991.

25 Gabriel Bonnot de Mably, *De la Législation, ou principes des lois*, Amsterdam, n.p., 1776, Pt II, Book IV, chap. 1, pp. 154–5.

26 Daniel Defoe, *Essay on Projects* (1697); facsimile of first edn., Menston, England, The Scolar Press Limited, 1969, p. 302.

27 'Girl's Lament', in *Gedichte von Philippine Engelhard geb. Gatterer* (1782); translated by W. Arndt, in Jeannine Blackwell and Susanne Zantop (eds), *Bitter Healing: German Women Writers from 1700 to 1830: An Anthology*, Lincoln, University of Nebraska Press, 1990, p. 195.

28 On the history of women's work in eighteenth-century Europe see in particular the recent contributions by Olwen Hufton, 'Women, work and family', in Davis and Farge, *A History of Women*, vol. 3; Elizabeth Fox-Genovese, 'Women and work', in Samia I. Spencer (ed.), *French Women and the Enlightenment*, Bloomington, Indiana University Press, 1984. See also Merry Wiesner, *Women and Gender in Early Modern Europe*, Cambridge, Cambridge University Press, 1993; Bridget Hill, *Women, Work and Sexual Politics in Eighteenth-Century England*, London and New York, Basil Blackwell, 1989.

29 Louis Sébastian Mercier, *Tableau de Paris*, vol. IX, Amsterdam, 1788, pp. 177–8.

30 On the 1723 debate, see Paolo Mantegazza, 'Il Problema dell'educazione della donna nel 1723', *Nuova Antologia*,1892, 124, 16, 16 August, pp. 689–701.

31 Dorothea Christiane Leporin, frau Erxleben, *Gründliche Untersuchung der Ursachen, die das weibliche Geschlecht vom Studieren abhalten, darin deren Unerheblichkeit gezeiget und wie möglich, nöthig und nützlich es sey, dass dieses Geschlecht der Gelahrheit sich befleisse*, Berlin, Rüdiger, 1742, reprinted 1975,

102 *Karen Offen*

Hildesheim and New York, Georg Olms Verlag, with an afterword by Gerda Rechenberg.

32 See Sylvia Harcstark Myers, *The Bluestocking Circle: Women, Friendship, and the Life of the Mind in Eighteenth-Century England*, Oxford, Clarendon Press, 1990.

33 See Jeanne Hageman, 'Elizabeth Wolff & Agatha Deken', in Kristiaan P. Aercke (ed.), *Women Writing in Dutch*, New York and London, Garland Publishing, 1994. This novel is still read by schoolgirls in the Netherlands today.

34 Dena Goodman, 'Enlightenment Salons: The Convergence of Female and Philosophic Ambitions', *Eighteenth Century Studies*, 1989, 22, 3, Spring, pp. 329–50; quotations pp. 332–3.

35 Dena Goodman, 'Governing the Republic of Letters: the politics of culture in the French Enlightenment', *History of European Ideas*, 1991, 13, pp. 183–99.

36 François Poulain de la Barre, *The Woman as Good as the Man; Or, the Equality of Both Sexes* (1673), edited with an introduction by Gerald M. MacLean, Detroit, Wayne State University Press, 1988, pp. 123–4. On Poulain de la Barre, see chapter 4 in this book.

37 Pierre Carlet de Marivaux, 'La Colonie', *Le Mercure*, June 1750, as translated by Peter V. Conroy in *Signs* , 1983, 9, 2, Winter, pp. 339–60.

38 See Josephine Grieder, 'Kingdoms of women in French fictions of the 1780s', *Eighteenth-Century Studies*, 1989–90, 23, Winter, pp. 140–56.

39 Mably, *De la Législation*, p. 155; Samuel Johnson to the Reverend Dr Taylor, 18 August 1763, as reprinted in George Birkbeck Hill (ed.), *The Letters of Samuel Johnson, LL.D.*, 2 vols, Oxford, Clarendon Press, vol. I, p. 104. I am grateful to Lisa Jadwin for this latter reference.

40 Montesquieu, *Mes Pensées*, in *Oeuvres complètes*, 2 Vols, Paris, Gallimard, 1949–51, vol. I, p. 1076.

41 Nicholas-Edmé Restif de La Bretonne, *Les Gynographes; ou Idées de deux honnêtes femmes sur un projet de règlement proposé à toute l'Europe pour mettre les femmes à leur place, & opérer le bonheur des deux sexes*, The Hague, 1777.

42 Perhaps the most notorious example is *A Father's Legacy to his Daughters*, by the Scottish physician Dr John Gregory, London, W. Strahan, T. Cadell, Edinburgh, J. Balfour, W. Creech, 1774, which was widely republished both in England and North America and subsequently denounced by Mary Wollstonecraft. For many others, see Vivien Jones (ed.), *Women in the Eighteenth Century: Constructions of Femininity*, London, Routledge, 1990.

43 Voltaire, 'A M.le Chevalier Falkener (Séconde épitre dédicatoire)', in *Zaïre: Tragédie en cinq actes* (1736), *Oeuvres complètes de Voltaire*, vol. I, *Théatre*, Paris, Furne, 1877, p. 551.

44 Condorcet, *Lettres d'un bourgeois de New Haven à un citoyen de Virginie* (1787), in A. Condorcet O'Connor and F. Arago (eds), *Oeuvres de Condorcet*, vol. 9, Paris, n.p., 1847, p. 15.

45 See Sylvia Tomaselli, 'The Enlightenment Debate on Women', *History Workshop*, 1985, 20, pp. 101–24; Jane Rendall, 'The Enlightenment and the Nature of Women', in J. Rendall, *The Origins of Modern Feminism*, New York, Schocken, 1984, and chapter 3 in this book.

46 Charles-Irénée Castel, Abbé de Saint Pierre, *Projet pour perfectionner l'éducation des filles* (1730), in *Oeuvres diverses de Monsieur l'abbé de Saint-Pierre*, Paris, Briasson 1730; quotation p. 96.

47 Pierre-Joseph Boudier de Villemert, *L'Ami des femmes* (1758), in English translation as *The Ladies Friend from the French of Monsieur de Gravines*, London, W. Nicoll, 1766.

48 Nicolas Baudeau, 'De l'Education nationale', in *Ephémérides du Citoyen, ou*

Reclaiming the Enlightenment for feminism 103

Chronique de l'esprit national, 1766, 4, 4, 12 May, as translated by Karen Offen in Bell and Offen, *Women, the Family and Freedom*, vol. I, doct 1.

49 Jean-Jacques Rousseau, *Julie* (1761); *Emile* (1762), Book 5.

50 Frederick the Great, 'Lettre sur l'éducation' (1770), *Oeuvres de Frédérick le Grand*, vol. IX, Berlin, translated by Karen Offen.

51 Prince Adam Kazimierz Czartoryski, 'Drugi List Imc Pana Doswiadczynskiego do przyjaciela swego wzgleden edukacji corek', in *4 Listy Imco Pana Doswiacaynskiego* ('Four Letters by Mr Experience'), Warsaw 1782, reprinted in Stefan Woloszyn (ed.), *Zrodla Do Dziejow Wychowania i Myscli Pedagogicznej*, Warsaw, 1965. Unpublished translation by Bogna Lorence-Kot.

52 Madame de P***, *Conseils à une amie*, n.p., 1749.

53 D'Epinay, *Histoire de Madame de Montbrillant*.

54 Madame de Montanclos, in Gelbart, *Feminine Opposition Journalism*, pp. 187–8.

55 Madame de Coicy, *Les Femmes comme il convient de les voir*, 2 vols, London and Paris, Bacot, 1785.

56 Stewart, *Gynographs*, pp. 201–3.

57 C. F. Koch (ed.), *Allgemeines Landrecht für die Preussischen Staaten*, Berlin 1862, originally published 1792–4, Part II, Title II, Arts 67 and 68. As translated in Bell and Offen, *Women, the Family and Freedom*, vol. I, doct 7.

58 Marie-Anne de Roumier, dame Robert, *Voyage de Milord Céton dans les sept planètes; ou, le Nouveau Mentor . . .*, The Hague and Paris, chez tous les libraires, 1765–6. Quotation as translated by Gelbart, *Feminine and Opposition Journalism*, p. 146.

59 Anon. [attributed to Stephanie-Félicité du Crest, comtesse de Genlis], *Le Club des dames; ou le retour de Descartes. Comédie en un acte en prose*, Paris, Au Bureau de la Bibliothèque des Romans, 1784.

60 See Janet Burke, 'Freemasonry, friendship, and noblewomen: the role of the secret society in bringing Enlightenment thought to pre-revolutionary women elites', *History of European Ideas*, 1989, 10, pp. 283–94; Margaret Jacob, 'Freemasonry, women, and the paradox of the Enlightenment', in Margaret Hunt *et al.*, *Women and the Enlightenment*, New York, Haworth Press, 1984, pp. 69–93; reprinted as chap. 5 in Margaret Jacob, *Living the Enlightenment; Freemasonry and Politics in Eighteenth-Century Europe*, Oxford, Oxford University Press, 1991.

61 See, for example, Londa Schiebinger, 'Why mammals are called mammals: gender politics in eighteenth-century natural history', *American Historical Review*, 1993, 98, 2, April, pp. 382–411; Lisbet Koerner, 'Goethe's botany: lessons of a feminine science', *Isis*, 1993, 84, 3, September, pp. 470–95.

6 Culture as a gendered battleground
The patronage of Madame de Pompadour[1]

Inge E. Boer

The wave, in its literal and metaphorical meanings, is a particularly suitable term to introduce the central figure of this article: Madame de Pompadour. Associated with rococo,[2] the 'wavy' style in mid-eighteenth-century French art, Madame de Pompadour exerted a power in culture not to be underestimated. Painted in pale pinks and blues, amidst undulating garlands of flowers and cupids, Madame de Pompadour could easily be dismissed, as the historiography about her shows, as being as capricious as the rococo style itself. When Jeanne Antoinette Poisson, the later Madame de Pompadour, was presented at the French court in 1745 as the official mistress of Louis XV, it caused an uproar. She evoked a host of contrasting and contradictory comments, marked by overt hostility or acknowledgment of her considerable qualities. I will argue that class is often invoked to explain this controversy, whereas her expert handling of culture as a domain of influence and contestation was just as much at issue.

I will argue, then, that it was through the channel of culture that Madame de Pompadour created a space of her own at the French court, contesting the terms and boundaries with which culture was associated. If we look only at the 'hardware' of feminism, inquiring for example who promoted social and political change or the aims of feminism directly,[3] we might actually miss the role women played in effecting changes in the politics of culture. Two sets of paintings will serve as the framework of my argument. First, I will juxtapose Louis Tocqué's (1696–1772) portrait of Marie Leczinska (1740) and that of Madame de Pompadour (1750–1) by Maurice Quentin de La Tour (1704–88) (both at the Louvre, Paris: figures 6.1 and 6.2). Second, I will analyse two paintings by Carle Vanloo, *Une sultane prenant du café* ('A sultana drinking coffee') and *Deux sultanes travaillant à la tapisserie* ('Two sultanas at work on tapestry') (both 1755 at the Musée des Arts Décoratifs, Paris: figures 6.3 and 6.4), commonly believed to represent Madame de Pompadour. The two sets of paintings show Madame de Pompadour as an in-between, negotiating her position at the court and her role in the politics of culture.

From a post sixth-wave feminist perspective, then, questions concerning culture and gender have relevance for politics as well. Culture was, and

Culture as a gendered battleground 105

remains to be, evaluated in political terms. Just as the eighteenth-century *salonnières* had to weather criticisms about their prominently visible role, Madame de Pompadour's role was perceived in terms of the public sphere. After her death the balance was literally drawn up in financial terms asking 'how much she cost the nation' or in arguments clothed in class terms. Focussing on culture shows in what ways Madame de Pompadour was aligned with the salon society, where she cannot be equated with the *salonnières*, and makes it possible to interpret her position within this broader framework.

WOMEN AT THE FRENCH COURT: ROLES AND FUNCTIONS

Louis Tocqué's portrait of Marie Leczinska is as striking as Madame de Pompadour's portrait by Maurice Quentin de La Tour. Marie Leczinska, married to Louis XV in 1725, is depicted in full state in a flowered dress 'à grands panneaux', an ermine mantle around her shoulders. She is painted in an environment which combines rich decorations on the table on the left, the chair on the right, the ceiling and the draped curtain, but which conveys an atmosphere of austerity as well. The pillars on the right and the tiles on the floor are not exactly the attributes for a feminine portrait. Most interesting as a feature in the painting however is the gesture with which Marie Leczinska points at the crown, placed on a little cushion. Why, one might ask, this gesture, as so many details already indicate that we are dealing with a royal figure? Is it not enough to demonstrate by the ermine mantle and the proliferating fleurs de lys that this woman is not just any woman, but the queen herself? So why the abundance of references to royalty, why this hysterical repetition of the fleurs de lys as if to drum their importance into our heads?

In semiotic terms, we might see the gesture that Marie Leczinska makes as an index. An index can be defined as a sign which on the basis of contiguity is connected to the meaning.[4] An example of an index might be a signature which stands for an individual. Because of the uniqueness of a signature, we take it to belong to a particular person, or we suppose it does. By following the gesture of Marie Leczinska, we arrive at the crown. The crown itself is a symbol for royalty, but as we have already had so many references to royalty, what makes the crown so special that it needs extra attention?

One possible and preliminary explanation might be inferred from Krzysztof Pomian's study on collectors, amateurs and the so-called 'curieux', in which he outlines what a collection is. In his view, collections have to do with a relation between the visible and the invisible. Objects are kept in store for private use and sometimes shown to a public or the public at large. The objects fulfil a role as intermediaries between those who look at them and invisibility. Pomian asserts that invisibility represents something which is either removed in space or time, or what is buried or divine. That is, objects can represent cultures that cannot be seen directly, but they can also point at

106   *Inge E. Boer*

a past or the future as invisible phenomena.[5] All sorts of objects can belong to a collection, but often they have a specific link to rituals and are used as artefacts in those rituals. Take a relic which is carried around in a public space once a year and after that is carefully stored away again, guarded from public scrutiny for another year. It is in these terms that Pomian refers to the regalia of the king which after his death used to be paraded around in funeral processions.[6] Following Pomian's argument, the crown, as part of the royal regalia, would then function as an intermediary between the spectator and what remains invisible. I will argue, however, that this crown, so prominently displayed and reinforced by the gesture, does not point at royalty as such, but at the function of the crown in relation to the person depicted.

In the pastel by Maurice Quentin de La Tour, Madame de Pompadour is seated in a completely different decor: an intimate space lined with gilded panels, one of which is painted with a landscape, and a curtain at the left-hand side. Madame de Pompadour is surrounded by a musical instrument, on the chair behind her, books, a globe, sheets with engravings, a Chinese vase underneath the table and a music score in her hands. Unadorned by jewellery, but in an elaborately decorated dress, she looks away as if interrupted in the act of reading the score. If we take a closer look at the books on her table we can read the titles on their backs: the *Encyclopédie*, the *Henriade* by Voltaire, *De l'esprit des lois* by Montesquieu and a volume on natural history. Here a woman of obvious intelligence with intellectual and artistic interests is depicted.[7] What struck the attention in the portrait of Marie Leczinska – the numerous references to royalty – strikes home in the case of Madame de Pompadour in the references to the arts. The queen's gesture to the crown might be compared to Madame de Pompadour's holding of the score. Comparing the two, what the portraits convey is a strong sense of identification: Marie Leczinska *is* the queen, Madame de Pompadour *is* the lover of the arts.[8] Another similarity between the two portraits is their insertion into a tradition dominated by male figures. The portraits of French kings in full state, such as Hyacinthe Rigaud's portrait of Louis XIV (Louvre, Paris, 1701) are summoned up in Tocqué's painting of Marie Leczinska. More interesting even is Madame de Pompadour's pose as a lover of the arts, recalling for example Holbein the Younger's *The Ambassadors* (London, The National Gallery, 1533), who are equally portrayed with all the necessary attributes to indicate their status as art lovers and collectors. Note the resemblance with an earlier portrait by Quentin de La Tour of *Le Président Gabriel-Bernard de Rieux* (Geneva, Private Collection, 1741) of which Georges Wildenstein has argued that it served as a model for the pastel of Madame de Pompadour a decade later.[9] What interests me in particular is Madame de Pompadour's aspirations to enter the domain – a male-dominated domain – of art lovers and collectors, of those who protect and stimulate the arts. As we will see, she became a formidable player in the field.

Possible differences between the two portraits are clearly present as well.

Culture as a gendered battleground 107

Figure 6.1 Louis Tocqué, *Portrait de Marie Leczinska*
Source: Paris, Louvre
Note: Courtesy Photo R.M.N.

If we recall the environment in which Marie Leczinska was depicted, she seemed to occupy a peculiar space. She was surrounded by elements that emphasize a certain monumentality: huge pillars and wall decorations of a neoclassical character. The curtain on the left-hand side is apparently drawn aside to provide the spectator with a view of this monumental background.

108 *Inge E. Boer*

Figure 6.2 Maurice Quentin de La Tour, *Portrait de la marquise de Pompadour*
Source: Paris, Louvre
Note: Courtesy Photo R.M.N.

Other elements such as the chair and the table, for instance, try to create more of a personal touch. Taken together, the various attributes – not forgetting the crown – model Marie Leczinska in a semi-public space, neither inside nor outside. Madame de Pompadour's space is unequivocally private, although we can notice references to the outside, the globe and the landscape for example, but these are not direct indications of a public sphere.

Culture as a gendered battleground   109

This brings me to another difference between the two portraits and a second explanation for Leczinska's gesture towards the crown. Madame de Pompadour came to the court in 1745, when she was established as the official mistress of Louis XV. Around 1751 or 1752 their relationship cooled and changed into a comradeship that lasted until Madame de Pompadour's death in 1764. The queen and the mistress sorted out a delicate balance in their personal contacts, but in their function they were very different. Guy Chaussinand-Nogaret emphasizes how the position of the king's mistress was both fixed and transitional. In comparison to the queen, related to the king by force of an arranged marriage, the official mistress derived her position from his desire. For the mistress to maintain her status, which Chaussinand-Nogaret evaluates as marginal and central at the same time, she will continually have to stimulate the king's desire. As soon as the king loses interest, the mistress' privileged position will be jeopardized and ultimately taken up by the next mistress. Chaussinand-Nogaret interprets the difference in function between the queen and the mistress as follows:

> Thus a disequilibrium is created between the queen and the mistress: for the one [the queen] indifference and respect, for the other love and influence. . . . A distribution of roles, a specialization of functions therefore exists between the women of the king. The queen embodies order, legitimacy, orthodoxy, and immobility. The mistress, on the contrary, is pleasure, movement, and creation.[10]

It is this division of functions which is visible in the two portraits. Marie Leczinska gestures towards her crown, because the crown provides her with a *raison d'être*, the officially assigned position of queen, and Madame de Pompadour, the playful and entertaining mistress displays what her function requires of her, that is playfulness and entertainment. Yet, as I will show, playfulness was not a goal in and of itself.

A SPACE OF ONE'S OWN

If Madame de Pompadour were just another mistress of Louis XV, why then did she evoke such controversy? I will argue that her expert handling of culture as a domain of influence and contestation, critiquing notions of the natural, touched upon political and class sensibilities. Jeanne-Antoinette Poisson was brought up in a bourgeois family of considerable means and educated to render her a suitable party for a good marriage. Through her mother, Jeanne-Antoinette came in touch with a brilliant society which surrounded Madame de Tencin and Madame Geoffrin in their salons. In the salon at which Madame de Tencin presided, she encountered Fontenelle, Montesquieu, the Abbé Prévost, Helvétius and Marivaux. She took lessons in singing and declamation with the best teachers available.

Carolyn Lougee has argued that in seventeenth-century France salons had as their function 'to propagate the culture, values, and manners which

110   *Inge E. Boer*

supplemented and legitimated acquired nobility', and that, in fact, they maintained and preserved the aristocratic structure of French society.[11] For the eighteenth century, Joan Landes and Tjitske Akkerman,[12] among others, have argued that the salons provided an intermediary space, an assimilating space for aspiring bourgeois to acquire aristocratic manners necessary for upward mobility. Connections, rather than formal invitations provided one with access to a good salon. Landes asserts, 'conversation, new works of art, bureaucratic patronage, status, wealth, and even daughters were exchanged at these gatherings. Wit, urbanity, conversation, politesse, and pleasure were the earmarks of salon society'.[13] Landes describes the process of assimilation in terms of women, the *salonnières*, presiding over the education of bourgeois men. The young Mademoiselle Poisson, however, was just as much formed by this engaging society which might have helped her to acquire the aristocratic manners, something Landes attributes only to male salongoers, and provided her with an example on which to model, but not imitate in every respect, her own activities at the court later on. And yet, despite her money, her good connections to Charles Le Normand de Tournehem, a rich, well-connected bourgeois financier who was close to her family, her upbringing, her marriage to Seigneur d'Etiolles, none of these factors could protect her against the uproar and overt hostility with which she was received by the aristocratic members of the court.

In his preface to Edmond and Jules de Goncourt's biography of Madame de Pompadour, Henri Montaigu argues that she was a rather ruthless social climber. From '*demi-bourgeoise*' by birth to '*demi-aristocrate*' through her marriage to Seigneur d'Etiolles, then making herself available to Louis XV, his account gives her all the traits of a calculating woman. In a much-quoted story about her careful planning to appear before the eyes of a lonely king in search of company, and enticing him with her radiant beauty into a personal meeting, Madame de Pompadour manages to realize a life-long attachment to the king. As soon as she has established herself at the court, she renders herself, to quote Montaigu

> indispensable, good to all, she is the favourite and minister, channel of favours and offices, superintendent of the House of the Queen, moreover a marquisate was bestowed upon her under the honorable patronyme of a family of high birth that had become extinct at the beginning of the eighteenth century, she finally was made a duchess which is the pinnacle of the Versailles ritual. She is a sultana, almost a vizir, and altogether a goddess.[14]

The Goncourt brothers pay much attention to the clash between the classes resulting from Madame de Pompadour's installation at the court. She caused a shock to existing patterns of behaviour and thought, and to the etiquette so ritualized in Versailles that aristocratic sensibilities needed considerable time if they were to adjust to this new situation at all. How hurt these sensibilities were becomes clear with the Marquis d'Argenson[15]

Culture as a gendered battleground 111

who describes her as a 'grisette' and a 'robine', both terms indicating the enmity that goes beyond personal grudges, but is directed toward class-based references.[16] Often in the historiography on Madame de Pompadour there is emphasis on the aristocratic stance, where she is taken as a representative of a class despised in many ways by the courtiers. Many of the later biographers and critics of Madame de Pompadour tried to give an explanation of her position. Some of the themes in their criticism have already been mentioned. She was seen as a social climber, as a *petite bourgeoise* avid for power, fame and influence. The Goncourts seek the answer in a quest for glory and immortality, for a place in history, a quest in which she did not succeed:

> Of all the disappointments of the favourite, let us recall, the biggest was the failure of her life's dream: she had to give up on glory. . . . The favourite did not at all scorn the memory of her name. She was concerned with and attended to history. She had pursued and sought, during the entire period as a favourite, above all glory with the passion and wilfulness of a woman.[17]

Others would literally draw up the account of her expenses, as a publication after her death by Le Roi shows. Under the title 'How much she cost the nation', Le Roi carefully categorizes the spending on dresses, servants, châteaux, food and of course the art works she commissioned.[18] It is an emphasis of which the Parliament of Paris also never grew tired when relating Madame de Pompadour to the bad condition of the state's finances. Danielle Gallet gives prominence to the sacrifice of Madame de Pompadour in order to anchor in some way the volatility of the king's interest, implying thus that de Pompadour did not serve her self-interest.[19]

The Goncourts, for example, explain how class formed a barrier never to be transgressed and which expressed itself in, 'The lack of that distinction that cannot be taught nor be obtained, but that is passed on like a natural tradition in the blood of a caste, the lack of lineage', [20] with all the connotations lineage implies in racial and ethnic categories as well. Lack of lineage can, of course, not be repaired by titles; distinction is inbred and can never be learned if it is dealt with as something natural. The contrast between this so-called natural behaviour of the aristocracy and what must, by necessity, remain unnatural, could not be resolved by contesting nature, and thus lineage, as such. Culture did provide viable ways to do so, and as we will see, the clash between nature and culture is emblematized in the two paintings by Carle Vanloo.

Danielle Gallet has pointed out how Madame de Pompadour 'arrived at the court as if in a foreign country'.[21] Crossing the boundaries of classes, as if they represented the borders of different nations, one experiences that a different sign system is at work too. I want to argue that Madame de Pompadour did not choose to enter the aristocratic sign system completely, but instead created a space of her own. It is a space where her bid for a

112 *Inge E. Boer*

recognized position was less tainted by lineage and fixed rules. She used culture as a means to enact and create a space, which, to a certain extent, acknowledged the restrictions that came with her function and simultaneously opened up the possibilities for transgressing the boundaries of class and gender imposed on her. Taste, which is not dependent upon birth or blood, became the vehicle for expression in the realm of culture with which she could compete. In the eighteenth century, taste had something natural to it, but its naturalness was not determined by birth. A sense of taste could exist, but had to be supplemented by study. Taste rendered culture, as Madame de Pompadour used it, into a gendered battleground and into a means to justify the breaking of the barrier between the rigorous rules of Versailles and her bourgeois background. As a woman of considerable standing, she established a patronage of the arts which was unsurpassed. Patronage of the arts was an area still dominated by men, mostly aristocratic and court members, but gradually more and more bourgeois men came to belong to the circle of those collecting art, and commissioning paintings and other works of art. In eighteenth- and nineteenth-century references to collectors and patronage, women of the eighteenth century are barely present. A study in this field is badly needed.[22]

One of the examples of her activities in the realm of culture is the staging of plays and operas in the so-called Théâtre des Petits Appartements beginning in 1747. Madame de Pompadour was an excellent singer and performed in many of the stagings herself. Starting out as a small intimate source of amusement, it soon became a matter of honour and of recognition of one's valued position at the court for a courtier to be invited as a spectator. The spectacles proved a tremendous success as they were new and exciting, drawing together a circle of courtiers and able singers, musicians and actors, mixing people from bourgeois and aristocratic backgrounds, and mixing genders. Opponents of Madame de Pompadour would point at the high costs involved and would hold her directly responsible for this considerable financial burden to the state.

In other interpretations, Madame de Pompadour's entertainment is analysed as a means of alleviating the constant boredom from which Louis XV suffered.[23] The continuous change of atmosphere was meant to keep the king from experiencing the ennui so threatening to the existence of the royal mistress. In light of the extensive contacts that Madame de Pompadour maintained with many of the important *philosophes*, these interpretations focus on the continuation of the relationship between Louis XV and Madame de Pompadour. But why would she risk the acquaintance of those *philosophes*, who often asked for her intervention and protection, if not to propagate a politics of culture? The *philosophes* were given housing in the royal palace and pensions, and were supported in their bid for membership in the Académie.[24] Crébillon the younger and Rousseau were endorsed through the publication and performance of their work, Montesquieu acquired the cooperation of Madame de Pomapadour in suppressing a refu-

Culture as a gendered battleground 113

tation of his *De l'esprit des lois*. Diderot and d'Alembert were successful in obtaining her support for the publication of the *Encyclopédie*. Marmontel was a protégé and so was Voltaire. Many of the now well-known figureheads of the Enlightenment were often threatened by imprisonment or the suppression of their work for its subversive nature, so Madame de Pompadour was treading on slippery ground.[25] Playwrights, *philosophes*, natural historians and novelists were not the only ones she supported and protected. There was also a host of painters, sculptors, engravers, gilders, woodcarvers, gardeners, florists and potters. In all of the castles that Louis XV bought for her or that she obtained herself, she would bring in artists to work on their redecoration and embellishment.[26]

One of the best documented castles is the Château de Bellevue. Madame de Pompadour had commissioned Falconnet and Adam, well-known sculptors, to produce two statues, Oudry to paint hunting scenes for the dining room, which were repeated in the woodcarving by Verbreck. Carle Vanloo painted six allegories to adorn a large room for gatherings and parties; Boucher was asked for two paintings for the room where Madame de Pompadour took her baths. She had her own apartment decorated by Boucher and Vanloo.[27]

GENDERED SPACE: THE *CHAMBRE A LA TURQUE*

I propose to consider Madame de Pompadour by analysing two paintings that were present in her own room in the Château de Bellevue. Because of the paintings the room was called the *chambre à la turque* ('the Turkish room').[28] The paintings clarify something about her in-between position, through the way in which they thematize issues of space, culture, gender and genre. The two paintings, *Une sultane prenant du café* and *Deux sultanes travaillant à la tapisserie* were commissioned by Madame de Pompadour. Carle Vanloo, a fashionable painter in the mid-eighteenth century, executed the paintings which are commonly referred to as 'turqueries'. The turqueries form a subset within the Orientalist tradition of representation that denotes a style of ornamentation characterized by intricate patterns and an extensive use of motifs identified as Oriental. Turqueries are the peculiar genre where the Oriental elements present might draw the attention first. In *Une sultane prenant du café*, we see a woman in a dress partially covering wide trousers, a pipe in her hand, her hair braided with pearls and a small table in Oriental style on which the long pipe rests. The painted pair of sultanas in *Deux sultanes* display similar details in clothing, and a rug with Oriental motifs covers the floor.

Looking at the paintings, we are led, through various devices, to interpret them as portraying the Orient. But these paintings, serving as examples for a larger corpus of turqueries, have something in common which tends to be ignored in other analyses: their overt fictionality. They belong to a pictorial tradition in which both Western men and women would have themselves painted *as if* they were Oriental. The *as if* situation depicted might best be

114 *Inge E. Boer*

Figure 6.3 Carle Vanloo, *Une sultane prenant du café*
Source: Paris
Note: Permission Musée des Arts Décoratifs

described by the term *cultural cross-dressing*, a term which conveys a sense of blurring the boundaries not only in gender roles but also in cultural roles.[29] Moreover, by using the term cultural cross-dressing I want to stress the fact that it is directed towards the assumption of a culturally constructed model, i.e. the Orient. Cross-dressing also implies an act in which one consciously and for a period of time takes up a particular form of dress.

Une sultane prenant du café and *Deux sultanes travaillant à la tapisserie* were so-called *dessus-de-porte*, located above doors, for Madame de Pompadour's room in Turkish style in the Château de Bellevue. The relation between the two paintings is emphasized in both their function and their subject matter. The *dessus-de-porte* were commissioned as pendants. Traditionally, pendants were two paintings, often portraits, that were related in their representation or were meant to indicate a mutual bond. The subject matter of the two canvasses is related in the repetition of various elements, most notably the window, the flowers and the negotiation going on between the women in both paintings.

The window seems to be the same in both paintings, although it is taken

Culture as a gendered battleground 115

Figure 6.4 Carle Vanloo, *Deux sultanes travaillant à la tapisserie*
Source: Paris
Note: Permission Musée des Arts Décoratifs

at closer range in *Deux sultanes* and functions as the source of light in both. Its presence indicates the division between the outside world and the interior scene that we as spectators perceive. The window functions as a framing device, seemingly overdetermining the message. Because the window is explicitly included in the scene, it emphasizes even more our awareness of being inside. I think, however, that yet another issue is addressed by the window in combination with the flowers in the pendants. In *Une sultane prenant du café* the woman seated on the right wears flowers on her headdress, and a vase containing flowers is placed on the windowsill. Although the flowers are natural, in both instances of their use in the painting they have been cut. Cut flowers signify cultivation, as the still-life-like arrangement of the flowers in the vase also suggests. The relation with still-life painting is reinforced by the combination of different flowers in the vase, a commonplace established through Dutch still-life painting of the seventeenth century.[30] The positioning of the vase on the windowsill – inside, but next to the window indicating the dividing screen between inside and outside – focusses our attention on the 'cultivatedness' of the flowers. By extension,

116   *Inge E. Boer*

it also points to the 'cultivatedness' of the person wearing the flowers on her headdress. This element of cultivation is repeated in *Deux sultanes* through the transposition of the world beyond the windowpane into the flowers in the tapestry, and the flower and leaf motives on the cushions and the drapery. In general, I want to suggest that both paintings pose the question of inside versus outside, in terms of culture versus nature.

But this apparent set of rigid oppositions is questioned by the situation of negotiation in both paintings. In *Une sultane* an arrested moment is depicted – not any moment in time, however, but the exact point in time at which an exchange takes place. By the title we are alerted to this particular situation which enhances the legibility of the painting. The negotiation is represented in the steaming cup of coffee, handed to the sultana by what we at first might interpret as the servant, and in the look between the two women. Coffee, introduced in the 1660s by the ambassador of the Ottoman sultan, had become a fashionable commodity in French eighteenth-century society, albeit only for upper-class consumers.[31] Meanwhile it maintained at least a part of its 'outside' property for the French population at large. There is another quality of coffee that I want to stress. As Lane indicated, coffee needed careful preparation, both of the beans and of the coffee itself. With reference to Lévi-Strauss's distinction between the raw and the cooked, coffee can be considered not a raw item, but a highly refined commodity.[32]

The cup of coffee embodies both inside qualities (a refined cultured commodity) and outside qualities (a culturally alien element imported in France). As such the window can be aligned with the coffee cup, each pointing at the difference between inside and outside, nature and culture. In that respect, the black woman would seem to be firmly placed in the realm of nature, outside the cultivated space depicted. The display of white and black women in paintings has a long tradition. Therein the roles for both were defined in antithetical ways. The black women were mostly depicted as servants, the white women as mistresses. The black women were represented as active, displaying and adorning their mistresses. This is how oppositions in class and race were represented. In opposition to this binary scheme, I would argue that the black woman occupies a mobile position, an ability to move both in inside and outside spaces. She is part of the interior scene, but she has entered the Oriental space created in this room from outside, while the sultana is maintained within the seclusion of the harem.

In *Deux sultanes* the negotiation seems less obvious except for the look the two women exchange. Yet, the gestures of the women are significant. The woman on the right leans forward, she extends her hand, and her legs are bent as if to reinforce the argument she tries to convey to the woman on the left. The latter is in a position of listening. She sits in a more relaxed way, while holding the needle of her tapestry work. Interestingly enough, in the engraved version of the painting by Jacques-Firmin Beauvarlet, the title is changed to *La Confidence* ('The Confidence', in the sense of being confidential with someone and usually suggesting erotic secrets). The change is

Culture as a gendered battleground 117

significant in that it foregrounds the nature of the exchange: one woman confiding in another. I like to suggest that the speech of the woman on the right is reworked at the same moment. This is done by way of the knots the woman on the left ties on the tapestry as she is the only one holding a needle.[33] This reworking and questioning of the nature–culture opposition by way of positing negotiation as a consistent pattern in the paintings leads me again to consider Madame de Pompadour as the cultural cross-dresser in these particular paintings. It is significant that both paintings are *dessus-de-porte*, marking the boundaries between this room where Madame de Pompadour 'is' a sultana and other spaces where she has other functions. Yet we might perhaps see de Pompadour's cultural cross-dressing as inspired by a different motivation, that is the desire to overcome strict demarcations in function and power, transgressing boundaries of class and gender.

Madame de Pompadour can be seen as an 'in-between', occupying a provisional space between the king and the queen. It is striking in that light to see her represented as a sultana, the highest position of a woman in the harem of the sultan, but a position not defined by lineage. Any woman in the harem could become a sultana, a function which does not imply the demarcations existing between queen and mistress at the French court. The legitimacy embodied by the queen – emphasized in her official function of bearing the royal heir – is displaced onto the sultana, who bore the sultan's children. Moreover, the sultanas often played an important part in the polit-ical powerplay of the seraglio in which the procuration of their children to the line of succession was but one aspect of the intrigues. Ultimately, their political role could result in actual access to power.[34]

The imagery in relation to Madame de Pompadour is striking in light of the paintings as such and is used by Montaigu, who mentioned Madame de Pompadour as a sultana. The nuncio of the Pope wrote in May 1753 in similar terms: 'All signs indicate that the favourite sultana is losing credit. The more the new infatuation for the young Irish woman picks up force, the more his coldness toward her increases'.[35] Now I am not interested in conflating the two notions into the view that Madame de Pompadour *is* a sultana; a more fruitful way to follow is to look at the ways space, genre, gender and culture are thematized. In each of these aspects – space, genre, gender and culture – the public and private domains are at play. The turqueries connected the private and the public spheres in other ways as well, implicating Madame de Pompadour's patronage and the gendered connotations of rococo painting. In the developing field of art criticism in the mid-eighteenth century, genre paintings, among which turqueries were ranked, were given a particular position in the hierarchy of painting: from history paintings, portraits and genre paintings down to still-life and land-scapes.

The history painter, as La Font de Saint-Yenne and many others after him pointed out, is the painter of the soul; the others paint just for the eye. Mourning the decline of history painting after the death of Charles Le Brun

118　*Inge E. Boer*

in 1690, critics such as La Font de Saint-Yenne made a plea for a reevaluation of the grand and heroic themes of mythology and French history.[36] *Le grand goût* ('grand taste', 'superior sensibility'), with its masculine connotations of national glory and heroic acts, had suffered:

> Sensualism has taken the place of intellectualism, feminine imaginations, gracious, and courteous, supplanted or blunted thoughts that would want to be virile, strong and sublime. . . . It was the victory of the 'pretty' over the 'beautiful,' of the 'petty manner' over the 'grand taste'.[37]

Genre paintings, consistently connected to the feminine and ranking lower in the hierarchy, thus clashed with the aim of redirecting attention towards history painting. Madame de Pompadour, as one of the most visible patrons of the despised elaborate and ornamental style of rococo painting, was targeted in particular. She became inextricably bound up with its connotations in the triad: 'Vanloo, Pompadour, rococo', a rallying cry in the anti-rococo sentiment of the times. Her patronage might be considered a personal affair – commissioning works of art for the embellishment of her residences – depicting her in a private sphere. But inserting herself in the domain of art collectors and publicly aligning herself with some of the most famous rococo painters of the time, rendered Madame de Pompadour a highly visible player in the cultural field.

CONCLUSION: CULTURE, CLASS AND GENDER

Joan Landes quite easily equates highly visible women of the court and the city, who were being targeted as the most extreme examples of aristocratic excess and imposture. Male hostility towards women who were active in the cultural field expressed itself in attacks on mannerisms, artifice and stylistic excess, as Landes asserts.[38] Madame de Pompadour's background as a *bourgeoise* was never forgotten, and thus she cannot be readily assembled under the same heading as the *salonnières*. She could use her salon education at the court and carve out a space for herself where culture became a powerful instrument for self-assertion. She did share the criticisms in gendered terms for the kind of art she supported and commissioned. Yet, the emphasis in the historiography about Madame de Pompadour on class and finances does not appear in the same way in criticisms about the *salonnières*. This emphasis has occluded the perception of the vital links between the *salonnières* and Madame de Pompadour in the public sphere, but also perception of the ways in which Madame de Pompadour used culture and, as a concomitant factor, taste to negotiate her position at the court. I like to think of the reworking of nature into culture in the two turqueries by Vanloo as another example of how self-evident categories of reason, self-evident categories of where one belonged in a hierarchy of class, gender and culture, become subverted. As Madame de Pompadour has herself represented as a lover of the arts, the natural given of lineage is replaced by taste

Culture as a gendered battleground 119

and the capability to distinguish on different grounds, thus rendering culture into a gendered battleground.

NOTES

1 The research for this article was funded in part by the National Foundation for Scientific Research and the Belle van Zuylen Institute, University of Amsterdam. All translations are mine, unless indicated otherwise.

2 The Goncourt brothers characterize Madame de Pompadour as 'the godmother and queen of rococo'. E. et J. de Goncourt, *Madame de Pompadour*, Paris, Olivier Orban Éditions, 1982, p. 309; see P. Stein, 'Madame de Pompadour and the harem imagery at Bellevue', *Gazette des Beaux-Arts*, 1994, 6th series, 123, pp. 29–44, for a similar argument on the connection between arts and politics.

3 It might be quite easy to deride influential eighteenth-century French women, such as Madame de Tencin and Madame de Pompadour, for not having exerted the right kind of influence, as Susan P. Connor asserts in equating women and politics with intrigue. It certainly backfires on women, but also turns a blind eye to the politics of culture in which both women, the former a *salonnière*, the latter salon-educated, participated actively. S. P. Connor, 'Women and politics', in S. Spencer (ed.), *French Women and the Age of Enlightenment*, Bloomington, Indiana University Press, 1984, pp. 49–64.

4 For a concise definition of an index as a semiotic term, see C. Peirce, 'Logic as semiotic: the theory of signs', in R. E. Innis (ed.), *Semiotics: An Introductory Anthology*, Bloomington, Indiana University Press, 1985, pp. 12–16.

5 K. Pomian, *Collectionneurs, amateurs et curieux. Paris-Venise: XVIe-XVIIIe siècle*, Paris, Editions Gallimard, 1987, p. 35.

6 Pomian, *Collectionneurs*, p. 29.

7 For a description of her library, see J. Bastien, 'Madame de Pompadour bibliophile et curieuse', in *Madame de Pompadour et la floraison des arts*, Montréal, David M. Stewart Museum, 1988. The Goncourts consider her library as essential for her knowledge in state affairs, history, politics and culture. De Goncourt, *Pompadour*, p. 270.

8 See D. Gallet, 'La belle que voilà . . . ', in *Madame de Pompadour et la floraison des arts* and Goncourt, *Pompadour*, pp. 311–12 for similar conclusions.

9 G. Wildenstein, *Un pastel de La Tour, le Président de Rieux*, Paris, Chez Emile-Paul, 1919, p. 15.

10 G. Chaussinand-Nogaret, *La vie quotidienne des femmes du roi: D'Agnes Sorel à Marie-Antoinette*, Paris, Hachette, 1990, p. 16. See also P. de Nolhac, *Versailles et la cour de France: Louis XV et Madame de Pompadour* (1904), Paris, Louis Conard, 1928, p. 135.

11 C. Lougee, *Le Paradis des Femmes. Women, Salons, and Social Stratification in Seventeenth-Century France*, Princeton, Princeton University Press, 1976, p. 212.

12 J. Landes, *Women and the Public Sphere in the Age of the French Revolution*, Ithaca, Cornell University Press, 1988, pp. 24–5; T. Akkerman, *Women's Vices Public Benefits: Women and Commerce in the French Enlightenment*, Amsterdam, Spinhuis, 1992, pp. 4–8.

13 Landes, *Women and the Public Sphere*, p. 25.

14 H. Montaigu, 'Introduction', in Goncourt, *Pompadour*, p. 6.

15 Quoted in Goncourt, *Pompadour*, p. 31.

16 *Grisette* means 'jeune fille coquette de petite condition', that is 'flirtatious young maiden of modest birth'. *Robine* is the female form of *robin*, designating a member of the *noblesse de robe*, noble officials whose title was frequently

120 *Inge E. Boer*

acquired upon their purchase of an office; their 'nobility' was thus lacking true lineage and marked by the stain of venality.

17 *Ibid.*, p. 284.

18 J. A. Le Roi, *Relevé des Dépenses de Madame de Pompadour*, Versailles, Impr. de Montalent-Bougleux, 1853. The Goncourts dish up with obvious relish how much the maintenance of the châteaux that Madame de Pompadour possessed cost, but they see the small army of artists as another major source of spending: 'What was incredibly expensive and costs France thirty-six million, was the whole group of painters, sculptors, marble-cutters, gilders, founders, earthenware makers, carpenters, flower makers, and gardeners that the favourite dragged along behind her in each of her new properties', Goncourt, *Pompadour*, p. 92.

19 D. Gallet, *Madame de Pompadour ou le pouvoir féminin*, Paris, Fayard, 1985, p. 111.

20 De Goncourt, *Pompadour*, p. 32.

21 Gallet, *Madame de Pompadour*, p. 49.

22 For descriptions of well-known eighteenth-century collections, see Pomian, *Collectionneurs*, and L. Clément de Ris, *Les amateurs d'autrefois*, Paris, Plon, 1877.

23 See Goncourt, *Pompadour*, pp. 47–50 and Gallet, *Madame de Pompadour*, p. 111.

24 Danielle Gallet describes Madame de Pompadour's role with regard to the *philosophes* and writers as indirect, though offering crucial support. Voltaire wrote to d'Alembert: 'At the bottom of her heart, she is one of ours, she protected the letters as much as she could', quoted in Gallet, 'La belle que voilà . . . ', p. 25.

25 See R. Darnton, *The Literary Underground of the Old Regime*, Cambridge MA, Harvard University Press, 1982, for descriptions of the repeated emprisonments of some of the *philosophes* mentioned.

26 One challenging way to connect Madame de Pompadour in a more direct sense to patronage and the cultural domain in general, is Danielle Rice's argument on paying more attention to collaborative efforts in the arts. Rice perceives the works commissioned by Madame de Pompadour for her residences as 'comprehensive works of art'. D. Rice, 'Women and the Visual Arts', in Spencer (ed.), *French Women*, pp. 244–6.

27 Many descriptions focus on the decorations of the Château de Bellevue, see for example, Goncourt, *Pompadour*, p. 93; J. Bastien, 'Bellevue', in *Madame de Pompadour et la floraison des arts*; Gallet, *Madame de Pompadour*, pp. 134–5; and De Nolhac, *Versailles*, pp. 221–2.

28 See P. Biver, *Histoire du Château de Bellevue*, Paris, Librairie Gabriel Enault, 1933, for detailed descriptions.

29 E. Apter, 'Ethnographic travesties: colonial fiction, French feminism and the case of Elissa Rhais', in N. Zemon Davis and G. Prakash (eds), *Imperialism, Colonialism and the Colonial Aftermath*, Princeton, Princeton University Press, 1994, uses a different terminology, such as cultural masquerade and ethnographic travesty. See for an elaboration of cultural cross-dressing, Inge. E. Boer, 'This is not the Orient: theory and postcolonial practice', in Mieke Bal and Inge E. Boer (eds), *The Point of Theory: Practices of Cultural Analysis*, New York and Amsterdam, Continuum and Amsterdam University Press, 1994. And for a critical assessment of the Orientalist tradition in French painting, see Inge E. Boer, *Rereadings and Revisions: Gender in French Representations of the Orient*, Stanford, Stanford University Press, forthcoming.

30 See N. Bryson, *Looking at the Overlooked: Four Essays on Still Life Painting*,

Culture as a gendered battleground   121

Cambridge MA and London, Harvard University Press, 1991, for extensive analyses of Dutch still life.

31 P. Martino, *L'Orient dans la littérature française au XVII et au XVIIIe siècle*, Paris, Hachette, 1906, p. 348.

32 E. W. Lane, *An Account of the Manners and Customs of the Modern Egyptians* (1836), New York, Dover Publications, 1973, p. 138; C. Lévi-Strauss, *Le Cru et le cuit*, Paris, Plon, 1964.

33 N. Miller, 'The knot, the letter, and the book', in *Subject to Change: Reading Feminist Writing*, New York, Columbia University Press, 1988, pp. 125–62, has argued on the connection between women writers and the tying of knots as a way of writing for women.

34 In recent research the role of sultanas has received closer attention. See for example, L. P. Peirce, *The Imperial Harem: Women and Sovereignty in the Ottoman Empire*, Oxford and New York, Oxford University Press, 1993; F. Mernissi, *Sultanes oubliées: Femmes chefs d'État en Islam*, Paris, Albin Michel, 1990, and S. J. Shaw, *History of the Ottoman Empire and Modern Turkey*, vol. 1, Cambridge, Cambridge University Press, 1976, pp. 170, 191, 193–194, 204.

35 As quoted in Goncourt, *Pompadour*, p. 117.

36 See La Font de Saint-Yenne, *Reflexions sur quelques causes de l'état présent de la peinture en France*, La Haye, Chez Jean Neaulme, 1747, and *Sentiments sur quelques ouvrages de peinture*, La Haye, Chez Jean Neaulme, 1754. The Collection Deloynes in the Cabinet d'Estampes of the Bibliothèque Nationale in Paris harbours some of the most interesting contributions in this debate.

37 As the arguments are summarized by J. Locquin, *La peinture d'histoire en France de 1747 à 1785: étude sur l'évolution des idées artistiques dans la seconde moitié du XVIIIe siècle* (1912), Paris, Arthena, 1978, p. xxviii.

38 Landes, *Women and the Public Sphere*, p. 47. For a critique of Landes, see D. Goodman, 'Public sphere and private life: toward a synthesis of current historiographical approaches to the old regime', *History and Theory*, 1992, 31, pp. 1–21.

7 A woman's struggle for a language of enlightenment and virtue
Mary Wollstonecraft and Enlightenment 'feminism'[1]

Virginia Sapiro

Feminists and feminist scholars have often been overly dutiful daughters. Despite our critical stance, and attempts to create our own thoughts and theories, feminist scholars have sometimes gone too far in accepting the definitions and views of dominant theoretical traditions as they have been shaped and applied in clearly male-dominated and non-feminist communities. This influence has sometimes warped our interpretations of our own intellectual history. This is certainly true with respect to dominant views of 'Enlightenment feminism' in feminist scholarship.

Feminist theory developed as a self-conscious enterprise in the 1970s and 1980s, when relatively rigid distinctions among theoretical schools were especially important. Communities of theory took on remarkably patriarchal forms. A cottage industry of feminist theory devoted itself to showing how one or another new theoretical formulation could now become the foundation for feminist theory. These formulations were usually named for their fathers, for example Marx, Freud or Lacan, or could be spoken of only in reference to their fathers, for example Rawls or Foucault. Feminists should be especially wary of expending too much effort in earning the right to take someone else's name. A few efforts to clarify the sources of feminist theory became unfortunately crystallized into a commonly accepted set of categories used to define types of feminist theory. Many observers continue to describe modern feminist theory as being divided into three types: liberal, socialist and radical.[2] These labels were often used not only to assess the historical complexity of varieties of feminism but to offer notions of competing formulations of the 'best' feminism. Feminist theorists tended to disagree about many things, but to agree on one: 'liberal feminism' and 'Enlightenment' influences on feminism were perhaps important historical forces, but they were so rooted in patriarchal assumptions as to be hardly feminist at all, perhaps not worth much serious feminist attention.

Categorization of theoretical traditions can be useful, but only in the same way as, for example, periodization of history. The name is a label chosen to abstract and represent a limited set of qualities identified by observers as especially important. Categorization of theoretical traditions, such as historical periodization, unfortunately sometimes takes on a life of

A language of enlightenment and virtue   123

its own, such that the labels begin to be taken as causes or explanations rather than as labels fitting to only varying degrees of comfort the cases they describe. Feminist scholars examining women's political and social history during the period roughly labelled 'the Enlightenment' are especially aware of the blinkers that sometimes limit the scope of feminist interpretation. My research on Mary Wollstonecraft and, in particular, on the history of interpretations of and reactions to Wollstonecraft brings the point home forcefully.

HISTORY

I have written about the ways in which the construction of Mary Wollstonecraft reflected the contemporaneous preoccupations of the various ages that interpreted her.[3] In contemporary feminist theory she is often seen through the lens of stereotypes of liberalism and the Enlightenment, described and dismissed quickly. Leading schools of feminist scholarship dismiss – or attack – the Enlightenment and anything that could be labelled 'liberal' on a number of well-known grounds that need no rehearsal here. Although in Anglo-American feminism especially Wollstonecraft is regarded as a key 'founding mother of feminism' (and indeed, her influence was geographically wider than that), her political and social theory are rarely seriously studied.[4] Probing the theme of this book, the languages of feminism, with respect to Wollstonecraft and the Enlightenment, raises an important historical problem. Danger lurks in the attempt to apply a label where no such concept existed. We face special problems in trying to understand a language of feminism in Mary Wollstonecraft's writing or that of the women who preceded her, because they preceded *feminism* as a self-conscious ideology or social movement. Mary Wollstonecraft is especially interesting because she has often been incorrectly labelled the first feminist theorist and because she stands at the historical moment just preceding the development of a feminist movement.

Karen Offen has done admirable work to help us sort out the historical meanings of feminism.[5] As historian Nancy Cott has written, some misreadings of women's history have resulted from the fact that the 'vocabulary of feminism has been grafted onto the history of women's rights'.[6] Although it is a matter for debate, I prefer these historical sensibilities to those that seem to imply that a historical figure like Wollstonecraft has little to offer because she did not know her Marx, Bahktin or MacKinnon very well. One reason we have failed to learn as much from some of our predecessors as we might have done is that some of the key theoretical impulses within feminist theory have tended to abstract and de-historicize the theory and the theorists. While the overarching emphasis on language within feminist theory is correct, studying language by abstracting it out of its material, political and social conditions has led us astray in important ways. Western, white, middle-class feminist theorists have worked hard to become sensitive to cultural and

124   *Virginia Sapiro*

national difference; they also should become more sensitive about *historical* difference.

There are a number of historical facts necessary to understanding Wollstonecraft and her work. Certainly it is difficult to imagine trying to comprehend her writing on the family, sexuality and work without attending to the historical structures of work, family, conception and birth in her day. The language she used to talk about these things must be grounded in the different world in which she lived. It should also be fascinating to feminist scholars pursuing the political and intellectual history of women to study this particular feminist, who lived before feminism as a conscious theory, ideology or social movement had been invented. There was no such term as 'feminism', 'feminist' or even 'womanist'. In Wollstonecraft's day, no woman that we know of had made a consciously named ideology or 'Ism' of her gender. There was no mass social movement, or none of which she was aware, of women who were acting in their own names for and on behalf of women. Thus one way of reading her work is to engage in watching a woman struggling with how to identify, name, and analyse the wrongs and rights[7] of woman's condition at a time in which she had no prepackaged language or analysis on which to draw. Feminists and feminist scholars today have a language that has been developed by others – even if not entirely adequately – which they can use for their own purposes.

Not only did Wollstonecraft not have the benefit of a movement, she did not have a 'history'. Readers are sometimes surprised to see that Wollstonecraft made no comments about many important (in our eyes) predecessors, such as Mary Astell or Christine de Pizan.[8] How would she have known about these women? Why would she know any more about them than our much more educated students schooled in an era of women's studies know about Charlotte Perkins Gilman, Anna Julia Cooper, Ellen Kay – or for that matter, Mary Wollstonecraft?[9] From what libraries, teachers or writers would she have learned about her feminist past?

These observations indicate that Wollstonecraft's life and career offer a glimpse of the struggle for a language of feminism at the most basic level in the context of the Enlightenment. That is, she was a thinker groping towards the very notion of feminism where the most radical languages generally at her disposal at the time which could be used as tools in this search were the various forms of Enlightenment political thinking, including both 'liberalism' as it is often conceived, and republicanism. Wollstonecraft's political and intellectual context gave her some general tools to use to think about the specifically gendered wrongs and rights of society. But she had to struggle to find the words to cast the problems and solutions in gendered terms. She had to seek for herself a way to make what she saw comprehensible to herself and to others who had no language of feminism. She had to find a language when, given her historical placement, she would have to discover for herself that language itself was indeed a problem for women.

Mary Wollstonecraft is a study in the very problems of enlightenment she

A language of enlightenment and virtue 125

investigated. She was certainly not the only woman in her time or before to do this. But there is a huge difference between the mere existence of similarly situated women and a community of people. Intellectual communities and traditions are social phenomena. The intellectual isolation of women is an important part of their intellectual history and to twentieth-century feminist theory, 'feminism', strictly speaking, must incorporate some consciousness of collectivity.

Wollstonecraft's writing on women is, as many have claimed, an application of Enlightenment principles. During most of her brief but productive writing career, she was a member of a London-based community of intellectuals, writers and artists, one of whose major distinguishing features was that they were religious Dissenters, and thus personally understood the denial of civil and political rights despite their generally high levels of education and despite, in the case of a few of them, their wealth. They also stood on the left wing of the political spectrum (as evidenced by the names Paine, Price, Priestley, Blake, Barlow and Godwin, among others), and they were avid supporters of that most unpopular and un-English revolution in France. This context is important because it not only helps to reveal the *roots* of her writing, but also its *audience*, and this should make a difference in our interpretation. Wollstonecraft wrote primarily *of* and *to* the left. Then as now, publishers aimed their products at specific markets. Her publisher produced books and pamphlets that were largely of interest to Dissenters and the left.

Thus, it is not surprising that her entire corpus of work shares the language and preoccupations of this socio-political group. She was deeply concerned with the problems of reason, independence, virtue, progress, education and enlightenment. Like her friends and colleagues, she was vehemently opposed to slavery, standing armies and many elements of political patriarchy such as primogeniture, aristocracy, and probably monarchy. She, like many of her friends, spent her intellectual life trying to figure out how a free and virtuous society might be constructed. Among the thinkers of the past whose work most influenced her, as it did them, were John Locke and Jean-Jacques Rousseau. At the same time, she continually demanded in print that her audience, this group of dissenting radicals, must expand and alter the terms of their analysis, in large part by applying their just principles more consistently and coherently to incorporate individuals excluded from their political analysis – women and children – and to incorporate a social institution that had been excluded from the terms of their analysis: the family.[10] If this struggle to incorporate gender into individual and institutional social analysis is a minor feat, then feminism itself must be defined as a trivial enterprise.

126 *Virginia Sapiro*

REASON

A brief vocabulary lesson may identify some of the especially enlightening struggles. I begin with a key term so often misunderstood in her writing: *reason* and its relatives *passion* and *education*. These terms cause trouble for those not very familiar with this period, especially for those who understand them through a post-nineteenth century perspective. These concepts are regularly interpreted in a twentieth-century sense quite different from that used by Wollstonecraft and her contemporaries. Some of these historical differences of language alter dramatically how we might understand Wollstonecraft.

Wollstonecraft and other liberal feminists are often chastised by our contemporaries for accepting masculine cold, hard, mechanical *reason* as the central mode of understanding the world. As Wollstonecraft's works on education, as well as her two vindications make clear, she shared with some of her friends an understanding of Reason derived clearly from David Hartley (1705–57) and Claude-Adrien Helvétius (1715–71).[11] For them, Reason was not a kind of abstracted mathematical play with words, but a matter of what they called the 'association of ideas', the process by which people learn to turn sense impressions into ideas, and combine these to create thoughts and judgments. It refers to the active process of reaching understanding from experience, not to a set of formulations found in a logic textbook. Reason is possible only if we learn to exercise our minds to gain their strength and independence, much as we might exercise our bodies to gain their strength and independence.

Wollstonecraft defined thinking as an active process in which the mind is trained not to substitute faith, obedience, imitation, unexamined habit or first impressions for real thinking. Unfortunately, she believed, most people regularly substitute these former processes – what she called 'prejudice' – for reason and thought. The fact that Wollstonecraft, like other Enlightenment thinkers, understood the mind as defined and shaped by experience led her to understand the nature of thinking and prejudice in an institutional and social context as well. All forms of inequality and social subordination that she could detect – what she called 'unnatural distinctions' – militated against the possibility of developing the strength and independence of mind necessary for reason. All forms of social subordination, including those based on rank, property, religion, race, age and gender, required such mechanisms as obedience and faith, ceremonies and rituals, fear and disdain, all of which barred all parties to these social relationships from being able to develop strength and independence of mind.

Thus, Wollstonecraft's work, especially when we consider all of her major works and not just the *Vindication of the Rights of Woman*,[12] is one of the earliest to grapple with the key issue of social change that feminists and other political activists confront: by what means can we, members of an inegalitarian, corrupt, and unenlightened society based on prejudice develop

A language of enlightenment and virtue 127

a more enlightened vision of society for ourselves, and then attain that vision in reality? One answer – the key one that the Enlightenment suggested – was employing the development of mind and reason. In this model we work through education to strip away the prejudices of past ages, reach a higher level of understanding of how we should be, and reform our minds, our ideas, our culture to conform to this improved notion.

Here it is important to examine this idea of education and the role it played in Wollstonecraft's work. Certainly, she spent her entire writing career probing problems of education. But for her, as for many of her contemporaries, education did not refer just to formal training received in schools. Although the small handful of pages in her *Vindication of the Rights of Woman* devoted to discussion of schooling and school systems is probably the most famous of all her work, if we take account of her entire corpus of writing, it is clear that for Wollstonecraft, education more often means much what the term 'socialization' means to us today: a broader concept of the development of the individual through all her experiences. Wollstonecraft was attentive to the breadth of experiences from which we learn – not just from schools, but from the structure of the institutions in which we live, from ceremonies and rituals, from our modes of dress and the way we eat. The problem – of which Wollstonecraft was well aware – was that if the structure and culture of the society around us so shapes how we think, how do we actually achieve an adequate vision of the virtuous alternative? And how do we change people's habits of mind if the structure of society has not yet changed? Despite her emphasis on education broadly and narrowly construed, her understanding of the effects of the unnatural distinctions that structured society led her to write in her famous *Vindication*, that 'It may . . . fairly be inferred, that till society be differently constituted, much cannot be expected from education'.[13]

While attending to reason as a means of change, she saw little possibility for real change unless there were more radical changes in the structure of society, especially the end to subordination by rank and gender. But her experience with the French Revolution, and especially the Terror, which she witnessed first hand, also led her to be uneasy about the likely nature of radical change that flowed from ideas developed in a basically corrupt society. The French Revolution, she believed, was part of the human destiny for improvement, but it proved to Wollstonecraft that the path to that goal was treacherous. Even as she hailed the revolution in often poetic terms, she worried about the outcome. As she thought about the now-silent palace of Versailles she felt glad of its demise as a symbol of tyranny, but also detected

> the vestiges of thy former oppression; which, separating man from man with a fence of iron, sophisticated all, and made many completely wretched; I tremble, lest I should meet some unfortunate being, fleeing from the despotism of licentious freedom, hearing the snap of the

128　*Virginia Sapiro*

guillotine at his heels; merely because he was once noble, or has afforded an asylum to those, whose only crime is their names – and, if my pen almost bounds with eagerness to record the day, that levelled the Bastille, the recollection, that still the abbey is appropriated to hold the victims of revenge and suspicion, palsies the hand that would fain do justice to the assault.[14]

The revolution was good, but it was born of a corrupt society, and thus must itself contain elements of that corruption. The problem, her writing suggested repeatedly, is that the solution must be found by the mutual enlightenment of equals who can imagine a virtue that can only come from the system not yet created. She explicitly denied that a specially enlightened vanguard could offer the solution; people are the products of their environment.

SOCIAL STRUCTURE

Wollstonecraft's basic enlightenment understanding of reason, virtue and experience, mixed with close examination of specific cases of subordination, led her to begin to probe a set of questions that have been central to feminist analysis since then: the tensions between social structures and individual psychology or between material and culture as the thread to pull when trying to unravel an old society and create a new one. This aspect of her work is most clear with respect to her understanding of women in her final manuscript, *The Wrongs of Woman, Or, Maria*, which lay unfinished on her desk when she died. The text weaves together the life histories of three people who find themselves in an insane asylum: one woman born poor, one man born wealthy and one woman born middle class. Each had been subjected to the special violences common to his and her own class and gender in an oppressive patriarchal system. The main character, Maria, has been locked up by her husband, who also took her child from her. The text that is available to us was compiled and edited by William Godwin, who found it as loose sheaves. Wollstonecraft's notes suggest at least five alternative plot courses for the unwritten conclusion.

Wollstonecraft's letters indicate she found this her most difficult work to write.[15] The *Wrongs of Woman* contains many unresolved problems. They are unresolved because the book was never finished, but the book was never finished partly because the problems were not resolved. I believe this lack of resolution was caused by Wollstonecraft's ever-increasing grasp of the systemic and enveloping nature of the structure of gender relations in their individual, cultural and institutional complexity. The author of this book understands physical and psychological violence against women and children in the context of intimate relationships that stems both from learned individual patterns of thinking and behaviour, and from the logic of social institutions as they are constructed by law.

A language of enlightenment and virtue 129

The gothic convention of the insane asylum/prison from which one might conceivably escape, but only with great luck, craft or assistance is given life through the figurative and more inescapable prisons of marriage and property law, and the corruptions of mind and heart. Here is perhaps the one instance in which a comparison of Wollstonecraft and Godwin is truly appropriate. Maria's observation that 'Marriage had bastilled me for life'[16] – this crucial political term for this private institution – harkens back to Godwin's most famous passage in *Caleb Williams*,[17] his fictional rendition of his *Enquiry Concerning Political Justice.*

> 'Thank God,' exclaims the Englishman, 'we have no Bastille! Thank God, with us no man can be punished without a crime!' Unthinking wretch! Is that a country of liberty, where thousands languish in dungeons and fetters? Go, go, ignorant fool! and visit the scenes of our prisons! witness their unwholesomeness, their filth, the tyranny. of their governors, the misery of their inmates! After that, show me the man shameless enough to triumph, and say, 'England has no Bastille!'[18]

The dark scenes of Maria's vain attempts to escape from her husband are reminiscent of Caleb Williams' escape attempts from his prisonkeeper. Wollstonecraft, in contrast to Godwin, extended her political analysis very clearly into the family, identifying it as an extension of the state, with the husband not just as the patriarch in the little commonwealth, but as its police as well.

The incidents in the characters' lives are plausible under the law of the time. But Wollstonecraft also recognized that oppression worked through the mind and heart as well as through law and material inequality. Oppression is not just a cage – it reaches into people's minds, destroying any simple notion of escape. Jemima, an impoverished woman who has suffered most forms of violence known especially to woman, has had her spirit crushed. Maria claims her own independence, but the court is there to stop her. Maria seems to try to save herself from the tyranny of one marriage by entering another as though that were the solution, but Wollstonecraft's notes for her unchosen conclusion suggest a strong likelihood that that 'solution' would prove the wrong one.

CHARACTER

The mechanisms of the mind in a corrupt society also point to another problem raised in Wollstonecraft's work: The character of women. Wollstonecraft is well-known for the negative things she had to say about women's character, especially their weaknesses and their use of beauty and sexuality as cunning instruments of tyrannical power. A short-sighted view understands her criticisms as the mere deficiencies of victim blaming. But in fact much of her work – especially the two vindications, but also her history of the French Revolution and her final fiction – emphasized the corrupting

130   *Virginia Sapiro*

influences of unnatural distinctions or social subordination on all parties to the inequality.

Self-preservation is a natural instinct. And for Wollstonecraft, those who are raised without reason, either because they are unnaturally raised to positions of power or unnaturally lowered to positions of subordination, are especially likely to be self-regarding and unjust in their relations with others. With each form of social subordination Wollstonecraft investigated – those based on rank, property, age and gender – she showed how the character and minds of both the dominant and subordinated partner within dominance relations become corrupted into a self-regarding short-term rationality framed by these unjust relations. She consistently framed her discussion of gender relations with metaphors of power and tyranny that would be more immediately politically comprehensible to the men around her than arguments about gender; the tyranny of men over women and its resulting effects on both men and women were like the tyranny of kings over their courtiers, to the profound corruption of both.

Woman's 'problem' is not just that she has been kept from an education that trains her mind and gives her substance; it is that her entire experience, like that of men, is shaped by unjust power relations. Women, when they are not entirely crushed by men's tyranny, too often turn to cunning, especially in the use of their bodies and sexuality, because that is the only weapon they have for survival in this system. As Wollstonecraft explained, 'this exertion of cunning is only an instinct of nature to enable them to obtain indirectly a little of that power of which they are unjustly denied a share'.[19] Both women and men are corrupted by this system of subordination, but she laid the lion's share of the blame at men's feet.

> From the tyranny of man, I firmly believe, the greater number of female follies proceed; and the cunning, which I allow makes at present a part of their character, I likewise have repeatedly endeavoured to prove, is produced by their oppression.[20]

She did not blame women for their relationship with men. She did, however, despise each of these relationships. This is a very different view from that of contemporary feminist commentators who sometimes seem to suggest that despite living within corrupt and unjust power relationships, and social institutions, women nevertheless have remained essentially distinctly nurturant and just, and that the only thing that stands between women and the goal of making heaven on earth is the men that won't let us do this.

Thus far we have followed a very few threads from Wollstonecraft's use of a basic Enlightenment vocabulary to her analysis of gender relations. Hers was an era that initiated a tremendous critique of institutions such as churches and governments and, with the help of Mary Wollstonecraft among others, the family. These people asserted the importance of the dignity of the individual human being, and the individual human mind and conscience against patriarchal institutions.[21] Wollstonecraft's main contribution here was that she would not let her friends leave women and the family out of this picture. The key to the complexity is that she was not focussing on disembodied reason, but reason driven by and embedded in experience, which creates a powerful political psychology. (It is no coincidence that her century gave birth to psychology and, more generally, social science.) That political psychology raises many of the issues that are central to the feminism that followed.

LANGUAGES OF FEMINISM: CONCLUSION

Finally, let us consider 'languages of feminism' in a narrow sense. I have asserted repeatedly that Wollstonecraft's feminist theory must be understood as one that preceded feminism as a named self-conscious entity and thus that it preceded the time in which a community of women had already worked out a basic vocabulary for naming their problems and searching for solutions. Consider an important implication: given Wollstonecraft's historical position, living in a great revolutionary era in which some of the leaders of the great nineteenth-century feminist movements were literally just about to be born, her work can be seen as a struggle towards a vocabulary, a recognition that there are special problems with language itself that must be solved before women can have justice. What follows are some illustrations.

One of Wollstonecraft's methods was to probe the meaning of key terms of social discourse. She asked whether they have the same or different meaning for women and men, and if different, why. Clearly, much of her discussion of reason and related terms falls into this pattern. She also, however, offered intriguing discussions of the gendered meanings of 'virtue', 'modesty', 'honour' and 'heroism'. She showed little trust in the words used by her political opponents, and assessed them very critically. She saw ordinary language as a tool of oppression:

> 'As a philosopher, I read with indignation the plausible epithets which men use to soften their insults; and as a moralist, I ask what is meant by such heterogeneous associations, as fair defects, amiable weaknesses, etc.?'[22] She saw these as phrases 'men condescendingly use to soften our slavish dependence'.[23]

Her belief in the development of the mind as the habitual association of ideas meant that such 'heterogeneous associations' or morally contradictory ideas could be bound together in people's minds, thus allowing the good and bad to be confused.

In the *Rights of Woman* Wollstonecraft both noted the power of corrupt associations of ideas, and attempted political polemic through analysis of language. The words 'feminine' and 'masculine', she argued, were used as weapons against women. Wollstonecraft concluded that the common sense of 'masculine' included the human virtues of reason, strength and independence

132 *Virginia Sapiro*

she so valued. The term itself could therefore be used to help deny women the opportunity to become virtuous. She believed 'the word masculine is only a bugbear; there is little reason to fear that women will acquire too much courage or fortitude'.[24]

In the end, Wollstonecraft herself remained caught in a gender-bound language that was not, as she herself indicated, merely external drapery to different thoughts, but a part of the mechanism of her own thinking.[25] She showed signs of trying to free herself from the confines of gender-structured (and therefore structuring) language. In the *Rights of Woman*, for example, she remarked on Catherine Macaulay's book:

> I will not call hers a masculine understanding, because I admit not of such an arrogant assumption of reason; but I contend that it was a sound one, and that her judgment, the matured fruit of profound thinking, was a proof that a woman can acquire judgment, in the full extent of the word.[26]

Wollstonecraft also worked out some 'heterogeneous associations' of her own, revealing her resistance and occasional sabotage of common gendered understanding. By the time she wrote the *Rights of Woman*, she was most likely to accuse men of being unmanly when they were acting most as men were expected to act, especially towards women. She referred to the apparently most masculine of characters as feminine, including the military and men engaging in common courtship rituals. But she certainly had no well-worked theory of language and no clear alternative.

One superb indication of her struggle with a language of feminism can be found in a generally neglected passage in which, I argue, a distinctly feminist voice appears to be on the point of emerging, and in which she begins to exemplify a feminist politics. I say 'exemplifies' rather than 'discusses' (or any similar word) because she demonstrates through incompleteness. For this, we return to her last work, *The Wrongs of Woman*. Consider this passage, in which Maria addresses her daughter as she writes her memoirs.

> Addressing these memoirs to you, my child, uncertain whether I shall ever have an opportunity of instructing you, many observations will probably flow from my heart, which only a mother – a mother schooled in misery, could make.
>
> The tenderness of a father who knew the world, might be great; but could it equal that of a mother – of a mother, labouring under a portion of the misery, which the constitution of society seems to have entailed on all her kind? It is, my child, my dearest daughter, only such a mother, who will dare to break through all restraint to provide for your happiness – who will voluntarily brave censure herself, to ward off sorrow from your bosom. From my narrative, my dear girl, you may gather the instruction, the counsel, which is meant rather to exercise than influence your mind.[27]

A language of enlightenment and virtue 133

This passage may appear innocent of politics at first, perhaps a mere example of conventional sentimentalism. But Maria is telling her daughter that her misery is not random, unique or exclusively personal, but rather that it falls systematically on the shoulders of women because of the 'constitution of society'.

Something else about Maria's statement of misery endows her words with a political significance that was rare before a woman's movement was available to foster gender-based political consciousness among women. It is 'only such a mother, who will dare to break through all restraint to provide for your happiness – who will voluntarily brave censure herself, to ward off sorrow from your bosom'. Maria will defy the restraints placed on her by law and social convention due to her sex, and despite the punishments she knows she must receive because she hopes to relieve the burdens on the younger woman. Maria knows the limits of the counsel. Mere individual enlightenment is insufficient because the 'state of society' will not have changed. And further, she *will not* tell her how to live. But the 'exercise' of the daughter's mind with respect to these restraints may give her the strength to make her own choices.

The narrator of the *Wrongs of Woman* did not play the role of authoritative reasoner as she did in the *Rights of Woman*; in the former she took the part of a woman speaking with love to her daughter. Nevertheless, Wollstonecraft instructed her readers to understand this story 'as (rather) of woman, than of an individual'.[28] We should not take the letter from mother to daughter at face value. Wollstonecraft seemed to be reaching towards the means to a shared political consciousness with her female readers. As Maria and Jemima, women from different classes, share their personal stories, they begin to realize that the sources of and possibly the solutions to their problems are not individual and personal. Perhaps the same might happen if Maria had a chance to share with her daughter the personal narrative that is, in truth, their shared story.

I emphasize that Wollstonecraft appeared *in the process* of finding the means to the leap from personal narrative to political consciousness. She was, literally, not in the position of the informed narrator unfolding an already known story. We, on the other hand, are readers informed by the passage of two centuries of feminist history since Wollstonecraft struggled with her manuscript. In the nineteenth century, and even more in the late twentieth century, one of the most powerful means by which feminism as ideology and practice developed was through the process of women sharing their common personal stories. In the late 1960s this process was adopted and refined as a political strategy and given a name – consciousness-raising – but the process was not invented whole. It evolved out of the personal conversations among female friends and kin that, in particular historical contexts, became political. In Wollstonecraft's writing we see the glimmerings of the idea of a political practice that later became instrumental in the development of feminist politics.

134 *Virginia Sapiro*

It would probably make sense to Wollstonecraft that discussion of 'private' pains within a particular oppressed social group could lead to a special form of enlightenment: realization of the underlying principles that unify social and individual human life to foster or inhibit the development of virtue. What Wollstonecraft did not seem to imagine was how this enlightenment might be translated into political action. But then, of the women who eventually conceived of a gender-based political movement, only a couple were even born during Wollstonecraft's lifetime, and they were still babies when she died.

In her last manuscript the text suggests that Wollstonecraft did indeed feel 'bastilled'. The development of her political and social ideas was closing her in, driving a wall between her own beliefs and the era of light. She had not yet found a way out of this story, just as she was not sure of a way out of the story of despotism and the Terror or, indeed, the story of her own life. We can learn from that. Political theory, including especially democratic feminist theory is not written in hindsight. By definition, if one is willing at all to accept any terms of enlightenment, it is done partly in the dark.

NOTES

1 This discussion is drawn substantially from my book, *A Vindication of Political Virtue: The Political Theory of Mary Wollstonecraft*, Chicago, University of Chicago Press, 1992. I refer the reader there for elaboration of the argument and more extensive documentation.

2 One of the most useful and intelligent examples of this approach is found in A. Jaggar, *Feminist Politics and Human Nature*, Ottowa, NJ, Rowman and Allanheld, 1983.

3 Sapiro, *A Vindication of Political Virtue*, chap. 8.

4 In contrast, there is an extensive literature of literary criticism of Wollstonecraft. See the Bibliography in Sapiro, *A Vindication of Political Virtue*. One – perhaps too personalized – indication of the undervaluing of Wollstonecraft as a political thinker in feminist circles is that *A Vindication of Political Virtue*, the first full-length work devoted entirely to the subject of Wollstonecraft's work specifically as feminist political theory, published in 1992 by a major scholarly publisher, was never (at least through spring 1996) reviewed by a single journal or periodical that identified itself as 'feminist'.

5 K. Offen, 'Defining feminism: a comparative historical approach', *Signs*, 1988, 14, pp. 119–57.

6 N. F. Cott, *The Grounding of Modern Feminism*, New Haven, Yale University Press, 1987, p. 3.

7 Here I use the term 'rights' in an ordinary generic way, not as a juridical term.

8 Mary Astell (1668–1731) was a British writer best known for *A Serious Proposal to the Ladies for the Advancement of their True and Greatest Interest*. Christine de Pisan (*c.* 1364–*c.* 1430) is best known for *The Book of the City of Ladies*.

9 Charlotte Perkins Gilman (1868–1935) was an American feminist writer whose best-known works include *Women and Economics* (1898), *The Man-Made World: Our Androcentric Culture* (1911) and *Herland* (1915). Anna Julia Cooper was an African American writer and educator whose best-known work was *A*

A language of enlightenment and virtue   135

Voice from the South (1892). Ellen Key (1849–1926) was a Swedish social feminist who wrote and lectured widely on feminist subjects.

10 One of the best works on this group is I. Kramnick, *Republicanism and Bourgeois Radicalism: Political Ideology in Late Eighteenth-Century England and America*, Ithaca, Cornell University Press, 1990.

11 The most relevant works would be Hartley's *Observations on Man, his Frame, his Duty, and his Expectations* (1749) and Helvétius' *De l'esprit* (1758). Both of these were extremely influential. In 1775 Joseph Priestley published *Hartley's Theory of the Human Mind, on the Principle of the Association of Ideas*, an abridgement of Hartley's earlier work. Elie Halévy claims this is the work that made Hartley so popular among the moral scientists; see Halévy, *The Growth of Philosophic Radicalism*, Boston, Beacon, 1955, p. 8.

12 This work has been reprinted in many editions. It, along with almost all of Wollstonecraft's other known writings except her correspondence, can be found in J. Todd and M. Butler (eds), *The Works of Mary Wollstonecraft*, London, Pickering, 1989.

13 M. Wollstonecraft, *A Vindication of the Rights of Woman*, in Todd and Butler, *The Works of Mary Wollstonecraft*, p. 90.

14 M. Wollstonecraft, *An Historical and Moral View of the Origin and Progress of the French Revolution; and the Effect It Has Produced in Europe*, in Todd and Butler, *The Works of Mary Wollstonecraft*, p. 85.

15 Her correspondence can be found in R. M. Wardle (ed.), *Collected Letters of Mary Wollstonecraft*, Ithaca, Cornell University Press, 1979.

16 M. Wollstonecraft, *The Wrongs of Woman*, p. 146.

17 W. Godwin, *Caleb Williams*, New York, Norton, 1977, p. 188.

18 W. Godwin, *An Enquiry Concerning Justice*, New York, Penguin, 1976.

19 M. Wollstonecraft, *A Vindication of the Rights of Woman*, in Todd and Butler, *The Works of Mary Wollstonecraft*, p. 68.

20 *Ibid.*, p. 265.

21 In *A Vindication of the Rights of Men*, in Todd and Butler, *The Works of Mary Wollstonecraft*, p. 11, she wrote that *reason* and *conscience* are synonymous.

22 M. Wollstonecraft, *A Vindication of the Rights of Woman*, in Todd and Butler, *The Works of Mary Wollstonecraft*, p. 103.

23 *Ibid.*, p. 75.

24 *Ibid.*, p. 76.

25 On this point, see M. Poovey, *The Proper Lady and the Woman Writer: Ideology as Style in the Works of Mary Wollstonecraft, Mary Shelley, and Jane Austen*, Chicago, University of Chicago Press, 1984.

26 *Ibid.*, p. 175.

27 M. Wollstonecraft, *The Wrongs of Woman*, in Butler and Todd, *The Works of Mary Wollstonecraft*, p. 22.

28 *Ibid.*, p. 83.

8 French utopians
The word and the act

Claire G. Moses

This chapter identifies utopian feminism as a distinctive period within the history of feminism. Utopians were most influential from the late 1820s to the repression that ended the European revolutions of 1848. They did not, however, call themselves 'utopians'; that was Marx's term for them and is explained less by their other-worldliness than by Marx's determination to gain political advantage by deriding his competitors. The groups themselves either identified by their leaders' names (Saint-Simonians, Fourierists, Cabetians, Owenites, for example) or used the new word 'socialist', invented at this time, to distinguish their programme from that of the late eighteenth-century Revolutionaries.

Their concern, they patiently explained, was 'social' rather than 'individual'. Their attention consequently shifted away from the kind of individual rights of citizenship including political rights that had concerned late eighteenth-century Revolutionaries, to new ways of organizing enduring social networks, intimacy, sexuality and reproduction, as well as production. Their social change strategy was to create alternative communities intended not only to collectivize households and the workplace, but also to provide a peaceful means for change that would present a distinct contrast to the more violent Revolutionary ethos. The New World would be constructed alongside the Old, and people – merely by observing the far preferable utopian life – would be won over to join with socialists in replicating these alternative communities.

In France, the most visible of these early socialists were the Saint-Simonians.[1] Organized somewhat on the model of a religious community, they appropriated the language and symbols of the Catholic Church and the bourgeois family, although their 'doctrine' (in Saint-Simonian terminology) challenged both. Prosper Enfantin and Saint-Amand Bazard were the Fathers of the Church. Then, after a schism, in November 1831, Enfantin alone bore the title of Pope; an empty seat alongside him signified the awaited female messiah who would rule one day as 'Pop-esse'. Until 1833, the inner circle of Saint-Simonians lived collectively in several *maisons de famille* and pooled their financial resources. Income needs were covered by contributions. Meals were collectively prepared and served for an even larger group of adherents.

French Utopians 137

Saint-Simonians were enormously popular, not only in France but also throughout Europe, and in Egypt and the Americas. Were one to conclude from a description of the group's activities that they were simply one sect among the many new religions of the early nineteenth century, one would miss the broad reach of their message, beyond their adherents, and erroneously underestimate the impact of their thinking on the future of feminism and socialism.[2]

One explanation for their popularity, especially among workers, was the failure of liberals and republicans to address workers' interests. The Revolution in France in 1830, for example, had brought to attention issues such as the appropriate size and basis for the electorate and the proper relationship of the legislature to the king. But these issues were of little concern to the artisans and skilled workers whose role on the barricades had forced Charles X's abdication. In their frustration workers turned away from the dry rationalism of republicans to the Saint-Simonians who blended Romantic rhetoric, in their emphasis on sentiment and physical beauty, with a vision for a new social and economic order. A peaceful relationship between the sexes, the classes and the nations would replace social conflict; inheritance of wealth would be abolished; and property would be held only as a public trust rather than an individual right, implying that the property of owners who did not place the means of production at workers' disposal would be confiscated.

The popularity of the Saint-Simonians lay also in their mastery of propaganda. They published several newspapers and distributed, often at no charge, numerous pamphlets plus the more weighty two-volume *Exposition of the Doctrine of Saint-Simon*. Oral propaganda was also important, especially in reaching the working classes at a time when illiteracy was still widespread. In Paris, in the early 1830s, Saint-Simonians were holding nine meetings a week in large, public lecture halls to present their ideas on the economy, religion, the arts and science, and on the emancipation of workers and women. They organized 'missions' to spread the doctrine to French cities beyond Paris. Outside France, their most successful missions were to Germany, Belgium and England (where their feminism was avidly covered in the Owenite press and applauded by the youthful John Stuart Mill). At the height of their popularity, crowds in the indoor lecture halls usually numbered in the hundreds and, outdoors, in the thousands. In 1831, letters from readers to their daily newspaper ran at more than a thousand a month.[3]

In Paris, Saint-Simonians also organized special teaching programmes, cooperative workshops (one for tailors and one for seamstresses), and a health programme for workers (led by one pharmacist and one doctor for each of the working-class neighbourhoods). Once a week, a Saint-Simonian lecture was delivered in Italian to reach immigrant workers.

138   *Claire G. Moses*

FEMINISM

The feminism of the Saint-Simonians was integral to their pacifism and to their economic programme. They viewed sexual equality as a natural consequence of their project to reorganize the globe by replacing the rule of 'brute force' with the rule of so-called spiritual powers. Women, who represented peace and love in their cosmology, would share leadership with men in the 'new age'. At first, early in the movement's history, the more rationalist elements of their theory on social and economic justice were emphasized, but when in the late 1820s Saint-Simonians began to emphasize more Romantic elements, and especially to develop their ideas for a 'new Religion' based on love, woman and the socio-sexual relationship between the sexes became the movement's central concern. This is the moment when social and economic equality – most generally – were linked to the equality of the sexes and to sexual liberation. This is the moment of greatest interest to us as historians of feminism.

It is the women among the French utopians who have attracted my attention.[4] In part, this may be due to the joy of discovery. When I first began my studies of the history of French feminism, I began with later, republican feminists who organized a liberal movement in the late 1860s. In so doing, I was following the lead of Simone de Beauvoir, who, in the *Second Sex*, identified 1869 as the beginning of French feminism and Léon Richer – whose name, by the way, she gets wrong – as the 'true founder'. Beauvoir's knowledge of feminism's history was sketchy, to say the least, although she did seem to know the names of at least a few earlier feminists – Christine de Pizan, Poulain de la Barre, Condorcet. Among the utopians, she identified Charles Fourier and the Saint-Simonian group, but called them 'unreasonable'.[5] Other sources, especially the several histories by Léon Abensour in the 1910s and 1920s, provided more information about the French utopians and were certainly more appreciative, but limited their attention to the theoretical work of the celebrated leadership of these groups – all men.[6] No one seemed interested in exploring the theoretical works published by the women – yet their materials were readily available in the same archival collections that Beauvoir and Abensour must have consulted for their work.

When I came upon the works of the women among the utopians, I was dazzled; and my fascination with them continued long beyond the first excitement of discovery. In large measure this was due to my identification with their life experiences and political practice. In turning our attention now to the women, I will be arguing that they are our forbears and that their rediscovery and placement in our history of feminist discourses is crucial to our understanding of the past. I will not, however, ignore the more famous men; understanding their contribution is necessary for contextualizing the women's history. I do hope to make clear, however, that there is good reason to give prominence to the less well-known women; it is in their work and

French Utopians 139

experiences that we recognize ourselves. It is they who grappled with issues that concern us still.

The first women to hold positions of influence in Saint-Simonianism were relatives – spouses, sisters, cousins – or close family friends of the male leaders. They were young (the oldest among them were only in their early thirties; most were in their twenties), and bourgeois in background, values and education, although none were high society. Within the movement, they served in the various degrees of the hierarchy and as co-directors for the practical activities; they wrote propaganda for the Saint-Simonian newspapers and pamphlets, corresponded with potential women recruits and hosted the soirées where new ideas were discussed. Evidently their propaganda and other outreach efforts were quite successful; at the height of Saint-Simonian activism, it is estimated that about half of the total audiences (400–500) of the almost daily lectures were women.[7]

Among the new recruits were many working-class women. In late 1832, after the movement ran into trouble with the police and split apart in disagreements over the issue of a new sexual morality, the Saint-Simonians' intricate hierarchical organization was dissolved. Although this was devastating to the movement, it was liberating for these working-class women who had not been part of the movement's hierarchy in any case. They began to hold their own meetings to discuss doctrinal issues and then launched a newspaper, which was first titled *La Femme libre*, but then was retitled several times – *Apostolat des femmes, Femme nouvelle* – before taking the title that I use, the *Tribune des femmes*. They did not, at first, consider themselves a breakaway group of dissidents. Their work, they maintained, was in response to the movement's 'call to women' to speak out on the question of the relationship between the sexes and they called themselves 'apostles', the name reserved for Saint-Simonians who devoted themselves to the cause. But in appropriating the men's emancipatory vision for their own needs, they transformed it.

A study of these working-class Saint-Simoniennes changes our understandings about the past of feminism in several significant ways. First, in tracing the origins of feminism to the organized liberal movements of the later nineteenth century, as used to be our practice, we had constructed a history of feminism that appeared to develop in a straight, evolutionary line, beginning with nineteenth-century movements, theories and strategies of seemingly narrow scope, and enlarging over time until the present when the concerns of feminism are seen to involve all aspects of human existence. But in shifting the focus of the origins of contemporary feminism to an earlier period, our sense of a linear progression is jarred and another striking pattern is revealed. The Saint-Simonian feminists of the 1830s have little in common with the liberal feminists of the late nineteenth and early twentieth centuries, but they do bear some remarkable similarities to contemporary radical feminists. Like their descendants, they were sexual radicals who analysed the repression of women's bodies as structurally fundamental to a

140   *Claire G. Moses*

system of social and economic oppression. And also like their descendants, they chose as a strategy of liberation the development of a separate women's cultural movement and, in particular, a feminine practice of the written word. One of these Saint-Simonian writers, Claire Démar, called this a 'parole de femme' ('word of woman'), a term that was resurrected in the 1970s.[8] In the first issue of their newspaper, the *Tribune des femmes*, it was announced that the journal would 'publish articles only by women'. Theirs was likely the first consciously separatist women's liberation movement in history.

A second way that knowledge of the Saint-Simonian women changes the historical narrative of feminism is through their socio-economic class. It is usually assumed that the origins of feminism lie in middle-class aspirations, but these Saint-Simonian women were working class, embroiderers and seamstresses mostly. Their coming to political consciousness was spurred not simply by the recognition that men's theorizing failed to explain their situation as women, but also by the recognition that the middle-class Saint-Simonian leaders – both male and female – had failed them as women workers. True, Saint-Simonian doctrine had addressed the concerns of workers as well as the concerns of women, but in the doctrinal view workers were men only: men's situation required a 'science of society', or class analysis, and a restructuring of the system of production. The doctrinal view that men – not women – were workers reflected *bourgeois* values; in contrast, the French working class – male and female alike – continued, in the 1830s and 1840s, to assume that women worked, and were even identifying women by their work.[9] But for the bourgeois Saint-Simonian leaders, women *qua* women had no class interest. Women's concerns were unified; their liberation required a restructured sexual morality. In the new world order, women would be empowered morally, raised up from the damnation of original sin by a theory that we today would call 'free love', but the problem of their dependency on men was not addressed. Men workers were promised that the productive investment of wealth that would spur industrial growth would provide them with sufficient work at sufficient wages to lift them out of poverty; the problem of women's poverty was ignored. The abolition of inheritance would provide men workers with the opportunity to enter the 'directing classes'; opportunities for women in the new order were undefined. Thus, working-class Saint-Simonian women were left in a position of double jeopardy: as women, they were still dependent on men, and as workers they were disempowered even within the Saint-Simonian new world order.

Saint-Simonian working-class women who had come together initially to address the sexual question, as called upon by the Saint-Simonians, soon recognized that they could not separate this question from what they called the material question. They turned at this point to the Fourierists for inspiration, for Fourierists, in the 1830s, linked women's liberation to productive work. But these working-class women surpassed both Saint-Simonians and

French Utopians 141

Fourierists; they alone linked women's liberation to sexual expression, family restructuring *and* work.[10]

In bringing attention to these women's reconfiguring of Saint-Simonianism by integrating their needs and interests as workers into the doctrine, one need not play down the importance of sexual issues. In fact, the sexual aspect of the working-class Saint-Simoniennes' views is rightly stressed, for it further demonstrates their significance for a rewriting of the history of feminism. It is usually assumed that when working-class women joined feminism – which is commonly but wrongly assumed to be much later than the 1830s – they limited themselves to issues of economic justice without concerning themselves with issues of sexuality. But the Saint-Simoniennes show us, on the contrary, a class-conscious, working-class feminism that predates middle-class feminism *and* that gives sexuality an integral role in their politics.[11] They identified the nuclear, privatized family as the source of sexual as well as economic oppression, and claimed the right to create other kinds of personal ties. Sex outside marriage, most certainly, but also motherhood outside marriage were claimed as alternatives. They denounced patronyms – 'we must not take men's names', they wrote – and they denounced paternity. Claire Démar even denounced 'maternity', by which she meant the institution of motherhood, in Adrienne Rich's sense of the term 'institution'.

Sexuality is perhaps the most compelling aspect of their theorizing and their practice; one reads their published writings and their private letters on this subject with intense interest. Significantly, their published writings suggest a freer, more liberated sexuality than their private writings, which, in contrast, convey an experience of sexual alienation. And even though they were more consciously woman-centred than any other feminist group prior to the 1970s, they do not seem to have considered the possibility of women loving women. Yet, other French women in this same decade did. Flora Tristan, for example, who came to know these women in the late 1830s, writes very explicitly and positively about her erotic attraction to one particular woman and about erotic relationships between women more generally in her private letters.[12] Their views on sexual morals were breathtakingly radical as was their recognition that women's sexual repression figured in women's oppression, but the language to express and probably to experience sexual pleasure was wanting.

In describing the Saint-Simoniennes' views on women as workers, on sexuality and on family structure, one underscores yet another way that our recovery of the working-class Saint-Simoniennes' history rewrites conventional histories of feminism: their role in initiating a radically socialist feminism. This challenges the older view of tracing the origins of socialist feminism to Engels' *Origins of the Family, Private Property, and the State*. Many of the Saint-Simonian women's writings, such as Claire Démar's *My Law of the Future* and certain articles in the *Tribune des femmes*, already – fifty years earlier than Engels' treatise – contain the most valuable elements

142   *Claire G. Moses*

of Engels' theory, while remaining free of the elements we now consider outdated. The feminists of the 1830s analysed the relation between private property inheritance, the patriarchal nuclear family, and women's oppression, but without Engels' mechanical stages or his dubious anthropology. Moreover, their theory goes further than Engels' later version, in that it not only advocates an end to the nuclear family and to dominance by the father, but also brings into this interrelated complex of factors women's sexual repression, analysing its role in women's oppression in general.

Moreover, in taking the Saint-Simonians into account, we are forced to change our understanding of the connection between nineteenth-century French feminism and religion. Recall that historians such as Barbara Berg, Ellen DuBois and Nancy Hewitt, who have looked at nineteenth-century American feminism, especially up to about the immediate post-Civil War period, and historians of British feminism, such as Jane Rendall, Barbara Taylor and Sally Alexander, have all granted a significant role to religion in inspiring feminism.[13] But one usually associates French feminism – at least the feminist movement of the second half of the nineteenth century – with secularism in general and anti-clericalism in particular. Saint-Simonian feminists, however, were deeply committed to a politics that was religious. True, they created a 'new religion' that was to challenge traditional Christian theology and the organized Catholic Church, but they called themselves 'apostles' and linked their ideology to theology. Their Saint-Simonian 'Church' was to be headed by a couple-pope, they awaited a female messiah, God was 'God, the Father and the Mother'. The words in the subtitle of this chapter, 'The Word and the Act', appear frequently in their writings. Of course, we can read them as 'their writings and their activities' or 'theory and practice', but the point is that they intentionally chose words that would resonate with New Testament rhetoric.

EQUALITY AND 'RADICAL DIFFERENCE'

Finally, there is the question of equality. What did Saint-Simoniennes envisage for this, what were their arguments for equality, who was to be included or excluded? It is a vexing question because their rhetoric extolled women's *difference* from men, and in our writing of feminism's history, the rhetoric of 'difference' has often been opposed to equality. But again, the Saint-Simoniennes' history results in a rewriting of the history of feminism. The rhetoric of 'difference' is unmistakable in their words, not simply emphasizing and valuing difference but also emphasizing and valuing *essential* difference. Throughout Saint-Simonian writings one finds the recurrent image of the male who represents 'reflection' and the female who represents 'sentiment'. Women and men were, by nature, different: men were rational; women were emotional, gentle and poetic. And their differences were essential, linked in their writings to 'nature' or to their biological potential for maternity. As Désirée Veret, one of these Saint-Simoniennes, wrote: 'What

French Utopians 143

[women] have to say is as different as the natures of man and woman are different from each other.'[14] Or elsewhere: 'The banner of women is universal, for are they not all united by the same bond of motherhood?'[15]

When I first examined the feminism of this group, I related their essentialism to the 'newness' of feminism at that time and judged the Saint-Simonians quite conservative. This suited my 'progressive' view of a linear history of feminism (here again I was influenced by Beauvoir's grand narrative). But my judgment related as well to our feminist theorizing in the 1960s to 1970s which had determined that our task was to challenge beliefs that women were innately 'different', 'other', more 'moral' or 'motherly' than men. This was the explanation we crafted to explain nineteenth-century feminists' failure to complete the revolution of women's liberation: because they had rarely challenged the idea of women's essential difference, women were still confined to the domestic sphere.

But judging the Saint-Simonians conservative was not very satisfying. First, their concept of womanhood – however different from manhood – was not a concept of what Barbara Welter called 'True Womanhood'. They celebrated women's maternity, but criticized socially 'real' mothers, especially, one should note, their own. The mother they celebrated was an idealized mother and, unlike their own, an active mother. And their dualisms were used to argue the necessity for a public role for women, never for a separate sphere of activity for them. In the governance of their movement, for example, Saint-Simonians practised what they preached, establishing co-directorships of women and men in all their practical enterprises – the health clinics, cooperative workshops for tailors and seamstresses, and the communal dining halls.

Moreover, Saint-Simonian women, who were generally young, unmarried and self-supporting, aspired to improved work opportunities and a different relationship to their work and employers. They were little interested in – indeed, never mentioned – a domestic role removed from the wage-earning workforce. Instead they challenged traditional domestic relationships as well as capitalist work relationships, proclaiming their right to non-marital sexual relationships and to have children without marrying. They celebrated women's moral force, but never to uphold the repressive bourgeois moral order. Essentialism was instead used to argue for change. Women's sexuality, they maintained, is too diverse for the strict moral codes of men, and since sexuality is essential and therefore unchangeable, it is men's moral codes that must be changed. In other words, the Saint-Simoniennes' 'difference' was different. They were neither individualists nor accepting of the sexual division of labour.[16] They championed equality, but they also argued that only through the association of differentiated sexes would women be able to attain full equality. They argued *for* equality *from* difference.

Some contextualizing will help us to understand their concept of difference. In arguing for equality from difference, the Saint-Simonian women were clearly influenced by Romanticism – especially by Romanticism's

144   *Claire G. Moses*

valuing of difference above sameness, the particular and the unique above the uniform or the universal. 'Feminine' characteristics were valued, even idealized, among Romantics. In Saint-Simonianism, feminine virtues were not simply prized, they were appropriated by the male leaders to buttress their own power.[17] But Saint-Simonian women then used essentialist arguments to recover the feminine even from those men who would appropriate female virtues for a new kind of male dominance. They responded enthusiastically to a theory that promised a recovery of the feminine for women. In writing of God the Mother and Father (not, it should be noted, a sexless or even androgynous God, but rather a God who is composed of two distinct elements), Suzanne Voilquin exclaimed:

> [Woman] is no longer drawn from a rib of man; she no longer is confounded with his glory; she descends, like him, directly from *her* God, father and mother of all men and all women. . . . In the future, she will find her own place; she will have her own life; she will no longer, like in the past, be merged into an other's existence.

The Saint-Simoniennes responded enthusiastically to a discourse that held out the promise of empowerment: 'Woman, discovering her model and guide in *her* God, can now develop *active* virtues; no longer will she be reduced to a passive role as was the ideal of Christian perfection.'[18]

The discourse of Saint-Simonian class analysis was also influential. Borrowing from Romanticism, it too valued the particular over the universal. Saint-Simonian women, who were immersed in the discourse of class analysis, not surprisingly came to recognize its applicability to the situation of women. In their view, women's interests, like workers' interests, were particular rather than universal. Indeed, women's interests could conflict with men's, like workers' interests conflicted with employers'. It was this discourse of difference, then, that supported the development of the first consciously autonomous women's movement, and the first practical attempts at consciousness-raising and theory building on the basis of some distinctive 'women's experience'.

RADICAL 'DIFFERENCE' AND THE FAMILY

Their theorizing on the family exemplifies the originality of their views. At this time, in France, views on the family were at the very centre of political debates – in part, but only in part – because the legislature was debating a variety of divorce bills. From the monarchist Right (Joseph de Maistre and Louis Bonald) to the anarchist Left (Charles Fourier), and including any republican or communitarian in between, everyone had a family reform politics. At first the working-class Saint-Simonian women applauded the most radical of the various competing views – those which had been formulated by Prosper Enfantin. Enfantin's intention was to redirect the family debates and to focus them on love and sexual unions rather than on economic

French Utopians 145

interest and marital unions. He had come to focus on sexuality in the course of developing his 'new religion'. Fundamental to this was a metaphysical innovation – the denunciation of the traditional Christian separation of spirit and matter. For Saint-Simon, the 'rehabilitation' of the material world, denigrated by the 'old' Christianity, had involved a re-evaluation of work and workers, and even, as one recent historian puts it, of 'machines, canals, factories, banks'.[19] For Enfantin, however, this new doctrine also involved a re-evaluation of the physical expression of love and a rejection of the Christian concept of original sin – changes that the Saint-Simonians connected in turn to the re-evaluation and ultimately the emancipation of women.

Saint-Simonians did not reject the traditional view that women are quintessentially temptresses. But what Enfantin did was to regard this image of women in a new light – in effect turning it upside down – by elevating sexual passion to a virtue. In a 'teaching' to the Saint-Simonians, Enfantin set forth a new morality for the new Christianity. The realities of human affections, he declared, required three different but equally valid moral codes: 1) that of the so-called constants; 2) that of the 'mobiles'; 3) the synthesizing love of a couple-pope, who would combine 'unity and variety'. Their special charge was to harmonize all social relations by 'rekindling the numbed feelings' of the constants and moderating the 'unruly appetites' of the mobiles.[20]

In plain language, it seems that what Enfantin had in mind was simply monogamous, lifelong marriage for some and divorce and remarriage for others – hardly a shocking proposition, even in nineteenth-century France. The radical aspect was in the role he envisaged for the couple-pope. This couple would form one lifelong union with each other but also experience variety in their sexual partners. The example of their enduring relationship would teach constancy to those among the 'mobiles' who might otherwise become dissolute. But they would also teach the joys of sexual pleasure to the 'constants', both by their example and by their willingness to have sexual relations with these 'constants'. Moreover, certain ambiguous statements left unclear whether the so-called synthesizing love would be possible only for one couple-pope or for an indefinite number of priests and priestesses.

The Saint-Simonian women readily agreed with Enfantin that the connection between economic interests and marital unions should be ruptured and that love alone should be the basis for forming personal unions. And they seemed more than willing to consider the pleasures of the erotic. But in focussing on their situation as women, they had to deal with circumstances that mattered little to the men. They alone risked social ostracism for practising a new morality, for example. The tight community the Saint-Simonians built could have shielded women from this; but it was not, unfortunately, long-lasting. By 1833, the *maisons de famille* had been closed. Worse, it seems that the Saint-Simonian sexual radicals could not even count on the support of other Saint-Simonians. In their private correspondence,

146   *Claire G. Moses*

there is much evidence that many felt injured by the disapproval of their friends and colleagues.[21]

Their experience as women also made it harder for them to pursue sexual pleasure as an end in itself. Birth control and 'family planning' were widespread in France, already in the 1830s, but these practices were still controlled by men. The most common forms of 'contraception' were coitus interruptus or abstinence. Abortion, it is thought, became common only at the end of the century, and among women of the working class the pessary was still unknown.[22] To lessen the probability that they would become pregnant, then, they would have to persuade their male partners to accede to their wishes. Statistics on fertility rates for single and married women suggest that men were most likely to acquiesce in the use of contraception within marriage. Single women, like these Saint-Simoniennes, were thus more likely to have unplanned pregnancies. From their correspondence, it is clear that they felt disempowered in sexual relationships: many had experienced coerced sex, and all seemed to assume that sex was inevitably linked to reproduction.[23] In their private correspondence, which is amazingly frank, I have found only one mention of birth control.

Within their autonomous movement, the Saint-Simoniennes took the family and sexuality debates in new directions. Pauline Roland proposed that the family should be based on 'the mother *alone*'.[24] Reine Guindorf, following Fourierist views, proposed collectivized households.[25] Claire Démar proposed that women should head households and men raise children: 'I truly have faith that the Saint-Simonian Religion will have power only when these two points are accepted by the Family.'[26]

And in contrast with the men's theorizing, the women connected sexual liberation to their demands for economic (they said 'material') autonomy. In time – certainly by 1848 – these same women began to sound less radical in their ideas about sexuality. It is interesting to follow the trajectory of their views through nearly two decades of sexual/political practice. Sexual liberation – at first at the centre of their politics – eventually ceased to be a priority. The stigma attached to free love for women was too severe, birth control was still too unreliable, the possibility for women's sexual pleasure was still too commonly limited by bodily injury incurred in childbirth or from venereal disease, and women's ability to support themselves was still too fragile to sustain their sexual radicalism.

The exploration of sexuality is but one example of the new directions their theorizing from difference took them. There are others. For example, the women, in organizing their own movement, developed a model quite different from the highly structured and very hierarchical Saint-Simonian movement. Unlike the religious structure, with popes and a hierarchy, first and second degrees, a dogma and a doctrine, Saint-Simoniennes worked collectively. Over and over, they repeated that all views that women held must be valued, and they practised this tolerance by publishing articles that were highly critical of their own statements or of Saint-Simonianism gener-

French Utopians 147

ally. Also, while the Saint-Simonian Church waited for the female messiah and some Saint-Simonian men set off to the East (Turkey, then Palestine) to search for her, the women determined that the female messiah was

> not one woman; she is all women. . . . We must take care not to fall into the trap that has ensnared men and which they lay for us in turn. – NO! – They will not find the ideal they seek so long as their narrow view does not expand to see it in all women.[27]

In time, their focus on their difference led to a kind of declaration of independence from all men's movements: 'Women alone shall say what freedom they want. . . . Men have advised, directed, and dominated us long enough. It is now up to us to advance along the path of progress without tutelage.'[28]

CONCLUSION

In coming to appreciate the Saint-Simonians and their discourse of 'difference', however, we should not simply turn the traditional historical narrative of feminism on its head. Gender neutral discourses have also served liberatory purposes, while arguments from 'difference' were adopted by rather conservative feminists later in the nineteenth century. The gender neutral discourse has been useful, especially in arguing for the rights of citizenship. To French Revolutionary feminists in the late eighteenth century and liberal republican feminists around the world in the late nineteenth and early twentieth centuries, women's exclusion from new regimes based on universally applicable laws was untenable once the rule of law replaced that of an arbitrary ruler, and once reason replaced superstition. But if a gender neutral discourse was useful in arguing for the rule of law, it was inadequate for the task of reordering relationships of production between workers and capitalists, or of reordering the sexual relationship between women and men. For this, it was necessary to pull apart the components of relationships and to identify the particularities of class and sex.

Conservative 'difference' feminists, in proclaiming an essential unity of women, often overlooked the differences among women. In arguing for their kind of 'couple-centred' feminism – the bourgeois couple – they were accepting the sexual division of labour. How unlike the working-class Saint-Simoniennes who, even while proclaiming the unity of women, were exploring and analysing the differences among women that related to class and sexual desires.

Feminists have constructed their arguments deploying both kinds of analysis – that which we call 'equality' and that which we call 'difference' – to achieve far-reaching goals. The Saint-Simonian experience, however, suggests the usefulness of a new kind of analysis that challenges the separate spheres doctrine, the sexual division of labour and even nuclear families. Their discourse permits us to imagine a feminism that affirms women's difference (whether based on biology, psychic development or social and

148   *Claire G. Moses*

historical experience) *and* women's autonomy in more subtle and nuanced ways. Indeed, it permits us to imagine a feminism that more successfully advances women's autonomy *because* it addresses women's difference. It models a feminism that recognizes, even values, sexual difference, and allows us to challenge heterosexism, racism and class inequality as well.

NOTES

1 See R. B. Carlisle, *The Proffered Crown: Saint-Simonianism and the Doctrine of Hope*, Baltimore, Johns Hopkins University Press, 1987; S. Charléty, *Essai sur l'histoire du Saint-Simonisme*, Paris, Hachette, 1896; G. Lichtheim, *The Origins of Socialism*, New York, Frederick A. Praeger, 1969; and R. P. Locke, *Music, Musicians, and the Saint-Simonians*, Chicago, University of Chicago Press, 1986.

2 See F. Manuel, *The Prophets of Paris*, New York, Harper and Row, 1962, p. 153: 'even in death Saint-Simonianism remained one of the most potent emotional and intellectual influences in nineteenth-century society, inchoate, diffuse, but always there, penetrating into the most improbable places'.

3 The Bibliothèque de l'Arsenal in Paris has an extraordinarily rich collection of materials on the Saint-Simonians. Upon the death of Enfantin, the Saint-Simonian archives – carefully collected, recopied, annotated and catalogued by Enfantin, Fournel, Dufour, Laurent and Guéroult – were donated to the Arsenal. This Fonds Enfantin includes many cartons of personal correspondence, sermons and other propaganda, such as the 'enseignements' and all of their newspapers. See in particular the carton 'Correspondance du *Globe* (Dames) – 112 letters from women describing their conversion to Saint-Simonianism'.

4 See C. G. Moses, *French Feminism in the Nineteenth Century*, Albany, State University of New York Press, 1984; and C. G. Moses and L. W. Rabine, *Feminism, Socialism, and French Romanticism*, Bloomington and Indianapolis, Indiana University Press, 1993.

5 S. de Beauvoir, *The Second Sex*, translated and edited by H. M. Parshley, New York, Bantam, 1953, p. 113. Beauvoir identifies the women's newspaper *La Femme nouvelle*, but erroneously identifies Claire Bazard as the editor; her comments about its contents – she states it focussed solely on improving women's education – leave no doubt that she never actually consulted the newspaper.

6 L. Abensour, *Le Féminisme sous le règne de Louis Philippe et en 1848*, Paris, Plon–Nourrit et Cie, 1913; *Histoire générale du féminisme*, Paris, Librairie Delagrave, 1921; *Le Problème féministe*, Paris, Aux Editions Radot, 1927.

7 For the number of women, see Enfantin to Fournel, 26 October 1830, Fonds Enfantin 7644, 'Archives', 2:33:4. See Charléty (*Essai sur l'histoire du Saint-Simonisme*, p. 115) for his estimate that at this time Saint-Simonian audiences were usually between 400 and 500 persons.

8 Claire Démar, *Ma Loi d'avenir*, Paris, Au Bureau de la *Tribune des femmes*, 1834. The entire text of *Ma Loi d'avenir* is translated in Moses and Rabine, *Feminism, Socialism, and French Romanticism*, pp. 178–203.

9 J. A. DeGroat, 'Women's work identity: female labor in the transitional manufacturing economy of July monarchy Paris', paper presented at the 38th Annual Meeting of the Society for French Historical Studies, El Paso, Texas, March 1992; J. Scott, *Gender and the Politics of History*, New York, Columbia University Press, 1988, p. 107.

10 For the feminism of the Fourierists, see Moses, *French Feminism in the*

French Utopians 149

Nineteenth Century, pp. 90–8. Fourierists emphasized productive work and played down the importance of sexual liberation, in marked contrast to the earlier writings of their founder, Charles Fourier. Fourier's classic feminist text, originally published in 1809, is *Théorie des quatre mouvements et des destinées générales: Prospectus et annonce de la découverte*, reprint, Paris, Jean-Jacques Pauvert, 1967.

11 The same is true for subjectivity, writing, and culture – the other supposedly middle-class concerns. See L. W. Rabine, 'Feminist texts and feminine subjects', in Moses and Rabine, *Feminism, Socialism, and French Romanticism*, pp. 85–144.

12 Flora Tristan to Olympe Chodzko, London, 1 August 1839, reprinted in *Flora Tristan: Lettres*, S. Michaud (ed.), Paris, Seuil, 1980, pp. 104–5.

13 B. J. Berg, *The Remembered Gate: Origins of American Feminism: The Women and the City*, New York, Oxford University Press, 1978; E. C. DuBois, *Feminism and Suffrage: The Emergence of an Independent Women's Movement in America, 1848–1869*, Ithaca, Cornell University Press, 1978; N. Hewitt, *Women's Activism and Social Change: Rochester, New York, 1822–1872*, Ithaca, Cornell University Press, 1984; J. Rendall, *The Origins of Modern Feminism: Women in Britain, France, and the United States, 1780–1860*, London, Macmillan, 1985; B. Taylor, *Eve and the New Jerusalem: Socialism and Feminism in the Nineteenth Century*, New York, Pantheon, 1983; and J. Scott, 'Women in 'The Making of the English Working Class', in *Gender and the Politics of History*, pp. 75–9.

14 J. Désirée [Veret] to the Father, 20 October 1832, 'Archives', 4:388 verso, Fonds Enfantin 7646.

15 *Tribune des femmes*, 1, p. 39.

16 This is Karen Offen's term for feminists who used gender-neutral arguments. See K. Offen, 'Defining Feminism: A Comparative Historical Approach', *Signs*, 1988, 14, pp. 119–57.

17 See L. Rabine, 'Essentialism and its contexts: Saint-Simonian and post-structuralist feminists', *Differences*, 1989, 1, pp. 105–23. See also A. Richardson, 'Romanticism and the colonization of the feminine', in A. K. Mellor (ed.), *Romanticism and Feminism*, Bloomington, Indiana University Press, 1988, pp. 13–25.

18 Both quotes from *Tribune des femmes*, 1, pp. 222–3.

19 See Carlisle, *The Proffered Crown*, p. 152.

20 Enfantin, 'Enseignements fait par le Père Suprème,' *Réunion générale de la famille: Séances des 19 et 21 novembre 1831*, Paris, Bureau du Globe, 1832.

21 See Moses, *French Feminism*, pp. 76–9.

22 A. McLaren 'Abortion in France: women and the regulation of family size, 1800–1914', *French Historical Studies*, 1978, 10, pp. 461–85.

23 See especially S. Voilquin, *Memories of a Daughter of the People*, translated in Moses and Rabine, *Feminism, Socialism, and French Romaticism*, pp. 156, 159, 160.

24 Pauline Roland to Algaé Saint-Hilaire, 24 June 1834, Fonds Enfantin 7777, no. 29.

25 *Tribune des femmes*, 1, pp. 36–9.

26 Démar to Enfantin, 29 December 1832, 'Archives', 5:518 verso–520, Fonds Enfantin 7647.

27 *Tribune des femmes*, 2, p. 153.

28 *Tribune des femmes*, 1, p. 45.

9 Equality and difference
Utopian feminism in Britain

Ruth Levitas

Contemporary feminist political theory has as a central theme the relationship between equality and difference. These are seen as contradictory for two reasons. First, the dominant liberal problematic sees equality as implying sameness, and therefore as opposed to difference. Second, the practical issues which are being theorized are those of the implementation of 'equal opportunities' in segmented labour markets where men and women compete under plainly unequal conditions, so that there is a practical contradiction between claims for equality and the recognition of the specific needs resulting from the reality of women's lives. Feminists seek a basis on which they can claim treatment which is fair; equality cannot mean sameness where there is a difference of circumstance (women become pregnant, men do not; women have responsibility for childcare which men do not have in the same way or to the same extent). The centrality of 'difference' also derives from the influence of French feminisms, where sexual difference is in various ways seen as the basis of women's identity. Difference is also prioritized in order not to impose the values and concerns of white, western middle-class feminists upon others. Postmodern theorists see the differences among women as sufficient to deconstruct the category 'woman' altogether. Contemporary British theorists seek to resolve the perceived tension between equality and difference by reference to alternative values of justice, fairness and parity.[1] In the 1990s, unlike the 1970s or the 1830s, they rarely challenge the existence of labour markets and capitalist economies, and less and less attention is given to the question of domestic labour.

This chapter addresses the relationship between equality and difference in utopian feminism in Britain between 1820 and 1840, an issue which Moses has explored in relation to the Saint-Simoniennes in France in the same period.[2] I argue that in Britain, although the meaning of 'equality' was wide in scope, there was an assumption of sexual difference leading to a natural sexual division of labour. 'Equality' and 'difference' were not seen as opposed. As Barbara Taylor has observed, this sometimes led to inconsistencies: women were seen as having a special moral mission to perform, although the Owenite 'doctrine of circumstance' implied the social construction of character for both men and women. Taylor argues that there was an

Equality and difference 151

'unresolved tension between the desire to minimise sexual difference and the need to reassert it in women's favour', that this tension was particularly acute in Owenism, and could only be resolved by a doctrine of circumstance which implied the transformation of both masculinity and femininity.[3] I want to argue that although there was an implied critique of masculinity, this could not resolve the tension between equality and difference and that this tension becomes clear because claims to equality are pushed further in utopian feminism than elsewhere. However, residual ideas of difference involved not only a special moral and maternal role for women, but a sexual division of labour in which women's exclusion from paid work was challenged, but men's freedom from domestic labour was not. Squaring this particular circle depended on the abolition of domestic work through associated labour, and the application of technology, the communalization of childcare and the breaking of the wage relation. Rereading key utopian feminist texts in the light of contemporary debates both highlights the specificity of the early arguments, and underlines the liberal assumptions of present-day debates.

Because the consideration of the meanings of equality and difference requires the detailed examination of specific texts, I focus on two main sources, with occasional reference to related material. The first main source is the *Appeal of One Half the Human Race, Women, against the Pretensions of the Other Half, Men, to Retain them in Political and thence in Civil and Domestic Slavery* (hereafter the *Appeal*). The *Appeal* has been described as 'the most important book in the history of the struggle for women's rights to appear between Mary Wollstonecraft's *Rights of Women*, published in 1792, and John Stuart Mill's *The Subjection of Women*, published in 1869'.[4] It appeared under the name of William Thompson in 1825 but is known to be the joint work of Thompson and Anna Wheeler. Thompson (1775–1833) was an Irish landowner whose estate had been reformed after his inheritance in 1814 on principles similar to those of Robert Owen at New Lanark. While Thompson became the principal economist of Owenism, publishing several books, he was also influenced by the Saint-Simonians.[5] Wheeler (1785–1848) was also born into the Irish gentry, and married at fifteen or sixteen to a dissolute teenager whom she left twelve years later, having had six children of whom only two survived. She was active in radical circles in England, Ireland and France from 1812 until the mid-1830s; this included involvement with Saint-Simonians in Caen as early as 1818, and connections with Fourier and with Flora Tristan, as well as activity in the Owenite movement in Britain.[6]

The second source is *The Pioneer* which was published from 1833–4, the first British journal to have a separate woman's page, which Taylor describes as the 'single most important platform for working-class feminist ideas' in Britain in the 1830s, and which was also the main Owenite journal promoting the Grand National Consolidated Trade Union (GNCTU).[7] As with the *Appeal*, there are questions about authorship. While *The Pioneer* contains a range of contributions from women, including some identifiable

152　*Ruth Levitas*

pieces from Frances Morrison writing as 'Bondswoman', it is impossible to assess the extent of her role in the unattributed articles in the woman's pages, or of her influence on some of James Morrison's editorials. If Thompson and Wheeler were unequivocally members of the Irish gentry, the Morrisons were English and working class. Frances (1807–98) was the 'illegitimate daughter of a Surrey land girl', who fell in love at fifteen, more propitiously than Anna Wheeler, when she met James (1802–35), a Birmingham house-painter tramping for work.[8] Prior to editing *The Pioneer*, James Morrison was active in the Operative Builders Union. After his death (from a fall) in 1835, Frances became an Owenite missionary, and later a schoolteacher.[9]

UTOPIAN FEMINISM AND UTOPIAN SOCIALISM

Utopian feminism was part of the wider phenomenon of utopian socialism, the generic term used for the ideas of Saint-Simon, Fourier and Owen, and the movements following them.[10] The designation 'utopian' was not self-ascribed, but imposed by Marx and Engels in 1848, on the grounds that they all espoused voluntaristic rather than materialist models of social change; the utopian socialists did not regard themselves as utopians, since the term was understood by all to imply 'unrealistic', and all regarded themselves as scientists. Moreover, they were not a group, but individuals who disagreed on important issues.[11] But provided that we clearly understand that 'utopian' is used to imply not impracticality, but an orientation to radical social transformation, it is useful to retain the term utopian feminism. The alternative, where Britain is concerned, is to use the term 'Owenite feminism', following Taylor's transformation of previous readings of Owenism by demonstrating the extensive participation of women. While in Britain Owenism was without doubt the most influential force in general terms, where feminism is concerned the three strands of Owenism, Fourierism and Saint-Simonianism are inextricably interwoven. The influence of Fourier is generally underestimated, as is that of the Saint-Simonian movement, and Anna Wheeler herself was an important link between French and British socialism and feminism. Thus the term 'Owenite feminism' is both too restrictive and misleading.

An attack on bourgeois marriage as tantamount to legal prostitution was an element common to all the utopian socialists, as was the pursuit of harmony, community and association. Both Owen and Fourier proposed the collective care of children and the socialization of domestic labour; they regarded single-family households as irrational and wasteful. In Owen's case, this was linked to his belief that character was formed by circumstance, since education was too important to be left to the vagaries of parents. In Fourier's case, it resulted from the quite contrary belief in the fixity of individual personality, determined by an innate mix of the twelve fundamental passions. Fourier believed harmony would be achieved not through ratio-

Equality and difference   153

nality, but through the proper mix of personalities and the resultant forces of 'passionate attraction'. Varied and attractive work was a central element in this – and unattractive work was to be carried out by children, the 'Little Hordes', two-thirds male, who had a natural affinity for dirt. Fourier's scheme was less economically egalitarian than Owen's. It was also more sexually radical. Unlike Owen, Fourier rejected heterosexual monogamy altogether; he was opposed to sexual repression for either men or women, believed sexual variety to be necessary to happiness, and argued that all sexual tastes could be met consensually in a community where the right mix of human types prevailed. Although their challenge to the position of women was extensive and radical, neither Fourier nor Owen clearly rejected the sexual division of labour in relation to the care of very young children, or in relation to domestic labour. Although these were to be socialized, liberating some women for other kinds of work, they remained women's province: it was never suggested that adult men should take responsibility for domestic labour.

How far utopian feminism derived from the views of Owen and Fourier, and how far it was a formative element in their construction, is an open question. The issue of women's legal, civil and economic subordination through marriage was central. Yet because of the close connection between feminism and socialism, the meaning given to the term 'equality' was broad: it went beyond claims for equal opportunities, and political, legal, moral and educational equality to insist on the importance of economic equality. In the following section, we examine some of the facets of equality claimed in the texts under scrutiny.

POLITICAL EQUALITY

The *Appeal* takes the form of a reply to James Mill's *Article on Government* (1820) in which he claimed in a virtual aside that women could be denied political representation 'without inconvenience' because their interests were subsumed under those of their husbands and fathers. The *Appeal* systematically takes this claim apart. The central point in Thompson and Wheeler's reply to Mill is that women should have equality of political representation, since their interests are not adequately – if at all – represented by those of their husbands and fathers (even if they have them). Indeed, women need political rights precisely to protect themselves from abuse by those Mill deems to represent their interests:

all women, and particularly women living with men in marriage and unavoidably controlled by their superior strength, having been reduced, by the want of political rights, to a state of helplessness, slavery, and of consequent unequal enjoyments, pains and privations, they are *more in need* of political rights than any other portion of human beings, to gain some chance of emerging from this state.[12]

154 *Ruth Levitas*

Paradoxically, although the question of political equality necessarily dominates this text, and is argued to be essential, this is not because political equality is consistently prioritized as the most fundamental issue in the *Appeal*; in the end, as we shall see, economic equality is most important.

Taylor argues that Owenite feminists generally supported female suffrage. However, when we turn to the columns of *The Pioneer*, we find that political equality does not, in fact, figure prominently. This reflects the ambiguous relationship between Owenism and Chartism. Many Owenites supported the Charter, but Owenism implied the limited relevance of representation within a system fundamentally flawed and corrupt. James Morrison argued both that 'productive labour must, indispensably, take its seat in the senate', and that there was a danger of being 'mocked . . . with the mere shadow of enfranchisement'.[13] Socialists should not stop demanding the franchise, but this must be secondary to changing wages to a fair share of profits: 'wages is a term of purchase; it means the piecemeal purchase of your blood, and bones, and brains, at weekly payment; it is the present name for *Saturday's market price of man, woman and child*'.[14] Thus, while political equality might be claimed, it was not always the central priority.

MARRIAGE

The *Appeal* starts from the utilitarian claim that women have an equal right to happiness, to the 'command of enjoyments', a right which they are unable to exercise.[15] The central obstacle is marriage, in which

> for the mere faculty of eating, breathing and living, in whatever degree of comfort husbands may think fit, women are reduced to domestic slavery, without will of their own, or power of locomotion, otherwise than as permitted by their respective masters.[16]

With at least as much vehemence as Owen or Fourier, Thompson and Wheeler attack marriage for the legal constraints it imposes upon women and the indefensible powers conferred in law and in practice upon men (including violence against women). The role of public opinion, of ideology, is important too, in conferring actual power beyond what is legally given, especially on fathers over unmarried daughters. But marriage is the main problem:

> Woman is . . . compelled, in marriage, by the possession of superior strength on the part of men, by the want of knowledge, skill and wealth, by the positive, cruel, partial, and cowardly enactments of law, by the terrors of superstition, by the mockery of a pretended vow of obedience, and . . . by the force of an unrelenting, unreasoning, unfeeling, public opinion, to be the literal unequivocal *slave* of the man who may be styled her husband.[17]

At the core of feminist arguments was the necessity to abolish the inequality of the marriage code. This was the central issue for utopian feminists, and the subject of many of their lectures, which drew audiences of hundreds of women throughout the country. Marriage was clearly seen as a market in which women were bought and sold. (James) Morrison, in an editorial addressed to employers who sacked workers for union membership, rails at them that 'your daughters ... are ... bought and sold for money; contracted for like bales of cloth; the deed or instrument a marriage ceremony, which feeds *respectability* with legal prostitutes'.[18] The woman's page says 'Woman is made a hireling; ... she finds a purchaser. She is sent to market like a calf, and appropriated by the highest bidder. She is not equal to her wooer, either in political or pecuniary influence'.[19]

The attack on marriage was an attack on the legal disabilities of married women, on the immorality of marriages contracted or sustained for economic reasons – as being effective prostitution – and indeed on an economic situation which drove large numbers of women into actual prostitution; it was not an attack on heterosexual monogamy. Margaret Reynolds defended Owen's views on marriage in the pages of the *New Moral World*: 'Mr Owen's system, by its certainty of producing abundant wealth and equal distribution, does away with all restraint upon marriage from pecuniary considerations, and does away with all temptation to form marriages from any other motive than affection.' She reiterates his claim that in a rational society, divorce would be rare, since only a few people would fail to make a good initial choice of partner. The general system of education advocated by Owen (which Reynolds claims includes sex education) will reduce promiscuity, especially among the young, by leading them 'to perceive the evils of premature indulgence'. An editorial note adds:

> It is important to note that Mr Owen *will not have his system of marriage and divorce acted upon under the existing state of things*; for he maintains that beings must be much better educated than they now are, before *all* those principles which should lead to virtuous marriages can be excited.[20]

Frances Morrison herself endorsed these views in a lecture in 1838.[21] Some Owenites ignored this advice, and implemented their own 'marriage' ceremonies, just as they introduced alternatives to christening. Others went further, and advocated complete sexual freedom. But, as Anna Wheeler observed in 1833, whatever the theoretical arguments, the practical consequences of flouting convention and acting on the principle of free love could be severe: 'the individuals who attempt to brave the public scorn, or to force it to reverse its decrees, only engage in a struggle which will finally end in the destruction of their happiness, and the injury of their cause'.[22]

SEXUALITY

The *Appeal* is quite clear that 'equality' includes women's equal right to sexual pleasure. Even Owen, though he was more puritanical than Fourier or the Saint-Simonians, argued that celibacy was a crime against human

156 *Ruth Levitas*

nature, and that all human nature was basically good. He contrasted the 'false chastity' of marriage with the 'real chastity' which would result when sexuality could be freely expressed within relationships based on genuine affection. The *Appeal* complains that the pleasures of the senses, primary among which are those of food and sex (pure Fourier, this), are generally deemed immoral in women; this is particularly true of sexual pleasure. The repression of women's sexual desire is repeatedly noted.[23] It is not just that no one will publicly admit women's sexual desire; the way in which male sexuality is socially constructed often forbids women to express sexual pleasure, as well as making it unlikely that they will actually experience it:

> The great bulk of men, however, from the wretched training in which they have been brought up, necessarily pursue mere individual selfish gratification on the very bosom of love, their sexual feelings having nothing of sympathy in them. Nay, some are brutal enough to associate – and to the point of morals too! – antipathy towards their companions who presume to share unreservedly and affectionately in their enjoyments: passive endurance being in their minds the perfection of conduct in their slaves.[24]

The argument for equality therefore includes the 'perspective of intelligence, beneficence, and happiness which would result equally to both sexes from the banishment of sexual morals, sexual laws'.[25]

EDUCATION

If political, legal and sexual equality figure prominently in the claims of the *Appeal*, so too does educational equality. The importance of this is two-fold. First, education and knowledge are seen as important in their own right, as aspects of fully human development, currently denied to women: 'From no class of human pleasures are women in general and wives in particular more systematically excluded.'[26] This leads men to an unwarranted contempt for women's intellectual capacities, and denies women happiness resulting from respect. Second, withholding education also withholds from women the possibility of economic independence.[27] Equality therefore includes the 'establishment of equal education between women and men'.[28]

Education is a key theme in the columns of *The Pioneer* as well. Here, however, the arguments focus predominantly on the moral role of women as mothers – especially as mothers of *sons*; daughters are less visible. Frances Morrison writes:

> No wonder at the present state of affairs, when the mothers of the most able, most useful of England's sons, have been denied the acquisition of truth of every kind. The mother is the first to sow the seed of instruction in the youthful mind; and if the seed is bad, what can we expect from the fruits?[29]

Similar arguments can be found elsewhere in the journal: the problem is the lack of education of those who are 'the wives, the helpmates,

Equality and difference 157

the companions of the men of today' and 'the mothers, the nurses and the first instructors of those who will be the men of tomorrow', 'the mothers and nurses of the next race of artisans and labourers'.[30] The importance of the education of women is here tied to their role as wives and mothers.

EQUAL PAY

The *Appeal* asserts a need for economic independence for women; part of the case for equal access to education is that only if this is available can women be free from the necessity of marrying for economic reasons. The arguments for economic equality, however, move quite quickly on to the role of associated labour (see below pp. 161–3) in ensuring this. The principle of equal pay for equal work could be seen to be implicit in the *Appeal*; but equal pay receives more extended treatment in *The Pioneer*.

The views expressed in *The Pioneer* cannot be assimilated to a single argument of the coherence of that put forward in the *Appeal*. Moreover, they are responses to specific political struggles. Two issues which dominate columns of *The Pioneer* are the Derby Lock-out and the arrest and transportation of the Tolpuddle Martyrs. Both of these major events in trade union history gave rise to national attempts to raise money, comparable to the 1984/5 miners' strike. The second set of subscriptions was for the defence of the convicted men and the support of their families. The first was more centrally aligned with Owenite objectives, being for the purchase of machinery to put the Derby textile workers back to work on a cooperative basis as well as for the relief of hardship. One of the interesting aspects of the coverage of the Derby Lock-out is the vacillation between recognizing women and children as workers in their own right and assuming that they are dependants of male workers.

A third issue reported and debated in *The Pioneer* was the exclusion of women from tailoring by unionized male workers,[31] and it is here that the issue of equal pay surfaces. What is striking is the clarity with which Frances Morrison, who refers to women as 'our class', sees that women's work is paid badly, irrespective of its skill, because it is done by women:

> In manufacturing towns, look at the value that is set on woman's labour, whether it be skilful, whether it be laborious, so that woman can do it. The contemptible expression is, it is made by woman, and therefore cheap? Why, I ask, should woman's labour be thus undervalued?[32]

James (or Frances?) Morrison sees the low price put upon women's labour as something imposed by patriarchal power and sustained by ideological means. He cites the argument put forward by male tailors that

> The women have always been worse paid for their labour than the men; and, by long habit and patient acquiescence, they have been taught to

158   *Ruth Levitas*

regard this inequality as justice. They are, therefore, content with merely a portion of man's wages, even where their work is equally valuable.

But Morrison contends that 'the low wages of woman are not . . . the voluntary price she sets upon her labour, [but] the price which is fixed by the tyrannical influence of male supremacy'.[33] Moreover, it is a tyranny by male trade unionists, who rail against the unjust authority of employers over them, but are keen to preserve their own privileges over women in the labour market.[34] This propensity of men to defend their own privilege is not confined to their labour-market position. The arguments for equal value even hint at the value of unpaid domestic labour:

> A woman's wage is not reckoned at an average more than two-thirds of a male . . . (and wives have no wages at all). Yet, is not the produce of female labour as useful? . . . The industrious female is consequently well entitled to the same amount of remuneration as the industrious male.[35]

This last assertion, however, occurs in the context of an argument about sexual difference, a recurrent theme, and one which is to be found also in the *Appeal*.

SEXUAL DIFFERENCE

What are the natural differences which render insufficient all the forms of equality outlined above? According to the *Appeal*, they are first, the superior strength of men, which in itself gives them an advantage in the competition for wealth; and second, the fact that childbirth means that women's exertions in paid labour are necessarily interrupted. In a competitive system, the result of these differences is that women will necessarily be economically worse off than men: '[t]wo circumstances – permanent inferiority of strength, and occasional loss of time in gestation and rearing infants – must eternally render the average exertions of women in the race of the competition for wealth less successful than those of men'.[36]

The central thesis of the *Appeal* is that women's interests cannot be assimilated with those of men, either individually or collectively. The authors claim that not only difference, but hostility to difference are natural. Dissimilarity leads to antipathy, similarity to sympathy. Sexual difference therefore produces antipathy between the sexes, which is only partly overcome by heterosexual attraction:

> Were no source of pleasure connected with the difference of organization of men and women, it is very probable that the antipathies between them would have been such that they would either have formed different communities, or that the weaker would have been condemned exclusively to the occupations of the greatest drudgery and toil. . . . The general effect of difference of organization is to decrease the sympathy and render more unfeeling and capricious the control [of men over women];

Equality and difference   159

the alleviation from sexual sympathy being, particularly in the forced state of marriage, partial and trifling in the extreme.[37]

The Pioneer also asserts a difference of interests between men and women. It is not wholly clear whether this is seen primarily as a social construct, or whether it is the outcome of natural difference, but the actual situation is one of conflict. The interests of men and women are opposed, collectively if not individually:

> There is a strife to come between man and woman, the one has rights to claim, the other concessions to make. . . . The individual is very different from the sex collectively. The individual is a lover; the sexes collectively are not lovers; they are merely political parties, who eye one another with jealousy, and whenever an opportunity is afforded of a fair encounter, they will separate from each other like master and slave, the one to insist on her rights to equality, the other to insist upon her obligation to obey.[38]

This argument continues with the claim, paralleling that in the *Appeal*, that it is only heterosexual attraction which prevents men from treating women even more badly.

In the *Appeal*, other consequences are argued to follow from reproductive difference, particularly an inclination for women to have a narrower outlook than men:

> [f]rom the physical organisation of women, as regards the bearing and rearing of children, (suppose that even the rearing terminated with weaning or at a year old) they must on average be more engaged in and more inclined to affairs of domesticity than men.[39]

They are thus inclined to attach too much importance to domestic and selfish as opposed to social concerns. Two points are important here. First, like most writers who presume a natural sexual division of labour following from reproductive difference, the authors here run together childbirth and childcare. This elision is however not as extreme as is commonly the case: it is suggested that children (described, in Fourier's terms, as a 'neutral' sex) brought up collectively might be supervised by either men or women, and that boys and girls should be educated together and identically, from a very early age. Second, there is a general belittling of the personal and domestic concerns of women, coincident with a continuing socialist tradition which defines domestic labour as petty, unskilled and trivial, women's concern with personal relationships and the 'emotional work' they perform in society as narrow, and their conversation as gossip. But the *Appeal* argues that since, from the 'casualties of gestation', women are more stationary and confined than men, and 'more inclined to mere local and personal sympathies', it is particularly important that society should be so ordered as to lead them away from these concerns into wider ones. Women's minds must be led away from 'an eternal association with mere childhood and childish toys, from

160   *Ruth Levitas*

isolation and stupidity, to high intercourse with minds of men equally cultivated and beneficent with their own'.[40]

This is not simply a deficit model of woman, since there is also a critique of masculinity. Equality with 'such creatures as men now are' is not an acceptable goal. Men currently expect to be regarded as superior on the basis of 'the strength of their arm and the lordly faculty of producing beards attached by nature to their chins'. They seek from women only 'the pleasures of mere animal appetite [and] the pleasures of commanding'; these are 'the only pleasures which their education and the hypocritical system of morals with which they have been necessarily imbued, permit them to expect'.[41] The argument does rely heavily on a social constructionist view of gender difference: 'all [women's] present peculiarities and defects, like those of men, are the mere result of the vicious circumstances surrounding and acting on them'.[42] The *Appeal* equivocates about the extent to which observable differences are biologically determined, while arguing that women are thereby more, not less, fit to govern than men.[43] Nevertheless, the assumption remains that reproductive difference and men's greater strength have profound consequences for the possibility of social equality.

A much stronger argument about 'separate spheres' is identifiable in *The Pioneer* – partly because it is later, partly perhaps because it is more closely tied to the reality of working women's lives, and also because claims are sometimes made for the political necessity of a separate space in which women can organize. Again, the key issues are women's reproductive role and men's greater strength: 'Man has his particular sphere and so ought women'; but man has filched more from woman as a result of superior physical strength.[44] 'Gertrude' writes that '[o]ur talents and duties are very properly to be exercised in making domestic life easy and comfortable . . . while man, from his stronger frame, can better buffer the stormy world without'; although she goes on to say that 'there are neutral grounds . . . there is no sex in the mind, or in conversation, instruction, advice and other operations of the intellect'.[45]

Despite reiteration of the doctrine of circumstance in general, and many specific claims about the effects of so-called civilized society on the characters of men and women, the pages of the journals of the 1830s reveal an extensive belief in natural sexual difference, and women's special role – particularly their maternal role, and their moral influence on the young, and upon men. The need for women to exert their influence is sharply expressed:

> [W]omen have the principal guidance in the common affairs of life. . . . The reform of . . . abuses must begin with the women themselves; they ought to train their little male brats to think properly of their mothers, and sisters, and aunts, and the whole of their feminine acquaintance, and to instruct the little Pollys and Sallys at the same time not to be quite so afraid of masters Jacky and Tommy.[46]

Equality and difference 161

Although *The Pioneer* supported the political organization of women, even the woman's page argues that they are to consult about 'their own affairs': 'let them make rules and regulations for managing domestic matters, morals, &c., or any other matters which particularly interest them as women'.[47] Indeed, they are exhorted to 'make a legislation for yourselves, a woman's law – a law for mind and morals, which shall put the body law to shame, and claim the supremacy of mind over matter'.[48] The proper sphere of influence of married women is limited:

> We do not advise politics or trade to matrons. If they are not traders, why should they interfere with trade? Neither do we advise them to go and spout at meetings, or make themselves public in any way. We only advise them to associate with each other, and communicate with each other upon subjects connected with woman alone.[49]

Mind you, if association with others is likely to produce such ill effects in women as 'becoming gossips, gadders, busy bodies, spouters', men had better be careful; for 'if union is to produce such a corrupting effect, then, for heaven's sake let men beware of it; for man and woman are one nature, and are refined or corrupted by the same means'.[50]

As Taylor has commented, there was a tendency for the 'good' aspects of women's characters to be deemed 'natural', and the 'bad' the result of circumstances. Thus Frances Morrison also argues that education will remove the grounds for complaining of women's narrowness and tendency to gossip:

> Then will we cast the foul aspersions that have been heaped on our sex into oblivion. The itch for scandal, tattling and other vices, which we are said to possess, placed in the scale of truth, with affection, sincerity, perseverance, ingenuity, and many other virtues; these, properly culti-vated, will ever outweigh the vices that have been forced into our naturally noble minds.[51]

But in both the *Appeal* and *The Pioneer*, there is an assumption of natural difference. It is a difference far less than that produced by the present inequality of circumstance, but it is nonetheless one which means that women cannot compete on equal terms with men. There is indeed a tension here between equality and difference.

SQUARING THE CIRCLE: ASSOCIATED LABOUR

We have seen that alongside assertions of natural difference, there are claims for legal, civil, sexual and educational equality, together with claims for political equality, and equal pay for women in employment, to be found in the writings of utopian feminism. So far, the claims for equality outlined largely correspond to liberal feminist agenda for equal rights and equal opportunities. But both the *Appeal* and *The Pioneer* go further. They are

162   *Ruth Levitas*

able to reconcile commitment to equality and belief in difference – but only by a rejection of capitalism and the assertion of the merits of associated labour.

In general, there is more emphasis on women's domestic role in the journals than in the *Appeal*, both descriptively and prescriptively. The descriptions refer to the impossibility of carrying out the role 'properly' as a result of overcrowding, poverty, lack of education, and the necessity to deal simultaneously with the incompatible demands of housework and children. Cooperation is extolled as a solution to this: children should be sent to infant schools; communal laundries should be set up. Such strategies would transform the lives of women even without the establishing of a society based on associated labour. Difference implies separate spheres, but associated labour will reduce the burden of work for women, as well as ensure the economic security of all. The general argument for associated labour is central to the agenda of *The Pioneer*. Women are to achieve a fair reward for their labour 'by the very same means by which the men will prevent the tyranny of the master'.[52]

The central importance of associated labour, and the inadequacies of equal opportunities agenda, are set out with blistering clarity in the *Appeal*. This text departs from a liberal argument in insisting that equal opportunities cannot result in equality of enjoyment between women and men as long as there is economic inequality and competition. Under such a system, women will, as a result of natural difference, always be disadvantaged. Consequently, the commitment to equal enjoyment and equal happiness leads in the end to an insistence on breaking the wage relation. No reconciliation between equal opportunities and natural difference is possible under a capitalist system.

Only under 'associated labour' can the inequalities resulting from natural difference be overcome: 'this scheme of social arrangements is the only one which will complete and for ever insure the perfect equality and entire reciprocity of happiness between women and men'.[53] Women's lesser strength and time lost through childbirth are no longer an issue in the acquisition of wealth; 'all possessions and means of enjoyment being the equal property of all – individual property and competition for ever excluded – women are not asked to *labor* as much in point of muscle with men'.[54] Children will be supported by the whole community, so mothers will not be dependent on individual men for the support of their children: 'the whole Association educate and provide for the children of all: the children are independent of the exertions or the bounty of any individual parent'.[55] Economic equality will make it impossible for men to tyrannize over women in any way, and will eliminate the double standard of sexual morality – although the *Appeal* is less emphatic than Owen that this will result in 'natural chastity'. The basis of men's power over women, which is ultimately economic, must be abolished, since 'it is not in human nature . . . to abstain on all occasions from the abuse of . . . power', and it is impossible for there

Equality and difference 163

to be a real equality where one has power to constrain, and the other is economically dependent.[56]

This early utopian feminist argument, however, does not, like some later socialist ones, suggest that come the revolution everything will be allright, and in the meantime women should simply support the cause. Utopian socialism was not a revolutionary movement but a gradualist one, dedicated to constructing an alternative economy alongside the existing capitalist one in the belief that the superiority of socialism would be self-evident, and capitalism would crumble. The reader is exhorted to support equal rights, while not being deluded into thinking that this is an adequate solution:

> [Y]ou should everywhere advocate, first, that partial equality which is that all equal laws, political and civil, equal morals, and an equal system of education can give you under the scheme of isolated individual, or family, exertion, now prevalent, and . . . you should also advocate, with an energy not inferior, the new social system. . . . The scheme of Association or mutual Co-operation, where all useful talents and efforts for the common good will be equally appreciated and rewarded, is the true haven for happiness of both sexes, particularly of women.[57]

Equal rights are not simply a trivial issue: even within the competitive system, they would transform the situation of women beyond all recognition:

> Though nothing short of 'voluntary association,' or the 'mutual coopera-tion of industry and talents in large numbers,' would entirely heal the flagrant evils of our present artificial social system, and particularly the desolating injustice practised on women; yet would the mere removal of restraints, of exclusions and unequal laws, so improve their situation and the general aspect of human intercourse, that they would be no longer recognised for the same. There are two great advances in the progress of human improvement, the one positive, the other negative: the negative consisting in the removal of restraints; the positive in the voluntary estab-lishment of co-operative associations.[58]

CONCLUSION

It is clear that the meaning of equality for utopian feminists in Britain between 1820 and 1840 was wide-ranging, incorporating political, legal, educational and sexual equality, as well as demands for equal pay. This was not seen as contradicting a belief in natural difference, which towards the end of the twenty-year period, underpinned an increasing emphasis on 'separate spheres'. Economic equality was essential to the Owenite argu-ment, yet seen as an impossibility under a capitalist system because natural difference implied a maternal and domestic role for women. This tension was resolved in two ways. First, by arguing that the extent to which women need be confined to such roles was limited, since childcare could be collectivized,

164   *Ruth Levitas*

and domestic labour minimized by socialization and mechanization, and/or by making the young of both sexes do it[59] – anything, in fact, except expecting adult men to do it! Second, by arguing that since women would otherwise still be at a disadvantage, the wage relation must be abolished. Sexual equality and capitalism were incompatible. The *Appeal* is a particularly useful text both because the different aspects of equality are so explicitly dealt with, and because the overall argument is so coherent and complete. A view of difference which incorporates a natural sexual division of labour in which domestic labour falls to women is set alongside a commitment to equality. The relationship between equality and difference, and the resolution of the tension between them through breaking the wage relation under associated labour, is particularly clear.

A return to these arguments is, I think, salutary for contemporary feminists who struggle with the tension between equality and difference, and with the question of how far equal opportunities may be a route to equality, almost entirely from within a liberal, individualist framework. Because these arguments now rarely confront the questions of the fundamental nature of capitalism or the possibility of alternatives to it, they lack the clarity of vision which Thompson and Wheeler certainly had about the limits of equal opportunity agendas. Moreover, the limits of the utopian feminist analyses, in insisting on a version of natural difference which exempts men from domestic labour, might remind us that the question of the sexual division of domestic labour, so central to feminist thought in the 1970s and so marginal now, also needs to remain a priority. Above all, contemporary feminists should take very seriously indeed the argument that equality between men and women, and a decent society for women, children and men, depends upon the elimination of the wage relation and thus upon the elimination of capitalism.

The relevance of these utopian feminist arguments to contemporary debates about equality and difference, and the relationship between equality and equal opportunities, is easily apparent. Yet to make that connection raises theoretical and methodological questions. In asking 'what did equality mean then?' we always implicitly ask 'and how, if at all, does that differ from what it means now?'. Like all histories, that of feminism is necessarily an account generated by the interplay of the questions of one generation and the concerns of another; the continuities arise from the extent to which these questions and theories do in reality overlap. Some continuities can be demonstrated. We know, for example, that Anna Wheeler had read Mary Wollstonecraft's *Vindication of the Rights of Women*.[60] The *Appeal* has disappeared and reappeared more than once, in successive phases of feminism: it was reprinted in serial form in *Woman's Signal* in 1898/9,[61] and in full in 1983 (on both occasions under the sole authorship of William Thompson) and in 1994, attributed formally for the first time to both authors. Fourier, whose visibility in this text has been obscured by its attribution to the Owenite Thompson, was a major influence on a continuing

Equality and difference 165

tradition of materialist feminism in the United States, a tradition synthesized by Charlotte Perkins Gilman and fed back by her into Fabianism and the British cooperative movement.[62]

But the question of causality is an awkward one. Do we have a developing tradition of feminist thought, building (despite the interruptions of lost sources) on those who have gone before? A materialist analysis of feminism would stress less the evolution of a complex of ideas, and place more emphasis on a recurrent set of responses to recurrent conditions – raising the question of what specific social conditions govern the changing expressions of women protesting against patriarchy. And poststructuralist suspicion of grand narratives would reject both approaches, arguing that there are only accounts generated from the different standpoints of different historians. These three perspectives all reveal and obscure important facets of the complex processes whereby feminism is continually recreated as an active political force; and part of that recreation involves the construction and reconstruction of a feminist tradition.

NOTES

1 C. Cockburn, *In the Way of Women: Men's Resistance to Sex Equality in Organizations*, London, Macmillan, 1991; G. Bock and S. James, *Beyond Equality and Difference: Citizenship, Feminist Politics and Female Subjectivity*, London, Routledge, 1992; A. Phillips (ed.), *Feminism and Equality*, Oxford, Blackwell, 1987.

2 C. G. Moses and L. W. Rabine, *Feminism, Socialism and French Romanticism*, Bloomington and Indianapolis, Indiana University Press, 1993.

3 B. Taylor, *Eve and the New Jerusalem*, London, Virago, 1983, pp. 30–1.

4 M. Foot and M. M. Roberts, 'Introduction' to W. Thompson and A. Wheeler *Appeal of One Half the Human Race, Women, Against the Pretensions of the Other Half, Men*, Bristol, Thoemmes Press, 1994 – citing R. Pankhurst, *William Thompson 1775–1833*, London, Watts, 1954 (reprinted London, Pluto, 1991).

5 For further details of Thompson's life, see Pankhurst, *William Thompson*.

6 On Anna Wheeler, see Taylor, *Eve and the New Jerusalem*, pp. 59–65; Pankhurst, *William Thompson*; and R. Pankhurst, 'Introduction' in Thompson and Wheeler, *Appeal of One Half the Human Race, Women, Against the Pretensions of the Other Half, Men*, London, Virago, 1983. There is dispute about whether Wheeler was fifteen or sixteen when she married: see M. M. Roberts, 'Introduction' to Rosina Bulwer Lytton, *A Blighted Life: A True Story*, Bristol, Thoemmes Press, 1994, p. x. See also D. Dooley, *Equality in Community: Sexual Equality in the Writings of William Thompson and Anna Doyle Wheeler*, Cork University Press, 1996.

7 Taylor, *Eve and the New Jerusalem*, p. 97; R. Frow and E. Frow, *Political Women*, London, Pluto, 1989, p. 213.

8 Taylor, *Eve and the New Jerusalem*, p. 75.

9 *Ibid.* See also J. Saville, 'J. E. Smith and the Owenite movement', in S. Pollard and J. Salt (eds) *Robert Owen: Prophet of the Poor*, London, Macmillan, 1971.

10 On Saint-Simonianism, see Moses and Rabine, *Feminism, Socialism, and French Romanticism*; and C. G. Moses, *French Feminism in the Nineteenth Century*, Albany, State University of New York Press, 1984. On Fourier, see J. Beecher and R. Bienvenue, *The Utopian Vision of Charles Fourier: Selected Texts on Work, Love and Passionate Attraction*, University of Missouri Press, 1983. On

166　*Ruth Levitas*

Owenism, see Taylor, *Eve and the New Jerusalem*; J. F. C. Harrison, *Robert Owen and the Owenites in Britain and America*, London, Routledge and Kegan Paul, 1969; J. Saville, 'Robert Owen on the family and the marriage system of the old immoral world', in M. Cornforth (ed.), *Rebels and their Causes: Essays in Honour of A.L.Morton*, London, Lawrence and Wishart, 1978; G. Claeys (ed.), *Selected Works of Robert Owen* (4 vols), London, William Pickering, 1993.

11　See V. Geoghegan, *Utopianism and Marxism*, London, Methuen, 1987; R. Levitas, *The Concept of Utopia*, London, Philip Allen, 1990.

12　Thompson, *Appeal*, p. 107.

13　*The Pioneer*, 17 May 1834, 14 June 1834.

14　*Ibid.*, 14 June 1834.

15　Thompson, *Appeal*, p. xxvii.

16　*Ibid.*, p. xxvii.

17　*Ibid.*, pp. 66–7.

18　*The Pioneer*, 24 May 1834.

19　*Ibid.*, 17 May 1834.

20　Cited in Frow and Frow, *Political Women*, pp. 128–30. The *New Moral World: a London Weekly Publication Developing the Principles of the Rational System of Society* began publication in November 1834 and continued until November 1845. It was edited by Robert Owen (and others), and survived rather longer than most radical periodicals, many of which lasted only one or two years.

21　F. Morrison, *The Influence Of The Present Marriage System Upon The Character And Interests Of Females Contrasted With That Proposed By Robert Owen, Esq.*, Manchester, A. Heywood, 1838.

22　Cited in Frow and Frow, *Political Women*, p. 121; see also Moses and Rabine, *Feminism, Socialism, and French Romanticism*.

23　Thompson, *Appeal*, p. 64.

24　*Ibid.*, p. 94.

25　*Ibid.*, p. 117.

26　*Ibid.*, p. 82.

27　*Ibid.*, p. 34.

28　*Ibid.*, p. 117.

29　*The Pioneer*, 25 January 1834.

30　*Ibid.*, 28 September 1833.

31　See Taylor, *Eve and the New Jerusalem*.

32　*The Pioneer*, 8 February 1834.

33　*Ibid.*, 5 April 1834.

34　*Ibid.*, 22 March 1834.

35　*Ibid.*, 12 April 1834.

36　Thompson, *Appeal*, p. xxvi.

37　*Ibid.*, pp. 97–8.

38　*The Pioneer*, 17 May 1834.

39　Thompson, *Appeal*, p. 177.

40　*Ibid.*, pp. 123, 179.

41　*Ibid.*, pp. xxviii–xxix.

42　*Ibid.*, p. 93.

43　*Ibid.*, p. 141.

44　*The Pioneer*, 31 May 1834.

45　*Ibid.*, 7 June 1834.

46　*Ibid.*, 31 May 1834.

47　*Ibid.*, 8 March 1834.

48　*Ibid.*, 15 March 1834.

49　*Ibid.* 22 March 1834.

Equality and difference   167

50 *Ibid.*, 29 March 1834.
51 *Ibid.*, 8 February 1834.
52 *Ibid.*, 22 March 1834.
53 Thompson, *Appeal*, p. 199.
54 *Ibid.*, p. 199.
55 *Ibid.*, p. 200.
56 *Ibid.*, pp. 203, 96.
57 *Ibid.*, p. 202.
58 *Ibid.*, p. 151.
59 See, for example, John Gray, *Lecture on Human Happiness* (1825), London, LSE, 1931.
60 Foot and Roberts, 'Introduction'.
61 M. Ramelson, *Petticoat Rebellion*, London, Lawrence and Wishart.
62 A. Brisbane, *Social Destiny of Man or Association and Reorganisation of Industry* (1840), New York, Augustus Kelly, 1969; D. Hayden, *The Grand Domestic Revolution*, Cambridge, MIT Press, 1981; A. Thomson, 'Domestic drudgery will be a thing of the past: cooperative women and the reform of housework', in S. Yeo (ed.), *New Views of Co-operation*, London, Routledge, 1988; R. Levitas, 'Who holds the hose? Domestic labour in Bellamy, Morris and Gilman', *Utopian Studies*, 1995, 6, p. 1.

10 Liberalism and feminism in late nineteenth-century Britain

Tjitske Akkerman

The tendency to regard liberalism and socialism as conflicting ideological traditions has sometimes distorted our perception of the history of feminism. The rise of working-class women's organizations at the end of the nineteenth century has thus been regarded as a development which divided and weakened feminism. Ideological confrontations between liberal individualism and socialist collectivism in particular were held responsible for its eventual decline.[1]

However, in this respect the history of feminism has varied according to national contexts. While class divisions were sharp in Germany, for instance, this was certainly not the case all over Europe.[2] At the other end of the spectrum was England, where liberal feminism appeared to be particularly flexible and where coalitions between the two strands of feminism proved relatively successful. In England there was no clear ideological cleavage between liberal individualism and socialist collectivism. Such a view, underestimates the collectivizing tendency in early and mid-Victorian liberalism, as well as the survival of various types of individualism into the twentieth century.[3]

We should also reconsider the thesis that feminism was weakened by the shift to socialism. This argument may be plausible for the period after 1918, when party politics and parliamentary representation became more important for feminists, while at the same time the Liberal Party and the Labour Party went their separate ways. Whereas the Liberals turned away from social reform, Labour stressed its autonomy. This certainly heightened tensions within feminism between gender and class loyalties, but it remains to be seen whether this was also true for the period up to World War I.

This examination of the development of liberal feminist thought and policy in England, when faced with these new challenges, will focus on certain major thinkers and leading liberal feminists. First, I would like to sketch the position of the mid-Victorian liberal feminists John Stuart Mill and Millicent Garrett Fawcett. I will then go on to set the liberal and individualist outlook of Mill and Fawcett against the way in which T. H. Green and Helen Bosanquet took a stand in the evolving debate in the last quarter of the nineteenth century between individualists and collectivists. And

Liberalism and feminism 169

finally I will turn to the youngest generation of liberals, who called themselves liberal socialists, concentrating particularly on the ideas of one of these New Liberals, Leonard T. Hobhouse.

MORAL REFORM AND VICTORIAN LIBERALISM

Millicent Garrett Fawcett was the last of the Victorian feminists to remain active after World War I. A pragmatic leader of the suffragists, she was apt to change her strategies. In 1912, for instance, she decided to ally with the Labour Party, but did not fundamentally modify her liberal principles, which had been formed in the mid-Victorian era.[4] Throughout her life she firmly believed in free trade – a conviction which had made her decide to break with the Liberal Unionists when Joseph Chamberlain changed his policy in 1903. She also remained opposed to protective labour legislation for women throughout her life. When the debate about family allowances entered the public arena in the 1920s, Millicent Fawcett belonged to the minority who spoke against it. As an enduring advocate of laissez-faire economics she had opposed family allowances since first encountering suggestions for 'subsidizing motherhood'. To her this constituted a 'Socialist nightmare of abolishing the ordinary responsibilities of marriage and substituting them with State salaries for mothers'.[5] Throughout her long career as a leading feminist Millicent Fawcett remained committed to the principles of mid-Victorian individualist liberalism.

But it is this individualism that needs to be examined if we are to understand some of her ideas and activities which at first sight did not fit in with liberal individualism. Barbara Caine, for instance, has argued that Fawcett's involvement with moral reform was at odds with the general liberal framework of her thought.[6] Millicent Fawcett's liberalism did, however, contain a consistent commitment to moral reform. Her arguments against state intervention were not so much based on a merely negative concept of liberty, but on an ideal of individual and public morality. The end of liberty in her view was the development of character, a development to be directed at learning to master one's desires. In this respect, the mid-Victorian liberalism of Fawcett, which was to some extent inspired by John Stuart Mill, stressed ethical rather than economic goals.[7]

Millicent Fawcett's liberal and feminist ideas were formed in the late 1860s and 1870s, beginning in 1867 when she became involved in the struggle for women's suffrage as a young woman of twenty. She worked closely together with John Stuart Mill from 1867 until his death in 1873. To Millicent and for her husband Henry Fawcett, a professor in political economy at Cambridge and a Liberal MP, Mill was to become a life-long intellectual and spiritual mentor. Their commitment to feminism was based on common principles. John Stuart Mill and Millicent Fawcett both supported women's struggle against sexual exploitation. Both were arguing for far more than the removal of legal impediments for married women,

170 *Tjitske Akkerman*

regarding existing marriage arrangements as a form of sexual slavery. Their concern for the moral quality of sexual relations also came to the fore in their opposition to the Contagious Diseases Acts (1862, 1864). Although they agreed that Josephine Butler's repeal movement had to be kept apart from the struggle for suffrage, this was a tactical rather than a principled decision. They were no less committed to this cause than those suffragists who did decide to ally with Butler.

Their opposition to these acts cannot be regarded merely as an expression of their concern for state invasion of individual liberty. Mill's evidence to the Royal Commission on the Acts in 1871 showed that his chief objection was that they proved to be a public endorsement of vice.[8] In his view the government used the Acts to license immoral behaviour. Millicent was also strongly opposed to the Acts, and she had to be persuaded by her husband to keep the campaign for women's suffrage separate from Josephine Butler's repeal movement. In the 1880s Millicent became publicly involved in the battle against the sexual exploitation of young girls, and she showed an uncompromising commitment to moral reform in endorsing vice tests for prospective members of parliament. The 1880s and 1890s, of course, witnessed a general upsurge in moral reform, but this preoccupation can already be found in Mill's and Fawcett's earlier positions and, more importantly, it fitted well within their framework of mid-Victorian liberalism. This strand of liberalism contained a strong commitment to the ideal of a public morality to which the acquisition of moral rectitude, self-control, temperance and thrift were crucial.

POLITICAL AND SOCIAL REFORM

Political reform was the chief aim of Fawcett, Mill and other liberal feminists of the mid-Victorian period. Their views of the suffrage movement and of democracy in general were also inspired by ethical ideals. Democracy was not primarily about protecting private interests, although Mill and Fawcett sometimes made use of such arguments. Mill saw the extension of the vote as a means of political education. Only active participation would enable the mass of the people to broaden their views and to refine their judgments.[9] His arguments in favour of the vote for women also rested on an educational aim. The vote would help women to broaden their outlook beyond the narrow sphere of private life.

Such views also inspired Millicent Fawcett's enduring struggle for women's suffrage. She wrote that she wanted the franchise for women partly because their specific rights and interests were often disregarded, but even more so because:

> It is a great tonic to character, it tends to check the tendency to take a mean and too personal view of the interests of life. . . . We want the electoral franchise not because we are angels oppressed by the wickedness of

Liberalism and feminism 171

'the base wretch man' but because we want women to have the ennobling influence of national responsibility brought into their lives.[10]

Here again, her individualist outlook did not primarily mean protection of the private sphere and of private interests, but was inspired by an ideal of individual and public morality. Her confidence that the individual development of character was fundamentally in harmony with the development of 'national responsibility' was to become a major principle of the later collectivists as well.

Social reform was to become the battleground for the debate about individualism and collectivism. In this respect Mill and Fawcett can be labelled individualists in the sense that they rejected the idea that the poor had a right to assistance and protection. They were opposed to philanthropy, which in their view discouraged self-improvement and sustained 'indolence and improvidence'. Of course the state was responsible for providing relief to the poor, as in the Poor Law for example, but this relief should be punitive and instructional in nature. Mill, for instance, argued that those dependent on poor relief were to be disenfranchised, and that those who were too poor to support a family should be prohibited from marriage.[11] Millicent Fawcett wrote that low wages, insecure employment and high costs of living might make it difficult to meet the duty to support oneself and one's family through labour, but nevertheless one 'should remember that vast numbers, who at the present time do not save, could save if they had the inclination to do so'. She added the familiar argument that millions were annually spent in excessive drinking, and that this sum could provide adequate insurance to support their widows and other dependants.[12]

Improvements in education were regarded by both Mill and Fawcett as being of the utmost importance. Their contributions to discussions about education paved the way for the Education Act of 1870 and the eventual introduction of compulsory education in 1876. Together with her husband, Millicent Fawcett had published a volume of essays and lectures in 1872, in which education was a central theme. Although the Fawcetts declared themselves against state intervention, – 'the more it can be avoided the better', wrote Henry Fawcett – they made an important exception in the case of children. If parents failed to meet their responsibilities, the state should intervene. The Fawcetts were therefore in favour of such policies as labour protection for children, and of compulsory education. They stressed however that state intervention should be aimed at fortifying character and responsibility. Millicent Fawcett thus argued that if parents could not pay their school fees they should be punished and treated as paupers.[13]

This individualist approach to social reform, with its emphasis upon the improvement of character, became more marginal at the end of the century, but it was never to disappear completely. In the 1880s and 1890s, when social reform became a major issue, the liberalism of Mill and Fawcett became in some respects outdated. The growing recognition of the extent of poverty,

172   Tjitske Akkerman

and the acceptance that poverty was to a large extent due to circumstances and not to character, induced progressive liberals to distance themselves from the older tradition of individualist liberalism. Such new insights superseded Mill's and Fawcett's feminism. They had, for instance, both opposed protective labour legislation for women. Until the 1890s this view enjoyed widespread support in the women's movement, but in the last decade of the century the feminist opposition against protective labour legislation withered away as women's trade unions began to support the idea. Millicent Fawcett had been on the whole fairly supportive of women's trade unions. In 1881 she became actively involved in Emma Paterson's Women's Protective and Provident League. She agreed with the League's policy of opposing protective labour legislation for women. But in the 1890s, when its successor the Women's Trades Union gave up its resistance to protective labour legislation, Millicent Fawcett did not comply.[14] Like Mill, who also rejected protective measures for women, she was committed to equal opportunities for women in the labour market. In their view, protective legislation deprived women of their status of rational adults capable of determining their own interests.

To discuss this evolving debate about protective labour legislation for women exclusively in terms of gender versus class loyalties does not sufficiently explain why Mill's and Fawcett's views with respect to protective labour legislation for women became outdated in the 1890s. It is true that by that time the family wage had become the major bargaining counter of the general labour unions and sweated workers; the ability to support a wife had become a measure of working-class male respectability.[15] In this context an outright rejection of protective labour legislation on the part of feminists committed to working-class politics became much more difficult to sustain. However, liberal feminists came to accept the 'breadwinner model' too, but not solely due to the pressure of labour unions.

THE END OF THE CENTURY

Perhaps the most important difference between mid-Victorian feminists like Fawcett and the younger generation of feminists was that Fawcett had no intimate knowledge of working-class life, in contrast to those feminists who became increasingly involved in social work. The growing recognition of widespread poverty developed alongside the growth of charity organizations, and in 1893 it was estimated that some twenty thousand women were working as paid officials in philanthropic work.[16] In the 1880s, when settlement houses were first founded, middle-class women began to live in working-class neighbourhoods. Fawcett's relations with working-class women had however been restricted to the level of committees. Her views became outdated in the eyes of those feminists who began to revise the predominant ideas of poverty, and the role of the family and the state in the 1890s, after their confrontation with poor working-class life in London's East End and other neighbourhoods.

Liberalism and feminism 173

The 1880s witnessed a growing belief that a category of poor people were powerless to help themselves, however hard they tried and whatever inducements were offered. Although there had been economic recessions in the mid-Victorian period, they never received the official recognition and status with which the agricultural depression of 1873 and the trade and industrial depressions of 1879 and 1886 were endowed by the Royal Commissions appointed to investigate the state of the economy.[17] Public debate was also stimulated by various pamphlets and reports in which poverty was 'rediscovered'. The recognition that large sections of the poor were powerless to help themselves became an important factor in forcing the social policy debate into an issue of state responsibility or 'high politics'.

In the mid-Victorian era social policy had been largely confined to the sphere of local government. Until 1900 the vast bulk of social legislation was still administered and financed by local government, but in the period 1906–14 twelve major items of social policy legislation were introduced under the Liberal government, of which only three were implemented through local authorities.[18] This transition of social policy from the local to the national level after 1900 had important implications for the women's movement. With the evolution of the debate about the centralization of social reform, not only issues concerning women's welfare were at stake, but a new dimension was also added to the fight for suffrage.

Women's activities in social reform had been accompanied by growing political participation in local government. While in 1870 only three women had been elected to public office, this number increased gradually to more than three thousand in 1914. Women's suffrage in local government had met surprisingly little resistance compared with the battle for the parliamentary vote. The winning of the vote at local level exemplified a pattern of an increasingly important role being accorded to women as social workers: they were elected to school boards and Poor Law boards, and eventually to city councils.[19] During the last quarter of the century liberal and socialist feminists were still broadly committed to the local administration of social work and to participation in local government. Only after 1900, with the centralization of social policy, did the arguments for the parliamentary vote become more urgent.

The evolving debate about social reform did not, however, simply reinforce the divisions between liberals and socialists. From the 1880s onwards there was a widespread acceptance among progressive liberals that they 'were all socialists now'. This did not imply any commitment to the class struggle or to the abolition of private property, it merely implied an obligation to promote social reform. Progressive liberals all recognized that acts of charity towards the poor were no longer sufficient. Socialism, in its typical English form, became synonymous with social reform. Joseph Chamberlain, for instance, declared that of course 'every kindly act of legislation by which the community has sought to discharge its responsibilities and its obligations to the poor is Socialism'.[20] In this period, that is

174 *Tjitske Akkerman*

from the 1880s to World War I, the terms individualism and collectivism acquired currency.

T. H. GREEN AND HELEN BOSANQUET

The shift on the part of progressive liberals towards collectivism was to some extent intellectually inspired by T. H. Green, who studied and lectured at Oxford from 1855 until his death in 1882. At Oxford, in the 1870s and 1880s, he inspired a younger generation of liberals who began to dissociate liberal theory from laissez-faire individualism. During the 1880s, Green's Idealism enjoyed a brief reign as the dominant philosophical school in Britain.[21] Idealism is traditionally characterized by its 'organicism', that is its emphasis upon society as a moral unit rather than an aggregate, and upon the supreme role of the state as the expression of the general will of the community. It is thus regarded as crucial to the development of the collectivist liberalism of Hobhouse and other New Liberals.[22] Other of T. H. Green's followers, however, remained strongly committed to individualism and opposed a collectivist approach to social policy. Green's intellectual heritage was ambiguous with respect to the debate about individualism and collectivism. Although he followed Hegel in his understanding of the state as the spiritual focus of community, his emphasis on morality as the result of free will and pure motivation was clearly Kantian, and not a very suitable standpoint from which to support the enforcement of moral goals by the state.[23]

Equally ambiguous was Green's intellectual background regarding feminism. He did contribute to the emancipation of women in several ways, witness his efforts for the education of girls and establishing women's colleges at Oxford. More importantly, however, Green inspired the settlement movement, in which women gradually came to outnumber men. The ideals of community and spirituality which figured so largely in the women's movement, particularly in the settlement movement and the women's colleges, were to a large extent inspired by the climate at Oxford, where Green, Canon Samuel Barnett and Toynbee had turned social reform into a vocation.[24] The ambiguity of Green's contribution to feminism becomes clear when we examine some of his heirs. The Bosanquets lent a rather conservative twist to his ideals of community and spirituality, while Leonard Hobhouse radicalized his views.

Bernard Bosanquet was one of those students of Green who abandoned his fellowship in order to take up social work in the Charity Society Organisation (COS) and the university settlements. In 1895 he married Helen Dendy, a district secretary in the COS. Both jointly and separately they published numerous essays on the subject of charitable work and social theory. The Bosanquets can be characterized as transitional liberals. They were collectivist in invoking Rousseau and Hegel in their conception of society as an organic community in which the state embodied the general

Liberalism and feminism 175

will. There could therefore be no antithesis between liberty and state intervention, as earlier liberals had supposed. The Bosanquets did, however, remain solidly individualist in their rejection of social rights, which they feared would sap individual will and initiative.

The Bosanquets were not so much moral reformers as what might be termed 'moral regenerationists', believing that social imperfections were essentially defects in individual conduct and that the remedy therefore was the 'remoralization' of character.[25] They rejected the new perception of poverty, refuting Charles Booth's theory that the majority of the poor were not immoral. Helen Bosanquet rejected the notion that a man could be 'out of work through no fault of his own' and argued that every man was responsible for his own circumstances.[26] The Bosanquets were collectivist in their emphasis on the importance of the social whole, stressing the place of the individual as a function in the social organism. The communities to which one belonged, and foremost the family, were to shape the cooperative qualities of individuals, without which the evolution and survival of moral standards were impossible. 'Broadly speaking, the co-operative individual, as demanded by civilized life, can only be produced in the family', Helen Bosanquet wrote in her book *The Family* (1906).[27] She evoked an ideal of the traditional patriarchal family, in which cooperation had been based on the ownership of land. Although this form of cooperation had been eroded by industrialization, it lingered on in the functional division of labour, according to which the wife was assigned the care of home and children, while the husband and adult children provided an income.[28] This division of labour also implied that the man should represent the family in the community, that is have the right to vote. Bosanquet did not oppose the vote for women, but restricted it to unmarried women. Notwithstanding this communitarian view of the position of women in the family and in the community, Helen Bosanquet was in many respects closer to the individualist liberalism of Fawcett than to the collectivist bent of new liberals such as Hobhouse. Like Fawcett she stressed the punitive character of poor relief, and the importance of education for the improvement of the opportunities of women on the labour market, but in Helen Bosanquet's case the latter applied only to unmarried women. [29]

A fundamental difference in views can be detected between Millicent Fawcett and Helen Bosanquet. Whereas the first was committed to the principle of equal opportunities for women on the labour market – not only for single women but also for married women – Bosanquet did not encourage working-class wives to earn a living. On the other hand, while proffering a 'breadwinner model' based on her organic view of the family, she also rejected collectivist solutions such as the 'subsidizing of motherhood'. When compared with the individualism of Fawcett on the one hand and the collectivism of the New Liberals on the other hand, Bosanquet's middle path was particularly unattractive to married working-class women. While endorsing a gendered division of tasks within the family, she merely stressed the duties

176   Tjitske Akkerman

of wives and mothers but rejected their claim to social rights. Her rejection of 'state subsidies' brought her into conflict with Beatrice Webb, when they were both members of the Royal Commission on the Poor Law in the period 1905–9. She remained committed to the individualist view that individual will and strength of character were the sole means of combating poverty. Outdoor relief for mothers therefore remained in her view an issue of charity and not one of justice.[30]

Followers of T. H. Green, like the Bosanquets, were not altogether in agreement with the evolving shift within women's organizations to collectivist claims such as state subsidies for mothers. T. H. Green also inspired a half-hearted support of the women's cause with respect to the fight for suffrage. Green had inspired the belief that 'the growth of women's power in such a state as England should be through local government'.[31] He never campaigned for votes for women, and he may well have indirectly inspired the Anti-Suffrage Appeal of 1889, signed by some female members of Green's intimate circle, including his wife Charlotte and Mrs Humphrey Ward. The anti-suffragists were 'heartily in sympathy' with the extension of women's powers as members of school boards, boards of guardians and other local public bodies, but when it came to questions of parliamentary policy, they argued, the experience of women could not provide them with 'sound judgment'. [32] Most of these anti-suffragists changed their mind when the struggle for the vote reached its zenith in the course of the first decade of the twentieth century.

The position of these Greenite anti-suffragists should be seen in the context of a broader commitment to the primacy of local self-government. There was a strong current in liberalism, from Mill to Green, for regarding the reinforcement of local democracy as the most effective path towards active citizenship.[33] The last quarter of the century witnessed a marked increase in social work and women's participation in local government. This was the period in which even the Fabians and the Social Democratic Federation were still committed to the local administration of poor relief.[34] The practical involvement of the Greenite circle in social work therefore provided a context in which the parliamentary vote was regarded as unimportant and even undesirable, being beyond women's sphere and competence.

After 1900 the campaign for women's suffrage became even more complicated by the increasing involvement of working-class women. Through women's trade unions, the Women's Co-operative Guild and the Women's Labour League the suffrage organizations increasingly recruited women of the working class. This development brought to the fore the recurrent issue of whether to relate the demand for equal votes for women to Labour's demand for adult suffrage. This became an important test case for coalitions between feminists and socialists. On the whole, feminism not only became a broader movement around 1900, but also a much more complicated and potentially divided movement. Social reform issues such as labour protec-

Liberalism and feminism 177

tion and family allowances, as well as the parliamentary vote for women, tested the flexibility of liberal feminism.

GENDERED RIGHTS AND DUTIES

Leonard Hobhouse (1864–1929) was the most important political theorist of the New Liberal generation. An Oxford student and fellow in the 1880s and 1890s, he became a journalist in the late 1990s, before returning to teaching in 1907, when he accepted the first chair in sociology at the University of London, a post he retained until his death in 1929.[35] In the early years of the new century he began to class himself as a liberal socialist or a New Liberal, emphasizing on the one hand the continuity of liberal thought, and on the other hand the affinity of liberal and socialist goals.

Hobhouse tried to reconcile the potential conflict between liberal and socialist goals, or rather between claims to individual rights on the one hand and to the requirements of social welfare on the other, by formulating an organic conception of society. Following Green's theories he argued that the individual could enjoy no right that conflicted with the common good. Hobhouse seemed to be suggesting that a proper understanding of the common good would bring this into harmony with self-development. A true harmony of individual self-development and collective progress was perhaps difficult to realize, he admitted, but it was imperative that a conscious effort be made to strive for this ideal.[36] Green had reformulated liberty as positive freedom in order to demonstrate that certain forms of state intervention – against drunkards for instance – were justified to further the common good. Hobhouse continued this argument, suggesting that state coercion was legitimate in cases where individuals or minorities obstructed the realization of conditions necessary for the welfare of the community; an example was the expansion of industrial legislation. These and other principles were applied to support a greatly increased regulatory role of the state. Many of the measures Hobhouse advocated, such as the introduction of old age pensions and health insurance, were in line with the policy of the Liberal government from 1906 onwards.

Most interesting for our discussion of feminism, however, is Hobhouse's support of the *Minority Report on the Poor Law*, and his backing of women's suffrage. Hobhouse was an ardent supporter of social rights and had always protested against the severity of Poor Law charity. In his view every member of society was entitled to a guaranteed minimum standard of living. Such rights, however, depended on a reciprocal relation between the individual and the state. The state recognized these rights as far as each man and each class fulfilled the various functions which were necessary to maintain the well-being of society. Hobhouse used this functionalist view of rights and duties in order to support such radical measures as a minimum wage, but it could also have rather conservative implications. Those who failed to perform any social function forfeited their rights, were subject to

178 *Tjitske Akkerman*

punitive discipline and might even be treated as criminals. There are still traces of the moral severity of the Poor Law's treatment of 'idlers' in Hobhouse's treatment of the 'undeserving poor'.[37] His justification of state endowments in exchange for the service of individuals to the community was also invoked to support the way the minority of Poor Law commissioners dealt with widowed and deserted mothers. In his best-known work, *Liberalism* (1911), Hobhouse supported the *Minority Report* on this case. He stated:

> The newer conception of rights and duties comes out clearly in the argument of the commissioners, that if we take in earnest all that we say of the duties and responsibilities of motherhood, we shall recognize that the mother of young children is doing better service to the community and one more worthy of pecuniary remuneration when she stays at home and minds her children than when she goes out charring and leaves them to the chances of the street. We no longer consider it desirable to drive the mother out to her charring work if we possibly can, nor do we consider her degraded by receiving public money. We cease in fact to regard the public money as a dole, we treat it as a payment for a civic service.[38]

Hobhouse, like many other Progressives, was involved with Beatrice Webb's *Minority Report*, participating as he did in a Committee for the Break-Up of the Poor Law, which Webb had founded to win support for her position in the Royal Commission on the Poor Law.[39] Webb shared Hobhouse's thesis that poor mothers were entitled to public assistance. In her version of the *Minority Report* she wrote that as the choice had been made to organize society in such a way that it was to the man that the income necessary for the support of the family was paid, the community was to keep its end of the bargain in case of death, desertion, illness or unemployment of the breadwinner. The concern of the community for children required public funds for sustenance 'conditional on the mother's abstaining from industrial work, and devoting herself to the care of the children'.[40] Webb therefore recommended a 'home allowance', on the principle that mothers should be formally regarded as non-able-bodied, and that such an allowance should not imply the loss of other rights such as old-age pensions.[41] She and Hobhouse thus differed from the opponents of the *Majority Report* – of which Helen Bosanquet was the most significant – in their endorsement of rights to assistance in exchange for the social service of raising children.

This principle implied that Hobhouse and Webb never supported unconditional rights; the latter argued for instance that it was legitimate to remove children from the care of the mother altogether if she failed to devote herself to their care or to provide a suitable environment by indulging in cruel habits.[42] We should not forget however that in this period liberals and socialists did not demand that social rights be unconditional. Moral standards were widely applied by liberals and socialists alike, not only to the poor but also to the 'immoral' habits of the rich who did not earn their income. Not

Liberalism and feminism   179

until 1918 did a socialist dare to make the shocking suggestion that the nation's wealth was sufficient to provide everyone, immoral or not, with a minimum subsistence.[43] Nor was the principle of unconditional rights endorsed by feminists in this period. Even after the war the paternalist element lingered on in the campaign for family allowances, for instance in the view of the Family Endowment Committee that allowances were only to be paid to a mother with a certificate proving that the general condition of her children was satisfactory.[44]

Among the socialist organizations the Women's Co-operative Guild was most consistently in support of benefits for mothers.[45] The Guild's secretary, Margaret Davies, was a lifelong friend of Hobhouse. As early as 1902 he discussed with her the possibility of a union of the New Liberals and Labour.[46] The Guild, together with the People's Suffrage Federation, published a pamphlet about mother's pensions in the United States, emphasizing that they were paid directly to the mothers, and that no discrimination was made between unmarried mothers and deserted mothers.[47] On the issue of the 'endowment of motherhood' there was no clear-cut division between socialist and liberal feminists. This is not to say that the *duty* of motherhood was generally accepted. Labour women, for instance, accepted in 1907 the principle that 'mothers with children dependent upon them shall receive continued adequate support to enable them to attend to the children without having to work'. The argument that 'endowment' would make women attend to the highest duty of motherhood, however, gave rise to heated debate.[48] Yet, New Liberals, feminists and socialists displayed a remarkable level of agreement on the collectivist strategy of 'subsidizing motherhood'. Although the movement for family allowances reached its peak during the 1920s, even in the period before 1914 feminists were observing that the endowment of motherhood was 'coming to be realized more and more clearly as the ultimate ideal of the feminist movement'.[49]

When the Labour Party resolved in 1905 to support only adult suffrage, 'believing that any Women's Enfranchisement Bill which seeks merely to abolish sex disqualification would increase the political power of the propertied classes', adult suffrage became an important test case for the coalition between feminists and socialists.[50] The People's Suffrage Federation (PSF), presided over by Leonard Hobhouse's sister Emily, united socialist feminists and liberal feminists by supporting adult suffrage together with the vote for women. Margaret Davies, also a member of the Federation, coined the term 'democratic suffragist' to designate the alliance between these two demands. Leonard Hobhouse wrote the pamphlet *Government by the People* for the Federation, in which he argued that the disenfranchisement of large numbers of the working class and of women should be abandoned. His argument for equal representation rested on the same principle as his argument for social rights, that is the principle of reciprocal obligation. In his view, social rights had to be met by the obligation of political participation. Now that the state 'enters more and more into the working of everyday life

180   *Tjitske Akkerman*

its control becomes a concern to every man and woman', Hobhouse argued. With the extension of social legislation women's suffrage was more necessary than ever.[51] His pamphlet, like others published by the PSF, painstakingly argued for the common interests of the working class and women.

Sandra Holton has argued that it was the successful realization of a democratic suffrage strategy in feminist labour alliances which ensured the vote for women in 1918. The People's Suffrage Federation, together with other suffrage organizations like the Women's Freedom League and sections of the National Union, played a crucial role in bringing about an alliance with the Labour Party in 1912, in transforming the demand for the vote into a mass social movement and in allying the cause of suffrage with that of social reform.[52] Although the crucial role assigned to this alliance between liberals, feminists and socialists in the final securing of the vote may be somewhat overrated, these alliances certainly indicate that English feminists succeeded rather well in minimalizing the potential conflict between class and gender loyalties in the period prior to World War I.[53]

CONCLUSION

Looking at the evolution of feminist thought from 1860 to 1920, it is clear that, at least in England, liberal ideas remained dominant throughout this period. The liberal intellectual tradition was still remarkably vital at the turn of the century. With the rise of working-class women's organizations, feminists succeeded in bringing about successful alliances. It is very plausible that the realization of a 'democratic strategy' in feminist labour alliances was possible because it could build on an older tradition of British radicalism. Demands for the extension of the franchise to the people had been traditionally a very important element in radical movements, from the Chartists to the popular liberalism of Gladstone and the early Labour Party.[54] In the term 'democratic suffragist', coined to designate the alliance between feminists and labour, we may hear the resonance of this older, radical commitment to government for and by the people. In the 1880s and 1890s radicals and liberals were to a large extent still committed to local government. Among feminists this commitment even inspired support for an anti-suffrage strategy, but after the turn of the century the hostility to national politics receded. Yet, from Millicent Fawcett to Margaret Davies, or from John Stuart Mill to Leonard Hobhouse, the extension of the franchise – whether local or parliamentary – implied a support of women's suffrage *and* of the cause of the people.

From the 1890s to World War I, liberal and socialist feminists were able to reach broad agreement on a social policy based on the principle of a family wage. The crucial issue was that of social rights for working-class mothers, and here again liberal and socialist feminists allied in demanding the endowment of motherhood. A collectivist view of society had now

Liberalism and feminism 181

become very influential among feminists. Social liberalism succeeded surprisingly well in providing the intellectual arguments for a moderate collectivism. The turn to collectivism certainly implied that Victorian 'individualism' became outdated in some respects – Millicent Fawcett belonged to the minority opposing family allowances – but on the other hand the new liberalism was not altogether new. The belief that individual liberty was to be in harmony with public morality was one of the outstanding continuities in feminism throughout this period. The Victorian 'individualism' of Millicent Fawcett implied a commitment to moral reform, and in this way it was clearly different from the dogmatic individualism of laissez-faire liberalism – whether in its nineteenth-century version or its revival in the 1980s.

NOTES

1 Olive Banks put forward the thesis that an ideology of class struggle – with socialist-feminists defending a collectivist view and liberal feminists defending an individualist view – weakened feminism in England. See O. Banks, *Becoming a Feminist: The Social Origins of 'First Wave' Feminism*, Brighton, Wheatsheaf, 1986. Richard Evans asserted in general that liberalism itself changed under pressure of the rise of working-class women's organizations, causing a disintegration of liberal individualism, and opening the way for conservative ideologies. See R. J. Evans, *The Feminists*, London, Croom Helm, 1977.

2 In Holland ideological class struggle was not dominant either. See U. Jansz, *Denken over sekse in de eerste feministische golf*, Amsterdam, Sara/Van Gennep, 1990.

3 Moreover, there is no simple one-to-one relation between the rise of Labour and a shift towards collectivism. Within the Labour movement indifference and even hostility to state intervention and centralized social legislation remained. See J. Harris, 'Political thought and the welfare state 1870–1940: an intellectual framework for British social policy', *Past & Present*, 1992, 135, pp. 116–42; J. Harris, 'The transition to high politics in English social policy, 1880–1914', in M. Bentley and J. Stevenson (eds), *High and Low Politics in Modern Britain*, Oxford, Clarendon Press, 1983, p. 62; P. Thane, 'Labour and local politics: radicalism, democracy and social reform, 1880–1914', in E. F. Biagini and A. J. Reid (eds), *Currents of Radicalism. Popular Radicalism, Organised Labour and Party Politics in Britain 1850–1914*, Cambridge, Cambridge University Press, 1991, pp. 244–71.

4 See R. Strachey, *Millicent Garrett Fawcett*, London, John Murray, 1931; D. Rubinstein, *A Different World for Women: The Life of M. Garrett Fawcett*, Hemel Hempstead, Harvester/Wheatsheaf, 1991; D. Rubinstein, 'Victorian Feminists: Henry and Millicent Garrett Fawcett', in L. Goldman (ed.), *The Blind Victorian. Henry Fawcett & British Liberalism*, Cambridge, Cambridge University Press, 1989, pp. 71–147; B. Caine, *Victorian Feminists*, Oxford, Oxford University Press, 1992, pp. 196–239; Millicent Garrett Fawcett, *The Women's Victory and After: Personal Reminiscences, 1911–1918*, London, Sidgwick and Johnson, 1920.

5 *Economic Journal*, 1907, September, p. 376. Millicent Fawcett's opposition to family allowances did not keep her from supporting the Women's Co-operative Guild's claim for a maternity benefit. See D. Rubinstein, *A Different World*, p. 208.

6 B. Caine, *Victorian Feminists*, p. 218.

7 On this ethical aspect of Mill's liberalism, see S. Collini, *Public Moralists.*

182 *Tjitske Akkerman*

Political Thought and Intellectual Life in Britain 1850–1930, Oxford, Clarendon Press, 1991; R. Bellamy, *Liberalism and Modern Society*, Cambridge, Polity Press, 1992; J. Gibbins, 'J. S. Mill, liberalism, and progress', in R. Bellamy (ed.), *Victorian Liberalism. Nineteenth-century Political Thought and Practice*, London and New York, Routledge, 1990, pp. 91–110; R. J. Halliday, *John Stuart Mill*, London, Allen and Unwin, 1976; H. S. Jones, 'John Stuart Mill as Moralist', *Journal of the History of Ideas*, 1992, 53, pp. 287–309; B. Semmel, *John Stuart Mill and the Pursuit of Virtue*, New Haven and London, Yale University Press, 1984.

8 See the minutes of evidence of J. S. Mill before the Royal Comission of 1870, in 'The Contagious Diseases Acts', in F.E.C. Priestly (ed.), *Collected Works*, vol. XXI. *Essays on Equality, Law and Education*, Toronto, University of Toronto Press, 1984, pp. 351–71. See also S. Collini, *Public Moralists*, pp. 153–5.

9 The radical liberalism of Mill and the Fawcetts was accompanied by a commitment to working-class politics. Henry Fawcett was looked upon by leaders of the labour movement as an uncompromising champion of the working class. See L. Goldman, 'Henry Fawcett and the Social Science Association: Liberal politics, political economy and the working class in mid-Victorian Britain', in L. Goldman (ed.), *The Blind Victorian*, pp. 161–3; Mill was also admired and respected as a representative of 'the people'. His intervention in the Hyde Park riots proved how much he was trusted by the working class, an intervention which on the other hand induced Emily Davies to warn against an identification of the women's suffrage cause with the name of Mill. See A. Rosen, 'Emily Davies and the Women's Movement, 1862–1867', *The Journal of British Studies*, 1979, XIX, 1, Fall, p. 113; F. B. Smith, *The Making of the Reform Bill*, Cambridge, 1966, p. 131.

10 *Women's Suffrage*, A speech delivered to the Women's Debating Society, Manchester, 13 February 1899, pp. 4–5, (Fawcett Collection).

11 J. S. Mill, 'Representative government', in H. B. Acton (ed.), *Utilitarianism, On Liberty and Considerations on Representative Government*, London, Dent, 1987, pp. 299–317; J. S. Mill, 'On liberty', in S. Collini (ed.), *On Liberty and other writings*, Cambridge, Cambridge University Press, 1989, pp. 105–9.

12 H. Fawcett and M. G. Fawcett, *Essays and Lectures on Social and Political Subjects*, London, Macmillan, 1872, p. 85.

13 H. Fawcet and M. G. Fawcett, *Essays and Lectures*, pp. 50–67.

14 The League's decision to support the regulation of laundry hours in 1891 marked the shift away from laissez-faire policy. See N. C. Soldon, *Women in British Trade Unions 1874–1976*, Dublin, Gill and Macmillan, 1978, p. 35.

15 See J. Lewis, *Women in England 1870–1950*, Brighton, Wheatsheaf, 1984, p. 49; J. Lewis, 'The working-class wife and mother and state intervention, 1870–1918', in J. Lewis (ed.), *Labour and Love. Women's Experience of Home and Family, 1850–1940*, Oxford, Blackwell, 1986, p. 105.

16 M. Vicinus, *Independent Women. Work and Community for Single Women 1850–1920*, London, Virago, 1985, p. 212.

17 In the 1880s several reports, pamphlets and articles on social questions appeared. The largest inquiry was that held by the Royal Commission on Labour (1892–94), in 49 vols. See C. Loch Mowat, *The Charity Organisation Society 1869–1913. Its Ideas and Work*, London, Methuen, 1961; G. Himmelfarb, *Poverty and Compassion. The Moral Imagination of the Late Victorians*, New York, Knopf, 1991.

18 Harris, 'The transition to high politics'.

19 P. Hollis, *Ladies Elect. Women in English Local Government 1865–1914*, Oxford, Clarendon, 1987; C. Rover, *Women's Suffrage and Party Politics in Britain 1866–1914*, London and Toronto, Routledge and Kegan Paul, 1967. See also

Liberalism and feminism 183

H. Blackburn, *Women's Suffrage in the Light of the Second Reading of 1897*, London, Williams and Norgate, 1898.

20 M. Freeden, *The New Liberalism. An Ideology of Social Reform*, Oxford, Clarendon Press, 1978, p. 27; M. Freeden, 'The new liberalism and its aftermath', in R. Bellamy (ed.), *Victorian Liberalism*, London, Routledge, 1990, pp. 175–93.

21 See M. Richter, *The Politics of Conscience. T.H. Green and His Age*, London, Weidenfeld and Nicholson, 1964; A. Vincent and R. Plant, *Philosophy, Politics and Citizenship: The Life and Thought of the British Idealists*, Oxford, Blackwell, 1984.

22 Green also continued the tradition of radical liberalism of Bright and Mill. See R. L. Nettleship, 'Memoir', in R. L. Nettleship (ed.), *Works of Thomas Hill Green*, vol. III, London, Longmans, Green and Co., 1886, p. xxiv; J. H. Muirhead, *The Service of the State. Four Lectures on the Political Teaching of T. H. Green*, London, John Murray, 1908, p. 85.

23 S. Collini, 'Hobhouse, Bosanquet and the State: Philosophical Idealism and Political Argument in England 1880–1918', *Past & Present*, 1976, 72, pp. 86–112.

24 Martha Vicinus has shown in her already classic book, *Independent Women*, how important these ideals were in these sections of the women's movement. See M. Vicinus, *Independent Women* ; O. Anderson, 'The feminism of T. H. Green. A late-Victorial success story', *History of Political Thought*, XII, 4, pp. 671–94.

25 P. Clarke, *Liberals and Social Democrats*, Cambridge 1978, Cambridge University Press, p. 15. The remedy for the improvement of the economic position, in particular 'the starvation wage', of women was, according to Helen Bosanquet, education. Mrs Bernard Bosanquet, *Rich and Poor*, London, Macmillan and Co., 1896, p. 116; see also A. M. Mc Briar, *An Edwardian Mixed Doubles. The Bosanquets versus the Webbs. A Study in British Social Policy 1890–1929*, Oxford, Clarendon Press, 1987; J. Lewis, *Women and Social Action in Victorian and Edwardian England*, Aldershot, Elgar, 1991.

26 H. Bosanquet, *Strength of the People. A Study in Social Economics*, London, Macmillan, 1903, pp. 51, 55.

27 H. Bosanquet, *The Family*, London, Macmillan and Co., 1906, p. 234.

28 *Ibid.*, p. 200.

29 However, her antipathy to state intervention in the case of labour legislation was overridden by her knowledge of and concern for the working conditions of women in sweated trades, and in 1897 she cooperated with Beatrice Webb in writing a pamphlet on the need to extend factory legislation. J. Lewis, *Women and Social Action*, p. 172.

30 See H. Bosanquet, *The Poor Law Report of 1909. A Summary Explaining the Defects of the Present System and the Principal Recommendations of the Commission, so far as relates to England and Wales*, London, Macmillan and Co., 1909.

31 M. A. Ward, *A Writer's Recollections*, London, 1918, p. 52. Cited in O. Anderson, 'The Feminism of T. H. Green', p. 688.

32 'An appeal against female suffrage', *The Nineteenth Century*, 1889, CXLVIII, June.

33 Both J. S. Mill and Millicent Garrett Fawcett valued local citizenship. Nevertheless, for Fawcett and Mill this did not in any way diminish the importance of the parliamentary vote. Millicent Fawcett criticized the anti-suffragists, and argued that their commitment to municipal suffrage was rather meagre compared to their negative object of opposing women's suffrage. See M. G. Fawcett, *Women's Suffrage*, London, p. 47.

184   Tjitske Akkerman

34 Mc Briar, *An Edwardian Mixed Doubles*, p. 98; P. Thane, 'Labour and local politics', in Biagini and Reid, *Currents of Radicalism*.

35 See P. Clarke, *Liberals and Social Democrats*; S. Collini, *Liberalism and Sociology. L.T. Hobhouse and Political Argument in England 1880–1914*, Cambridge, Cambridge University Press, 1979; R. Dahrendorf, *LSE. A History of the London School of Economics and Political Science 1895–1995*, Oxford, Oxford University Press, 1995; J. A. Hobson and Morris Ginsberg, *L. T. Hobhouse. His Life and Work*, London, Allen and Unwin, 1931; P. Weiler, 'The new liberalism of L. T. Hobhouse', *Victorian Studies*, 1972, XVI, 2, December, pp. 141–61.

36 L. T. Hobhouse, 'Liberalism', in J. Meadowcroft (ed.), *Liberalism and Other Writings*, Cambridge, Cambridge University Press, 1994, pp. 60–5; L. T. Hobhouse, 'The individual and the state', in J. Meadowcroft (ed.) *Liberalism*, pp. 152–4; see also C. M. Griffin, 'L. T. Hobhouse and the idea of harmony', *Journal of the History of Ideas*, 1974, XXXV, pp. 647–61.

37 Hobhouse, *Liberalism*, p. 99; see also Collini, *Liberalism and Sociology*, p. 139.

38 Hobhouse, *Liberalism*, p. 87.

39 B. Drake and J. Cole (eds), *Our Partnership, by Beatrice Webb*, London, Longmans, Green and Co., 1948, vol. I, p. 430.

40 Sydney and Beatrice Webb, *The Public Organisation of the Labour Market: Being Part Two of the Minority Report of the Poor Law Commission*, London, Longmans, Green and Co., 1909, p. 211.

41 Sydney and Beatrice Webb, *The Break-Up of the Poor Law: Being Part One of the Minority Report of the Poor Law Commission*, London, Longmans, Green and Co., 1909, p. 340.

42 *The Public Organization of the Labour Market*, p. 21. The Minority Report may be regarded primarily as an expression of the Webbs' quest for efficiency; see G. R. Searle, *The Quest for National Efficiency. A Study in British Politic and Political Thought 1899–1914*, Oxford, Basil Blackwell, 1971, pp. 235–57.

43 McBriar, *An Edwardian Mixed Doubles*, p. 92.

44 See J. MacNicol, *The Movement for Family Allowances 1918–45: A Study in Social Policy Development*, London, Heinemann Educational, 1980, p. 24. See also H. Land, 'Eleanor Rathbone and the Economy of the Family', in H. L. Smith (ed.), *British Feminism in the Twentieth Century*, Aldershot, Edward Elgar, 1990, p. 111.

45 The Guild played an important role in securing the inclusion of a maternity benefit in the Insurance Act of 1911. See J. Gaffin and D. Thoms, *Caring & Sharing. The Centenary History of the Co-operative Women's Guild*, Manchester, Cooperative Union LTD, 1983, pp. 68–73.

46 J. A. Hobson and Morris Ginsberg, *L.T. Hobhouse. His Life and Work*, London, Allen and Unwin, 1931, p. 63.

47 'Mothers pensions', (collection of pamphlets, Fawcett Library).

48 P. Thane, 'Visions of gender in the making of the British welfare state: the case of women in the British Labour Party and social policy, 1906–1945', in G. Bock and P. Thane, *Maternity & Gender Policies. Women and the Rise of the European Welfare States 1880s–1950s*, London and New York, Routledge, 1991, pp. 107–9.

49 See C. Dyhouse, *Feminism and the Family in England 1880–1939*, Oxford, Basil Blackwell, 1989, p. 93.

50 D. Morgan, *Suffragists and Liberals. The Politics of Woman's Suffrage in Britain*, Oxford, Balckwell, 1975, p. 34.

51 Hobhouse, 'Government by the People', in *Liberalism and Other Writings*, p. 134.

Liberalism and feminism 185

52 S. S. Holton, *Feminism and Democracy. Women's Suffrage and Reform Politics in Britain 1900–1918*, Cambridge, Cambridge University Press, 1986.
53 Even though some authors would also give some credit to the suffragettes, there is broad agreement that the role of the WSPU has been rather overrated. See J. Liddington and J. Norris, *One Hand Tied Behind Us. The Rise of the Women's Suffrage Movement*, London, Virago, 1978; M. Pugh, *Women's Suffrage in Britain 1867–1928*, London, The Historical Association, 1980; B. Harrison, 'Women's suffrage at Westminster 1866–1928', in Bentley, *High and Low Politics in Modern Britain*, pp. 80–123; C. Rover, *Women's Suffrage and Party Politics in Britain 1866–1914*, London, Routledge and Kegan Paul, 1967.
54 See E. F. Biagini and A. Reid, 'Currents of radicalism, 1850–1914', in Biagini and Reid *Currents of Radicalism*.

11 Feminists and sex
How to find lesbians at the turn of the century[1]

Martha Vicinus

Lesbians are seemingly invisible in feminist history. In order to bring the lesbian back to the centre of women's history, I want to suggest that we need to look beyond feminist organizations, movement leaders or famous writers and shift our focus to cultural images, theatre stars, fashion and the ephemera of an age. Through this documentation we can see, I believe, the ways in which substantial changes in attitudes and behaviour towards women, and more specifically, lesbians occur. Let me begin with a discussion of what I see as certain limits in the ways in which we research and write lesbian history and, by implication, feminist history. Then, through an example drawn from the period 1890–1925, I will suggest an alternative way of writing about lesbianism and feminism in modern European history.

Lesbian history has always been characterized by a 'not knowing' of what could be its defining core. Over a decade ago I pointed out a paradoxical tendency: writers appeared to be both reticent to name same-sex desire and yet over-hasty to categorize and define women's sexual behaviours; unfortunately, this still remains true.[2] Our current models all privilege either the visibly marked mannish woman or the self-identified lesbian; romantic friendships, once the leading example of a lesbian past, are now either reconfigured in terms that fit these categories or labelled asexual. Historians seem to accept only what is seen and what is said as evidence. These limitations have shaped both how we know and how we imagine the lesbian. I want to argue for the possibilities of the 'not said' and the 'not seen' as conceptual tools for the writing of lesbian history and, by implication, feminist history. Recognizing the power of not naming – of the unsaid – is a crucial means for understanding a past that is so dependent upon fragmentary evidence, gossip and suspicion. A present limited to the visible, self-identified lesbian reduces our understanding of both the daily life of the homosexual and her multiple relationships with the dominant heterosexual society and its cultural productions. A more open definition of women's sexual subjectivity, and of same-sex desire, will enable us not only to retrieve a richer past, but also to understand the complex threads that bind women's actions and desires to the larger world.

The binaries that have dominated our conceptualization of sex and

Feminists and sex 187

gender have been rigorously questioned recently, but too often this questioning has yielded either polymorphous play or an unstable 'third sex' defined by crossdressing and marginal sexualities.[3] In contrast, I believe that the lesbian is never absent from any definition of women, whatever her avowed sexual preference. I am arguing here for the primacy of a continuum of women's sexual behaviours, in which lesbian or lesbian-like conduct can be both a part of and apart from normative heterosexual marriage and childbearing. I am not calling for a return to Adrienne Rich's notion of a continuum of 'woman-identified experience', in which all-female bonding is defined as unproblematic nurturance and love, in opposition to the divisions wrought by compulsory heterosexuality.[4] Instead, I seek to understand a continuum of women's sexual experiences that also contains an irreducible sense of the dangerous difference implicit in homosexuality. Perhaps no image – continuum, circle or margin – can embody a subject as pervasive as sexual desire. But I contend that the lesbian is at the centre rather than the periphery of any study of women and men. Women's same-sex love always remains a threatening affront to male sexual prerogatives; it is also a hazardous act that can unite and divide women.[5] I want to suggest that lesbianism can be everywhere without being mentioned; the withholding of the name 'lesbian' can reinforce its existence as a defined sexual practice.[6] In effect, we have what was unnamed in the past and our own reluctance to name that past; this determined ignorance reinforces homophobia and impoverishes both lesbian history and the writing of feminist history itself.

I find it ironic that 'lesbianism' continues to depend upon the evidence of sexual consummation, whereas heterosexuality is confirmed through a variety of ways. For example, we know of several unconsummated marriages among middle-class British intellectuals – I draw your attention to the Ruskins, Carlyles, and George Bernard Shaw and Charlotte Payne Townshend; these spouses may be failed heterosexuals, but they are not stripped of their sexual identity. Conversely, even when we have evidence of homosexual practices, it has often been reinterpreted as asexual sentimentality. The American sculptor Harriet Hosmer (1830–1908) made a specific distinction in her letters between kissing her close friends and the pleasures of 'Laöcooning' in bed with her female lover, but her most recent biographer insists that Hosmer was not like her lesbian friend, Charlotte Cushman (1816–76), the internationally admired American actress.[7] However difficult it may be to interpret the flowery language of letters written between friends by both women and men during the nineteenth century, are we not relying too much on a literal language of either sex or sentimentality? Why is an explicit statement seen as a truth statement and elision as uncertainty?

OBVIOUS IDENTITIES?

This insistence upon explicitness has led to a privileging of an identity model of lesbian history. We have focussed on two obvious categories of

188 *Martha Vicinus*

same-sex love: romantic friendships and butch-femme role playing. The former depends upon our present-day identification of these friendships as homoerotic, if not homosexual, while the latter depends upon self-identification by the women themselves. Romantic friends can be called the 'good girls' – educated, monogamous and gently loving of women. Numerous examples of these Sapphic loves can be documented throughout European and American history, for they were an established phase of a young girl's initiation into emotional maturity. As a result, it has been repeatedly claimed that 'once upon a time' women could love each other and society approved.[8] This rosy picture of social acceptance, while never fully endorsed by historians, has seemed boringly asexual to many lesbians of today. They preferred, in Alice Echols' phrase, the 'bad girls' from an immediate, retrievable past.[9] These 1950s working-class butches drank, fought and had fun; among lesbians a romantic nostalgia for the bar-dyke culture of this period is common. Self-identification as either butch or femme has become the defining sign of one's true identity.[10] Limiting lesbian sexuality to these two categories, romantic friendships and butch-femme roles, has led to a dreary narrowing of historical possibilities. Both are conceptualized so as to leave little room for women who might behave differently at different times, or who might belong to both categories of romantic friendships and butch-femme passion – or neither. How are we to define a married woman who falls in love with a woman? Or a lesbian who falls in love with a man?[11]

For Judith Butler the performance of gender, and especially the practices of butch-femme and drag, offer a more viable politics in our postmodern world than identity-based politics, which depends upon privileging one identity over another.[12] As a leading philosopher of queer theory, the most exciting theoretical approach that came up in the 1990s, Butler has fought vigorously against the notion of homosexuality as a miming of heterosexuality. In effect, she has taken the definitional uncertainty about 'what is a lesbian?' and argued for its radical potential. If all gender is a performance, then we historians need not seek a coherent lesbian identity in the past or present. Lesbians are a social construct produced in the process of relating to others. This is, of course, an immensely freeing notion for historians.

Nevertheless, the wholesale embracing of a theatrical metaphor denies the historicity of all lesbian roles, and their specific meanings at different historical times – indeed, even the possibility of their non-existence in the past.[13] Modern sexual behaviour cannot be divorced from its intersection with race, class and other social variables, nor can it be wholly a matter of fashionable metaphorizing. Moreover, the focus of queer theory upon performance is yet again a privileging of the visible, which returns us to some of the same difficulties that have characterized identity-based history. It is as if 'what is gender?' is still confined to 'what is *visibly* gendered?'. From its very inception lesbian studies has been concerned with 'making visible' the lesbian of the present and the past. This process of reclamation has focussed almost entirely upon the mannish women because she has been

Feminists and sex   189

the one most obviously different from other women – and men. What does this insistence on visibility do to notions of both femininity and feminism? Are we fixated on visibly marked difference, whether it be a 'performed' gender or a gendered identity, because the explicitness of our age demands clear erotic signals? No wonder so many postmodernist lesbians when they dress for a party go in butch drag or a campy femininity – the theatricality of each role provides the necessary erotic marker.

Historians are especially well situated to problematize the privileging of the visible as sexual sign. Did this defining of external physical signs as the crucial referent for sexual difference begin with the nineteenth-century medical profession? Early sexologists argued for an enlarged clitoris or excessive body hair, or similar physical 'deformations'.[14] Freud's theory of sexual difference depends directly upon the male child's *seeing* its mother's lack of a penis.[15] Carroll Smith-Rosenberg has pointed out that Richard von Krafft-Ebing made gender inversion physiologically manifest. The women who 'aped' men's roles looked like men. But even more, having rooted social gender in biological sexuality, Krafft-Ebing then made dress analogous to gender. Only by her dress would you know her.[16] There is a curious elision from presumed bodily deformities to the clothes one wears. In effect, difference becomes defined by what is visibly different – if we can't see the bodily hair or the deformed pudenda, we can see the cigarette, long stride and tie. What we see as 'different' means, for the sexologists, the mannish lesbian. But if only the visual marker of mannishness could signify sexual preference, a so-called femme would be distinct from a heterosexual woman only by her performance of an extreme form of femininity, as if to counteract Havelock Ellis' claim that such women were the homely leftovers rejected by men.[17] Recently, self-identified political femmes have refused an identity based solely on their relationship to a butch lover. As Lisa M. Walker has said, 'because subjects who can "pass" exceed the categories of visibility that establish identity, they tend to be peripheral to the understanding of marginalization'. Like Biddy Martin, she too examines the implicit racism of writers who reify marginalization in terms of 'the visible signifier of difference', whether it be race, class or 'mannishness'.[18]

The alternative to 'making visible' the lesbian is language.[19] But I want to suggest some of the ways in which we may be in danger of magnifying its importance in lesbian studies. For both Lillian Faderman and Esther Newton, the late nineteenth-century sexologists' language of genital sex made women sexually self-conscious. For Newton, this 'new vocabulary built on the radical idea that women apart from men could have autonomous sexual feeling', and thereby freed lesbians from the asexuality of romantic friendships.[20] Radclyffe Hall seemed to confirm Newton's generalization; her heroine, Stephen, cannot understand what is wrong with her until she stumbles upon an annotated copy of the work of sexologist Richard von Krafft-Ebing in her father's study. For Faderman, this provision of a sexual language was a disaster that took away the innocence of

190 *Martha Vicinus*

romantic friends. She describes late nineteenth-century women as 'fledgling human beings' who lacked the self-confidence to resist the sexologists' language of neurosis.[21] Both interpretations, though diametrically opposed, give inordinate power to language as either a freeing or a disabling means of self-identification for lesbians. Both critics also reinforce the common assumption that until middle-class women had a sexual vocabulary, their relationships were asexual or guiltily furtive.

As Terry Castle has noted, the lesbian is repeatedly treated as if she were a ghost, whose sexuality cannot be pinned down, and yet she repeatedly reappears, haunting the heterosexual imaginary. This ghosting of lesbian desire has enabled historians to deny its reality for too long. We need to learn from Castle that the 'apparitional lesbian' is not absent from history, but to be found everywhere and, as she suggests, we need 'to focus on presence instead of absence, plenitude instead of scarcity'.[22] As part of that plenitude, I return to my earlier argument: if we begin with the possibility of a continuum of sexual behaviours for all women, then the lesbian is neither marginal nor phantasmic, but central. We need to remind ourselves again – as queer theorists have claimed – that sexual behavior is polymorphous, changeable and impossible to define absolutely. It can only be understood in relation to the multifarious elements that make up a human identity. At the same time, we should not lose that sense of 'dangerous love', so eloquently defended by Elizabeth Wilson over a decade ago; risk-taking, romantic idealism and passionate hedonism are not limited to a heterosexual imagination.[23] Many more women from the past will be part of this sexual world, temporarily or permanently, when we recognize the sheer variety and richness of women's sexual desires – and actions. Truth-claims cannot be made, but a fuller history can be constructed. Lesbians and lesbian-like women have had a profound influence upon women and men, challenging them to rethink and alter their behaviour. Economic independence, alternative lifestyles, and sometimes non-traditional political and cultural activities characterize these women. Why then do they remain so peripheral to our definition of the past?

LESBIAN SUBCULTURE 1880–1920

Parallel to the growing feminist movement of the fin-de-siècle we find a growing lesbian subculture that interacted with, but grew apart from, the burgeoning (and highly visible) European male homosexual culture. Both groups of homosexuals drew their inspiration from the single most important form of popular entertainment: the theatre. In doing so, they recuperated current images and rewrote scripts that concluded with heterosexual marriage or tragic death for their own purposes. Contemporary homosexuals created their own self-image out of a bricolage of reworked classicism, popular theatre, decadent art and poetry.[24]

Historians have assumed that the years 1880–1920 were dominated by the

Feminists and sex 191

sexologists' definitions of so-called deviant sexuality, but homosexuals themselves remained largely impervious to their medicalization of desire. Not until the 1920s, and then only among one strand of homosexuals, did Richard von Krafft-Ebing, Havelock Ellis and Sigmund Freud become defining forces. The larger society, and especially the middle class, condemned homosexuality, but urban sophisticates were well attuned to its many semi-public manifestations. An elaborate code of recognition amidst concealment existed, which is only now being unravelled.[25] Without using 'the L-word' in public, women knew how to recognize each other. Women could also select their own fashion, 'mannish' or otherwise, from a range of visual imagery that suited particular occasions; all could – if they so wished – 'pass' as either homo- or heterosexual.

One of the most popular figures among homosexuals was the famous actress, Sarah Bernhardt, for she embodied neither an explicitly 'butch' appearance nor the bourgeois inflections of a Victorian romantic friendship. As a theatrical figure, in both senses of the word, imitating her seemed almost irresistible to countless admirers, whatever their sexual preferences. Cabaret parodies of Bernhardt's most famous roles were legion – and so too were her homosexual admirers.[26] This French-Jewish actress had revolutionized the French theatre with her unconventional interpretations of leading roles in such famous plays as *Phèdre, Hernani, La Dame aux camélias* and *Théodora*. In the 1870s and 1880s she had taken Paris, London and New York by storm. She never retired, bringing her lavish productions to English-speaking audiences year after year; the spectacle of this famous woman was sufficient to overcome any language barrier. Her well-publicized slim beauty, personal extravagance and sexual liaisons thrilled admirers everywhere; photographs, postcards (including pornographic versions of her most famous roles), card games, commemorative plates and other mementoes of the most famous actress of her time can still be found in antique markets. Bernhardt never feared controversy, publicly fighting with the Comédie Française, actively supporting Dreyfus, and openly praising the suffrage movement. She also included in her intimate circle the mannish artist, Louise Abbéma.[27]

In her fifties, at a time when most actresses retired or took supporting roles, Bernhardt shifted from her famous *femme fatales* to portray a series of tragic heroes. She chose her roles carefully, specializing in men who had 'a strong mind in a weak body', claiming that only an older woman was mature enough to interpret thought-wracked young men.[28] Her best-known roles were her self-consciously light-hearted 'black Hamlet' (figure 11.1) in Shakespeare's play (1899) and her popular anti-hero, the Duke of Reichstadt, son of Napoleon, or her 'white Hamlet', after the colour of his uniform (figure 11.2), in Edmond Rostand's *L'Aiglon* (1900). Bernhardt's vacillating heroes became successful and sexy spokespersons for homosexual freedom. A sexual desire that could turn to so few visual images drew from and altered theatrical transvestites.

Figure 11.1 Sarah Bernhardt as Hamlet
Source: Author's collection

Bernhardt was a favourite among the growing coterie of fin-de-siècle Paris lesbians. The American heiress, Natalie Barney (1876–1972), addressed a poem to Bernhardt after seeing her in *L'Aiglon*. The poem was published in 1900 as part of a collection of lesbian verse; as if to highlight her close identification with the Duke, Barney included a portrait of herself as a page.

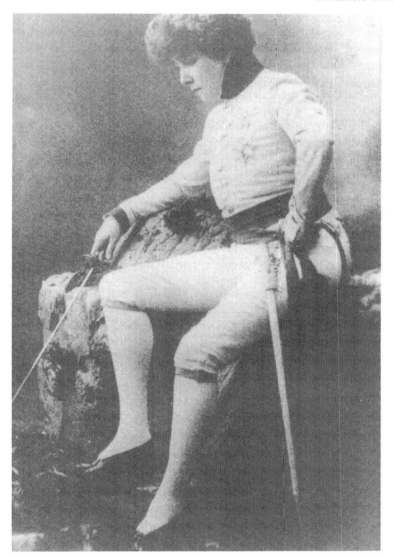

Figure 11.2 Sarah Bernhardt as the Duke of Reichstadt
Source: Author's collection

Her outraged father had the plates and all copies destroyed, though Barney managed to save a few.[29] But Albert Barney could not stop his daughter, who became one of the best-known lesbian hostesses and patrons of her day; she was also notorious for her numerous affairs. The courtesan, Liane de Pougy published a roman à clef, *L'Idylle saphique* in 1901, describing her tumultuous affair with the young Barney. In one scene, clearly drawn

194 Martha Vicinus

directly from their relationship, the two lovers watch Bernhardt play Hamlet. Rather than falling in love with her Hamlet, as so many heterosexual women did, they identified with him. The Natalie-figure compares the frustrations of women with Hamlet's impotent rage against tyranny, 'For what is there for women who feel the passion for action when pitiless Destiny holds them in chains? Destiny made us women at a time when the law of men is the only law that is recognized'.[30] The staginess of this speech echoes Bernhardt's own grandiose style of expression.

Natalie Barney and her friends took their identification with the male impersonator beyond literature and into the public domain. For Barney crossdressing was an erotic embellishment of lesbian play, and not the embodiment of her special nature; passing as male was bad form. The attractiveness of Bernhardt was as much due to her artificial style as her portrayal of anguished young men. Barney and her coterie took Bernhardt's tragic heroes and turned them into romantic exponents of lesbian love. Barney dressed as Bernhardt's Hamlet, but added a provocative garter, as if to draw attention to the erotic nature of her costume (figure 11.3). She and her various lovers celebrated lesbian passion by photographing themselves in costumes that ranged from nudity in the woods of Maine to the breeches and ruffles of eighteenth-century pages and the flowing gowns of Sappho's Greece. Renée Vivien, Barney's next lover, transformed herself from the upper-class Anglo-American Pauline Tarn into the mysteriously handsome page, who was re-née or reborn to a new life as a French-writing lesbian.

Bernhardt was also a cult figure among male homosexuals. The amateur actor, the Marquis of Angelsey, was photographed as the Duke of Reichstadt (figure 11.4) in 'a romantic pose and appropriate costume' in the gossip column of *The Sketch* in January 1902.[31] H. Montgomery Hyde describes the Marquis as 'the most notorious aristocratic homosexual', immediately following the Wilde trial; he was 'an extreme example of the effeminate transvestite type, and was a gifted female impersonator'.[32] Within six years of coming into his inheritance the Marquis had to declare bankruptcy and flee to Monte Carlo. The music hall male impersonator, Vesta Tilley, added to her male wardrobe by buying 'dozens' of waistcoats of 'delicately flowered silk' at the sale of his personal effects.[33] In the 1930s the lead role in *L'Aiglon* was taken over by a well-known homosexual, Jean Weber.[34] Weber was proud of his ability to play roles that had previously been exclusively *travesti* parts. He continued the tradition of exaggerated emotionalism and gender ambiguity in his portrayal of the Duke of Reichstadt, if the surviving publicity still is any guide.

Young suffragists, determined to gain women's political rights during the years 1903–13, also projected images of sartorial elegance which could embody lesbian desire, sexual independence – and political demands. They too borrowed from the theatre and, given their public actions, were subject to the accusations of deviant behaviour that the wealthy Paris lesbians managed to avoid by staging their theatricals in private. Although the

Figure 11.3 Natalie Barney as a Hamlet-like page
Note: Courtesy of George Wickes

196 *Martha Vicinus*

Figure 11.4 The Marquis of Angelsey as the Duke of Reichstadt
Source: *The Sketch*, 1 January 1902
Note: Courtesy of the British Museum

dominant image sought by such leaders as Emmeline Pankhurst, her daughter Christabel and Emmeline Pethick-Lawrence, was of unimpeachable high style, many of their followers adopted a more practical – more masculine – dress. Photographs of women who sold suffrage newspapers on the street show them dressed in tweed suits, sturdy boots and neat bow ties. Male impersonators had appropriated specific male symbols as shorthand for masculinity; they invariably sported such obvious phallic accoutrements

Feminists and sex 197

as a cigarette or cigar, sword or walking stick, or, at the very least, a tie. Now suffragists all seemed to be wearing a version of a man's tie. Photographs and illustrations of suffragists invariably include a woman with a tie. It spoke of political and sexual independence – and made a woman fair game for lewd jostling and obscenities.[35]

In the eyes of male journalists, medical men and most politicians, suffragists were assumed to be usurping male power, both in the bedroom and in parliament. Lesbian innuendo was pervasive. Rumours abounded about Emmeline Pankhurst's close relationship with the mannish composer Ethel Smyth. Commentators spoke darkly of the undue influence of the 'female celibate pedagogue' and medical men warned against the contagion of inversion.[36] To outsiders some women flaunted their sexual preference. Ethel Smyth was simply the most egregious example, but Cecily Hamilton and Edy Craig, known for their lesbian proclivities, also wore tweed skirts, shirts, jackets and flowing bow ties.[37] Their stylish appearance bears some resemblance to the trouser-suit of the 1970s, drawing attention to a sexual independence from men. Both women contributed their theatre expertise to the Cause, writing and producing suffrage plays, training volunteers for numerous events, and masterminding the vast, colourful pageants and marches. These women and others provided confirmation of preexisting assumptions about politically active women. The popular novelist, Marie Corelli, dismissed the suffragists with the comment, 'No man likes to be libellously caricatured and a masculine woman is nothing more than a libellous caricature of an effeminate man'.[38] What an earlier generation had left implicit was now explicit: the effeminate male homosexual and the ravening mannish lesbian endangered society.

Lisa Ticknor has described how long-standing iconographic shorthand, familiar from *Punch*, the music halls and comics, was used to portray the suffragist as an older, unattractive spinster with either a vindictive or an excitable nature.[39] Anti-suffragists rewrote theatrical male impersonation, turning fantasy into a savage burlesque. Young women in particular needed male protection, lest they fall victim to a coarse, man-hating virago. The womanly woman could be saved only by the intervention of paternal authority. This might be expressed, for example, as an open attack on the suffragist, portraying her as a hefty, ugly dame, in danger of leading astray a vulnerable boyish girl (figure 11.5).

The viciousness of this attack on suffrage women in parliament, the press and cartoons is a reminder that the positive expression of women's sexual desire, and specifically lesbian desire, was a dangerous imaginative act with potentially explosive political and personal consequences. Although early twentieth-century lesbians and suffragists successfully recovered the theatrical transvestite as an expression of sexual independence, they did so at a price. The wealthy lesbians who frequented Barney's soirées could afford to ignore momentary notoriety, but suffrage women – homosexual or heterosexual – found themselves largely unable to control negative publicity.

198 *Martha Vicinus*

Figure 11.5 'The Suffragette: Number 1 in a series of Present Day Types'
Source: Bystander, 31 December 1913
Note: Courtesy of the Mansell Collection

Feminists and sex 199

The fashionable elegance of their leaders was not sufficient to overcome the widespread assumption that when women took to the streets they assumed not only male prerogatives but also deviant sexual desires which were visibly encoded on women's bodies. By the 1920s some legislators were calling for legal action against lesbians.[40] Barney was shrewd enough to avoid political radicalism (she became a Fascist sympathizer during the interwar years); economic privilege and sexual radicalism made her, Radclyffe Hall and their friends politically conservative.[41]

CONCLUSION

The history of the lesbian moves from a ghostly presence without a name to one of overt persecution. But the process is more complicated than current historiography allows, for contradictory representations coexisted then and coexist now. By the 1920s the mannish *femme damnée*, originally drawn in part from Bernhardt's languid heroes, became the dominant image of the twentieth-century lesbian. Yet even this single figure had a complex history, drawn not only from medical texts but also the stage, poetry and fantasy. Instead of looking for versions of this single figure throughout history, we need to see how she came to be historically constructed, beginning with apparent invisibility and silence. A narrowly political or institutional interpretation of women's history cannot capture that important figure's origins. We need to turn to the field so despised by both nineteenth- and twentieth-century feminists, namely female fashion. Present-day feminist have by and large neglected fashion, drama and other forms of popular culture because they have seemed so apolitical or marginal to the concerns of nineteenth-century reformers. While many feminists of this period did play down their sexuality in order to be seen as citizens and rational beings, lesbians embraced the sexualized images of the theatre. But they did so with a difference: they imitated the vulnerable, dandified male impersonators, rather than the bosomy heroines dressed in lace and tulle. Early lesbians found no nourishment in either liberal feminism or utopian feminism, both of which seemed irrelevant to their concerns. As sexual radicals, they adhered to a conservative social agenda, feeling that it gave them greater personal freedom. The theatre, that orderly space for misrule, became a rich source for the fashioning of what we now call the modern lesbian identity.

NOTES

1 Portions of this essay have appeared previously in the *Radical History Review*, 1994, 60, and in Andrew H. Miller and James Eli Adams (eds), *Sexualities in Victorian Britain*, Bloomington, Indiana University Press, 1996. I am indebted to the National Endowment for the Humanities for a fellowship which enabled me to write and research on this subject.
2 'Sexuality and power: a review of current work in the history of sexuality', *Feminist Studies*, 1982, 8, Spring, pp. 150–1.
3 The most influential critics for these perspectives have been Judith Butler,

200 *Martha Vicinus*

> *Gender Trouble: Feminism and the Subversion of Identity*, New York, Routledge, 1990, and Sue-Ellen Case, 'Towards a butch-femme aesthetic', *Discourse*, 1988–9, 11, 1, pp. 55–73. For a discussion of the importance of 'the third sex', see Marjorie Garber's *Vested Interests*, New York, Routledge, 1991.

4 Adrienne Rich, 'Compulsory heterosexuality and lesbian existence', *Signs*, 1980, 5, 4, Summer, p. 649.

5 See Elizabeth Wilson's important intervention on behalf of the erotic power of deviance in 'Forbidden love', *Feminist Studies*, 1984, 10, 2, Summer, pp. 213–26. She also critiques Rich's lesbian continuum.

6 Annamarie Jagose, 'Springing Miss Wade: *Little Dorrit* and a Hermeneutics of Suspicion', unpublished paper, December 1993.

7 Doris Sherwood, *Harriet Hosmer: American Sculptor, 1830–1908*, Columbia, University of Missouri, 1991, pp. 169–71, 270–3.

8 The best-known argument for this position is Lillian Faderman's in *Surpassing the Love of Men: Romantic Friendship and Love between Women from the Renaissance to the Present*, New York, William Morrow, 1981, and her essentially unchanged position in *Odd Girls and Twilight Lovers: A History of Lesbian Life in Twentieth-Century America*, New York, Columbia University Press, 1991. See also the ways in which these generalizations have been unproblematically accepted by literary critics such as Tess Cosslett, *Woman to Woman: Female Friendship in Victorian Fiction*, Brighton, Harvester, 1988, and Betty T. Bennett in *Mary Diana Dods: A Gentleman and A Scholar*, New York, William Morrow, 1991.

9 See her *Daring to be Bad: Radical Feminism in America, 1967–75*, Minneapolis, University of Minnesota Press, 1989.

10 A sense of finding one's 'true identity' as a butch or as a femme, particularly in opposition to 1970s feminism, characterizes many of the 'coming out' stories in Joan Nestle (ed.), *The Persistent Desire: A Femme-Butch Reader*, Boston, Alyson Publications, 1992.

11 See Jan Clausen, 'My interesting condition: what does it mean when a lesbian falls in love with a man?', *Outlook*, 1990, 2, 3, Winter, pp. 10ff.

12 See not only Butler's 'Gender and subordination', in Henry Abelove, Michele Aina Barale and David M. Halperin (eds), *Lesbian and Gay Studies Reader*, New York, Routledge, 1993, pp. 307–20, but also her *Gender Trouble*. See also Case, 'Towards a butch-femme aesthetic'.

13 In 'Critically queer', *GLQ*, 1993, 1, 1, pp. 17–32, Butler partially responds to critics who have called her work ahistorical.

14 See George Chauncey, Jr, 'From sexual inversion to homosexuality: medicine and the changing conceptualization of female desire', *Salmagundi*, 1982–3, 58–59, Fall/Winter, pp. 114–46.

15 For a discussion of the implications of this, see Jacqueline Rose, *Sexuality in the Field of Vision*, London, Verso, 1986, pp. 227–8.

16 'The new woman as androgyne: social disorder and gender crisis, 1870–1936', in *Disorderly Conduct: Visions of Gender in Victorian America*, New York, Knopf, p. 272.

17 See Esther Newton's discussion of Ellis' conceptual contradictions in 'The mythic mannish lesbian: Radclyffe Hall and the new woman', in Martin Bauml Duberman, Martha Vicinus and George Chauncey, Jr (eds), *Hidden from History*, New York, New York American Library, pp. 288–9.

18 Lisa M. Walker, 'How to recognize a lesbian: the cultural politics of looking like what you are', *Signs*, 1993, 18, 4, Summer, 868, 888. See also Shane Phelan, '(Be)Coming out: lesbian identity and politics', *Signs*, 1993, 18, 4, Summer, pp. 765–90.

Feminists and sex 201

19 Jeffrey Weeks, *Sexuality and Its Discontents: Meanings, Myths & Modern Sexualities*, London, Routledge and Kegan Paul, 1985, pp. 171–2.
20 Esther Newton, 'The mythic mannish lesbian', p. 286.
21 Faderman, *Surpassing the Love of Men*, p. 249. This section reprints her 'The morbidification of love between women by 19th-century sexologists', *The Journal of Homosexuality*, 1978, 4, pp. 73–90.
22 Terry Castle, *The Apparitional Lesbian: Female Homosexuality and Modern Culture*, New York, Columbia University Press, 1993, p. 19.
23 Wilson, 'Forbidden love', pp. 220–3.
24 For a discussion of one figure used by homosexual men and women, see my essay, 'The adolescent boy: fin-de-siècle femme fatale?', *Journal of the History of Sexuality*, 1994, 5, 1, July, pp. 90–114, which looks at one of these created figures in literature.
25 For American male homosexuals, see Laurence Senelick, 'Lady and the tramp: drag differentials in the progressive era', in Laurence Senelick (ed.), *Gender in Performance: The Presentation of Difference in the Performing Arts*, Hanover, University Press of New England, 1992, pp. 26–45; and George Chauncey's introduction to his book, *Gay New York: Gender, Urban Culture and the Making of the Gay Male World, 1890–1940*, New York, Basic Books, 1994.
26 Gerda Tarnow, *Sarah Bernhardt: The Art within the Legend*, Princeton, Princeton University Press, 1972, p. 221, cites nine parodies of *L'Aiglon* alone, with at least a dozen more based on her other successes.
27 Biographies of Bernhardt are legion. See Tarnow, *Sarah Bernhardt*, p. 211, and Arthur Gold and Robert Fizdale, *The Divine Sarah: The Life of Sarah Bernhardt*, New York, Alfred Knopf, 1991. For her theatrical innovations and influence, see John Stokes, 'Sarah Bernhardt', in John Stokes, Michael R. Booth and Susan Basnett, *Bernhardt, Terry, Duse: The Actress in her Time*, Cambridge, Cambridge University Press, 1988.
28 The critical response to Bernhardt's numerous *travesti* roles – nine in the first thirty-two years of her career and eighteen in the last twenty-seven – are recounted in many biographies. The best summary is Tarnow, *Sarah Bernhardt*, pp. 210–27. Bernhardt's description of her three Hamlets as strong minds in weak bodies comes from her *The Art of the Theatre* (1929), H. J. Stenning (trans.), London, Geoffrey Bles, n.d., p. 141.
29 George Wickes describes the contents of *Quelques Portraits-Sonnets de femmes* in *The Amazon of Letters: The Life and Loves of Natalie Barney*, New York, G. P. Putnam's, 1976, pp. 45–6. The volume has never been reprinted.
30 Quoted and translated in Wickes, *The Amazon of Letters*, p. 40.
31 See *The Sketch*, January 1902, 403. *The Sketch* does not identify who the Marquis is imitating, but theatregoers of the day would never have missed the visual reference.
32 H. Montgomery Hyde, *The Love That Dared Not Speak Its Name*, Boston, Little Brown, 1970, pp. 153–4. He had married his cousin, Lillian Chetwynd, who left him on their honeymoon and received a decree of nullity.
33 Lady De Frece [Vesta Tilley], *Recollections of Vesta Tilley*, London, Hutchinson, 1934, p. 125. According to Hyde, p. 154, the sale of his jewellery and clothes (mostly women's or, like his waistcoats, effeminate) raised £88,000 for his creditors.
34 Gilles Barbedette and Michel Carassou, *Paris Gay 1925* Paris, Presses de la Renaissance, 1981, p. 66. See also the illustration of Weber in costume opposite p. 255.
35 Policemen often stuck their nightsticks up women's skirts, both to expose them and to hurt them. These and similar incidents are described in Martha Vicinus,

202 *Martha Vicinus*

Independent Women: Work and Community for Single Women, 1850–1920, Chicago, University of Chicago Press, 1985, pp. 262–8.

36 Ethel Coquhuon, 'Modern Feminism and Sex-Antagonism', *Quarterly Review*, 1913, 219, p. 155, and Walter Heape, *Sex Antagonism*, London, Constable, 1913, pp. 206–14. See also Sir Almroth E. Wright, *The Unexpurgated Case Against Woman Suffrage*, London, Constable, 1913, which argues that women could not lead the country because they suffered temporary monthly insanity.

37 See Cicely Hamilton's unrevealing autobiography, *Life Errant*, London, J. M. Dent, 1935; E. Adlard (ed.), *Edy: Recollections of Edith Craig*, London, Frederick Muller, 1949; and J. Melville, *Ellen and Edy: A Biography of Ellen Terry and her daughter, Edith Craig, 1847–1947*, London, Pandora, 1987. Edy and her partner were friends with Radclyffe Hall and her partner.

38 Quoted from Marie Corelli's *Woman,–or Suffragette?*, in Lisa Ticknor, *The Spectacle of Women: Imagery of the Suffrage Campaign, 1907–14*, Chicago, University of Chicago Press, 1988, p. 198.

39 Ticknor, *The Spectacle of Women*, pp. 162–74. See especially her astute discussion of the hysteric.

40 See Jeffrey Weeks, *Coming Out: Homosexual Politics in Britain, from the Nineteenth Century to the Present*, London, Quartet, 1977, pp. 106–7, for a discussion of efforts to criminalize lesbian sexual acts in 1920–1.

41 For a fuller discussion of these issues, see Shari Benstock, 'Paris lesbianism and the politics of reaction, 1900–1940', in Duberman *et al.*, *Hidden from History*, pp. 332–46.

12 Beauvoir's philosophy as the hidden paradigm of contemporary feminism[1]

Karen Vintges

'Her problems are my problems', 'I live exactly as Beauvoir', 'I *am* Beauvoir'... During years of research on the life and work of Simone de Beauvoir I frequently received such reactions from all types of feminists. Their passionate response to Beauvoir's writings and personality was miles away from the dismissive attitude of some major contemporary feminist theorists who had summarily condemned Beauvoir's thinking as outdated and 'male biased'.[2] Numerous 'ordinary feminists', however, enthusiastically identified themselves with Beauvoir, and it even appeared that she herself was among us!

In this article, we will examine why Beauvoir's life and work still have such an impact on women of our times. We will see that her philosophy already encompasses all the elements of contemporary feminism, and so much so that it can even count as its paradigm. This, however, is not immediately visible. To grasp the reasons for their continuing impact on women of our times we need to go into the philosophical backgrounds of her life and work. A different picture of Beauvoir from the usual then emerges, the usual one being that of the *pur sang* rationalist thinker. As she is usually seen as a follower of (the early) Sartre, she, as is he, is considered a genuine Cartesian, valuing consciousness above all, opposing bodily dimensions.[3] If one perceives any difference at all, then it is that she is more of a real Enlightenment thinker. Iris Murdoch, for instance, ranks her as a representative of Enlightenment optimism, the historical background being that 'she [Beauvoir] belongs to a race whose liberation can still be conceived as a proper task of Reason and one which is within its power'.[4]

Against these views on Beauvoir as a Cartesian and Enlightenment thinker I would like to present another, seemingly contradictory[5] interpretation: Beauvoir as a Rousseauist feminist. Beauvoir was extending to women what Rousseau claimed for men, and like Rousseau she bridged the gap between rationalism and romanticism, thereby constructing the paradigm of contemporary feminism. To demonstrate this thesis I shall first deal with the broader philosophical framework of Beauvoir's thinking and the philosophy of her feminist study *The Second Sex* more specifically. A closer look will be taken at her ethics as well as at her life as part of her ethical project. Finally, I shall try

204 *Karen Vintges*

to outline my new interpretation of Beauvoir in relation to contemporary feminism, especially in relation to its logic of 'equality and difference', a theme that proved crucial throughout the long history of feminism.

PHILOSOPHICAL FRAMEWORKS

The Second Sex (1949), Beauvoir's study on the situation of women, provoked much dispute and discussion in the sixth feminist movement, and this discussion continues this very day. Exploring the historic situation of women, Beauvoir concluded that they had been prevented from taking active control of their own lives. Woman has been the Other throughout culture, man has been the Self, the subject. Woman has been subjugated to man, who, partly with woman's consent, made her merely an extension of himself. For the first time in history, through the availability of contraceptives and the access to paid work, women have the chance to develop into a Self as well. *The Second Sex* is a passionate appeal to women to do so whenever they can.

The impact of *The Second Sex* in the fifties was non-existent. It was only twenty years after its appearance that the book was discovered by the new feminist movement which had its focus on 'body politics'. Shulamith Firestone in her *Dialectic of Sex* (1970) referred to Beauvoir explicitly; others like Kate Millett in her *Sexual Politics* (1971) were highly influenced by Beauvoir's *The Second Sex* , as Millett herself would only later acknowledge. The same goes for Betty Friedan, whose *Feminine Mystique* (1963) started the feminist movement in the United States. Only in 1975 did she admit that she 'who had helped start women on the new road', had been herself 'started on the road' by Beauvoir.[6]

Control by men of female sexuality and fertility were seen as central to the oppression of women, and free contraception and abortion on demand were a key issue. Economic autonomy was another. Women had started to enter the job market but the economic evolution of woman's condition, as Beauvoir had announced it in *The Second Sex*, had yet to be accomplished. Socialist feminism took up this theme and found its theoretical inspiration in Beauvoir as well. However, with respect to the theme of the liberation of female sexuality, after a few years the new women's movement radicalized into an explicit 'romanticism', stressing the difference between men and women, masculinity and femininity.[7] Women's capacities were regarded as superior, rather than inferior to men's. Instead of becoming equal to men, women should develop their own values, which would amount to a complete cultural revolution. Feminism would bring harmony by breaking down the barriers between mind and body, work and love, thereby bringing mankind a fuller freedom.[8]

On a theoretical level this view was expressed by an overtly disapproving reaction towards Enlightenment feminism: both socialist and liberal feminism were now seen as adapting women to male standards, encouraging

Beauvoir's philosophy   205

them to emancipate in order to become identical to men. Modern feminism aspired to be more than just another emancipation movement. It was not simply striving after social equality between men and women, and the abolition of women's oppression – it wanted to offer fundamental alternatives to the dominant culture. This so-called cultural feminism soon became dominant in feminist theory and Beauvoir's *The Second Sex* was marginalized and even criticized as extremely misogynist. Beauvoir had been embraced by part of the emerging women's movement in the 1960s, but now she was criticized intensely by other sections. *The Second Sex* was condemned as a 'male' view of women that had been superseded by the new, 'real' feminism. Psychoanalytical theory now became important as a source of knowledge about female sexuality – for instance in Juliet Mitchell's *Psychoanalysis and Feminism* (1974) – and as an inspiration for the articulation of a different form of thinking and writing compared with the masculine 'logocentric' approach. Feminist theoreticians such as Luce Irigaray and Julia Kristeva, as well as French writers, such as Hélène Cixous, sought to develop an *écriture féminine*, arguing that what lies outside the dominant subject form in Western society is femininity. Because it has been excluded from culture, the feminine would be culture-critical above all and its articulation was seen as a revolutionary project. These French feminists all mentioned Beauvoir in one way or another as an extremely important figure but distanced themselves from her so-called male philosophical point of view.[9] The dichotomy between equality and difference now became central to the agenda, and Beauvoir's work was seen as typical of the egalitarian approach.

However, it would seem that the philosophy of *The Second Sex* has generally not been recognized. On those rare occasions when the text is discussed from a philosophical perspective, only the Sartrean notions it contains are highlighted. Because Beauvoir applied the notions of Sartre's early work *Being and Nothingness* (1943), she is accused of unleashing Cartesian male thinking on (the subject of) women. Male values are said to dominate in her work because she is believed to place consciousness above the body, thinking above feeling, activity over passivity and transcendence above nature.[10] She is even said to have joined the ranks of our culture's long tradition of misogyny, insofar as she despises women and rejects the female body.[11] However, Beauvoir did not simply copy Sartre's ideas and her thinking does not fit his Cartesianism at all. By way of her ethical theory, she developed a new version of the existentialist philosophy in which solidarity with fellow human beings, corporality and emotion had a very great place.

Beauvoir's general philosophical framework can be traced back to an affinity with a 'phenomenological' perspective, especially in the field of philosophical anthropology, a perspective which approaches humans as situated beings. She shares this approach, which is influenced by Heidegger and others, with Merleau-Ponty and Lévinas. The point of departure of the phenomenological perspective is that humans are always involved in the world, and so can only be understood within the total, highly complex

206 *Karen Vintges*

context of that world. The person should thus be understood within his or her situation. Not only are humans always involved in the world but they are also seen as beings who continually give meaning to their situation. Thus, humans are objective subjectivity and subjective objectivity. Their bodily existence in time and place always has a signifying component. A work in which Beauvoir expresses this phenomenological approach most clearly is her essay on the Marquis de Sade, entitled *Must we burn De Sade?* (1952). Here she presents an entirely different concept of man compared to that of Sartre, which amounts to an altogether different concept of emotion. For Sartre emotion is 'bad faith' and self-deceit. For Beauvoir, on the other hand, emotion is a positive experience, through which contact with others occurs. In her essay on Sade, not being able to experience emotion represents a lack of full humanity. It is through emotion that we become a 'psycho-physiological unity' and achieve 'immediate communication' with the other. In the experience of emotion there is a confluence of body and mind, which can be contrasted to pure, individuated consciousness. Beauvoir herself says that she and Sartre disagreed about emotion from the start: 'He had no taste, he said, for all those disordered physical reactions – violent palpitations of the heart, trembling, or giddiness – which paralyse verbal communication.' Not only had Sartre no sense for emotion, he is contemptuous of it. Emotion is not authentic, because it is not lucid: 'If you gave way to tears or nerves or sea-sickness, he said, you were simply being weak.'[12]

Beauvoir, on the contrary, speaks of feelings as 'an experience of fulfilment'. For her, they are a 'direct contact with the world'.[13] We find the same leitmotiv in her discussions of ethics. Here, too, the emotional dimension emerges as the meeting-place with fellow human beings. Her ethical essay, *Pyrrhus et Cinéas* (1944) opens as follows: 'I knew a child who cried because the concierge's little son had died. His parents let him cry, but then became irritated: "He wasn't your brother". The child dried his tears.' But these parents were wrong, Beauvoir continues. True, the little boy is not my brother. But if I cry for him, he is no longer a stranger. Who my neighbour is cannot be determined in advance: 'my tears decide'. Here again, emotion resolves the difference between myself and the other.[14]

In *The Ethics of Ambiguity* (1946), Beauvoir argues that the world reveals itself to us only 'through rejection, desire, hate and love'. It is through them that we really meet other people. For Sartre meeting other people is an illusion because emotion belongs in fact to consciousness. To feel emotion is a free choice of the mind. Thus the splendid isolation of the lucid consciousness is always there and real contact with fellow beings is in the final analysis unthinkable. Beauvoir clearly rejects Satre's solipsism. Her essay *Must we burn De Sade?* should, in my opinion, be regarded as an indirect response to Sartre's solipsism. Both Sartre and Sade saw love as an impossibility and emphasized the conflict, the enmity and the separation between people. Beauvoir deplored Sade's inability to forget himself as a consciousness and

Beauvoir's philosophy 207

put forward emotion as the ability to achieve contact with the other. It would appear that we can replace Sade's name with that of Sartre, and that we can read the covert message of her article as: *Must we burn Sartre?*.

Beauvoir's position in her essay on Sade can be traced back to her earlier work, *The Ethics of Ambiguity*. This book contains in fact a consistent attempt to reconcile Sartre's thoughts about the ontological freedom of man with the phenomenological perspective in philosophical anthropology. In his work *Being and Nothingness* Sartre had affirmed a lucid, supremely conscious way of life as the only authentic human existence. In *The Ethics of Ambiguity*, Beauvoir on the contrary develops a theory of human beings as essentially situated. She argues that the human condition is ambiguous. As situated beings, we are a psycho-physiological unity. But, she continues, our ontological freedom, our status as pure and isolated consciousness, is always there at the background of our existence, and this is the reason why life is a continuous moral project. By a moral transformation of the will, a 'conversion', we continually have to *situate ourselves*, rising from this background of pure, individuated consciousness to the level of incarnated, i.e. situated, beings. Only in this way are we able to overcome the distance and separation between ourselves and others, and engage with them as our fellow human beings.

However, she adds that our situation can be such that we cannot realize our ontological freedom by such a moral conversion. The historical situation of women and slaves has stunted their ability to exercise fully their ontological freedom. Beauvoir emphasizes the influence of social circumstances on the life of individuals. Every person is always situated, i.e. embedded, in time and place, and as such every person lives as a psycho-physiological unity. But his situation can be such that he is unable to experience *actively* and realize the potentiality of his ontological freedom. Social freedom is therefore a necessary condition for situating ourselves on the basis of our ontological freedom. We may conclude that Beauvoir succeeded in reconciling Sartre's notion of ontological freedom with the idea of human beings as a psycho-physiological unities, a reconciliation Sartre himself did not achieve.

THE PHILOSOPHY OF *THE SECOND SEX*

Having sketched the philosophical stance of Simone de Beauvoir, we have cleared the decks to deal with the philosophy of *The Second Sex*. This seminal text should be placed in the context of Beauvoir's reworking of Sartre's theory in *The Ethics of Ambiguity*. But the two texts are rarely studied together from such a philosophical vantage point: when the philosophical framework of *The Second Sex* is at stake, only the Sartrean notions it contains are treated. Because Beauvoir applied these concepts she is accused of unleashing 'male thinking' on the subject of women.

Such a critique was formulated, for instance, by Genevieve Lloyd, in her

208　*Karen Vintges*

The Man of Reason (1984). According to Lloyd, transcendence in Sartre signifies nothing less than an abhorrence of the female body and therefore *The Second Sex*, in which Beauvoir uses this concept, is masculine and sexist as well. In the final section of *Being and Nothingness*, Sartre indeed regards the female body as a dangerous threat to freedom, that is to pure consciousness (the so-called *pour-soi*).[15] All 'holes' threaten the *pour-soi*. They seduce the subject into becoming mere flesh and so fill the hole. And Sartre continues:

> The obscenity of the feminine sex is that of everything which 'gapes open'. . . . In herself woman appeals to a strange flesh which is to transform her into a fullness of being by penetration and dissolution. Conversely woman senses her condition as an appeal precisely because she is 'in the form of a hole'. . . . Beyond any doubt her sex is a mouth and a voracious mouth which devours the penis.[16]

Thus the female body emerges as the opposite of transcendence, in fact as its enemy par excellence, and Sartre's philosophical framework seems sexist indeed, for it defines the female body in opposition to consciousness.

The question now is in which form Sartre's conceptual framework appears in *The Second Sex*: is it applied in its original form, and is the female body also seen by Beauvoir as the enemy par excellence of freedom? There are passages which would suggest this. Beauvoir sometimes speaks in very negative terms about female bodily functions, such as menstruation, pregnancy and labour.[17] In addition, however, we also find an emphasis on the fact that the body is not a thing, but an 'experienced' reality. The real human body, Beauvoir contends, 'is not the body-object described by biologists . . . but the body as lived in by the subject':

> It is not merely as a body, but rather as a body subject to taboos, to laws, that the subject is conscious of himself and attains fulfilment – it is with reference to certain values that he evaluates himself. And, once again, it is not upon physiology that values can be based; rather, the facts of biology take on values that the existent bestows upon them.[18]

Referring to the insights of Heidegger and Merleau-Ponty, she asserts that the body is not a thing, but a 'situation'.[19] By doing so, she approaches the body explicitly from the phenomenological perspective: the perception of the human being as objective subjectivity and subjective objectivity. Reductionist biological notions of woman are subjected to permanent and incisive criticism throughout *The Second Sex*. Women's bodies always contain a dimension of *meaning* for Beauvoir. She claims that the position of woman as 'Other' throughout history was by no means the inevitable consequence of woman's bodily functions. It was the outcome of an *historically contingent* process, in which the biology of woman has been appropriated by men to relegate her to the specific role of the 'Other'. It was

Beauvoir's philosophy 209

the oppression of women that made it impossible for them to develop into an autonomous Self.

Through the central role of the thesis of woman as *historic* Other in *The Second Sex*, it is clear that whenever Beauvoir talks about the female body, she has the situated body in mind, i.e. the body which is embedded in and experienced through socio-cultural practices and meanings. Her approach of woman as situated human being made it impossible for her to share Sartre's high-handed dismissal of the female body as the antithesis of consciousness. The real object of criticism in *The Second Sex* is not the female body but the traditional situation of women. If women gain active control over their own lives they will also experience their bodily functions including menstruation, pregnancy and labour in different ways.

Removing the female body from Sartre's dualistic ontology and ranking it at a socio-cultural level, Beauvoir not only transformed the very core of Sartre's sexist conceptual framework, but his Cartesianism as well. Cartesian thinking, with its strong distinction between mind and body, is left behind by phenomenology, fusing the two in the concept of man as always 'situated': a body in time and place which is always experienced and as such is a unity of flesh and consciousness. Therefore, Beauvoir's appeal to women to grasp their chances to develop into a Self cannot be considered a plea for women to become pure rational selves. Beauvoir wanted women to become autonomous selves, but her plea is for the sensitive 'situated' self, with true emotions. And here is our first clue to her Rousseauism. She – like Sartre – identified the good life with dependence on self. Human beings should live as self-responsible, authentic beings and not live 'through' others. But, in contrast to Sartre, it is not the rational, lucid self but the 'situated', sensitive self she is after. Beauvoir now claimed for women what Rousseau saw as the prerogative of men: to develop a sensitive self with its own sentiments and inclinations.

As Charles Taylor puts it, Rousseau was *bridging* rationalism and romanticism because his discourse on emotions and the sensitive self was forged against the background of the view of man as a disengaged rational self, developed by Descartes and Locke among others. Rousseau remained on the modern side of the watershed, because he presupposed the triumph of the new identity of disengaged reason over the premodern notion of personal identity as embedded in an ontic logos. Only in this context could our subjective sentiments acquire a decisive value.[20]

The parallel with Beauvoir's mission is very clear in this respect. She also formulated her view of (wo)man as sensitive self against the background of the disengaged rational self that dominated Sartre's theory, bridging rationalism and romanticism in a way similar to Rousseau. The impact of Rousseau's work was enormous in his time. People wept and embraced each other. It was his appeal to become a sensitive self that moved them and that they somehow recognized as 'being in the air'. Beauvoir also articulated something that was 'in the air'. But this time it was for women. They now

210 *Karen Vintges*

felt the longing to become autonomous selves as well. Beauvoir voiced her plea to women not only in *The Second Sex* but also in her philosophical novels and her autobiography. There, she expressed it very attractively, with all the romantic melancholy and feelings of solitude that had also made Rousseau's writings so alluring. It is this appeal that still moves women all over the world and inspires in them a desire to become 'selves'. Like Rousseau, Beauvoir received a flood of letters from readers who wrote that she had saved their lives. Her work has had a resonance with women world-wide, who recognize themselves in her words and recognize each other in having read them. Her funeral was crowded and flowers are always on her grave.[21]

'ART OF LIVING'

We shall now look at Beauvoir's ethics more specifically. We saw that she spoke in terms of a moral conversion: man is an ontologically free being but has to search situatedness by a moral conversion. According to her, only life as an incarnated, sensitive being is ethical because only thereby is man *fully realizing* his ontological freedom. In the first part of *The Ethics of Ambiguity* Beauvoir underpinned this idea theoretically. She introduced a distinction between 'being free' and 'willing oneself free' (*se vouloir libre*, also: *vouloir vivre*), between 'ontological' or 'original' freedom on the one hand, and 'moral' freedom on the other. By willing ourselves free we identify positively with the fact that we *are* free and have to make choices continually. We don't turn away from the world indifferently, but we commit ourselves by actively involving ourselves with other people. But why should we call this a moral attitude? If we will ourselves free and become actively involved with the world and people around us, can't we then equally become involved in 'evil doings'? This is, however, impossible, because 'willing oneself free' also implies that we want freedom as such: we take up a position against every form of oppression, both of ourselves and of others. Willing oneself free thus entails a positive involvement with other people that is not passive in nature. We do not adopt a noncommittal attitude to others, but oblige ourselves to become concerned with their fate and welfare. This is why Beauvoir saw 'willing oneself free' as a moral attitude and why she spoke in terms of a moral conversion.

Through the configuration of conversion, Beauvoir brought together both the continuing presence of ontological freedom, and the active involvement with other people. Given the ever-present ontological freedom of man, the element of pure consciousness he carries within himself, radical separation will always be the background of our existence. This means that in the end we can never speak for another person and universalizing moral theories are invalid. In opposition to such an abstract moral theory, Beauvoir introduced a different approach, an 'ethics of ambiguity'. Man's ambiguous condition is the reason why universal moral laws cannot exist. However, the

Beauvoir's philosophy 211

existence of the concrete can certainly be the locus of a moral dimension. In this way, Beauvoir managed to retain the sting from Sartre's existentialism – his idea of the radical separation between people – and to achieve a reconciliation between that existentialist barb and a moral perspective.

At the end of *The Ethics of Ambiguity*, Beauvoir was still seeking to ground a positive morality. Later she distanced herself from this 'moralism'. The universal side of her ethics is thereafter only found in the form of a negative moral code which states that no person may be oppressed. For the elaboration of a positive ethics we must turn to her literary work and her autobiography. For Beauvoir, philosophical literature was an essential part of philosophy. In this genre, the subjective truth, i.e. the truth of concrete experiences of people in concrete situations, can be explored without forcing them into abstract schemes or formulas. Because Beauvoir also saw the subjective dimension as the location of ethics, her novels can be seen as the continuation of her philosophical reflections on the foundations of ethics.

If we look at her novel *The Mandarins* (1954), this becomes immediately apparent. Not only are moral decisions the central theme in the novel, we also witness the emergence here of a specific type of positive ethics: the notion of a personal morality in the form of a self-identity that is shaped by a specific life-project. Beauvoir even introduces a separate term for this type of project. One of the young people in the social milieu depicted in the novel, Lambert, for whom the writer Henri has an exemplary function, urges the latter to write novels which can provide a leitmotiv for personal actions: 'First of all,' Lambert asserts, 'we need an ethics, an art of living.' Later on, he implores of Henri: 'You have a sense of what is real. You ought to teach us how to live for the moment.' At first, Henri protests:

> 'Formulating an ethics, an art of living, doesn't exactly enter into my plans.' His eyes shining, Lambert looked up at Henri. 'Oh, I stated that badly. I wasn't thinking of a theoretical treatise. But there are things that you consider important, there are values you believe in.'[22]

In the end, Henri makes it his task to capture a coherent identity for himself and decides to start writing again. Beauvoir introduced the concept 'art of living' here as an equivalent to ethics. This concept expresses in compact form how moral decisions are made: it not only articulates the fact that ethics take on the form of a concrete, individual approach to life, but also represents the attitude that moral decisions come about in a continual creative process without the application of general methods, moral laws or rules. In *The Mandarins* ethics take on the form of a fully open ethos (with the negative moral code that no person may be oppressed, continuing to work in the background). Beauvoir considers man an open collection of heterogeneous elements. His life is 'pulverized by events, scattered, broken'.[23] However, it is man's task to bring together that abundance of elements into a unity.

In two lectures, *Que peut la littérature?* ('What is the power of literature?',

212   *Karen Vintges*

1965) and *Mon expérience d'écrivain* ('My experience as a writer', 1966), Beauvoir emphasized that human life is fragmented, or 'detotalized': we are never the total of our experiences. One emotion will always escape us as we experience another. Our memory is incapable of forging the diversity of all recollections into a unity. Only literature can succeed in reconciling the irreconcilability of all our experiences. Literature alone is able to pursue two themes simultaneously, just as a symphony can develop various themes at the same time. Literature is the means by which we can fashion an identity out of our countless, dispersed experiences: writing is self-creation. However, this does not concern the creation of a psychological entity. Beauvoir never lost her disgust for the 'inner-self'. The 'I' is a construction in writing. Henri realizes that: 'The truth of one's life is outside oneself, in events, in other people, in things; to talk about oneself, one must talk about everything else.'[24]

Beauvoir's concept of the necessity of a conscious construction of one's own identity out of a heterogeneous collection of elements is diametrically opposed to Sartre's thinking. In essence, his theory requires us to *remain free from* an identity. Consciousness has to remain empty because otherwise we would become a thing, and our human existence would not be authentic. It is true Sartre also saw man as a being who creates himself, and he stated every human life is characterized by a *projet fondamental*. But this fundamental project can only be reconstructed in retrospect from a person's actions. For Sartre, self-creation cannot form a way of living. We must not live as though there is an 'I' which guides our actions and to which our experiences manifest themselves. We have to be aware of the emptiness of our consciousness, and of the task of continually creating ourselves. No identity can be stuck on us, either by ourselves, or by others. Compared to the anarchism or nomadism of Sartre, Beauvoir emerges as a 'moralist'; in her thinking, everything a person does should contribute to his own identity.

> Renouncing all previous anger and desires and giving preference to the emotions of the moment means smashing human existence into worthless fragments, erasing the past. [Instead,] it is the task of everyone to realise his individual unity by involving his past in aims for the future.[25]

Man should assume his responsibility for a specific collection of moral values by providing himself with a coherent identity. This does not imply a finished or closed identity; it remains open to the future, although being based on the past, this openness is limited.[26] Reflecting on the past, we have to remain conscious of who and what we are. Beauvoir stated that she wrote her autobiography because she loved constructing herself so that she could continue to create herself from a firm base.[27] Life for her was 'an undertaking that had a clear direction'.[28] In this light, Beauvoir's autobiographical work emerges as the core of her oeuvre. It forms the conscious construction of an individual identity and way of life and as such reflects her attitudes to ethics as an art of living. We should interpret her autobiography as ethical

Beauvoir's philosophy 213

self-creation rather than as self-analysis. For Beauvoir, the self is something to be stylized on the surface rather than examined in depth. Her autobiography is not aimed at revealing an inner world beneath or behind her active life, but at charting and styling that active life. She used the inventory technique in order to weigh and determine herself continually. According to the task she had set herself within the framework of her art of living ethics, she thus designed a coherent identity for herself as she went along.

In her autobiography Beauvoir told us that Rousseau was one of her most beloved writers and that she read and reread his *Confessions* endlessly. Rousseau created himself in his autobiography as well. Although he spoke in terms of confession and truth, he also mentioned the character of autobiography as fiction. Gutman, in my view, correctly states that in his *Confessions* Rousseau wanted 'to create a "self" which can serve to define himself, to himself and to others, in the face of a hostile social order'. To create a unitary self Rousseau used the self-technique of 'enumeration of each and every experience that has made one what and who one is.'[29] It is also in this respect that Beauvoir can be seen as a Rousseauist feminist, trying, by the self-technique of writing, to create a self as a woman intellectual in the face of a hostile social order.[30]

BEAUVOIR'S PHILOSOPHY AS PARADIGM OF THE 'SIXTH FEMINIST WAVE'

Finally, I would like to discuss the relationship of *The Second Sex* to contemporary feminism, focussing on the equality-difference debate in feminist theory. Should women be considered as different from men, or is this way of thinking an essentialist trap and should we merely think in terms of 'sameness' between men and women? We have seen that equality and difference were two main approaches in contemporary feminism. However, a third important point of view came to the fore in the course of the debate. Out of 'Romantic' feminist thought that stressed the difference between man and woman, a so-called postmodern feminism emerged, which carried the deconstruction of the subject 'woman' a stage further. Contemporary postmodernist thinkers such as Jacques Derrida and Michel Foucault harboured a deep suspicion towards the supposed unity of the subject, and they sought to escape from the restrictions of the unitary self. According to this Neo-Nietzschean philosophy, all ethics and morality are themselves already a power mechanism; they limit man to being a creature with a so-called inner life, a creature who can and must continually give an account of his actions. In this way man acquires an identity and as such becomes predictable and controllable: the self is fashioned into an 'ordre interieur' that is actually the mainstay of the dominant social order. To move beyond this invisible prison-house, other ways of living and forms of subjectivity have to be developed.[31]

Feminist theoreticians, such as, for instance, Rosi Braidotti in her

214   *Karen Vintges*

Nomadic Subjects (1994) retheorized the feminine subject in a similar way. If we assume that a unitary subject is unavoidably a product of power mechanisms, we can no longer speak in terms of 'woman' as an essential feminine subject who has to be liberated. Moreover, we may no longer assume the identity of the feminine as an essence that can be articulated. Instead, we should unravel and deconstruct fixed meanings of femininity, so that an open space is created that permits the shaping of new ways of thinking and living. Postmodern feminism, with its suspicion of any fixed subject 'woman', expresses the political mood of the feminist movement as we approach the end of the twentieth century. Differences between women have come to dominate the agenda of the women's movement, and universal similarities between women are no longer taken for granted. Postmodern feminism can thus be seen as the third important approach in contemporary feminism, paradoxically stressing the difference between women rather than their common identity.

In my opinion, Beauvoir's philosophy in many ways prefigures and anticipates postmodern feminism, and it may help us to clarify the meaning of all three varieties of contemporary feminist thought discussed above. Let us begin to look at the first two approaches through the prism of *The Second Sex*. Equality and difference are frequently thought of as contradictory ideas, even though some have advocated combining them in a pragmatic way.[32] Beauvoir's philosophy, however, enables us to perceive the linkages between the two approaches and thereby clarifies the way they go together in the feminist movement. The universal demand for social freedom, necessary for people to develop into a self, provides the negative moral code of *The Second Sex*. Equality between men and women – equality in not being oppressed – is the background against which new personal identities of women can emerge. In *The Second Sex*, we find no ready-made model for a common, new identity for women; only the prediction that cultural differences between men and women will remain, following the disappearance of women's oppression:

> There will always be certain differences between man and woman; her eroticism, and therefore her sexual world, have a special form of their own, and therefore can not fail to engender a sensuality, a sensitivity of a special nature. This means that her relations to her own body, to that of the male, to the child, will never be identical with those the male bears to his own body, to that of the female, and to the child; those who make much of 'equality in difference' could not with good grace refuse to grant me the possible existence of differences in equality.[33]

Equality and difference are interwoven in the philosophy of this text in a way that perfectly captures their continuing dialectic in contemporary feminism. The two seemingly contradictory principles can be quite well combined when one is seen as the precondition of the other; social and political equality are a necessary but not a sufficient condition for the emer-

Beauvoir's philosophy 215

gence of new female, but not perforce feminine, identities. Both can be seen as part of a larger project that aims at enlarging the freedom for women to decide for themselves how they will live.

The Second Sex was severely criticized by cultural feminists who thought it merely implied the injunction for women to become identical to men. A closer scrutiny of the text discloses that its aim is exactly the opposite, namely to make women free so that they can create new situations, new cultural meanings and new ways of experiencing what life as a woman can be. Surveying the entire corpus of Beauvoir's philosophy, including her auto-biographical writings, we feel confident to affirm that she really was a thinker of our times, as even the crucial themes of postmodernism are integral to her thought. She, like Sartre, was thoroughly familiar with Surrealism and other modernist movements from which postmodernism inherited its suspicion of the unitary deep self. Beauvoir shared Sartre's disgust for the 'deep inner self', but in addition she distanced herself from his ideas of man as a subject. She knew people did not live the lives of such a self at all; women *are* not a self, they have to *capture* one in a bitter contest against all kinds of constraints that are still powerfully present. But what they must win is a 'situated' self, instead of chasing after the mirage of the deep psychological one.

In her own life Beauvoir wanted to develop an 'art of living' that could be *inspiring* to other women and would give them guidance on how to give meaning to their own lives. She wanted to develop an experimental style, a model of what life as an active and creative woman could be like. She herself sought to live in accordance with the ideas developed in *The Second Sex*, but she did so as a singular and contingent project – an *art* of living. In this way she reconciled *avant la lettre* the postmodernist aversion of the fixed subject *and* the cultural feminist project to develop alternatives for the dominant patriarchal culture.

Beauvoir's philosophy thus encompasses all three approaches of contemporary feminism. Between three and four million copies of *The Second Sex* have by now been sold.[34] It must surely be considered the most important theoretical work in contemporary feminism. As we have pointed out above, her autobiographical oeuvre ought to be seen as an integral part of her philosophical 'system'. Taking a close look at her thought, it becomes clear that all the themes of contemporary feminism were already present in her work. In this sense we feel justified to conclude that Beauvoir has set the agenda for the women's movement of the late twentieth century, and that her philosophy can be called paradigmatic for contemporary feminism. She and her texts will remain with us for some time to come.

NOTES

1 I wish to thank Margaret Simons and the editors for their comments on earlier versions of this chapter. My treatment of Beauvoir is based on my book

216 *Karen Vintges*

Philosophy as Passion: The Thinking of Simone de Beauvoir, Bloomington, Indiana University Press, 1996.

2 Margaret Simons deals with this anti-Beauvoirism in her 'The moral philosophy of Simone de Beauvoir', paper presented at the American Philosophical Association, New York, 1987. See also her 'Introduction' in M. Simons, (ed.), *Feminist Interpretations of Simone de Beauvoir*, Pennsylvania, Pennsylvania State University Press, 1995, pp. 1–28.

3 When we deal with Sartre's philosophy here we always refer to his pre-Marxist 'existentialism'.

4 See Iris Murdoch, *Sartre, Romantic Rationalist*, Cambridge MA, Yale University Press, 1953, p. 53.

5 Rousseau was a sexist himself.

6 *Saturday Review*, 14 June 1975, p. 71. Quoted in: Sandra Dijkstra, 'Simone de Beauvoir and Betty Friedan: the politics of omission', *Feminist Studies*, 1980, 6, Summer, pp. 290–303.

7 For the long history of romanticist feminism, see Ursula Vogel, 'Rationalism and romanticism: two strategies for women's liberation', in J. Evans (ed.) *Feminism and Political Theory*, London, Sage, 1986, pp. 17–45.

8 For a picture of its romantic cultural context, especially that of Paris 1968, see Charles Taylor, *Sources of the Self*, Cambridge, University of Cambridge Press, 1989; Richard Holmes, *Footsteps*, London, Hodder and Stoughton, 1985.

9 See Ieme van der Poel, *Une révolution de la pensée: maoïsme et féminisme à travers* Tel Quel, Les Temps modernes *et* Esprit, Amsterdam, Rodopi, 1992.

10 See Mary Evans, *Simone de Beauvoir – A Feminist Mandarin*, London, Tavistock, 1985, pp. 56–7, xi; Naomi Greene, 'Sartre, Sexuality and *The Second Sex*', *Philosophy and Literature*, 1980, Autumn, p. 205; Jean Leighton, *Simone de Beauvoir on Woman*, Rutherford, Fairleigh Dickinson University Press, 1975, p. 213; Genevieve Lloyd, *The Man of Reason*, London, Methuen and Co., 1984; Charlene Haddock Seigfried, 'Gender-specific values', *The Philosophical Forum*, 1984, 15, p. 441; Margaret Walters, 'The Rights and Wrongs of Women: Mary Wollstonecraft, Harriet Martineau, Simone de Beauvoir', in J. Mitchell and A. Oakley (eds), *The Rights and Wrongs of Women*, Middlesex, Penguin Books, 1977, pp. 377, 359.

11 See Suzanne Lilar, *Le malentendu du deuxième sexe*, Paris, Presses Universitaires de France, 1970; Toril Moi, *Simone de Beauvoir – The making of an intellectual woman*, Cambridge MA and Oxford, Blackwell, 1994.

12 *Prime of Life*, Peter Green (trans.), Harmondsworth, Penguin, pp. 39, 129.

13 *Force of Circumstance*, Richard Howard (trans.), 1968, 1987, pp. 671 and 661 respectively.

14 *Pyrrhus et Cinéas*, Paris, Gallimard, 1944.

15 *Being and Nothingness*, London, Routledge, 1990, 1993. He at first starts talking about 'the slimy' which threatens the *pour-soi*, then speaks about the slimy as a 'moist and feminine sucking', a 'sickly-sweet, feminine revenge'. Many authors have already referred to these phrases of *Being and Nothingness*.

16 *Being and Nothingness*, pp. 609 and 614 respectively.

17 See e.g. *The Second Sex*, H. M. Parshley (trans.), Harmondsworth, Penguin, 1974, 1984, I, pp. 61–2; II, pp. 512–13.

18 *Ibid.*, pp. 69 and 68–9 respectively.

19 *Ibid.*, p. 66.

20 See Taylor, *Sources of the Self*, p. 301.

21 Vogel argues that Mary Wollstonecraft already was a Rousseauist feminist because she aimed 'to *extend* to women what Rousseau has asserted with regard to men' (Vogel, 'Rationalism and romanticism', p. 44n.3). However, I consider

Beauvoir's philosophy 217

Simone de Beauvoir's direct appeal to women to do as she did and develop an authentic self decisive for a characterization as Rousseauist feminist.

22 *The Mandarins*, first edn., Cleveland, World, pp. 180, 182. In these quotations we do not follow the current English translation exactly because 'une morale' and 'art de vivre' are translated imprecisely as 'a set of principles' and an 'approach to life', respectively.

23 *Force of Circumstance*, p. 287.

24 *The Mandarins*, p. 341.

25 'L'Oeil pour l'oeil', in *L'Existentialisme et la sagesse des nations*, four essays, Paris, Nagel, 1948, pp. 88, 87–8.

26 See *All Said and Done*, Patrick O'Brian (trans.), Harmondsworth, Penguin, 1988, p. 10.

27 See Francis Jeanson, *Simone de Beauvoir ou l'entreprise de vivre*, Paris, Editions du Seuil, 1966, p. 289.

28 *All Said and Done*, p. 8.

29 See Huck Gutman, 'Rousseau's *Confessions*: a Technology of the Self', in M. Foucault, L. Martin, H. Gutman, P. Hutton (eds), *Technologies of the Self*, London, The University of Massachusetts Press, 1988, pp. 103 and 107, respectively.

30 I cannot go into the position of the woman intellectual in Western society, but let me state briefly that she was mostly seen as a contradiction in terms (see chapter 1 of my *Philosophy as Passion*). As a woman intellectual, Beauvoir met a lot of hostility, which reached its peak after the appearance of *The Second Sex*.

31 Taylor, *Sources of the Self*, p. 462.

32 See e.g. the debate between Mieke Aerts and Aafke Komter in J. Hermsen and A. van Lenning (eds), *Sharing the Difference. Feminist Debates in Holland*, London and New York, Routledge and Kegan Paul, 1991.

33 *The Second Sex*, II, p. 740.

34 See Deirdre Bair, *Simone de Beauvoir. A Biography*, New York and London, Summit Books, 1990, p. 652.

13 Contemporary feminism between individualism and community

Jet Bussemaker

An analysis of contemporary feminism creates its own problems. There is no historical distance to help us analyse its peculiarities and its similarities to former 'waves', as we are still living in this wave, or at least in its wake. In addition the multiplicity of events and ideas makes it extremely hard to do justice to this richness. Since we already talk about feminism*s* in the case of other waves, we should certainly do so in the case of this one. In order to grasp its main ideas we could analyse the writings of important authors such as Betty Friedan, Kate Millett, Shulamith Firestone, Juliet Mitchell and Adrienne Rich. Or we might concentrate on central topics such as abortion, equal rights or sexual harassment, or on the organizational culture of the women's movement with its non-hierarchical structures and anarchic tendencies. Another possibility would be to focus on theoretical debates about the relationship between feminism and Marxism, the role of psychoanalysis, the concept of patriarchy, the relationship between equality and difference, or the differences between women in relation to sexuality, class and ethnicity.

Whatever the starting-point, the meaning of the concept 'feminism' must be brought into question. There is no universal language to describe the problems and needs of women; the debates on its definition are an inherent part of feminism itself. It matters whether one describes the position of women in terms of oppression or in terms of relative disadvantage. It also makes a difference whether preference is given to a language of equality or to one which highlights the differences between men and women. The idea that the meaning of feminism is obvious has, as Delmar writes, even 'become an obstacle to understanding feminism, in its diversity and in its differences, and in its specificity as well'.[1] A general working definition, as proposed in the introduction of this book, is only useful insofar as it opens up the plurality of historical feminisms for analysis.

I shall select one way of looking at contemporary feminism: the relationship between liberal, individualist visions of feminism on the one hand, and more socially and community-oriented perspectives on the other.[2] In order to show the specific meaning of 'sixth wave' feminism, I shall focus on two major factors affecting the formation of national feminisms: the context of

Contemporary feminism 219

expanding welfare states and the development of political cultures. The development of welfare states made possible the demand of social rights for women as well as the ideal of self-development and personal autonomy, both of which could be formulated in a situation where the state guaranteed a 'decent, human life' to all its citizens.

Contemporary feminism presupposed a strongly egalitarian ethos that was extremely critical towards all traditional forms of power and authority and so, in a broader context along with other social and political movements, contributed to a debate on the foundations of social and political cohesion or 'community' that seriously affected the entire political culture of late twentieth-century Western society. Precisely how, depended greatly on geographical settings. If we restrict ourselves to the North Atlantic world, we can distinguish an Anglo-American society, where more acquisitive, market-place values predominate, as against continental Europe, with a greater influence of communal value orientations, both social democratic and Christian democratic. This distinction will be an underlying theme in my contribution. For example, to label women as a 'we', with a certain sense of group identity, may be interpreted differently in different nations. In the United States, tradition encourages people to identify themselves as Americans, with basic economic rights. In the Netherlands, however, personal identity tends to be more embedded in humanist values, and group identity is a strategy of dominant society for a peaceful coexistence of different belief systems, such as Protestantism and Catholicism. In France a tradition of political citizenry dominates: the only acceptable group identification derives from where one stands in political life.[3] Below, I will refer to such cultural differences, focussing on some less familiar examples from the Netherlands.

My main thesis is that, in the long run, notions based on an individualistic political culture and an individualist psychology have dominated contemporary feminism, but that the significance of these notions has differed greatly between the Anglo-American and the European continental societies. Even though socialist, Christian democratic and other communalistic and solidarity movements have contested the supremacy of individualism from time to time, it was the dialectic between feminism and individualism that gave the movement its radical edge in continental Europe. Anglo-American individualism was, by and large, more wedded to a market-oriented and atomistic view of society, which sometimes constituted a threat to, rather than an opportunity for, contemporary feminism.

FEMINISM, INDIVIDUALISM AND SOCIAL RELATIONS

The distinction between individualist and relational ideas on gender and society is, of course, not restricted to contemporary feminism. It can be traced back to the origins of modernity and was certainly relevant to nineteenth-century feminism.[4] In general terms we can describe the

220 *Jet Bussemaker*

differences as follows: the first approach privileges the rights and claims to self-development of individual persons who are endowed with an autonomous rationality, which is logically and morally prior to society. The second approach sees social relations as the basic reality, maintaining that the individual exists and *can* only exist in relation to others, and thus in communities. These relationships may vary from traditional heterosexual families to all other social arrangements and communities, but in all cases an individual can only become a morally responsible human agent through social interaction with others.

The distinction outlined above comes close to Karen Offen's opposition between individualist and relational feminism. In her view, individualist feminism traditionally emphasized abstract concepts of human rights and celebrated the quest for independence and autonomy in all fields of life, while playing down or even dismissing as insignificant most socially defined roles and minimizing discussion of gendered behaviour. By contrast, the relational tradition proposes, according to Offen, a gender-based but egalitarian vision of social organization. It features the primacy of a companionate, non-hierarchical, male-female couple as the basic unit of society, emphasizing women's rights as rights for *women* and insisting on women's distinctive contributions to civilization.[5] According to Offen, contemporary feminism has mainly drawn on the individualist tradition, formulating its primary demands in the language of equal rights and equal treatment, bypassing the socio-political context as well as the relational aspects of most women's lives. She criticizes this approach, because it denies the lived experience of many women and thereby leaves the realm of daily toil and trouble, as well as the field of compassion and love, effectively claimed by opponents who have succeeded in mobilizing public fear against the feminist movement. As an alternative, Offen proposes to reintegrate individualistic, rights-based claims into a more socially conscious relational framework that emphasizes responsibility to others. Offen thus puts relational feminism first, as a framework for individualist feminism. She is certainly right in her assertion that strong individualism prevails in Western society as well as in a major part of feminism, but she does not discuss the other available option: that of putting individualistic feminism first and integrating aspects of relational feminism within it – an option which needs serious consideration and to which I will return in my conclusion.

To appreciate the powerful impact of the individualist tradition, we can refer to the struggle of contemporary feminists in the legal-constitutional sphere. This struggle is especially relevant in the American case, where it is closely related to debates around individualism, communitarianism and group identity. But it is also important for European feminism – though in different ways, which are linked to differences in conceptions of citizenship, gender and legal traditions in European countries. Moreover, the supranational legislation of the European Union and the decisions of the European Court of Justice have been of particular importance in a number of gender-related issues. The differences between the American and European political traditions have also influenced the ways in which feminists on both shores of the Atlantic have formulated critiques of the darker sides of an 'atomistic' and 'egotistical' individualism. In comparison with Western European countries, especially the continental ones, individualism is more strongly developed, with much further reaching consequences in the United States. It is striking that Offen, as well as other authors from the US, are extremely critical towards individualism.[6] I doubt, however, if this criticism is transmittable to continental Europe. This does not mean, of course, that the distinction of individual versus relational feminism does not apply in the European case, but it does mean that European feminisms emerged in a great variety of political cultures, in which ideas about the individual and the role of the state differed from those prevailing in the United States.

THE CONTEXT OF THE WELFARE STATE

In postwar Western Europe the welfare state expanded rapidly. The new interventionist social policies fundamentally reshaped the relations between the individual, the family and the state. Gender is a crucial element in understanding these developments, which deeply affected the relationship between work and care, individual rights and community values.[7] In most European countries there was a widely shared belief that the male breadwinner/female carer family was the basic unit of society and should therefore be protected by the state. The ideology of the 'male breadwinner family' has historically cut across the established typologies of welfare states, and has been particularly entrenched in continental Europe and Britain.[8] Nonetheless, there are major differences between national welfare states, with some relying almost exclusively on the male breadwinner model, while others are more generous towards married or single women. Historical analysis of the strength of women's agencies, women's movements and welfare states – though more detailed for the prewar than for the postwar period[9] – has, however, revealed that there is no straightforward link between a strong feminist movement and welfare policies contributing to full citizenship for women.[10] The British case shows, for example, that a powerful feminist movement may, paradoxically, have contributed to the granting of family allowances and other provisions, which resulted in strong breadwinner-based arrangements.[11]

Women's movements originated in the sixties in different types of welfare states and breadwinner arrangements. What all these states had in common was a proliferation of institutions that concerned themselves with the quality of life, and especially with the quality of family life. In the emerging welfare states, 'politics' overflowed into a broad field of social regulation, which penetrated deeply into the web of society in a way traditional parliamentary legislation never did. The range and generosity of state welfare benefits do not appear to be of such crucial importance in this respect as the political culture, but the type of welfare state has to some extent influenced

222 *Jet Bussemaker*

the form and content of feminist thinking and organization. We might expect, for example, that countries with strong 'breadwinner regimes' may have given rise to a powerful women's movement with a clear focus on individual rights. As an example, I will examine the Dutch situation.[12]

The Dutch welfare state was characterized by strong 'breadwinner' arrangements, Christian Democrat domination, the phenomenon of pillarization[13] and by a great emphasis on community values. Moreover, the Dutch case is fascinating because, from a comparative perspective, the welfare state was not well developed before World War II, but became one of the most generous welfare states in the postwar period.[14] The immediate postwar years witnessed a broadly shared desire among political parties to revert to former patterns of home life as soon as possible. This explains the emphasis in the 1950s in political and public discourses on the importance of private domesticity, as well as the prevalence of a rather conservative family policy.[15] But while traditional values were prized when it came to morality and family life, the various political movements displayed great enthusiasm for modernization on economic issues. These two ideas must be seen as two sides of the same coin; a stable, traditional family life was thought of as a prerequisite for a dynamic economy.

In the 1950s there was a widely held belief that keeping housewives in the home was one of the victories of the welfare state. Catholics, in particular, who dominated the discussion on gender relations and family life, disseminated the idea of working women as contradictory to modern conceptions of good living, and incompatible with social virtues. One could say that relational frameworks were dominant with regard to social rights and family policy. Differences between male breadwinners and female carers were not presumed to be discriminatory, but a recognition of natural differences in ability, talents and tasks between men and women. The relationship between them was understood in terms of a Catholic tradition of equal dignity in difference – meaning that men and women had complementary tasks concerning the public good. Postwar welfare provisions were built on social and communitarian reasoning, and took serious account of people's social circumstances. These circumstances, however, presupposed the traditional family as the basic unit of society and thus legitimized gender inequality in social arrangements.

Together with the incorporation of gender differences in social rights, however, women – particularly married women – obtained some important civil rights. In 1947 joint parental control was formally legalized. In 1955 the marriage-bar, which prevented married women from working in the civil service, was withdrawn. In 1956 the civil disability of married women in legal contracts was abolished. In public parlance, the idea of a 'completed emancipation' became almost commonplace. This was part of a slowly developing, more general change in discourse on the relation between individuals and public life: citizens were regarded as responsible and emancipated individuals rather than as docile subjects. These changes paved

Contemporary feminism   223

the way for more egalitarian conceptions of gender relations, although no one could foresee the emergence of a new 'wave' of feminism in the late 1960s.

The rather slow and cautious changes of the late 1950s and early 1960s towards a more democratic culture in general, and more equal gender relations and family life in particular, have only recently begun to receive the attention of historians. I believe these changes to be significant since they help to explain the rapid spread of democratic and feminist vocabularies later in the 1960s. Feminism was part of a broad change in attitudes to social problems, such as the new urgency of personal autonomy, the democratic critique of an authoritarian-bureaucratic public administration and a social approach towards individual discontent and complaints, including the famous 'housewife syndrome'. The Catholics played an important role in paving the way for these changes. The Catholic Party in the Netherlands was especially interested in individual well-being, as well as self-expression and the political significance of personal feelings, whilst it criticized the welfare state for adopting too utilitarian an approach in the early 1960s. Femininity became a metaphor for empathy and social involvement in the public sphere, related to humanist values.[16] Whereas femininity had been restricted to family life and motherhood in the 1950s, its meaning was now extended to public life as a condition for social well-being and happiness, thus turning gender into a potentially politically relevant category.[17] The change in the vocabulary of Catholics was symptomatic of a broader transformation of political culture across Europe; the focus was on 'social equality' rather than 'natural hierarchy'.

Besides the occasional publication on women's problems,[18] neither a feminist vocabulary nor a feminist movement were as yet in place. It was Joke Kool-Smit, an Amsterdam journalist and university lecturer, who first turned the language of 'completed emancipation' into a vocabulary of women's liberation. This is one of the most striking features of contemporary women's liberation and feminism: the recourse to a new language – the language of liberation rather than of emancipation.[19] Kool-Smit's cautiously formulated 1967 article *The Discomfort of Women* is now commonly regarded as the starting-point for Dutch contemporary feminism. The article opens, like many others from that period, with a reference to Simone de Beauvoir. Kool-Smit analyses the problems of middle-class women, who should be happy but are not; whose existence extends no further than their house and who enjoy a tenuous contact with the outside world. Women, she writes, must become more like men. To this end, women must learn to think in terms and vocabularies that, traditionally, have been reserved for men: 'It is really time that women permit themselves the healthy egoism that has been taken for granted among men since time immemorial'.[20] Kool-Smit made a deliberate move from a language of female virtues to one about women's interests, and so extended the language of enlightened self-interest to women. Women should no longer see

224   *Jet Bussemaker*

themselves as docile citizens and obedient housewives but as individuals with their own interests.

The vocabulary of enlightened self-interest is, of course, part of the history of individualism. The quotation above exemplifies the ambiguous relationship between feminism and individualism: finding support in an individualist tradition of self-interest on the one hand, and criticizing this tradition on the other, due to its exclusion of women, as well as because of its emphasis on economic values. Kool-Smit distanced herself from a purely economic conception of self-interest. The 'healthy egoism' she proposes for women should be different. It is not a destructive passion but a respectable desire which will also be productive for others, particularly for men and children, who will gain a spouse and mother with her own thoughts and experiences. Kool-Smit regards feminism as an invisible hand which in due time will usher in a positive, generous society for all, an invisible hand which is accompanied by a 'morality of sentiments' in which personal relationships, trust and social values are high on the agenda. The attempt to encourage enlightened self-interest might be seen as a logical outcome of the (Dutch) welfare state, which promised greater well-being, self-development and full citizenship rights for all inhabitants. Feminism tended to follow the logic of the welfare state as far as equal rights and social justice were concerned, but it changed the unit of welfare and justice from the traditional family to individuals, that is to individual men and women. Feminist individualism, therefore, differed from a purely economic market individualism as well as from the 'rugged' variety prevailing in mainstream American culture.

AUTHORITY, EGALITARIANISM AND FEMINISM

Despite her radical vindication of egoism for women, Joke Kool-Smit was not radical in her politics. Her political programme remained within the limits of parliamentary politics – in her case the politics of the Social Democratic Party. In terms of political theory, her approach might be understood as belonging to the radical end of the liberal spectrum. Diana Coole describes liberal feminists as 'demanding the welfare provisions – nurseries and so on – that would allow more genuine equality of opportunity', and concludes that their exponents' goal has essentially been for a competitive society, with the sexual division of labour now largely rejected in favour of access to jobs on the basis of merit.[21] More radical in the sense of debunking theoretical frameworks, reclaiming language, recasting identities and criticizing parliamentary strategies were the left-wing Marxist and radical feminists. The first radical left-wing feminist group in the Netherlands was Dolle Mina ('Mad Mina') – a name inherited from a late nineteenth-century feminist, Wilhelmina Drucker. The Dolle Minas translated personal problems into political ones. In 1970 they asserted that 'the liberation of women *and* of men, as well as existing discrimination, are political phenomena', explicitly politicizing gender issues.

Contemporary feminism 225

Not only was the content of ideas radical but so was the form in which they were presented. Dolle Minas became well known through their public actions in which they burned bras, cordoned off men's toilets in order to demonstrate the lack of women's facilities, and whistled at men on the street. The eyes of the world were soon on them – often even to their own surprise. This was partly a consequence of their spectacular tactics, but it also demonstrated a certain international sensitivity to the issues involved. In those years, feminist demands were articulated throughout the Northern Atlantic world. Apart from shocking campaigns, Dolle Minas were also involved in more serious matters, such as the theorizing of patriarchy and gender oppression in Marxist terms. The Dolle Minas were typically highly educated women embarking on a career. Their aim was to speak not only for themselves but also for, and to, 'ordinary women in the street'. The majority of their ideas derived from American and British authors, such as Shulamith Firestone and Juliet Mitchell, whose work circulated on both shores of the Atlantic.

While the Dolle Minas frequently used a socialist language, the culture of the movement was rather individualistic, and sometimes even anarchistic. They rejected the model of a traditional political organization with formal membership and the election of official spokespersons. Later on, Dutch feminists went on to organize themselves into – again rather informal – 'fem-soc' (feminism – socialism) groups where they could experiment with new ideas and forms of political action. Many of them also set up consciousness-raising groups, privileging individual experiences and emotions. Anja Meulenbelt's book *De schaamte voorbij* ('The Shame is Over'), recounting her own personal history with men in the left-wing and Marxist movement, was extremely important to this phase of Dutch feminism.[22]

The women's movement was, of course, not the only movement criticizing traditional forms of power and authority. It was part of new value-orientations towards postmaterialism, self-development and autonomy, which political scientists have called 'the Silent Revolution'.[23] The forceful egalitarian ethos which emerged during the 1960s throughout the Western world, provided the political background for this change in political orientation. In the United States the black movement in particular was important, whilst in continental Europe the student movement was at the forefront of activities. Social movements radically challenged the authority of parliamentary decision-making.

As far as the Netherlands are concerned, we should add here a more general critique of the typical hierarchical social organization of a pillarized society in the 1960s. There was a broadly shared dissatisfaction in the 1960s with the notion of self-evident authority, whether it referred to the father, the priest or the official. This critique had several origins: the student movement, intellectuals and new elites, and initiators of new political parties. They were all extremely critical of the centralistic, high-handed culture of

226   *Jet Bussemaker*

public administration, which gave citizens very little opportunity to participate in the decision-making process, in which public debate was scarce and
in which authority could hardly be discussed. As this critique became louder
and more influential in the course of the 1960s, the situation was termed a
'de-pillarization' of Dutch society. In this context, feminists criticized the
despotic character of family relations and patriarchal power. As a result,
they castigated a specific form of communitarian and socially oriented organization: the oppressive, authoritarian and stifling variant found in Dutch
society in the 1950s.[24] The distinctive Dutch tradition of humanist values
and inter-group tolerance also gave rise to groups which criticized the traditional, pillarized society, from within the social welfare scheme of
operations, receiving attention and help through government subsidy to
establish new institutions, as was the case with a lot of feminist initiatives.
The effect of this development was two-fold: it was able to satisfy the
requirement for radical innovation on the one hand, but on the other often
meant traditional state control.[25]

However, the feminist critique of authority was not just one of many – it
added a critique of the relationship between the private and the public
sphere, as well as of the definition of the personal and the political. And of
course feminists contested notions of 'natural' differences between femininity and masculinity. From this perspective they not only defined gender
as a political category, but also defined as political the hierarchy between
men and women in the private sphere.

The radical critique of authority and power of contemporary feminism
manifested itself in two ways. First, feminist critiques of patriarchal power
and authority were not new. More contemporary critiques rested on the
revolutionary force of individualist thinking during the Enlightenment, and
its feminist spokespersons, who criticized the marriage laws, the authority of
fathers and the assumed parallel between the power of the father and the
king. Relations of hierarchy and obedience in the family as a model for
governmental structures had, of course, already come up for criticism.
Nevertheless, sixth-wave feminism rediscovered these criticisms as 'forgotten
history', and restated them loud and clear. The language of absolute power,
and notions such as the father's role as head of the family were radically
rejected and were replaced by a call for equal civil, political and social rights,
as well as for equal opportunities. Patriarchy manifested itself not only in
men's public power, but also in their dominant roles in the home. Feminists
have accused some more recent welfare policies of transforming private
patriarchy into public patriarchy of the state,[26] but patriarchy appears to
have undergone a clear transformation since the 1960s. Welfare provisions
are rarely patriarchal only and tend to combine both disciplinary and emancipatory goals.

A second manifestation of feminism's radical thinking was its critique of
modern, functionalist arguments about social cohesion in general, and
family life in particular. Modern functionalism with regard to family life and

Contemporary feminism 227

gender became influential in the postwar period, in Europe as well as in the United States. The development of psychological, sociological and pedagogical functionalist notions transformed both academia and society as a whole. Entire generations grew up under the influence of Spock and Bowlby. Their visions were less hierarchical than traditional thinking, but their notions of permissive, child-centred attitudes required a great deal of attention from mothers. Motherhood was presumed not only natural, but also something that had to be learned; rearing children had to be in line with psychological and pedagogical ideas. The 'psy-complex' generated new ideas of gender relations and family life founded on a notion of functionalism. Although the husband did not have absolute power over his spouse, a division of power was still presumed, based on arguments of necessity and practical organization. As a consequence, women's interests were subsumed under those of the family. As Okin makes clear, functionalism has played a clear role in history since Aristotle, particularly where gender and family issues are concerned, and it continues to do so. Taking Erik Erikson and Talcott Parsons as examples, Okin analyses the power of functionalist discourse:

> Through textbooks, advertising, child-rearing manuals, and countless other channels, the prescriptive 'nature' which was imposed on women by their reproductive biology, in combination with the assumption of the conventional family structures, was virtually unopposed by any alternative views.[27]

The 'modern' functionalist view was influential in many postwar welfare states. Although the expanding welfare state changed 'traditional' visions of authority within the family and helped erode the power of fathers, it also helped to spread new functionalist views of the relationship between the family and society, and thus of gender relations, through a network of social and psychological professionals. Feminism commented on both these traditions by putting authority and obedience up for discussion.

The egalitarian and anti-authoritarian ethos of sixth-wave feminism was part of a political culture that cleared the ground for the individualist-communitarian debate about the foundations of social and political cohesion or 'community'. The specific feminist contribution to this was a critique of the 'natural' character of the family as well as the notion that family life is governed by altruism and empathy in contrast to a competitive world of self-interest outside. Feminism radically changed views on family life, social cohesion and community values. What was to take its place, however, remained an unresolved issue.

FEMINISM, INDIVIDUALISM AND COMMUNAL THINKING

Of course, feminists had alternatives in mind. In the first instance, feminism expressed itself in a language of collectivism founded upon shared

228 *Jet Bussemaker*

experiences of oppression and discrimination as women, and upon notions of sisterhood and solidarity. In the second place, feminists developed ideas on new forms of non-hierarchical living arrangements, with and without children and men. They found inspiration in the ideas of the feminist utopian socialists. They shared a strategy of liberation through the development of a separate women's cultural movement, as well as radical ideas on solidarity and sisterhood, on sexuality and the oppression of the body, and on notions of sexual pleasure as a relevant topic for political discussion.[28] In the long run, and over the course of time, however, we might say that individualist notions dominated relational ones; contemporary feminism seems to have achieved more in terms of individual rights than in changing the structures of society.[29]

A strategy of individual rights has become popular since the 1970s. Equality policies have been implemented in many European countries, including the Netherlands. Women's participation in the labour market has grown rapidly, while traditional 'breadwinner' models have been abandoned in favour of formal equal treatment. In most European countries gender equality has become an important goal of governmental policies. Article 1 of the Dutch constitution states that discrimination on grounds of religion, philosophy, political conviction, race, sex or any other grounds is illegal. In 1994, after years of discussion and political struggle, the general law on equal treatment passed through parliament – a law based on individual rights, and not on discriminated or oppressed groups, thus fitting well with the individualist tradition. In the last decades, however, feminists have begun to doubt the ideal of equality and equal rights, which often seems to result in sameness, a double burden for women, or a decline of rights for women as well as men. Therefore, Dutch feminists coined the slogan 'as badly off is also equal'. Nonetheless, the strategy of individual rights has been rather successful.

Feminism has been less successful in changing structures. Women's joint role of employee and carer, for example, still proves problematic, due to a combination of labour-market structures, lack of public childcare facilities, and the accordance of a disproportionately large share of caring and child-rearing responsibilities in the private sphere to women. If progress is being made, it is well-educated middle-class women who tend to benefit rather than lower-class women, single mothers and migrant women. In general, feminism has not been very strong in the social and political articulation of more contemporary forms of community life.

As a result of the imbalance in achievements in terms of individual rights and in changing the structures of society, feminism, as well as other progressive movements, did not have a really strong defence against developments of market-oriented neoliberalism on the one hand and of family-oriented neoconservatism on the other, both of which became popular in the 1980s in various countries. During the 1980s individualism became a topic of discussion in itself, often being related to gender issues. While the support for

Contemporary feminism 229

individualism vis-à-vis the market was growing, the support for individualism in the context of the family and social relations declined.

In the Dutch case, the Christian Democrats (the result of the merger of several different denominational parties) are the best example of this shift in ideas. They supported more individualism vis-à-vis the market, but were extremely critical towards individualism vis-à-vis small communities, including the family. They associated feminism with individualism in a disparaging manner and championed community values such as personal responsibility and morality as an alternative. Such an argument poses problems for feminism because 'community' seems to refer, whether explicitly or implicitly, to traditional community networks such as the family and village life, while individual rights concerning female labour-market participation are associated with 'a monoculture of individual economic independence, which submits the whole society to a materialistic motif', as a Christian Democrat spokesman once said.[30] Although Dutch Christian Democrats, as well as most conservatives and liberals, still view the protection of the social fabric as a task of the state, some of them come close to the ruder versions of individualism which are associated with Reaganomics and Thatcherism.

From this perspective we might speak of a backlash against feminist ideals, spurred on by neoconservative and neoliberal rhetoric, as is most clearly the case in Britain.[31] But it could also be argued that the lack of a strong feminist critique of this rhetoric is an indication that many problems have been solved and that we should no longer seek the protection of the state. A vocabulary of individual independence has indeed won more attention in feminism and in the political culture generally. Although such a perspective is far more attractive to well-educated, middle-class women than to women who suffer discrimination on the grounds of race and class (a distinction however, which is less sharp in European continental countries than in the United States and, to a lesser extent, the United Kingdom), it demonstrates the huge influence of feminist ideas among younger generations, for whom feminism – whether or not one feels it necessary to refer explicitly to the 'ism' – has become one of the self-evident facts of life.

This does not mean, however, that there is either a simple 'backlash' or no feminism at all because all problems are by now believed to be solved. It is more a change in topics and style, as well as a change in generations. In line with developments in the United States, where younger women such as Naomi Wolf and Kate Roiphe publish on new ways of feminist thinking, the Netherlands now have their own pamphlet struggle. In 1994 the pamphlet *Macha Macha!* was published. The author blamed the older generation for victimizing women, exaggerating the differences between men and women and wanting too much (a career, children, a pleasant family life and public support). As an alternative, problems should be solved on an individual level, with or without a boyfriend or husband. A year later, a group of writers, calling themselves 'the Hard Core', responded with a brochure entitled *Indeed, feminist, but not emancipated*, in which they deplored the

230   *Jet Bussemaker*

continuing inequality between the sexes, but also argued for diversity within feminism and varied ways of living.[32]

Although neither publication succeeded in delineating a new or original perspective, or new strategies for achieving the much-advertised diversity, both received broad public attention. This indicates that the feminist debate is still – or rather, is once again – important for contemporary political culture. From this perspective it may be more accurate to look forward to a subsequent stage of modern feminism (or even of a 'seventh wave') than to regard these pamphlets as the harbingers of the impending end of feminism.

CONCLUSION

The relation between feminism, individualist visions and community-oriented visions of social and political life has not lost its meaning. Communitarianism has important things to say for feminism – the importance of the social context in which equality and justice are shaped, the meaning of civil society and notions about the importance of friendship and social relations with other people, to name but a few.[33] But in the historical context in which the sixth wave arose, feminism must also be seen as a critique on central notions of communitarianism, especially as long as the traditional family and village unit are held up as examples of community life. Feminism itself was the result of contradictions in the postwar political culture and the welfare state, with the emphasis on self-development and individual social rights on the one hand, and the stabilization of a classic model of family life on the other. In this historical situation, a defence of communitarian values can easily be incorporated in a neoconservative vocabulary of moral duties instead of rights.

From this perspective, the individualistic focus is logical and, in my opinion, still of value. Whilst I would not agree that feminism in most European countries has become individualistic in an egoistic and atomistic sense, I do believe that a number of acute problems still exist concerning the issues of how to handle gender differences in contemporary political culture and particularly in the restructuring of the welfare state. Communitarian notions of civil life and responsibility might be very useful in correcting individualist notions of equal rights and autonomy. In the same way, relational feminist arguments are vital to the process of analysing and discussing the possible dangers of an individualistic approach – such as, for example, an abstract idea of universalist rights which may occasion the denial of differences and responsibility for others. However, even though we should distrust strong vocabularies on individualism, we should not reject the concept of individualism wholesale. In any case, the overlap in terms of content (feminism owes a great deal to individualism) and in terms of historical background (feminism was part of a broader movement which put the individual centre stage) makes it impossible to reject individualism as such. To do so would amount to a denial of the emancipatory resources of

Contemporary feminism 231

abstract individualism for feminism and in the perspective of Western political history. From Mary Wollstonecraft to John Stuart Mill and beyond, feminists have built upon the emancipatory and revolutionary aspects of individualism, without abstaining from a critique of other aspects of the philosophical tradition of individualism.[34]

In the context of the contemporary European welfare states, I would like to put forward the reverse of Offen's recommendation to integrate individualist ideas into a framework of relational feminism.[35] The integration of relational and communal feminist ideas into a framework of individualist feminism might be more in tune with the historical background of the welfare state, as well as being in accordance with the main cultural trends of our time.

We should be aware of the enormous influence feminism has had upon society as a whole since the 1960s. Many women nowadays claim not to be feminists, and then proceed with arguments we might easily label as such (for example, claiming equal rights, independence and sexual pleasure). But this also shows that many women do not wish to be identified with a specific *image* of contemporary feminism; they do not want to be seen as victims of patriarchy or as opponents of or competitors with men. In one respect their language is more individualistic than that of leading feminists in the 1960s and 1970s, the emphasis now being on individual autonomy and independence. At the same time their language is more relational and communal, in terms of a concern for relationships with partners. In other words, the language of a younger feminist generation is predominantly individualistic, while it does not neglect relational constituents.

Integrating relational and communitaristic elements into a framework of individualism will change the concept of individualism itself. Instead of an abstract, egotistic, market-oriented or utilitarian notion of individualism, a democratic socially oriented variety of individualism may develop. This approach respects individualist values while trying to keep them in perspective, without neglecting the role of community. Fundamental values of moderate democratic individualism might include human dignity, autonomy, privacy and self-development. None of these values is considered an isolated attribute. Rather, each presupposes the existence of the others. In the final analysis, such a model of individualism relies on the willingness of citizens to contribute to the common good, as well as on their desire to exercise their freedom to contribute to the dignity, autonomy, privacy and self-development of others. This democratic individualism might profit from the opportunities of modern life and avoid some of its disadvantages. Among these opportunities are (economic) independence, equality and pluralism in living arrangements and lifestyles. Among the possible disadvantages are egotism, the rejection of difference, racism and – indeed – anti-feminism.

232 *Jet Bussemaker*

NOTES

1 R. Delmar, 'What is Feminism?', in J. Mitchell and A. Oakley (eds), *What is Feminism. A Re-examination*, New York, Pantheon Books, 1986, p. 8.
2 On other views of feminism, see S. Moller Okin and J. Mansbridge (eds), *Feminism*, Aldershot, Edward Elgar, 1994; A. Jaggar (ed.), *Living with Contradictions. Controversies in Feminist Ethics*, Oxford, Westview Press, 1994; J. Evans, *Feminist Theory Today*, London, Sage, 1995.
3 G. Pheterson, 'Group identity and social relations. divergent theoretical conceptions in the United States, the Netherlands and France', *The European Journal of Women's Studies*, 1994, 1, pp. 257–64.
4 See K. Offen, 'Defining feminism. a comparative historical approach', *Signs*, 1980, 14, pp. 119–57.
5 Offen, 'Defining feminism'.
6 See L. Gordon, 'Het individualisme en de kritiek op het individualisme in de geschiedenis van het feministisch denken', in *Jaarboek voor Vrouwengeschiedenis 1980*, Nijmegen, SUN, 1980, pp. 262–84. See also E. Fox-Genovese, *Feminism Without Illusions. A Critique of Individualism*, Chapel Hill, University of North Carolina Press, 1991. The focus on individual rights has, according to Fox-Genovese, produced a white middle-class feminism.
7 On the feminist critique of welfare-state literature, see A. Orloff, 'Gender and the social rights of citizenship: the comparative analysis of gender relations and welfare states', *American Sociological Review*, 1993, 58, pp. 303–28; J. Lewis and I. Ostner, *Gender and the Evolution of European Social Policies*, ZeS–Arbeitspapier Nr. 4/94, Bremen, Centre for Social Policy Research, 1994, p. 17. See also J. Lewis, 'Gender and the development of welfare regimes', *Journal of European Social Policy*, 1992, 2, pp. 159–73. An overview of mainstream and feminist approaches is J. Bussemaker and K. van Kersbergen, 'Gender and welfare states: some theoretical reflections', in D. Sainsbury (ed.), *Gendering Welfare States*, London, Sage, 1994, pp. 8–25.
8 Lewis and Ostner, *Gender and the Evolution of European Social Policies*.
9 See Th. Skocpol, *Protecting Mothers and Soldiers. The Political Origins of Social Policy in the United States*, Cambridge and London, Belknap Press of Harvard University Press, 1992; G. Bock and P. Thane (eds), *Maternity and Gender Policies. Women and the Rise of the European Welfare States 1880s–1950s*, London and New York, Routledge, 1991; S. Koven and S. Michel (eds), *Mothers of a New World. Maternalist Politics and the Origins of the Welfare State*, New York and London, Routledge, 1993. See also S. Koven and S. Michel, 'Womanly duties: maternalist politics and the origins of welfare states in France, Germany, Great Britain and the United States, 1880–1920', *American Historical Review*, 1990, 95, pp. 1076–108; L. Gordon (ed.), *Women, the State and Welfare*, Madison, University of Wisconsin Press, 1990.
10 Lewis, 'Gender and the development of welfare regimes', p. 170.
11 Koven and Michel, 'Womanly duties', p. 1080; Koven and Michel, *Mothers of a New World*, pp. 24–6.
12 See for Britain E. Wilson, *Women and the Welfare State*, London, Tavistock Publications, 1977 and from the same author *Only Halfway to Paradise. Women in Postwar Britain: 1945–1968*, London, Tavistock Publications, 1980.
13 Pillarization refers to a denominationally segregated society with a dominance of the confessional in the sphere of culture as well as politics. But, significantly, pillarization also referred to the social system; it means a segregation of social organizations, friendship networks, education, labour organizations, etc., which were all segregated along lines of (Christian) world views.

Contemporary feminism 233

14 See A. de Swaan, *In Care of the State, Health Care, Education and Welfare in Europe and the USA in the Modern Era*, New York, Polity Press, 1988.

15 This situation is similar to Germany. See I. Ostner, 'Slow motion: women, work and the family in Germany', in J. Lewis (ed.), *Women and Social Policies in Europe. Work, Family and the State*, Aldershot, Edward Elgar, 1993, p. 97.

16 J. Bussemaker, *Betwiste zelfstandigheid. Individualisering, sekse en verzorgingsstaat*, Amsterdam, SUA, 1993, p. 117.

17 The background to this idea of self-development and consciousness raising is often linked to ideas of spokesmen of the Frankfurt School and to other radical movements of the sixties. Oddly enough, a detailed analysis of Dutch political movements shows that it was also, or maybe even especially, the Catholics who opened up the way for thinking on self-development. See Bussemaker, *Betwiste zelfstandigheid.*

18 See I. Costera Meijer, 'Het onbehagen van een lotgenote. De ontwikkeling van een nieuw feministisch perspectief op vrouwen in de jaren zestig', in M. Schwegman *et al.*, *Op het strijdtoneel van de politiek: twaalfde jaarboek voor vrouwengeschiedenis*, Nijmegen, SUN, 1991, pp. 153–69.

19 Delmar, 'What is Feminism?', p. 26.

20 J. Kool-Smit, 'Het onbehagen bij de vrouw' (1967), in J. Smit, *Er is een land waar vrouwen willen wonen. Teksten 1967–1981*, Amsterdam, Sara, 1984, pp. 15–42.

21 D. Coole, *Women in Political Theory. From Ancient Misogyny to Contemporary Feminism*, Sussex, Wheatsheaf Books, 1988, pp. 234–5.

22 A. Meulenbelt, *De schaamte voorbij*, Amsterdam, Van Gennep, 1976 (translated into German and English).

23 R. Inglehart, *The Silent Revolution. Changing Values and Political Styles among Western Publics*, Princeton, Princeton University Press, 1977.

24 In a sense, Dutch pillarization was very communitarian, stressing the value of small communities and focussing on civic virtue, social control and normality.

25 See Pheterson, 'Group identity', p. 260.

26 See e.g. H. Holter (ed.), *Patriarchy in a Welfare Society*, Oslo, Universitetsforlaget, 1984, and B. Siim, 'The Scandinavian welfare states – towards sexual equality or a new kind of male domination?', *Acta Sociologica*, 1974, 30, 3/4, pp. 255–70.

27 S. Moller Okin, *Women in Western Political Thought*, London, Virago, 1980, p. 246.

28 See the contributions of Levitas (chapter 9) and Moses (chapter 8) in this collection.

29 See Gordon, 'Het individualisme'.

30 Bussemaker, *Betwiste zelfstandigheid*, p. 148.

31 See A. Jeffries, 'Britsh conservatism: individualism and gender', *Journal of Political Ideologies*, 1996, 1, pp. 33–52, and R. Lister, 'Back to the Family: family policies and politics under the Major government', in H. Jones and J. Millar (eds), *The Politics of the Family*, Aldershot, Avebury, 1995.

32 M. van Hintum, *Macha Macha!*, Amsterdam, Nijgh en Van Ditmar, 1995; De Harde Kern, *Wel feministisch, niet geëmancipeerd*, Amsterdam, Contact, 1996.

33 See E. Frazer and N. Lacey, *The Politics of Community. A Feminist Critique of the Liberal-Communitarian Debate*, Hemel Hempstead, Wheatsheaf, 1993.

34 See the contributions of Sapiro (chapter 7) and Akkerman (chapter 10) in this volume.

35 Offen comes close to Fox-Genovese, who seeks, in *Feminism without Illusions*, to formulate an alternative for individualism in proposing a concept of 'generous community life'.

Guide to further reading

GENERAL

Albistur, M and Armogathe, D. (1978) *Histoire du féminisme français*, Paris, Des Femmes.

Boxer, M. J. and Quataert, J. H. (eds) (1987) *Connecting Spheres: Women in the Western World*, New York, Oxford University Press.

Bridenthal, R., Koonz, C. and Stuard, S. (eds) (1987), second edn., *Becoming Visible: Women in European History*, Boston, Houghton Mifflin.

Fauré, C. (1991) *Democracy Without Women. Feminism and the Rise of Liberal Individualism in France*, Bloomington, Indiana University Press.

Duby, G. and Perrot, M. (eds) (1992–1995) *A History of Women in the West*, 5 vols, Cambridge MA, Belknap Press.

Kelly, J. (1982) 'Early feminist theory and the *Querelle des femmes*, 1400–1789', *Signs*, 8, pp. 4–28; reprinted in *Women, History and Theory: The Essays of Joan Kelly*, Chicago, University of Chicago Press, 1984.

Labalme, P. (ed.) (1980) *Learned Women of the European Past*, New York, New York University Press.

ON GENDER AND THE CANON OF (MALE) POLITICAL THOUGHT

Coole, D. (1993) *Women in Political Theory: From Ancient Misogyny to Contemporary Feminism*, New York, Harvester Wheatsheaf.

Elshtain, J. B. (1981) *Public Man, Private Woman: Women in Social and Political Thought,* Princeton, Princeton University Press.

Kennedy, E. and Mendus, S. (eds) (1987) *Women in Western Political Philosophy*, Brighton, Wheatsheaf.

Okin, S. M. (1979) *Women in Western Political Thought*, Princeton, Princeton University Press, 1979.

Pateman, C. (1988) *The Sexual Contract*, Cambridge, Polity Press.

MEDIEVAL

Brabant, M. (ed.) (1992) *Politics, Gender and Genre: The Political Thought of Christine de Pizan*, Boulder, Westview Press.

Cadden, J. (1993) *Meanings of Sexual Difference in the Middle Ages: Medicine, Science and Culture*, Cambridge, Cambridge University Press.

Guide to further reading 235

Edwards, R. R. and Ziegler, V. (eds) (1995) *Matrons and Marginal Women in Medieval Society*, Woodbridge, The Boydell Press.
Kay, S. and Rubin, M. (eds) (1994) *Framing Medieval Bodies*, Manchester, Manchester University Press.

SIXTEENTH AND SEVENTEENTH CENTURIES

Berriot-Salvadore, E. (1990) *Les Femmes dans la Société Française de la Rénaissance*, Genève, Droz.
DeJean, J. (1991) *Tender Geographies. Women and the Origin of the Novel in France*, New York, Columbia University Press.
Ferguson, M. W., Quilligan, M. and Vickers, N. J. (eds) (1986) *Rewriting the Renaissance. The Discourses of Sexual Difference in Early Modern Europe*, Chicago and London, University of Chicago Press.
Haase-Dubosq, D. and Viennot, E. (eds) (1991) *Femmes et pouvoirs sous l'ancien régime*, Paris, Rivages.
Harth, E. (1992) *Cartesian Women. Versions and Subversions of Rational Discourse in the Old Regime*, Ithaca and London, Cornell University Press.
Jordan, C. (1990) *Renaissance Feminism*, Ithaca and London, Cornell University Press.
Lougee, C. C. (1976) *Le Paradis des Femmes. Women, Salons, and Social Stratification in Seventeenth-Century France*, Princeton, Princeton University Press.
MacLean, I. (1977) *Woman Triumphant. Feminism in French Literature, 1610–1652*, Oxford, Clarendon Press.
Perry, R. (1986) *The Celebrated Mary Astell. An Early English Feminist*, Chicago and London, University of Chicago Press.
Reynier, G. (1929) *La Femme au XVIIe siècle. Ses ennemis et ses défenseurs*, Paris.
Rosso, J. G. (1984) *Etudes sur la feminité aux XVIIe et XVIIIe siècles*, Pisa, Libreria Goliardica, pp. 189–211.
Schiebinger, L. (1991) *The Mind has no Sex? Women in the Origins of Modern Science*, London and Cambridge MA, Harvard University Press.

EIGHTEENTH CENTURY

Akkerman, T. (1992) *Women's Vices, Public Benefits. Women and Commerce in the French Enlightenment*, Amsterdam, Het Spinhuis.
Applewhite, H. B. and Levy, D. G. (eds) (1990) *Women and Politics in the Age of the Democratic Revolution*, Ann Arbor, University of Michigan Press.
Gelbart, N. R. (1987) *Feminine and Opposition Journalism in Old Regime France. Le Journal des Dames*, Berkeley, University of California Press.
Goldsmith, E. C. and Goodman, D. (eds) (1995) *Going Public. Women and Publishing in Early Modern France*, Ithaca and London, Cornell University Press.
Goodman, D. (1994) *The Republic of Letters. A Cultural History of the French Enlightenment*, Ithaca, Cornell University Press.
Hoffman, P. (1978) *La femme dans la pensée des lumières*, Paris, Editions Ophrys.
Landes, J. B. (1988) *Women and the Public Sphere in the Age of the French Revolution*, Ithaca, Cornell University Press.
Rogers, K. M. (1982) *Feminism in Eighteenth-century England*, Brighton, Harvester Press.
Sapiro, V. (1992) *A Vindication of Political Virtue. The Political Theory of Mary Wollstonecraft*, Chicago, Chicago University Press.

236   *Guide to further reading*

Spencer, S. I. (ed.) (1984) *French Women and the Age of Enlightenment*, Bloomington, Indiana University Press.

NINETEENTH CENTURY

Banks, O. (1986) *Faces of Feminism*, Oxford and New York, Basil Blackwell.

Bidelman, P. K. (1982) *Pariahs Stand up! The Founding of the Liberal Feminist Movement in France, 1858–1889*, Westport and London, Greenwood Press.

Boxer, M. J. and Quataert, J. H. (eds) (1978) *Socialist Women: European Socialist Feminism in the Nineteenth and Early Twentieth Centuries*, New York, Elsevier.

Davidoff, L. (1995) *Worlds Between: Historical Perspectives on Gender and Class*, Cambridge, Polity Press.

Evans, R. J. (1977) *The Feminists. Women's Emancipation Movements in Europe, America and Australasia 1840–1920*, London and Sydney, Croom Helm.

Gerhard, U. (1992) *Unerhört. Die Geschichte der Deutschen Frauenbewegung*, Reinbek bei Hamburg, Rowohlt.

Grogan, S. K. (1992) *French Socialism and Sexual Difference: Women and the New Society, 1803–44*, Basingstoke, Macmillan.

Hausen, K. (1983) *Frauen suchen ihre Geschichte: Historischen Studien zum 19. und 20. Jahrhundert*, München, Beck.

Moses, C. G. (1984) *French Feminism in the Nineteenth Century*, Albany, SUNY Press.

Rendall, J. (1985) *The Origins of Modern Feminism: Women in Britain, France and the United States, 1780–1860*, Basingstoke and London, Macmillan.

Taylor, B. (1983) *Eve and the New Jerusalem. Socialism and Feminism in the Nineteenth Century*, London, Virago Press.

TWENTIETH CENTURY

Bock, G. and Thane, P. (eds) (1991) *Maternity and Gender Policies. Women and the Rise of the European Welfare States 1880s–1950s*, London and New York, Routledge.

Bock, G. and Jame, S. (eds) (1992) *Beyond Equality & Difference. Citizenship, feminist politics, female subjectivity*, London, Routledge.

Fox-Genovese, E. (1991) *Feminism Without Illusions. A Critique of Individualism*, Chapel Hill, University of North Carolina Press.

Githens, M., Norris, P. and Lovenduski, J. (eds) (1994) *Different Roles, Different Voices. Women and Politics in the United States and Europe*, New York, Harper Collins.

Koven, S. and Michel, S. (eds) (1993) *Mothers of a New World. Maternalist Politics and the Origins of the Welfare State*, New York and London, Routledge.

Mitchell, J. and Oakley, A. (eds) (1986) *What is Feminism. A Reexamination*, New York, Pantheon Books.

Phillips, A. (1991) *Engendering Democracy*, Cambridge, Polity Press, 1991.

Index

Abbéma, Louis 191
Abensour, Léon 138
abolitionism 21, 23, 125
abortion 146, 204
academic institutions, women and 12–13, 17–18, 68, 72, 73–5, 79, 80, 89, 93
Adam, Lambert-Sigisbert 113
Aganice 57
Akkerman, Tjitske 23, 110
Alain de (Alan of) Lille 43
Albert the Great 35–6
Alberti, Marcello 55, 64n34
Alembert, Jean Le Rond d' 89, 113
Alexander, Sally 142
Amar y Borbón, Josefa 90
Amazons 7, 11, 12, 28, 69, 78, 94
Angelsey, Marquis of 194, 196
anti-slavery movement 21, 23, 125
anti-suffrage movement 176, 197
Antoninus of Florence 40
Apologie pour la science des dames (1662) 70–1, 73
Apostolat des femmes 139
Applewhite, Harriet 18
Aquinas, Thomas *see* Thomas Aquinas
Argenson, René-Louis de Voyer de Paulmy, marquis d' 110–11
Arienti, Giovanni Sabadino degli *see* Sabadino degli Arienti
Aristotle 35, 69, 73, 227
Astell, Mary 1, 6, 7, 15, 34, 87, 89, 124
authenticity 26, 27
authority 9, 80; contemporary feminism and 219, 224–7; Enlightenment 94–5; late-medieval women and 37–9, 40, 46
autonomy 5, 26, 67, 76, 148, 219, 225, 231; Beauvoir's autonomous self 209–10; economic 204; *see also* independence

Ballard, George 53, 55, 56, 57–8, 59
Banks, Olive 15, 181n1

Barlow, Joel and Ruth 125
Barnett, Samuel 174
Barney, Albert 193
Barney, Natalie 192–4, 195, 197, 199
Bassi, Laura 89, 93
Baudeau, Nicolas 16, 96
Bazard, Claire 148n5
Bazard, Saint-Amand 136
Beatrice of Aragon 51
Beaumarchais, Pierre-Augustin Caron de 88, 92
Beaumer, Mme de 90
Beauvarlet, Jacques-Firmin 116
Beauvoir, Simone de 1, 27, 138, 143, 203–15, 223; ethics 206–7, 210–13, 215; philosophical frameworks 204–7; philosophy as paradigm of the 'sixth feminist wave' 213–15; philosophy of *The Second Sex* 207–10
Beguines 40–1
Belgiojoso, Cristina Trivulzio 25
Bennett, Judith 34
Berg, Barbara 142
Bergomensis, Jacobus Philippus 51, 62n8
Bernardino of Siena 40
Bernhardt, Sarah 4, 191–4, 199
Betussi, Giuseppe 51, 62n8
Beverwijck, Johan van 53, 54, 55, 57
Bisticci, Vespasiano da 51
Blackstone, Sir William 87
Blake, William 125
Bloch, Howard 36
Boccaccio, Giovanni 51, 52, 54, 62n8
body, woman's: Beauvoir and 205, 207–8; medieval perceptions 35–6, 47
Boer, Inge 4, 5, 12, 17
Boileau, Etienne 38
Bonald, Louis 144
Booth, Charles 175
Borbón, Josefa Amar y *see* Amar y Borbón
Bosanquet, Bernard 174–6

238 *Index*

Bosanquet, Helen (née Dendy) 168, 174–6, 178
Boucicaut, Jean de 43
Boudier de Villemert, Pierre-Joseph 96
Bovenschen, Sylvia 60
Bowlby, John 227
Braidotti, Rosi 213–14
breadwinner/carer model of family 172, 175, 221–2, 228
Bright, John 183n22
Britons 7
Buffet, Marguerite 13, 53, 70, 73–4
Bund Deutscher Frauenvereine 23
Burckhardt, Jacob 11, 51
Burke, Edmund 14
Bussemaker, Jet 25, 26, 27
Butler, Josephine 170
Butler, Judith 188, 199n3

Cabetians 136
Caine, Barbara 169
Cambridge School of political thought 8
capitalism, rejection by utopians 162, 163, 164
Carlyle, Thomas and Jane 187
Carter, Elizabeth 93
Cartesianism: Beauvoir and 203, 205, 209; social, of Poulain de la Barre 68, 76–8, 80; *see also* Descartes, René
Case, Sue-Ellen 200n3
Castle, Terry 190
catalogues of 'learned women' 11, 50–62
Catherine II of Russia 94
Catholicism: Dutch 222, 223; and education 88; and feminism 16, 23, 25; late-medieval women and 40–2; and marriage 39–40, 42, 86
Cattier, Philippe 74, 75
Catullus 43
Chamberlain, Joseph 169, 173
Chappuzeau, Samuel 75, 76
Charpentier, Gervais 72
Chartier, R. 86
Chartism 154
Châtelet, Gabrielle-Emilie Le Tonnelier de Breteuil, Mme du 17, 93, 95
Chaucer, Geoffrey 42, 44
Chaussinand-Nogaret, Guy 109
Chidley, Catherine 65n50
Chiesa, Francesco Agostino della 53
childcare: Enlightenment thought 85, 95–7; late-medieval thought 37; utopians and 151, 152, 159, 162, 163; *see also* education; motherhood
Chobham, Thomas 39–40
Christine of Sweden 55

Cicero 74
citizenship 147, 221; Enlightenment thought 91, 95; French Revolution and 18–20; late-medieval Cologne 39; local, in nineteenth-century Britain 173, 176; *see also* civil rights; social rights; suffrage
civic humanism, virtues 6, 15, 16
civil rights: Dutch 222; French Revolution 18; *see also* citizenship
civil society 80, 230
civilizing mission of women 24, 86, 95–7, 98, 220
Cixous, Hélène 205
class: and education 88; late-medieval women 37, 45; learned women and 58, 61–2; Mme de Pompadour and 104, 109–12, 118; seventeenth- century feminism 67–8
class struggle 181n1
Clement, Elisabeth Marie 13, 70, 71–2, 73
Cocceji, Samuel von 87
Code Napoléon 19
coercive heterosexuality 27
Coicy, Mme de 97
collectivism: evolution of, in nineteenth-century liberalism 168, 174–5, 177–81; of utopians 136, 146, 152, 159, 163, 180–1, 227–8
Cologne, citizenship 39
communitarianism 27, 175, 230
community, individual and 27, 218–31
Condorcet, Marie-Jean-Antoine-Nicolas de Caritat, marquis de 19, 85, 95, 138
Connor, S.P. 119n3
consciousness-raising 133, 225, 233n17
contemporary feminism(s) 2, 3, 25–8, 204–5, 218–31; authority, egalitarianism and feminism 224–7; Beauvoir's philosophy as paradigm of 213–15; context of welfare state 221–4; individualism and communal thinking 227–30; individualism and social relations 219–21; *see also* feminist philosophy; feminist political theory; feminist theory
contraception 146, 204
Coole, Diana 224
Cooper, Anna Julia 124
Corelli, Marie 197
Cornara, Helena-Lucrezia Piscopia 79
Corvinus, Gottlieb Siegmund 53
Cosson, Charlotte 53
Cott, Nancy 3, 123
courtly literature 42–5, 47
Craig, Edith (Edy) 197

Index 239

Crébillon, Claude-Prosper Jolyot, the younger 112
critical theory 99
crossdressing 4, 12, 187–99; *see also* cultural-crossdressing
cultural cross-dressing 114, 117
cultural difference and feminism 219
cultural feminism 205, 215, 228
cultural masquerade 120n29
cultural relativism 78
culture as gendered battleground in eighteenth-century France 17, 104–19
Cunitz, Maria 57
Currica, Ester Martini 25
Cushman, Charlotte 187
Czartoryski, Prince Adam Kazimierz 96

Dacier, Anne 54, 72
Danish catalogues of learned women 52
Davies, Emily 182n9
Davies, Margaret Llewelyn 179, 180
Dead White European Males 6
Declaration of the Rights of Man and the Citizen 19
Deffand, Marie de Vichy, marquise du 93
Defoe, Daniel 87, 92
DeJean, Joan 4, 11, 68
Deken, Agatha (Aagje) 93
Delmar, Rosalind 218
Démar, Claire 140, 141, 146
democracy 23, 25, 26, 28, 170
democratic individualism 231
democratic suffragist 179, 180
Derrida, Jacques 213
Descartes, René 55, 76, 77, 78, 97, 209; *see also* Cartesianism
Descrues, D.I.B. 79
DesHoulières, Antoinette 72
Diderot, Denis 69, 85, 113; *see also* *Encyclopédie*
difference: Enlightenment and 14, 15, 98; external physical signs as referent for sexual difference 189–90; modern sexism and 30; Renaissance feminism and 50; Saint-Simonians and 142–8; seventeenth-century views of 68, 73, 75, 76; women's movement and 204; *see also* natural difference
difference/equality debate 24, 27, 30, 50, 204; relationship of *The Second Sex* to 205, 213–15; Saint-Simonians 142–4, 147–8; utopian feminism in Great Britain 150–65
divorce 18, 87, 144, 145, 155
Dolle Mina 224–5

domestic work 22, 150, 151, 152, 153, 158, 159, 162, 164
dress 4–5, 12; lesbians and suffragists 187–99
Drucker, Wilhelmina 224
DuBois, Ellen 142
DuBos, Jean-Baptiste, abbé 67
Dubosc, Jacques 70
Dunn, John 6
DWEMs 6

Eastern Europe 24–5
Eberti, Johann Kaspar 53, 55, 57, 64n34
Echols, Alice 188
écriture féminine 205
education 30; Enlightenment thought 16, 86, 88–92, 96–7; learned women 55, 56, 61; liberal feminism and 22, 171, 174, 175; Mary Wollstonecraft and 14, 125, 126, 127; utopians and 155, 156–7, 161
Ellis, Havelock 189, 191
emancipation 91; superseded by liberation 223
emancipation movements, nineteenth-century 22–4, 29; *see also* suffrage; women's movement
emotion 15, 86, 206–7, 209
Encyclopédie 69, 79, 87, 106, 113
Enfantin, Prosper 136, 144–5
Engelhard, Philippine Gatterer 92
Engels, F. 21, 141–2, 152
England *see* Great Britain
Enlightenment 5, 30, 61; Beauvoir as Enlightenment thinker 203; feminist influence on 29, 80–1; patronage of Mme de Pompadour 104–19
Enlightenment feminism 2, 3, 10, 13–20, 22, 30, 85–99, 122–3, 204, 226; civilizing mission 95–7; critique of institutionalized marriage 86–8; critique of women's education 88–91; potential of women 91–4; women in public affairs 94–5; *see also* Wollstonecraft, Mary
Epinay, Louise de La Live d' 85–6, 97
equal opportunities 175; liberal feminism and 22, 172, 175; utopian socialism and 161–2
equal pay 157–8
equal rights 161, 163; *see also* natural rights; political rights; social rights
equality 5, 9, 10, 13, 14, 15, 26, 27, 28, 30, 228; Enlightenment and 85–6, 98; French Revolution 18–20; liberal feminism and 23, 24; in Netherlands 222–7; of Saint-Simonianism 138,

240 Index

142–4; seventeenth-century feminism 8, 67–81; spiritual 15, 73; *see also* difference/equality debate; natural equality; political equality

Erasmus, Desiderius 54

Erikson, Erik 227

Erxleben, Dorothea Christiane Leporin 93

ethics of Simone de Beauvoir 206–7, 210–13, 215

ethnographic travesty 120n29

Etiolles, Seigneur d' 110

European feminism 220–1

Evans, Richard 15, 181n1

existentialist philosophy 205, 211

Fabianism 165, 176

Faderman, Lillian 189–90, 200n8

fairness 150

Falconnet, Etienne-Maurice 113

family: churches and 86–7; contemporary feminism and 26, 221–2, 226–7, 228, 230; French Revolutionary feminism 18; late-medieval 46; liberal feminism and 172, 175–6, 180; Mary Wollstonecraft and 125, 129, 130–1; utopianism and 141–2, 144–7; *see also* childcare; family allowances; father; marriage; motherhood

family allowances 169, 177, 179, 181, 221

famous women 11, 20, 50–2, 69, 79

fashion *see* dress

father, as educator of learned women 54, 56

Fawcett, Henry 169, 171, 182n9

Fawcett, Millicent Garrett 168, 169–72, 175, 180, 181, 183n33

feelings *see* emotion

Feijoo y Montenegro, Benito Jeronimo 89

Female Rights Vindicated (1758) 89–90

femininity 189, 205, 214; codes of 4, 12; late medieval thought 35–6, 47; Netherlands 223; representations 4–5

feminism 1–30; definition 3–4; and history of political thought 5–6; as invention of tradition or recovery of suppressed evidence 7–9, 99; and modernity 28–30; periodization 2–3; use of term 2

feminist critical theory 99

feminist philosophy 6, 14

feminist political theory 150

feminist publishing 3, 7, 18, 20, 70; Dutch 229–30; Saint-Simoniennes 139, 140, 141; *see also Journal des dames*

feminist theory 122–4, 134, 143, 205, 213–15

femme damnée 199

Femme généreuse, La (1643) 69

Femme libre, La 139

Femme nouvelle, La 139, 148n5

femmes savantes see learned women

Fénelon, François de Salignac de La Mothe, archbishop 89, 92

Firestone, Shulamith 204, 218, 225

Fontenay, de 75

Fontenelle, Bernard le Bovier, sieur de 88, 109

Forge, de la *see* La Forge

Foucault, Michel 122, 213

Fourier, Charles 95, 96, 138, 144, 151, 152–3, 154, 155, 156, 159, 164

Fourierism 20, 22, 136, 140, 146, 152

Fox-Genovese, E. 232n6, 233n35

France 219; Enlightenment 5, 16–18, 86–98 *passim*; feminism in 3, 11, 16–21, 150; learned women 12, 52, 62n10, 68–76, 79–80, 88; liberal feminism 22, 23; medieval 38, 46; patronage of Mme de Pompadour 104–19; Revolution of 1789 16, 18–21 (Mary Wollstonecraft and 14, 125, 127–8); seventeenth-century 67–81, 87, 88, 89; utopians in 20–2, 136–48, 151

Frankfurt School 99, 233n17

Frawenlob, Johann 54

Frederick the Great 87, 96

Free Spirits 41

freemasonry 18, 98

Freud, Sigmund 122, 189, 191

Friedan, Betty 27, 204, 218

friendship, female 70, 230; *see also* romantic friendships

Fronde 12, 68, 69, 79

Fulbicke, Emerentia 65n56

Fulgosus, Baptista 51, 62n8

functionalist view of family rights and duties 226–7

Galen 35, 36

Gallet, Danielle 111

Gauls 7, 28

Gelbart, Nina Rattner 18

gender 5, 85; performance of 188–9

gender group identity 4

Genlis, Stephanie-Félicité du Crest, comtesse de 97

Geoffrin, Marie-Therèse Rodet, Mme 17, 93, 109

German-speaking feminism 3, 11, 22, 23, 24–5

Germany 55, 93, 168, 233n15

Geschichtliche Grundbegriffe 6

Gilman, Charlotte Perkins 124, 165

Girault, Mlle 75
Godonville, Monsieur de 74
Godwin, William 125, 128, 129
Goncourt, Edmond and Jules de 110, 111, 119nn2,7, 120n18
Goodman, Dena 93–4
Gouges, Olympe de 1, 14, 18, 19, 124
Gournay, Marie de 1, 6, 7, 10, 13, 55, 68–9, 74
Grande Mademoiselle see Montpensier, Anne-Marie-Louise d'Orleans, duchesse de
Gräserin, Eva Juliana 65n56
Great Britain, feminism in 3, 4, 15, 88, 221, 229; backlash against contemporary feminist ideals 229; Enlightenment feminism 87, 89, 90 (*see also* Wollstonecraft, Mary); liberalism and feminism in nineteenth century 22, 23, 168–81; utopian feminism 20, 21, 22, 150–65; women and work in late-medieval England 37
Green, Charlotte 176
Green, Thomas Hill 168, 174, 176, 177
Gregory, John 102n42
Guillaume, Jacquette 70, 72
Guindorf, Reine 146
Gutman, H. 213
Guyonnet de Vertron, Charles 79

Halévy, Elie 135n11
Hall, Radclyffe 189, 199, 202n37
Hamilton, Cecily 197, 198
Hampsher-Monk, Ian 6
Hartley, David 126
Hegel, Georg Wilhelm Friedrich 174
Heidegger, Martin 205, 208
Helvétius, Claude-Adrien 109, 126
heroic women 11, 68
heterosexuality 187
Hewitt, Nancy 142
Histoire des Femmes/History of Women project 5
Hobbes, Thomas 13
Hobhouse, Emily 179
Hobhouse, Leonard T. 169, 174, 175, 177–80
Hoccleve, Thomas 44–5, 49n26
Holbein, Hans, the younger 106
Holton, Sandra 180
Hosmer, Harriet 187
Hunt, Lynn 18–19
Hyde, H. Montgomery 194

identities, identity: Beauvoir and 212–13; and lesbianism 187–90

identity politics 27, 188
images 4–5; lesbianism 1880–1920 186, 190–9; Marie Leczinska and Mme de Pompadour 104, 105–9, 113–18
independence 91, 125, 231; *see also* autonomy
individual 130
individualism: and collectivism in late nineteenth-century Britain 168, 169–72, 174, 175, 181; and community 27, 218–31
inheritance customs 46, 125, 142
Irigaray, Luce 205
Italy 3, 11, 16, 20; learned women 17, 52, 72, 79, 93

Jacques de (James of) Vitry 41
Jaucourt, Louis Chevalier de 87–8
Joan of Arc 94
John of Salisbury 43
Johnson, Samuel 94
Jordan, Constance 11
Journal des dames 18, 90, 92, 97
Juliana of Cornillon 42
Juncker, Christian 64n30
justice 150

Kant, Immanuel 85, 99, 174
Kauffman, Angelika 93
Keil, Andreas von 59
Keil, Elisabeth Margaretha von 59
Kelly, Joan 9–10, 34
Key, Ellen 134n9
King, Margaret 59
Kingdom of Jerusalem 46
kinship 46; *see also* family
Knight, Anne 21
Kool-Smit, Joke 223–4
Krafft-Ebing, Richard von 189, 191
Kristeva, Julia 205
Krueger, Roberta 47

La Font de Saint-Yenne 117–18
La Forge, Jean de 70
La Forge, Louis de 70
La Porte, Joseph de 53, 55
La Tour, Maurice Quentin de 104, 105, 106, 108–9
Lacan, Jacques 122
Lambert, Anne-Thérèse de Marguenat de Courcelles, marquise de 17
Landes, Joan 110, 118
Lane, E.W. 116
languages of feminism 28–9, 231; late-medieval 42–7; Mary Wollstonecraft and 123–4, 131–4; Netherlands 223–4

242 Index

late-medieval feminism 2, 9–11, 34–47; clashing and intersecting discourses 45–7; dominant discourses on women and femininity 35–6; feminist language 42–5, 47; woman as moral guide and preacher 39–40; women as religious inspiration 40–2; women, work and authority 37–9
Launay, Gilles de 75
Le Brun, Charles 117
Le Normand de Tournehem, Charles 110
Le Prince de Beaumont, Jeanne-Marie 88
Le Roi, J.A. 111
learned women 11–13, 50–62, 69, 68–76, 79–80, 88, 92–4; catalogues of seventeenth-and eighteenth-century 54–5; education 56; social background and life 58–60; transition from famous to learned women 52–4; type of knowledge 56–8; *see also* salon culture
LeBermen, Louys 68
Leczinska, Marie, queen of France 104, 105–9
Lehms, Georg Christian 53, 55
Lerner, Gerda 99
lesbian studies 188, 189
lesbianism 4, 141, 186–99; identities 187–90; subculture 1880–1920 190–9
Lesclache, Louis 70, 75
Lespinasse, Jeanne-Julie de 17, 93
Levellers 28
Lévi-Strauss, Claude 116
Lévinas, Emmanuel 205
Levitas, Ruth 21
Levy, Darline 18
liberal feminism 2, 20, 22–5, 122, 161, 168–81, 199, 204, 224; and contemporary feminism 218–31; gendered rights and duties 177–80; moral reform and Victorian liberalism 169–70; political and social reform 170–2; social situation at end of the century 172–4; T.H.Green and Helen Bosanquet 174–7
liberalism 28, 124
liberation 228; Dutch feminism and 223
liberty 5, 9, 14, 28, 91–2
Lloyd, Genevieve 207–8
Locke, John 3, 9, 13, 125, 209
Lorris, Guillaume de 43, 44
Lougee, Carolyn 67, 109
Louis XIV, king of France 7, 68, 106
Louis XV, king of France 104, 105, 109, 110, 112

Mably, Gabriel-Bonnet, abbé de 16, 91, 94

Macaulay-Graham, Catharine 90, 132
McLean, Ian 67, 68
Maffei, Clara 25
Maintenon, Françoise d'Aubigné, marquise de 89
Maisonneuve, Catherine Michelle, Mme de 90
Maistre, Joseph de 144
male homosexuals 190, 194
male impersonators, and homosexuality, lesbianism 4, 191–9
male supremacy 3, 13, 30, 77, 85–6, 87; and women's work 158
Malebranche, Nicolas 88
manners 10, 12, 15, 16–17, 67, 73, 80
Maria Theresa of Austria 94
Marinelli, Lucrezia 69
Marivaux, Pierre Carlet de 94, 109
Marmontel, Jean-François 113
marriage: Dutch 222; Enlightenment thought 85, 86–8, 95; late-medieval 39–40, 46; learned women 59–60; liberal feminism and 21, 169–70, 175–6; seventeenth-century 69–70, 77; utopians, Saint- Simonians and 21, 145, 152, 153, 154–5, 161; *see also* family; family allowances; motherhood
Martin, Benjamin 66n62
Martin, Biddy 189
Martineau, Harriet 34
Martinus a Balthoven 54
Marx, Karl 21, 122, 136, 152
Marxist feminists 224–5
masculinity, critique of 131–2, 151, 160
materialist feminism 165
Matriarchs 7
medieval feminism *see* late-medieval feminism
Mehmed Efendi 67
Melanchthon, Philipp 56
Ménage, Gilles 53, 72
Menagius, Aegidius 54–5
Mercier, Louis-Sébastian 92
Mercure Galant 79
Merleau-Ponty, Maurice 205, 208
Meulenbelt, Anja 225
Meun, Jean de 43, 44
middle-class women 22, 61–2
military command, women and 78, 79, 94
Mill, James 153
Mill, John Stuart 1, 6, 22, 23, 137, 151, 168, 169–72, 180, 183nn22, 33, 231
Miller, N. 121n33
Millett, Kate 1, 204, 218
misogyny 3, 9–10, 12; of Beauvoir 205, 207–8; late-medieval and Renaissance

29–30, 36, 42–5, 46, 47; seventeenth-century French 68, 69, 73
Mitchell, Juliet 205, 218, 225
modernity, feminism and 28–30
Molière, Jean-Baptiste Poquelin de 12, 68, 70, 72, 75, 76, 88
Montaigne, Michel de 74
Montaigu, Henri 110, 117
Montanclos, Marie Emilie, Mme de 97
Montesquieu, Charles de Secondat, baron de 85, 87, 94, 106, 109, 112–13
Montpensier, Anne-Marie-Louise d'Orleans, duchesse de 7, 12
morality 6, 80; Beauvoir and ethics 206–7, 210–13, 215; liberal feminism and moral reform 169–70, 171, 175, 178–9, 181; moral role of women in late-medieval thought 39–40; moral role of women in utopianism 151, 156, 160; *Querelle des femmes* 10, 43, 44, 50
More, Thomas 54, 56
Morrison, Frances 152, 155, 156, 157, 161
Morrison, James 152, 154, 155, 157–8
Moses, Claire 21, 150
motherhood: contemporary feminism and 227; Enlightenment and 16, 18, 19, 86, 95–7, 98; learned women and 59; liberal feminism and 24, 169, 175–6, 178, 179, 180; utopians and 141, 143, 151, 156–7, 160
Murdoch, Iris 203
myth 7

national feminisms 218–19
nationalism 7–8, 25
natural difference 50, 142–3, 158, 159, 160, 161, 163, 226
natural equality 13, 14, 15, 50, 79, 86, 89–90
natural law 13, 77
natural rights 19
Nebrissensis, Antonius 56
Nebrissensis, Francisca 56
Necker, Suzanne, Mme 17, 93
neoliberalism, neoconservatism 228, 229
Neoplatonism 58
Netherlands 181n2, 219; feminism 3, 15, 23, 93; individualism and communal thinking and feminism 228–30; political culture of feminism 224–7; welfare state and feminism 222–4
New Liberals 169, 174, 175, 177–81
New Moral World 155
Newton, Esther 189
Nordenflycht, Hedvig Charlotta 90–1
novel(s) 86; female 11, 69, 88, 93, 94, 97,

193–4, 211; of Mary Wollstonecraft 128–9, 132–3

Offen, Karen 3, 8, 14, 15, 16, 123, 220, 221, 231
Okin, Susan 6, 227
Orientalism 113–14
origins, quest for 7, 34
Oudry, Jean-Baptiste 113
Ovid 36, 43
Owen, Robert 151, 152–3, 154, 155, 162
Owenism 21, 22, 136, 137, 150–65

Paine, Thomas 125
painters, female 60, 93
painting, representations of femininity 4–5, 104–18
Pankhurst, Christabel 196
Pankhurst, Emmeline 196, 197
Pantheon of World Fame (Burckhardt) 11, 51
parity 150
'parole de femme' 140
Parsons, Talcott 227
Paterson, Emma 172
patriarchy 27, 38–9; critique of 6, 13, 46–7, 67, 72, 80, 130–1, 225, 226
patristic literature 36, 43, 69
patronage, female, in eighteenth-century France 17, 104–19
Paullini, Christian Frantz 53, 57
Pellegrin, Nicole 4
People's Suffrage Federation 179, 180
Perez de Moya, Juan 51, 62nn6, 8
personal/political 226
Pethick-Lawrence, Emmeline 196
phenomenology, Beauvoir and 205–7, 208, 209
philosophers, women 54–5, 56
philosophes 17, 85, 112–13
Piéron, Henri 8
pillarization 222, 225–6
Pioneer, The 151–2, 154, 156–8, 159, 160–1, 162
Pizan, Christine de 1, 7, 9–11, 12, 34, 43–5, 50, 51, 124, 138
Pléiade, the 60
poets, female 60
Poland 25, 96
political: importance of education of women 91; significance of Mary Wollstonecraft's thought 132–4
political culture(s): of contemporary feminism 25–7, 219–31; and Enlightenment feminism 17, 94–5; French Revolution 18–19

244 *Index*

political equality: in Poulain de la Barre
78; in utopian socialism 153–4
political rights 18–19; *see also* citizenship;
suffrage
political thought 8; feminism and 5–6
Pomian, Krzysztof 105–6
Pompadour, Jeanne Antoinette Poisson,
Mme de 17, 104–19
Poor Clares 40
Port Royal 78
Porte, Joseph de la *see* La Porte
postmaterialism 225
postmodern feminism 27, 150, 213–15
postmodern lesbians 189
postmodernism 14, 188
poststructuralism 165
Pothier, Robert 87
Pougy, Liane de 193–4
Poulain de la Barre, François 1, 6, 8, 13,
68, 76–8, 80, 88, 92–3, 94, 95, 138
power 130, 214, 219; women's 17, 36, 40,
46, 94, 95; *see also* authority; patriarchy
précieuses 12, 68, 70
Prévost d'Exiles, abbé 109
Price, Richard 125
Priestley, Joseph 125, 135n11
Prieur, Monsieur 74
private/public *see* public/private
professions, women and 92–3
progress 10, 125
Protestantism: and education 88; influence
on feminism 15–16, 23–4, 125; and
marriage 86–7
Prussia 96, 97
psychoanalytical feminism 205
public role of women: in Enlightenment
thought 86, 94–5, 98; femininity in
Netherlands 223; at French court in
eighteenth century 17, 105–19; in
French Revolution 18–20; *see also*
authority; civilizing mission; political;
power; public/private
public/private 6, 37, 226
Puisieux, Madeleine d'Arsant de 97
Pure, Michel, abbé de 70
Pythagoras 74

Quakers 87
queer theory 188, 190
Querelle des anciens et des modernes 78, 79
Querelle des femmes 5, 9–11, 34, 42, 50,
67, 69
Querelle de la rose 42–4

radical feminism 139, 224–5
radicalism 28, 125, 151, 180, 233n17

Rang, Brita 3, 11
rationalist feminism 2, 10, 13, 14–15, 52,
68–81, 89–90; Mary Wollstonecraft and
14–15, 125, 126–8; *see also* reason
rationality *see* reason
Ravisius, Joannes *see* Textor, Johannes
Ravisius
Rawls, John 122
reason, rationality 14, 28, 99; late-medieval
view of women and 36, 41;
see also rationalist feminism
Reichenbach of Helmstedt 56
religion: late-medieval women and 40–2;
and marriage 86–7; Saint-Simonianism
and 21, 136, 138, 142, 144, 145, 146–7;
see also Catholicism; Protestantism
Renaissance feminism 2, 5, 9–12, 16;
famous and learned women 50–2,
58, 59
Renan, Ernest 21
Renaudot, Théophraste 73
Rendall, Jane 15, 23, 95, 142
Republic of Letters 5, 11, 17, 93–4
republicanism 6, 15, 16, 87, 124
Restif de la Bretonne, Nicolas-Edmé 94
Reynolds, Margaret 155
Riballier, Ambroise 53, 55, 56, 57, 58, 60,
64n34
Riccoboni, Marie-Jeanne 88
Rice, D. 120n26
Rich, Adrienne 141, 187, 218
Richer, Léon 138
Richesource, Jean de Soudier de 73–5, 76
Rigaud, Hyacinthe 106
rights 86, 123; *see also* equal rights; natural
rights; political rights; social rights
Rivet, André 69
rococo painting 104, 117, 118
Rohault, Jacques 75, 78
Roiphe, Kate 229
Roland, Pauline 146
romantic friendships 186, 188, 189, 190
romanticism 6, 204, 213; of Saint-
Simonians 137, 138, 143–4
Romieu, Marie de 58
Roper, Lyndal 38
Rosso, Jeanette 67, 82n32
Roumier, Marie-Anne de (dame Robert) 97
Rousseau, Jean-Jacques 16, 17, 18, 19, 85,
89, 91, 96, 97, 112, 125, 174; Beauvoir
as Rousseauist feminist 203,
209–10, 213
Royal Commission on the Poor Law 176,
177–8
Rubin, Miri 10
Ruskin, John and Effie 187

Russia 96

Sabadino degli Arienti, Giovanni 51
Sabine, George H. 6
Sade, Donatien-Alphonse-François,
    marquis de 206–7
Saint-Pierre, Charles-Irénee Catel, abbé
    de 96
Saint-Simon, Claude-Henri, comte de
    145, 152
Saint-Simonianism 20, 21, 22, 23, 136–48,
    150, 151, 152, 155
Saint-Yenne, La Font de see La Font de
    Saint-Yenne
Saliez, Antoinette de Salvan de 79, 80
salon culture, *salonnières* 12, 17, 18, 67, 69,
    93–4, 105, 109–10, 118
Sapiro, Virginia 14
Sardonati, Francesco 62nn6,8
Sartre, Jean-Paul 203, 205, 206, 207, 208,
    209, 211, 212, 215
Scala, Bartholomeo 56
Scandinavian feminism 3, 15, 23
Schurman, Anna Maria van 13, 55, 69, 74
scientific learning 12–13, 53, 57–8, 60–1,
    93; acquisition 56; debate in
    seventeenth century 74–5, 80, 89
Scottish Enlightenment 95
Scudéry, Madeleine de 69, 72
Scythian queens 74, 78, 79, 138
Second Sex, The (Beauvoir) 27; philosophy
    of 207–10; relation to contemporary
    feminism 204–5, 213–15
self, situated, of Beauvoir 207, 209–10,
    213, 215
self-development 26, 219, 220, 225, 230,
    233n17
self-interest, enlightened 15, 16, 224
self-knowledge 77
self-ownership 97
sentiment see emotion
settlement houses 172, 174
Sevigné, Marie de Rabutin-Chantal, Mme
    de 55
sex-gender system 27
sexism 27, 30
sexology, and sexual difference 189–90
sexual difference see difference;
    difference/equality debate; natural
    difference
sexual division of labour 22, 92; late-
    medieval 37; Poulain de la Barre and
    78; Saint-Simonians, utopians and 143,
    147, 150, 151, 152, 159, 175, 224
sexual equality see equality
sexual politics 27, 86

sexuality: Beauvoir and 204; feminists and
    186–7, 199; Saint-Simonians, utopians
    and 138, 139, 140, 141, 143, 145–6, 153,
    155–6
Sforza, Bianca Maria 51
Shaw, George Bernard 187
Sieyès, Emmanuel-Joseph, abbé 19
Simons, M. 216n2
Smith-Rosenberg, Carroll 189
Smyth, Ethel 197
Social Democratic Federation 176
social movements 225
social reform, liberal feminism and 24, 168,
    169–70, 171–81
social rights 176–80, 219, 230
social status see class
social structure: contemporary feminism
    and 228; Mary Wollstonecraft and
    128–9, 133
socialism 21, 136
socialist feminism 23, 27, 168, 176–80, 204;
    see also utopian-socialist feminism
socialization: of children 85–6, 95–7, 98,
    127 (see also education, motherhood);
    of domestic labour in Owenism 152,
    153, 164
Sophia (pseud.) 89
Spain 20, 52, 89, 90
Spartan ideal 16, 18
Speght, Rachel 34
Spock, Dr. Benjamin 26, 227
Stewart, Joan Hinde 88, 97
Stopes, Charlotte 7
Stuurman, Siep 13, 52
subject, in contemporary feminism 213–15
Suchon, Gabrielle 1, 13, 80
suffrage, female 19, 22, 24, 95, 191; liberal
    feminism and 169–80; Owenites
    and 154
suffragists 169; and lesbianism 4, 194–9
sultana, Mme de Pompadour and role of
    110, 113–17
Svetlà, Karolina 25
Swedish catalogue of learned women 52
Swedish feminism 90–1

Tarn, Pauline 194
Taylor, Barbara 142, 150, 151, 152,
    154, 161
Taylor, Charles 209
Taylor, Harriet 1, 150
Tencin, Claudine Alexandrine Guérin,
    Mme de 109, 119n3
Textor, Johannes Ravisius 51, 52, 62n8
theatre: and feminism in seventeenth and

246 *Index*

eighteenth centuries 12, 75–6, 88, 92, 97; and homosexuality 4, 190–9
Theon of Alexandria 56
Third World feminism 27
Thomas Aquinas 51
Thomasius, Johann 53
Thompson, William 151, 152, 153–64
Ticknor, Lisa 197
Tiepolo, Giovanni Battista 56
Tilley, Vesta 194
Tocqué, Louis, portrait of Marie Leczinska 104, 105–9
Tocqueville, Alexis de 14, 21, 26
Tomaselli, Sylvia 95
Tournehem, Charles Le Normand de *see* Le Normand de Tournehem
Townsheld, Charlotte Payne 187
Toynbee, Arnold 174
transvestism *see* crossdressing
Tribune des femmes 139, 140, 141
Triller, Daniel Wilhelm 55
Tristan, Flora 141, 151

Ulfeld, Leonara von 53
United Nations 27
United States of America 16, 22, 23, 165, 204, 219, 220, 221, 225, 229
universities, women and *see* academic institutions
utopian novels 94, 97
utopian-socialist feminism 2, 3, 20–2, 23, 199, 228; France 136–48; Great Britain 150–65

Vanloo, Carle 104, 111, 113–18
Verbreck 113
Veret, J. Desirée 142–3
Vertron, Charles Guyonnet de *see* Guyonnet de Vertron
Vicinus, Martha 4, 12, 183n24
Vigée-Lebrun, Elisabeth 93
Villemert, Pierre-Joseph Boudier de *see* Boudier de Villemert
Vintges, Karen 27
Virgil 43
virtue: civic 6, 15, 16; Mary Wollstonecraft's struggle for feminist language of 122–34
Vivien, Renée (Pauline Tarn) 194
Vogel, U. 216n21
Voilquin, Suzanne 144
Voix des femmes 20

Voltaire (François-Marie Arouet) 85, 95, 106, 113, 120n24
Vossius, Gerardus Johannes 54

Walker, Lisa M. 189
Ward, Mrs Humphrey 176
Webb, Beatrice 176, 178, 183n29
Weber, Jean 194
welfare state 26, 219, 221–4, 230
Welter, Barbara 143
Westonius, Elisabeth Johanna 54
Wheeler, Anna 151, 152, 153–64
Wiesner, Merry 38
Wildenstein, Georges 106
Wilson, Elizabeth 190, 200n5
Wolf, Naomi 229
Wolff, Elizabeth (Betje) 93
Wollstonecraft, Mary 1, 6, 14–15, 21, 34, 87, 90, 102n42, 122–34, 151, 164, 216n21, 231; and languages of feminism 123–4, 131–4; and reason 126–8, 131; and social structure 128–9, 133; and woman's character 129–31
woman intellectual 217n30
Woman not Inferior to Man... ('Sophia') 101n18
Woman's Signal 164
women: contradictions of postwar position 26–7; Mary Wollstonecraft and character of 129–31; *see also* body, woman's; femininity
Woman's Co-operative Guild 176, 179
women's movement 22, 24, 144, 172, 174; Beauvoir and 204, 205, 214, 215; in Netherlands 224–5; and welfare state 221–2; *see also* suffrage
women's political clubs 18
Women's Protective and Provident League 172
work, women and 92–3, 204; late-medieval 37–9; liberal feminists 169, 172, 175, 183n29; utopian feminists and 140–1; *see also* equal opportunities; equal pay
working-class, Saint-Simonians 137
working-class feminism 21–2; Owenites 151–65; Saint-Simoniennes 138–47
working-class women's organizations 168, 172, 176, 179, 180
Wright, Sir Almroth E. 202n36
Wright, Frances 21

Zmichowska, Narcya 25